WITHDRAWN

CHRISTENDOM AND CHRISTIANITY
IN THE MIDDLE AGES

Christendom and Christianity in the Middle Ages

The Relations between Religion, Church, and Society

Adriaan H. Bredero

Translated by
Reinder Bruinsma

WILLIAM B. EERDMANS PUBLISHING COMPANY
GRAND RAPIDS, MICHIGAN

First published as *Christenheid en Christendom in de Middeleeuwen.*
Over de verhouding van godsdienst, kerk en samenleving.
Copyright © 1986 by Kok Agora, Kampen.
Second edition 1987

First English edition copyright © 1994 by
Wm. B. Eerdmans Publishing Co.
255 Jefferson Ave. S.E., Grand Rapids, Michigan 49503
All rights reserved

Printed in the United States of America

Library of Congress Cataloging-in-Publication Data

Bredero, Adriaan Hendrik.
[Christenheid en christendom in de middeleeuwen. English]
Christendom and Christianity in the Middle Ages: the relations
between religion, church, and society / Adriaan H. Bredero;
translated by Reinder Bruinsma.
p.   cm.
Translation of: Christenheid en christendom in de middeleeuwen.
Includes bibliographical references and index.
ISBN 0-8028-3692-5
1. Christianity — Middle Ages, 600-1500.   I. Title.
BR252.B7313   ~~1993~~ 1994

270.4 — 4dc20   91-37168
                                                    CIP

Contents

❧   ❧

Preface   viii

Acknowledgments   xi

Abbreviations   xiii

I   Religion and Church in Medieval Society   1

    1. Introduction   1

    2. The Early Christianization   10

    3. The Eleventh Century and the Transition
      to the Twelfth   18

    4. Assimilation to the Urban Population   26

    5. The Fourteenth and Fifteenth Centuries   36

II   Against Misunderstanding the Medieval Mentality   53

III   Jerusalem in the West   79

IV   The Bishops' Peace of God:
A Turning Point in Medieval Society?   105

CONTENTS

V   Cistercians and Cluniacs   130

VI Saints and Sainthood   151
    1. Introduction   151
    2. Veneration of Saints and the Authority
       of the Church   158
    3. The Sainthood of Bernard of Clairvaux   181

VII Heresy and Church Reform   198
    1. The Transition from the Eleventh
       to the Twelfth Century   198
    2. Henry of Lausanne: From Reformer to Heretic   211

VIII Master Peter Abelard (1079-1141):
     The Misfortunes of a Single-Minded Teacher   225

IX The Beginnings of the Franciscan Movement
    and the Canonization of Its Founder   246
    1. The Structure of the Brotherhood   246
    2. The "Failure" of Brother Elias   251
    3. The Longing for the Return to the Time
       of St. Francis   255
    4. The Meaning of the Canonization of St. Francis   260
    5. The Beginnings of the Franciscan Movement
       in the Context of Its Time   265

X   Anti-Jewish Sentiment in Medieval Society   274
    Excursus: The Role of Theology in the Vilification
               of the Jews in the Late Middle Ages   307

XI Religious Life in the Low Countries (ca. 1050-1384)   319
    1. Introduction   319
    2. Church Membership   323
    3. God and His Saints   330

CONTENTS

4. Blessings and Penance   347

5. The Bilingualism of the Church
   and Its Social Consequences   355

Appendix: Reason in the Middle Ages   376

For Further Reading   382

Index of Names   390

Index of Subjects   397

Preface

❧   ❧

O N SUNDAY, September 29, 1963, the late Pope Paul VI ceremoniously
opened the second session of the Vatican II Council. In his address
to the episcopal fathers, the pope spoke about the purpose of the Council,
summarizing it in four points. One of these points, which concerned the
renewal and reform of the Church, regarded the tradition. It was the task
of the Council not only to underline its essential and valuable aspects, but
also to purge the Church of all those elements in its traditions which were
wrong or unworthy. The execution of such a purpose requires the obtaining
of historical insight into matters such as customs and conceptions which
were mostly the products of their time but which also added to the
traditions of the Church and afterward came to be considered part of the
transcendental norms and values of Christian belief, as if these customs
and conceptions integrally belonged to the tradition.

This supplementing and integrating of dated elements in the traditions of the Church, which continually took place and which will continue
to take place, is a process that is inevitable. This is because, without this
process of acculturation, Christian faith could not have taken shape in
human society as it did according to time and place. Without this sort of
continual acculturation, the experience of Christian faith has no future in
society. For the promotion of this *aggiornamento,* the traditions of the
Christian Church must continually be cleansed and purified from the
nonessential additions of earlier acculturations. This task is unworkable

without historical reflection, for there is the risk that in this cleansing valuable elements of the tradition may also disappear. At the same time, there is the risk that because of this fear the necessary purification of the tradition may be omitted.

This historical reflection has to be focused especially on the Middle Ages. Medieval society, in which the Church occupied an important social position and also obtained great and direct authority in politico-economic affairs, in later centuries still set its mark so strongly on the outward appearance of the Church, as well as on the practice and the awareness of the Christian religion, that the Enlightenment can be seen as being the first settling of scores with the medieval acculturation of Christianity. In reaction to this merciless reckoning, the Romantic period restored the "Christian Middle Ages" to its place of honor and considered it to be an ideal Christian era, to which humanity should return as soon as possible. Such idealization of medieval society influenced the judgments concerning those centuries for quite a long time.

This nostalgic point of view has been superseded, or at least weakened; historians who study the strongly interwoven relations between Christian experience of faith and the Middle Ages no longer speak of the "Christian Middle Ages" but prefer to speak about "medieval Christianity." To this they attribute the typical medieval awareness of the created reality, since from this idea form was given to the medieval Christian experience of faith. Some historians even tend toward giving so much attention to the overgrowth of these religious practices by medieval society that they are of the opinion that the popular religion of those days could not even be called Christian. Such an opinion of medieval Christianity may be considered exaggerated because much of medieval Christianity is still recognizable in the contemporary experience of the Christian faith, even outside Europe and the church of Rome.

This book deals with medieval Christianity in its relation to the Church and society. This relation also concerns medieval Christendom, which in that period had been molded ideologically by society into a collectivity. The author, who confesses this faith and is a member of this Church, but also is a scholar specializing in medieval history, has often, because of his professional reflections on medieval society, asked himself how medieval the Christianity of our times still is. The answer will be different according to the degree in which this medieval inheritance lives in each Christian. The differences should be seen less in respect to the normative prescriptions which are valid within the churches for their members concerning the practice of religion.

Still, answering the question of how much these prescriptions are based on earlier acculturations leads to an increasing difference of opinion among Christians, and this causes polarization because the discussion is carried on with presuppositions about the past. In order to avoid this polarization among Christians, it would be better to ask how medieval Christianity still is, and how much of this should be considered as belonging to the essential Christian tradition, or how much could be discarded in order to make the following acculturation possible. The author hopes to lay this question more specifically before the readers of this book.

❧   ❧

THE FIRST and second editions of this book appeared in the Netherlands, and the present work is a translation of the second Dutch edition. It is even more than a translation. The author has revised the text and added a new chapter: "The Beginnings of the Franciscan Movement and the Canonization of Its Founder." The bibliographical references in the annotations are as far as possible adapted to the language in which the book now appears. Most of the chapters were previously published in periodicals, sometimes within, sometimes outside the Netherlands. They were partially rewritten and adapted to the intent of this book as mentioned above. The translation of this work was time-consuming for Dr. Reinder Bruinsma, who was well prepared to carry out this delicate and extensive task. The author wishes to expressly thank him for his efforts.

Acknowledgments

☙   ☙

THE AUTHOR and publisher gratefully acknowledge permission to quote material from the following publications:

Edward Arnold, London
> *The Crusades, Idea and Reality,* by Louise Riley-Smith and J. S. C. Riley-Smith. Copyright © 1981.

Burns & Oates, London
> *The Letters of St. Bernard of Clairvaux,* tr. Bruno Scott James. Copyright © 1953.

Cistercian Publications, Inc.
> *On the Song of Songs,* 3, tr. Kilian Walsh and Irene M. Edmonds. Copyright © 1979.
> *Sermons on the Song of Songs,* 4, tr. Irene M. Edmonds. Copyright © 1980.
> *The Works of Bernard of Clairvaux,* vol. 1: *Treatises.* Copyright © 1974.

Clarendon Press, Oxford
> *The Ecclesiastical History of Orderic Vitalis,* ed. and tr. Marjorie Chibnall. Copyright © 1969-1980.
> *The Five Books of the Histories and the Life of St. William,* by Rodulfus Glaber, ed. and tr. John France. Copyright © 1990.
> *Scripta Leonis, Rufini et Angeli, sociorum s. Francisci: The Writings of*

Leo, Rufino and Angelo, Companions of St. Francis, ed. and tr. R. B. Brooke. Copyright © 1970.

T. & T. Clark, Edinburgh
"The early Cistercians and the old monasticism," by Adriaan H. Bredero, in *The End of Strife,* ed. David M. Loades, 180-99. Copyright © 1984.
The Writings of Tertullian, tr. S. Thelwall and P. Holmes. Copyright © 1870.

Columbia University Press, New York and London
Heresies of the High Middle Ages, by Walter L. Wakefield and Austin P. Evans. Copyright © 1969.

Franciscan Herald Press, Chicago
St. Francis of Assisi: Writings and Early Biographies, ed. Marion A. Habig, 4th ed. Copyright © 1983.

Medieval & Renaissance Texts & Studies, Binghamton, N.Y.
The Chronicle of Salimbene de Adam, ed. J. L. Bair, G. Baglivi, and J. R. Kane. Copyright © 1986.

Penguin Books, Harmondsworth
Augustine, *The City of God,* tr. Henry Bettenson. Copyright © 1972.
Mediaeval Latin Lyrics, tr. Helen Waddell. Copyright © 1962.
The Waning of the Middle Ages, by Johann Huizinga. Copyright © 1955.

Prentice-Hall, Englewood Cliffs
The Crisis of Church and State, 1050-1300, by Brian Tierney. Copyright © 1964.

University of Pennsylvania Press, Philadelphia
The First Crusade: The Chronicle of Fulcher of Chartres and Other Source Materials, ed. Edward Peters. Copyright © 1971.

Weidenfeld & Nicolson, London
The Early Growth of the European Economy, by Georges Duby. Copyright © 1974.

Abbreviations

ӿ   ӿ

CC	*Corpus Christianorum, Series Latina*
CCM	*Corpus consuetudimum monasticarum*
CCCM	*Corpus Christianorum, continuatio mediaevalis*
COD	*Conciliorum Oecumenicum Decreta,* ed. C. Leonardi, et al. 3rd ed.; Bologna, 1973
Constable	*The Letters of Peter the Venerable,* ed. G. Constable. Cambridge, MA, 1967
HE	*The Ecclesiastical History of Orderic Vitalis,* ed. and tr. M. Chibnall. 6 vols.; Oxford, 1969-80
James	*The Letters of St. Bernard of Clairvaux,* tr. B. S. James. London, 1953
Mansi	J. D. Mansi, *Sacrorum Conciliorum Nova et Amplissima Collectio.* 31 vols.; Florence, 1759-98; repr. in 35 vols., Paris, 1901-27
MGH	*Monumenta Germaniae Historica,* ed. G. H. Pertz. 5 vols.; Hanover, 1835-89
PL	*Patrologia Latina,* ed. J.-P. Migne. 221 vols.; Paris, 1844-64
Recueil	J. Leclercq, *Recueil d'Études sur Saint Bernard et ses Écrits.* 4 vols.; Rome, 1962-87
RHE	*Revue d'histoire ecclésiastique*
RSB	*Regula Sancti Benedicti,* Eng. tr. *St. Benedict's Rule for Monasteries,* tr. L. Doyle. Collegeville, MN, 1948
SBO	*Sancti Bernardi Opera Omnia,* ed. J. Leclercq, H. M. Rochais, and C. H. Talbot. 8 vols.; Rome, 1957-77

I

Religion and Church in Medieval Society[1]

❧   ❧

1. INTRODUCTION

THE DEATH of Emperor Henry II of the Holy Roman Empire on July 7, 1024 brought the dynasty of the Saxon emperors to an end. With the election of his successor the German princes continued the exercise of their electoral rights, which over time had enabled them to expand their influence over and against the emperors and had contributed to a disintegration of the empire.

The childlessness of Henry II had, therefore, far-reaching consequences, and was for him personally — though posthumously — of further importance: Because they produced no offspring, he and his wife Kunigonde were venerated as saints and eventually officially recognized as such. Henry received this distinction in 1146, partly due to the efforts of Pope Eugenius III, while Kunigonde was admitted to sainthood by Pope Innocent III. Naturally, an important role in their canonization was played by the pious works that they had undertaken during their lives, such as building the Cathedral of Bamberg. In that church they were buried, and their tombs drew visitors who experienced miracles and answers to prayer. This led to veneration of the emperor and his wife and no doubt further

1. The Dutch original of this chapter was first written for students in spring 1985 and later revised.

1

influenced those who stood to gain from this veneration, notably the bishops of Bamberg, to urge their canonization.

But the childlessness of Henry and Kunigonde was the basic reason for their veneration and canonization. In the early church only martyrs and confessors were regarded as saints, that is, those who had risked or lost their lives because of their willingness to witness to their faith. When persecution ceased, other criteria for the recognition of sainthood were established. Virtuous deeds — along with the power to work miracles — became the determining factor. The deciding question was whether a particular virtue was manifested in the same heroic way as had been the case when the martyrs had sacrificed their lives. The virtue of chastity came to assume primary significance, and the biographies of most saints contain at least one intriguing passage dedicated to heroic exercise of chastity. Henry and Kunigonde had manifested this virtue at its highest level, which resulted in their lack of offspring.

More rulers died childless then than now, but the records show that this was usually not their intention. Often, in fact, they tried to avoid this situation by having childless marriages annulled or by simply having extramarital affairs. But Henry had not chosen this option, and therefore it was assumed that in pursuit of virtue he and his wife had abstained from sexual intercourse and taken a vow of chastity. Thus they had exhibited virtue in a heroic way and deserved to be venerated as saints.

The veneration of saints was an important part of medieval religious life. It also served a social interest, traces of which are visible even today. No guild, brotherhood, or hospital could exist without the patronage of a saint. This was rooted in the conviction that saints possessed powers that enabled them to influence society. As a result the account of a medieval saint would be more concerned with events occurring after his or her death than with the events of his or her earthly life. The saints' interventions increased the esteem in which they were held, their shrines flourished more and more, stories about their miracles became increasingly abundant, and collections of their relics expanded.

To a significant degree the saints embodied the otherworldly powers held responsible for the many forces and phenomena that remained insufficiently understood or that were not fully accepted by society. Their power was concentrated in a special way in their relics. At first relics were limited to objects that had been in contact with their bodies or their tombs. In those days the grave of a saint remained unopened. In the West this practice began to change in the eighth century, when the remains of martyrs buried in the catacombs outside Rome were exhumed and reburied elsewhere to ensure their safety from the Muslims threatening the city. Thereafter, the martyrs' bones, hairs, and nails were considered relics *par excellence*. As the power attributed to them resided in every part of their physical remains, no saint's relics were kept together in one place.

Each church tried to collect relics. Possession of relics often determined to a considerable extent the patrocinium of a church, that is, the saint under whose protection the building was placed. Relics were kept in a reliquary or enclosed in an altar stone. In newly converted regions, especially in the Frankish kingdom and England, relics were in high demand and people were prepared to spend large sums of money for their acquisition. The English Queen Emma, for example, as the wife of King Canute the Great (†1035), paid many pounds of silver to purchase the arm of the apostle Bartholomew, offered to her by the bishop of Beneventum in southern Italy. He had taken it with him to England, where he had traveled to raise money to combat the famine in his diocese. The transaction was completed when the bishop had, under oath, confirmed the authenticity of the relic. On other occasions people traveled to Rome to acquire relics. A letter from Canute has survived in which, after his return from Rome, he tells his bishops about the many costly gifts he has brought with him. Some of these were mounted in gold and silver, which indicates that he was referring to relics.

The demand for relics frequently exceeded the supply, and sometimes it was necessary to sell relics, for instance, in times of famine. A trade in false relics, many from Italian cemeteries, was the inevitable result. The authenticity of the objects was "attested" by an accompanying *Vita* of a saint. But there were cheaper ways to obtain relics. At times they were stolen, under the protection, it was alleged, of the saint himself, who preferred his new shrine. Sometimes relics were found when an exhumed body appeared to be well preserved and free from the normal odors of a corpse. In such a case these human remains were assumed to have been those of a saint, who was expected to announce his identity. There was no room for doubt, for the Psalmist had written, according to the Latin Vulgate, "You do not give my soul up to hell or let your saint see corruption" (Ps. 16:10).

And so, already in the early Middle Ages, an unbridled cult of saints proliferated. Gradually the church attempted to exercise some control. In the tenth century, for example, it became customary for canonization to precede veneration. At first this could be arranged by the local bishop, but from the twelfth century on canonization came to be a privilege reserved to the pope. Local cults around objects that had no or little relationship with Christianity continued to develop, while the veneration of saints also took forms that, though based on old Christian traditions, evolved in rather unchristian ways. An example of such a local cult, one that has recently received a degree of attention that seems out of proportion, is found in what happened in the village of Neuville, near Lyon. There, from the thirteenth century onward, St. Cunefort was honored as the healer of children; the veneration centered around a dog that had died while saving a child.[2] The degeneration of a Christian tradition is seen in the commemoration of Holy Innocents. Besides the folklore that developed around this church festival, for the most part in the monastic schools, the number of Innocents was greatly augmented by inclusion of children who were found dead, who were believed to have been ritually murdered by Jews, and who thus became martyrs for their faith.

The veneration of saints and pilgrimages to their shrines were indissolubly linked together. Visits to these shrines were further stimulated by widely publicized answers to prayer, especially miracles experienced during such visits. Miraculous answers to prayer were recorded in miracle books. New shrines developed along the routes to important places of pilgrimage. When pilgrimages to Compostella began in the eleventh century, the Conques monastery in the Massif Central enjoyed sudden fame. There the relics of Sainte Foy — "Saint Faith" — were venerated. She was believed to have lived in the South of France and was regarded as a virgin-martyr of the third century. Since Conques lay along one of the important routes to Compostella and many pilgrims stayed there overnight, the interest grew considerably. Already in the eleventh century a new basilica was built for this saint.

※   ※

IN THE SAME CENTURY the urge to journey to places where relics were kept was also of use to the Peace of God movement (see chapter IV below on this movement). The bishops of France, first in the region between Bordeaux, Limoges, and Albi, made vigorous attempts to rein in the fighting spirit of the military elite. The lack of central authority and the fact that

---

2. J.-C. Schmitt, *The Holy Greyhound: Guinefort, Healer of Children since the Thirteenth Century* (Cambridge, 1983).

the Capetian kings were as yet powerless beyond their own central domain, enabled the members of this elite to fight private wars without fear of punishment. This fighting caused most harm to those who were not directly involved. For that reason the bishops tried, through the Peace of God movement, to confine the problem and attempted to assemble great masses of people to further such plans. The most effective method for mass involvement was to bring a collection of relics from different shrines to the place of assembly. Many would be enticed to come, since by traveling to just one place they could venerate all the relics that had been gathered.

Relics, like saints, did not all possess equal power. Power often depended on the influence attributed to a saint in God's dealings with the world. For example, even the Irish knew that St. Peter was a greater saint than St. Patrick. The most important relics were, of course, those of Christ himself. For that reason no pilgrimage could compare with a pilgrimage to Jerusalem. After the crusades, during which Jerusalem had become primarily a place of this-worldly significance, pilgrimage to Jerusalem became important again — and survived long after the Reformation. But even in the early Middle Ages Jerusalem had a special meaning for Christians. As a holy place it radiated a strong attractive force toward the West, such that it overshadowed Compostella, though Compostella drew more pilgrims. Jerusalem even surpassed Rome, even though Rome could boast many tombs of apostles and martyrs and many collections of relics. The objects venerated because of their connection with Christ's Passion — the shroud, the sudary, the wood of the cross, the crown of thorns, and the nails — authentic or not — were essential for many a shrine in the Latin Christian world. But even in this context Jerusalem played a role. The crypts in Carolingian and Romanesque churches symbolized the Holy Sepulchre, and Gothic cathedrals evoked images of the heavenly Jerusalem that one day would descend upon earth.

The pilgrimage to Jerusalem also influenced Christian spirituality. It contributed to a Christ-centered form of piety that continued to expand throughout the medieval period under the name of the imitation of Christ. The development of this spirituality then affected the veneration of saints. It can be recognized in the devotion to Mary as the mother of God and of the child Jesus. But the Jerusalem pilgrimage also had a more peripheral impact. Thus, the claim that the grave of the apostle James was in Compostella dates from when pilgrims were going to Jerusalem. Around the same time the shrine of Mary Magdalene was established at Vézelay, where her remains were believed to rest. In the South of France another cult developed: that of Saint Lazarus. He became the patron saint of the apparently dead, of grave diggers, and of lepers.

In addition to the saints who had lived with Christ on earth, other links were established with the earthly life of Christ. The abbey of Petersborough possessed remains of the swaddling cloths in which Christ had been wrapped after his birth, together with pieces of the manger. It also had some of the bread left over from the feeding of the five thousand. In Milan relics of the three Magi were venerated until around 1160, when they went to Cologne as spoils of war. There, in the cathedral, the altar still stands and is also a shrine attracting many visitors every day. But not all worship required relics. There were churches dedicated to the Trinity, and all Cistercian monasteries were under the patronage of the holy Virgin, without any interest in such objects.

❧   ❧

IT IS CLEAR BY NOW that the medieval veneration of saints was very wide in scope. It included unchristian aspects, but also touched the basics of the faith. It could be no more than a shield against such common threats as disease, bad weather, and other catastrophes, since people were otherwise completely helpless in the face of such misfortunes. But it could also express the Christian mystery of salvation in terms corresponding to the prevailing view of reality. Religion in those days was experienced most of all as participation of the sacred in earthly reality. As a result inexplicable aspects of this reality were attributed to otherworldly forces that had to be either warded off or placated. And this, it was thought, the saints did.

The gospel could be spread across Europe only if it could be assimilated in form and content to the way of experiencing reality current at the time. This did not present too many difficulties as far as form was concerned: The gospel, that is, the New Testament, was already written in conformity with that same sacral view of reality. Moreover, the gospel was preached by people who shared the same experience of reality — often men of great spiritual power who fearlessly encountered the hostile, strange world and were convincing through the very exceptional character of their lives. In proclaiming the gospel, however, more effort was required to recognize and then define the limits of this assimilation. For this sacral view of reality determined to a large extent the thinking of those who, as Christians, believed in a personal salvation that comprehended and transcended death. Since the idea of life after death was already commonly

6

accepted, it was far from simple to evoke the awareness that life after death was given to people only on the basis of their faith in God.

This close connection between the medieval view of reality and the Christian faith is evident in several ways. It is evident in the many church rituals of blessing to give fertility to the soil, to prevent crop failures or thunderstorms, to protect livestock from diseases, and to guard against snakes and other creatures. Numerous blessings also accompanied people during critical moments of life such as childbearing and birth, the beginning of a journey, marriage, and death. At baptism, marriage, and death, blessings were the liturgical accompaniments of sacraments.

Monumental church buildings standing today give us visible reminders of this convergence of the view of reality of that time with the Christian faith. Whatever role prestige may have had in their planning, such structures were designed, built, and embellished to direct people toward eternal salvation and to guard them against evil forces threatening them even in their earthly existence. Churches were regarded as places of refuge. Fugitives found sacral protection in churches, and whoever violated the asylum of a church building would find himself under a sacral threat.

Medieval religious expression included aspects having little or nothing to do with the Christian faith or the church. Some incidents of superstition were totally unacceptable to the church, and, on the other hand, there were manifestations of simple unbelief, indifference, and rationalistic doubt. Sects having nothing in common with the Christian faith also developed.

Nevertheless, the Christian faith, even if not completely orthodox, continued to occupy a central place in the religious experience of the time. It did because it presented itself in its spread across Europe as emerging from a tradition of civilization that was highly respected by the Germanic peoples and because the strength of this religion — from a sociological perspective — lay in its ability to relate to reality as it was experienced by that society. The military elite appeared to be open to the proclamation of the gospel. To live according to its demands required only some adaptation of their code of behavior. We are well informed about this assimilation. But Christianity was also assimilated to the lifestyle of the anonymous rural population, of which we know far less. But something can be gleaned from the church calendar, which combined a cyclical experience of time with an eschatological expectation of salvation. This calendar was not, to be sure, the church's exclusive invention. Important elements of it were derived from Judaism, while the social realities experienced by the rural population provided further contributions. The calendar confirmed an agricultural existence, in which scarcity was a recurring fact. The period of fasting, for example, fell in the season when supplies ran low, with little available except from the monastic storehouses. This may explain why St. Benedict's feast was celebrated on the first day of spring.

Christianity, thus shaped by society in those early years, also adapted itself to later sociological changes, including the growth and growing importance of towns and cities. But because Christianity came to be totally integrated into society, such adaptations and changes did not arise simply from Christian teaching. The need for adaptation was partly the result of pressure exerted by social changes. At times, however, Christian teaching itself was the germ of adaptation, since within its own changing social circumstances it could serve as a point of departure for criticism of society, sometimes even in revolutionary terms.

In this process of adaptation and change in Christianity the Roman Church also was a complicating factor, since it developed into an administrative and social institution, governed primarily by its own laws. The institutionalized church sometimes failed to keep up with new forms of Christianity that grew up in society. Its slow response led at times to protest movements outside the church. Usually these movements were not very successful, not primarily because of the coercive system developed to maintain the unity of Christendom, but because the laypeople were insufficiently educated. But more remarkable than all that was the ability of the medieval church to experience at crucial moments an *aggiornamento*, an adaptation that prevented its degradation from an institution of salvation into a relic of the past.

❧　　　　❧

WHAT WERE THE BASIC social transformations that called for ecclesiastical adaptation? The medieval world began as a society in which fighting was normal and was considered a means of subsistence. The economy of the fighting elite was based on plunder, which they could offer as sacrifice in order to placate otherworldly powers and grant to loyal vassals. This elite continued its military lifestyle until the late Middle Ages. But by then other economic patterns had developed, to which even this elite had to adapt. A first change led to the rise of an agrarian economy based on better use of the soil, which led to other changes, in, for instance, metallurgy: Forging plows was added to the smith's task of forging swords. Social change led to accelerated population growth, which may also have been a result of a more sedentary life. Agricultural surpluses stimulated trade, and that, in turn, resulted in the development of a money-based economy. This, in turn, helped to promote industry and the development of towns, which led to further changes. Tied in with this complexity of change was a series of modifications in religious life, a concurrence that indicates already the close relationship between religion and social life.

To what extent were social and religious change interdependent? It is easier to demonstrate how religion, the church, and Christianity were influenced by the world than, inversely, to explain how they influenced society. The development of a literary culture can perhaps be identified as one area in which the church influenced society. But even such claims remain debatable. All social changes involve numerous factors, religion being just one. Grain cultivation provides a good example. The medieval food supply was always extremely vulnerable, mainly as a result of the preference for growing grain, while growing beans would have reduced the risks. But grain was held in higher esteem because of the role of bread in the Eucharist.

Did this choice result from religious or cultural influences? Culture, in the first analysis, would seem to have been the determining factor, since the Christian religion had already traversed many cultures by the time it was preached to the Germans — most recently the culture of the Latin-speaking part of the Roman Empire. The fact that Christianity, as it was presented to the Germans, had already been integrated into Roman culture, made it attractive, as Germanic peoples wanted very much to participate in Roman civilization. This provides an important social explanation for their conversion, though other factors must also be considered. A precise delineation of the direct religious influence remains nearly impossible, considering the complexity of the social processes of change. But there is no reason to deny the possibility of such influence.

Another important example of the complexity that precludes any exact definition of the role of the church in social change is the disappearance of slavery in the early Middle Ages. Here the church played, without any doubt, an important role. But never did it condemn or forbid slavery as such. It only said that Jews could not own slaves who had been baptized. Likewise the church did not strongly object to other forms of social oppression or dependence. Serfs were usually barred from the priesthood, which is a clear example of adaptation to socially determined relationships, one that explains why revision of social structures did not get the degree of attention from ecclesiastical circles that it sometimes gets today.

9

One aspect of social adaptation on the part of the church that cannot be denied concerns the customs and methods current in the medieval judicial system. The Inquisition, about which little good can be said, must be seen against the background of the medieval judicial practices in terms of which it developed. That background consisted of an amalgamation of practices derived from Germanic tribal customs, such as trial by ordeal, and from the Roman law codes. The Roman codes made it possible to punish a heretic for lèse-majesté. The Inquisition must be understood in this context as an intermediate phase in the painful development of a public coercive power: It took considerable time for the administration of coercive justice, which at first operated through feuds and vendettas, to become the exclusive domain of civil government.

The complexity of social change — now better appreciated by historians due to the influence of the social sciences — has changed the approach of historians to the relationship between religion, church, and society in the Middle Ages, when compared to that of their Christian predecessors in the period between the World Wars. Those earlier historians strongly emphasized the impact of the Christian religion on society, but also usually presented it rather one-sidedly, assuming that the medieval world was preeminently Christian. They painted a flattering portrait of the role of religion and church, which had already been sketched out as an aspect of Romanticism.

Here we will distance ourselves from this view and limit ourselves mainly to drawing out the changes in the way the Christian religion was experienced in the midst of the developments in the medieval world. But we will make no more than an audacious attempt, especially since we can give in this chapter only an outline sketch.

2. EARLY CHRISTIANIZATION

In spite of all the opportunities for assimilation, one immediate consequence of the christianization of the Germanic peoples was a partial discontinuation of ancestor worship. Not wanting to discontinue it may sometimes have been a reason for refusing baptism. But though pagan ancestors lost their significance in this process of christianization, the ancestor cult continued. The nobility provided for Christian cult centers where their family members were buried, and thereby maintained ties to succeeding generations. With this in mind they built and patronized monasteries, which were already becoming numerous in the seventh and eighth centuries, both in England and in the Frankish kingdom. This Christian form of ancestor worship also provided economic benefits: It was no longer necessary to burn part of the harvest as a sacrifice or to put treasures in graves in view of the afterlife.

Conversion to Christianity had at first few consequences for the moral behavior of the members of these warrior clans. They behaved as before, or even worse, since the social control of the earlier ancestor worship was eliminated. Through their behavior, however, these new converts could easily find themselves excluded again from the Christian community, which excommunicated blatant sinners. Excommunication had long been practiced as part of the Christian penitential system. Since baptism provided pardon for sins and absolution from punishment for sin, many converts remained baptismal candidates or catechumens and were only baptized late in life, some only on their deathbeds. After much controversy the early church introduced the possibility of a second pardon for sins, the "second baptism." This exhausted the sinner's possibilities for reconciliation with the church. A flagrant sinner who had to avail himself of this second opportunity to reenter the Christian community would be excommunicated if he fell once more into sin.

This system, already difficult for those born of Christian parents, could no longer be maintained for Germanic converts. Irish missionaries who had come to Gaul introduced the practice of multiple confession, thus deviating substantially from earlier confessional practice. In so doing they also made infant baptism more attractive. Some act of penance was now imposed on the sinner who repented of his sins. After the completion of the act the sins were remitted through the granting of absolution. The punishment for the sins was endured in the act of penance.

Acts of penance were usually rather heavy. From what we know from confessional or penitential books of the time, the penitential tariffs were determined in a way that reflected Germanic tribal laws,[3] which included stipulations concerning wergild intended to limit feuds: The perpetrator of a crime paid an indemnity to the victim or his family, the amount of which was partly determined by the social status of the victim. In the penitential books the degree of punishment for each sin depended

3. J. F. McNeill and H. M. Gamer, *Medieval Handbooks of Penance: A Translation of the Principal* Libri Poenitentiales *and Selections from Related Documents* (1938; repr. New York, 1965).

on the status of the sinner (clergy, layperson, or child) and sometimes of the person with whom the sin had been committed.

Often a sinner, especially when he confessed on a regular basis, was unable to complete all the acts of penance within the remaining years of his life, though he could shorten the required time by, for instance, spending a day of fasting in a crypt. In view of this time pressure the assistance of others sharing in these penitential exercises was welcomed. This became a regular part of the task of the monasteries. Of course, a sinner could withdraw into a monastery to do penance through a holy life. But usually this was left to the monks, in which case the sinner would usually donate a piece of land to the monastery's patron saint, which assured the donor of being remembered as the monks' benefactor in their prayers.

One question regarding this penance by substitution was difficult to answer: Was all guilt remitted at the moment of death of the sinner whose penance was paid by substitution? Often the solution was found in a continuation of penance and prayer after the sinner's death, to safeguard his soul, especially if he was buried at a monastery. Prayer for the dead, already known in the early church, was now primarily intended to shorten the stay of the deceased's soul in purgatory. In the Carolingian era (roughly from the mid-eighth century through the mid-ninth century), when these prayers became accepted practice, where the soul abided for its purification remained a matter for speculation, but that such a third place existed in the beyond was generally believed.[4]

The intercessory monastic prayers strengthened the role of the monasteries in the Germanic Christian world. And monasteries were more than cultic centers where the bond between generations was preserved. They were also places of refuge for one whose life was threatened by others and where one could escape the punishments of an angry god. Entering a monastery just before death, the *conversio ad succurrendum,* was not uncommon. Monasteries also made suitable places of incarceration. When Pepin the Short staged a successful coup in 753, this discarded ruler, the last Merovingian, disappeared, with tonsure, into a monastery. Moreover, monastic life also provided an alternative for those who were ill-suited for the military.

The assistance of the parents of the potential monks and nuns was an important factor in the recruitment of the monastic population. Among

4. A. H. Bredero, "Le Moyen Age et le purgatoire," *RHE* 78 (1983), 429-53.

the elite it was an almost universal custom to dedicate one child to God and give that child at an early age to God's service. As a result the monasteries counted many children among their inhabitants. As oblates — persons dedicated to God — they waited until they were old enough to take final vows. This was neither an attempt to keep up the monastic population nor an alternative to killing unwanted disabled children. Dedicating one's children to God fitted in, with little tension, with the sacral experience of reality, and the right of children to decide for themselves was incompatible with existing family structures.[5]

Monasteries had been in existence from early Christian times, when they were places of refuge for those who fled from a society they rejected as corrupt. Monastic life functioned as a counterculture. Though the daily life of monks remained the same, over time their role vis-à-vis society changed. Monasteries were regarded as places towering above the world. Precisely because their population came primarily from the military elite, they were seen by that elite as allies supporting the warrior class with their prayers. The monks were the sacral guardians of the interests of this elite. Their fixed liturgy with its strict forms fitted perfectly the ritual needs of Germanic society. In matters of justice rituals determined who was guilty or not guilty. In a similar way the correct gesture and appropriate formula were indispensable in the people's relationship with God, who was their highest judge.

In spite of these many relationships between the religious[6] and the laity, two clearly distinguishable types of religious life developed. Those who remained in the world limited themselves to a life lived according to the moral codes, or, when they transgressed the moral codes, to acts of penance — assisted by others — and to invoking the saints. Behind this lay a wide realm of magical practices, known to us mainly from prohibitions issued by synods.

The other form of religious life lay outside the world of normal society and was practiced by those who had separated themselves from the world for its sake. For the monks this experience developed into a distinctive religious culture, which maintained its own language: Latin. The divergence in experience became especially visible in the fact that layper-

5. M. B. de Jong, *In Samuel's Image: Early Medieval Child Oblation* (Leiden, 1990).
6. The author uses *Geestelijken* here to speak of both monks and bishops, in keeping with early medieval distinctions and with Gregory's thought and his strategy of using monks as missionaries [ed.].

sons, who before the seventh century could sometimes exchange a worldly career for the episcopal office, were no longer able to make this transfer. The world of the clergy gradually closed itself to outsiders.

At first this division between laity and religious still knew its exceptions. In the Carolingian Empire the office of bishop or abbot offered possibilities for a career at the court, which explains why there were lay abbots. Appointment of them was a royal prerogative. They did not, however, fit in with the tenor of monastic life and often a monastery administered by a lay abbot was pictured in the contemporary sources as undergoing a period of decline — which was not always actually the case.[7] Such decline did, however, take place in the late Carolingian era, though there were also attempts at revitalization. Those who worked for reform naturally painted a dark picture. The lay abbot typically was attributed a negative role in the process of decline.

At least, this was the way things developed in France. In England hardly any monastic life survived the Viking invasions of the ninth century. Benedict Biscop founded abbeys in Warmouth and Jarrow in 674 and 685, after which a network of monasteries spread over the country. But his work was virtually obliterated between 793 and 870. One of the results was, according to a statement by King Alfred in 871, that nobody south of the Thames was still capable of following the Mass in Latin. Alfred then ,decided to found two monasteries for monks and nuns. The monastic population, including the abbot, the abbess, and the oblates, had to be imported from the Frankish kingdom.

The revival of English monastic life dates only from the middle of the tenth century. The initiative was mainly that of St. Dunstan. In 950 he was sent by his uncle to the abbey of Fleury on the Loire. In 957 he was recalled by King Edgar of Mercia, who appointed him bishop of Worcester. With the help of the young king and two other bishops, Dunstan was able to begin the reconstruction of Benedictine monasticism in England. The result proved to be impressive and eventually the impact of monasticism on English society was as strong as it had already been on the Continent.[8]

The separation between religious and laity in England during the period of monastic decline must have remained much more limited than it was on the Continent. In any case, the deterioration led to attempts to

---

7. F. J. Felten, *Aebte und Laienäbte im Frankenreich* (Stuttgart, 1980).
8. D. Knowles, *The Monastic Order in England* (Cambridge, 1963), 16-57.

translate writings from the patristic tradition into the English of the time. The translation of the *Regula Pastoralis* by Pope Gregory the Great (†604), commissioned by King Alfred, has survived, as have other such documents. We have at least thirty manuscripts of collections of Old English sermons aimed at proclaiming the gospel in the context of the Sunday Mass. It is noteworthy that these manuscripts contain many sermons of the Church Fathers, either in full or excerpted at length. The use of the vernacular disappeared again as monasticism further developed. With the increase in the knowledge of Latin, the separation between religious and laity increased proportionally.

Among the Franks the widening of the chasm between laity and religious was increased by Charlemagne's attempts to encourage literacy among the religious, especially monks, in his empire. This was part of the cultural reform known to us as the Carolingian renaissance. One of Charlemagne's objectives was textual uniformity among biblical and liturgical manuscripts. For that reason a uniform and easily readable script was developed and promoted, the Carolingian minuscle, which is even now found on every typewriter. There was also renewed study of classical Latin. All this increased the distance between the unlettered *(illiterati* or *idiotae)* laity and the educated religious. Charlemagne deemed this separation desirable because of the distinct task of a literate clergy, who needed to strive for the purest possible use of Latin to avoid answers to prayers that were the opposite of what they intended to ask of God. The fulfillment of one's desires, it was thought, depended on enunciating the correct formulas.

Reforms of liturgy and monastic life were also part of this program of renewal. Liturgical renewal had already been undertaken by Pepin the Short, Charlemagne's father. The renewal of monasticism was to be the work of Charlemagne's son, Louis the Pious, who delegated the task to Abbot Benedict of Aniane (†821). It was forbidden to follow other monastic rules than that of Benedict of Nursia (†543). As a result other rules, such as those of the Irish monks and of St. Martin of Tours (†397), disappeared. Moreover, a careful distinction was made between canons and Benedictine monks. Canons, usually connected with capitular churches — often cathedrals — followed the rule of St. Augustine (†430).

The difference in religious experience between laity and religious did not imply total ignorance on the part of lay people regarding the essence of the Christian faith. But we are better informed about their familiarity with moral instruction. Much can be learned from penitentials, and the way in which men and women were to relate to each other in marriage was also carefully prescribed, especially with regard to the period during which they were to refrain from sexual intercourse. These rules were primarily based on the spirit of the time rather than on biblical precepts, even though the Bible was appealed to. "The obsession of that time with sexual abstinence according to the church calendar and convictions regarding purity . . . were not in the least characteristic of a Christianity for all ages."[9]

The laity's ignorance of doctrine and religious experience was mainly in regard to the prayers offered by the clergy. The clergy prayed in Latin and their prayers remained untranslated. Even "Ave Maria" did not become "Hail Mary." Active lay participation in the liturgy was out of the question. The laity went to church mainly as spectators. Usually there was plenty to see. The walls of churches were covered with paintings depicting biblical stories. Even the creed was depicted as a series of stories. Admittedly, Charlemagne had taken the position in his *Libri Carolini* that pictures were superfluous, since the law of Moses was put in writing and not in pictures. But this concerned primarily the clergy. Charlemagne did also indicate that churches needed images as decorations and as reminders of past events. Frescoes dating from that time, such as are found in the crypt of the former abbey of St. Gavin sur Gartempe, suggest that stories from the Scriptures were also included in the notion of "images." Whether pictorial instruction was adequate remains questionable, and it is not clear by what standard its adequacy could have been measured.

❧   ❧

A TOTALLY DIFFERENT aspect of religion and the church originating in the Carolingian era was the formation of an ideology of Christendom. The term *christianitas,* referring to the community of believers, was already in use, though sparingly. Pope Boniface V (619-25) called Jesus Christ "the source and head of all Christendom."

"Christendom" as the state consisting of all Christians, of which Christ was the founder and leader, was first referred to by Augustine. In *City of God* he placed this city of Christendom in opposition to that of the world or of the devil, while giving a novel definition of the state *(res*

9. J.-L. Flandrin, *Un temps pour embrasser: Aux origines de la morale sexuelle (VIe-XIe siècle)* (Paris, 1983), 160.

publica). The current definition was: a community of people answering to the same laws. Augustine's description became: a community of people sharing the same purpose. This enabled him to differentiate between two states: the community seeking what is higher than what is human, the city of God, and the community that is utilitarian in its aims, seeking what is of benefit now, the terrestrial city.

Augustine never said clearly what state anyone belonged to, except, in general terms, the dead, who have received, he said, their definite citizenship in one of the two states. While on earth a person moves, he said, between the two states, so that the distinction between them is an abstraction. The (actual) state was a necessary evil, established because of human weakness.

In the Germanic world, where the capacity for abstract thought was still non-existent, Augustine's concept was understood differently and was adapted to one's particular social situation. Each person was part of a kinship unit and was hardly allowed to make personal decisions. When these kinship units disintegrated as they were incorporated in the Carolingian Empire, this remained unchanged: Concepts of communal relationships continued to be dominated by the idea of collectivity.

In his thinking about his empire, Charlemagne reverted to Augustine's doctrine of two cities. He identified his empire as the city of God, and its population as Christendom. Outside his empire was the state of the devil. The terms *Franci* and *christiani* became almost identical as terms for his subjects. Baptism was a prerequisite for both. His wars of conquest were holy wars, and the conquered not only saw their territory incorporated into his empire but were also forced to become Christians. Conquest and christianization went together and the preachers of the gospel worked in the service of the Frankish rulers. Boniface (†754) was somewhat of an exception, since he succeeded in maintaining his independence. But this was before the time of Charlemagne, who gave greater force to the conjunction of missionary and royal service. His coronation as emperor made his domain the *imperium christianum,* and Christendom — the subjects of his empire — thus became a political and ideological unit. Charlemagne did not apply the title of king or emperor of Christendom to himself, but some courtiers did.[10]

These courtiers were literate, belonging as they did to the clergy.

10. J. Rupp, *L'idée de chrétienté dans la pensée pontificale des origines à Innocent III* (Paris, 1939), 27-29.

In the traditions of the church they had an arsenal of material on which this ideological unity could be built. The Romans already referred to the Christians as a people in analogy to the Jewish people. The term took on ethnic color, and came to be interpreted by Christian authors in a spiritual sense. Augustine spoke of the Christian people *(populus christianus)*, elected to a position above that of the Jews.[11] Around 600 the All Saints' litany included the following supplication, "That You may give peace and unity to all Christians, Lord, hear our prayer." This prayer was sung in Latin at all church ceremonies and worked its way deep into the consciousness of the clergy. Thus it was that the political accomplishments of Charlemagne could be viewed as an answer to prayer.

But this answer to prayer proved to be of limited duration. Therefore, the concept of Christendom as an ideological unity found no further elaboration. Carolingian political unity ended in the ninth century, when the empire collapsed through invasions and internal discord. But the term "Christendom" survived in ecclesiastical discourse. "Church" was used to denote the clergy. Laity and clergy together constituted Christendom as a sacral community. This concept embraced more than the church; it also encompassed a political community.

When civil authority collapsed, that community sought refuge with the church, where it received a willing ear. This was the situation during the pontificate of John VIII (872-82).[12] Christendom looked for his protection against the barbaric invasions and the Muslims, and he, time and again, asked for assistance from the Byzantine emperor and the Frankish rulers. Christendom consisted of those countries, people, and events that were — or were supposed to be — under the influence of Christ. One had but to await the moment when the pope could claim leadership of this Christendom and could enforce this claim.

3. THE ELEVENTH CENTURY AND THE TRANSITION TO THE TWELFTH

THAT MOMENT WOULD COME in the eleventh century, when changes that had begun earlier came to have more visible effects. As we have noticed, a breakthrough in the agrarian economy influenced these processes of

11. *Enarratio in Ps. 77* ix = *PL* XXXVI, 990.
12. Cf. Rupp, 35-52.

change to a considerable extent. But the agrarian economy was highly vulnerable. Harvests remained relatively poor and crop failures could even carry the risk of losing the seed for the next planting season.

Moreover, farmers still had to fear looters, since a vacuum in central authority again gave the plunderers full opportunity to pursue their ways. The western part of the Frankish kingdom, that is, most of what we know as France today, was especially suffering from this anarchy. The Peace of God movement was not very successful. Pacifying the military elite proved to be difficult. Things improved when regional princes were able to establish their authority and were, to some extent, successful in imposing their will on the military. The contribution of the church to the pacification of society in the West consisted largely of its appeal to the military profession to take part in the crusades.

The first appeal was launched in 1095 by Pope Urban II during a council in Clermont-Ferrand. It was an expression of papal authority that apparently found receptivity in western Frankia. Papal authority had not yet been fully established and the struggle to obtain it — the investiture dispute — was still going on. The investiture dispute had been brought on by abuses arising from lay influence on ecclesiastical appointments. Spiritual offices were bought and sold, and this usually implied vassalage. Many of the clergy who found themselves in this double role paid hardly any attention to the obligations of their spiritual callings. These abuses were widespread in the western church in the first half of the eleventh century.

But the claims to papal authority had been clearly formulated, and the laity in particular agreed with them because of the need for reformation of the clergy. Heretical lay initiatives, born of a desire to improve the church, can be noted in the first half of the eleventh century, but no longer occurred when Rome itself undertook this reform, which we know as the Gregorian Reform, after Pope Gregory VII (†1085).

One can only tentatively determine the extent to which the laity felt involved in the affairs of the church. There is, however, another indication that Christendom had become a social reality. That is the surprisingly large response of the laity to that first call for a crusade. Several elements were, of course, involved in the response. Part of the reason was, no doubt, the significance that Jerusalem held for the West. A journey to Jerusalem was considered a last resort in a totally hopeless situation. That view was an expression of the Christian hope for salvation, and thus the First Crusade, contrary to the later crusades, was the expression of a religiously motivated popular movement, though some historians have found this interpretation

19

difficult to accept. They feel the participation of the people — of Christendom — must rather be seen as a sign of social unrest. Such discontent did indeed exist, but it expressed itself in popular uprisings during the investiture dispute. But these, too, were partly religiously determined.

During the eleventh century many abuses occurred due to the influence of a part of the laity on church appointments in nearly every region of the church's expansion in the West. Spiritual appointments were bought and sold because they were bound to vassalage. Many of the clergy who held these appointments did not pay much attention to the accompanying responsibilities. Resistance to this lay domination of the Church came from another part of the laity who turned against the feudalized clerical establishment, and it probably would not have tipped the balance had resistance not existed elsewhere within Christendom. Resistance developed in episcopal circles in Lorraine. Through Emperor Henry III this group gained influence in Rome. In mid-century Pope Gregory began to provide leadership for this reform movement. This reform program soon led to the schism between the Latin church and the Greek church, which was never to be healed, and to a long conflict with the German emperor: the investiture controversy.

※   ※

THE GREGORIAN reform movement was preceded by another, less notorious movement, which did, however, create the climate for the later movement, which was to free the church from lay rule over the clergy. This earlier, less sensational, reformation occurred in the monasteries, which had suffered immensely since the demise of the Carolingian Empire. Raiders destroyed numerous abbeys. Entire monastic communities had to flee and, with their relics, were on the move for years before finding places to settle. The reorganization of the monasteries sought by Louis the Pious had resulted in little more than a general introduction of the rule of St. Benedict. But it did not by any means guarantee strict compliance with that rule as it existed in those days. Moreover, with the loss of imperial protection, many monasteries had become lay property.

Reaction against lay ownership set in toward the end of the ninth century, though on a limited scale. In their desire to free themselves from lay rule, some monasteries had sought the special protection of St. Peter, that is, the pope. At that time the pope did not yet present himself as Christ's vicar, but as the successor of Peter, to whom the keys of heaven had been given. Petrine authority was exercised particularly in papal granting of privileges and in the sanctions that the pope could, as possessor of the keys, invoke against those who dared to violate such privileges. He could threaten them with damnation, as appears from the injunctions attached to such privileges.

One of the monasteries benefiting from papal protection was Cluny, which was founded in 910. The rule of life *(ordo)* at Cluny was clearly based on the incomplete reforms of the Carolingian era, notably with respect to the importance attributed to the liturgy and to choral prayer.[13] The monks' prayers were supposed to foster the interests of Christendom, specifically of that class of Christians with which they enjoyed special ties. Yet Cluny, as a result of its papal privileges, was free from secular authority and even fell outside episcopal jurisdiction. This "exemption" contributed greatly to the process that was to make Cluny such an important ally in Rome's struggle with the emperor and the princes, since Rome could not rely on bishops appointed by the princes.

Cluny needed a good scriptorium for adequate execution of the expansive liturgical task that it had taken on. This proved a heavy burden, especially because the obligations of prayer caused a neglect of the manual labor mandated by Benedict's rule. Consequently the monastery came to be dependent economically on those on whose behalf its prayers were offered. The monks hardly had time left to work the land and most income was derived from donations, especially harvest tithes.[14] Monastic life at Cluny was not overly ascetic, and many poor had to be fed every day, even when in the twelfth century donations and tithes declined.

Cluny was not simply an important abbey and the place where the largest church of Christendom was being built. It comprised hundreds of monasteries where the way of life of its monks, their *ordo,* was followed. Cluny developed into a monastic order, though it seemed less so in its organization. The abbot of Cluny served as the abbot of most Cluniac houses. But daily affairs were in the hands of priors appointed by the abbot. Monasteries that had been under lay authority were, out of pressure from the monks or as a result of the nascent reform movement, transferred to the abbot of Cluny. He was commissioned to revise the way of life in

13. Cf. A. H. Bredero, *Cluny et Cîteaux au douzième siècle* (Amsterdam/Maarssen, 1985), ch. 1 (pp. 1-26): "Cluny et le monachisme carolingien: continuité et discontinuité."
14. Cf. G. Constable, *Monastic Tithes from their Origins to the Twelfth Century* (Cambridge, MA, 1964).

these monasteries. Thus the abbots of Cluny, who during the eleventh century each ruled for a long period, became extremely powerful leaders in Christendom and were, after their deaths, venerated as saints.

The way of life for these monastic houses had come to be determined partly by written *customs,* which sometimes assumed more importance than the rule itself. They led to great rigidity from the eleventh century onward, at which time Benedictines gradually began to give more attention to the population tied in servitude to the land and providing labor for the monasteries. Improved agricultural techniques resulted in better harvests, from which not these workers but the monasteries, through the tithing system, benefited. But other monks realized what was happening and wanted to support themselves, as had earlier been the practice, through their own labor.

This desire for reform was also provoked by developments in spirituality. Christ received a more central place and many monks wanted to imitate more fully his earthly life in poverty. This did not yet entail a renunciation of material goods on the part of the monastic communities, as the mendicant orders would later require. But in an agrarian society, where working the land brought low profits and the possession of acreage did not result in high income, possessing large holdings only meant relative prosperity. Whoever wanted to live from the land, without being a serf, had to own land. So the desire for poverty did not yet lead to a rejection of monastic property. The individual monk had to live frugally with regard to food, clothing, and housing and had to follow the rule without paying attention to the formally prescribed *customs.*

❧   ❧

MEDIEVAL REFORMERS looked for a return to a primeval golden age. The last chapter of Benedict's rule pointed in such a direction with its counsel that those striving for perfection turn to the exhortations and precepts of the earliest monks, the desert hermits. At the end of the eleventh century many wanted to return to the life of the hermits, though usually not as individuals. They preferred to be together with kindred spirits.

Eremitic monasteries were established in remote places and enforced the rule far more strictly.[15] Manual labor and silence were once

15. H. Leyser, *Hermits and the New Monasticism: A Study of Religious Communities in Western Europe, 1000-1150* (London, 1984).

again stressed. Many such communities disappeared quickly, however, and some were absorbed into a wider network of related monasteries. The Carthusian order, founded in 1084 by Bruno, the canon of Cologne, deserves separate mention. At fifty-four years old he retired with some associates into the Alps near Grenoble, in the Grande Chartreuse, where even today some monks continue to lead their eremitic life in this almost inaccessible monastery.

The best-known and most successful initiative among the eremitic institutions was Cîteaux. This monastery was founded in 1098 in Burgundy, the same region where Cluny is located. So much has been written and so much energy expended in polemics about the earliest history of this abbey and the order that developed from it — the Cistercian order — that the smoke of scholarly dispute has not yet fully dissipated.[16] This much is clear: The monks of Cîteaux wanted to follow Benedict's rule unencumbered by the traditions that had developed around it. They therefore exchanged black hoods and garments, usually of good quality, for undyed habits. They were henceforth clothed in white, which soon became a symbol for them of greater perfection and for others of spiritual pride.

At first Cîteaux was extremely poor. It was located in a desolate, swampy area. Its monks were serious about manual labor and spent much time working the land. They refused to receive or pay tithes and did not have much time left for liturgy. Their churches were simple, but showed architectural refinement and had no distracting statues and paintings. One would have expected the same simplicity in their manuscripts, but they were, instead, often richly illuminated and contained multicolor miniatures. The rule required that each monk and lay brother read a book during Lent. Lay brothers often could not read, so for them instructive picture books were indispensable.

The Cistercians had no oblates. Their novices entered the monastery at the age of at least fifteen. The choir monks of the order received their education outside the monastery, often at cathedral schools. As a result their spirituality resembled what many of them had experienced in the world. This explains why their mystical authors so often focused on allegorical readings of the Song of Solomon, in which love for God is compared to a bride's devotion. This unique aspect of Cistercian spirituality constituted a significant factor in the development of the female

16. J.-B. Auberger, *L'unanimité cistercienne primitive: mythe ou réalité?* (Cîteaux Studia et Documenta 3; Achel, 1986).

branch of the order, which came a little later, though as early as the thirteenth century the order had more convents for women than abbeys for men.

The growth of the male branch began fifteen years after Cîteaux had been established. By the middle of the twelfth century there were already some 350 monasteries, spread over many countries. Clairvaux, founded in 1113, played a major role in this process. St. Bernard (†1153), the first abbot, strongly promoted this growth and was to become one of the most important leaders of Christendom of that time. Among other accomplishments, he ended a papal schism and launched the appeal for the Second Crusade. His influence — sometimes negative — was felt in practically all aspects of contemporary life. Through his writings, which were of excellent literary quality, he set the trend for Christian spirituality. For centuries his books were read, even in Reformation circles. Luther and Calvin knew and used his sermons and his influence on Pietism is unmistakable.

The enormous success of the Cistercian order was closely related to the growth of the agrarian economy, which led not only to higher profits but also to use of previously uncultivated lands, which was necessary because of population growth. The increase in population was due in part to the possibility of marrying at a younger age brought by a higher standard of living. And unwanted newborns were now abandoned rather than killed.

The Cistercian monasteries were often built in remote areas and had an important role in the development of marginal lands. Their communities included, apart from choir monks, also lay brothers, the *conversi*, who worked in the fields and lived during the week in outlying farm buildings, coming only on Sundays to the abbey to attend Mass. They contributed in a major way to the prosperity of this well-organized order, which itself played a significant role in the changes in society occurring in Western Europe. Religious motivations were mixed with other factors in these changes.

The *conversi* were at least partly motivated by religion in their work, which had a strong impact on society, notably because it involved claiming marginal land for agriculture. From a base in Ter Doest in Flanders, they were responsible for creating polders in Voorne-Putten in the southern Netherlands. Much is also known about their work in Frisia. How they went about their work depended on their location. Depending on the type of soil, they also began some industries. So some abbeys had salt mines, ovens for bricks and tiles, marlpits, iron mines, or smithies. But the *conversi* continued to work on the land, while, where possible, increasing the acreage. Those who worked on the Vaulerent grange of the Chaalis abbey from the thirteenth century onward provided food for a major section of Paris.[17]

                ≈   ≈

THE EREMITIC MOVEMENT, which gave rise to the Cistercians, led to another initiative that involved the common laity more: the activities of popular preachers. The lifestyle of these preachers resembled that of hermits, but they traveled while preaching. They opted for poverty out of solidarity with the poor. For that reason they were highly critical of the wealth of the church and of the behavior of the higher clergy, of bishops and canons. They were allies of those who supported the ecclesiastical reform movements and so during this period were tolerated by the bishops, though they were viewed with suspicion. As a result of their criticism, administration of the sacraments by unworthy priests came to be viewed as invalid. This view had long been regarded as heresy, but the reformers tried to keep people from confessing to such priests and from attending church when unworthy priests were reading the Mass.

Another reason for suspicion was the popularity of these preachers with women. Often a preacher would have a number of women in his entourage. The preachers repeatedly showed their concern for prostitutes, sometimes providing dowries. But there were also women who, struck by the call for repentance, wanted a totally different lifestyle. They came from all walks of life and had not all been obvious sinners. The popular preachers were able to avoid conflicts on this issue by founding convents where their female followers could continue their lives of repentance in a more orderly fashion.

The eremitic movement not only criticized the wrongdoings of the clergy, but was also opposed to the status of the clergy in the church. They were, however, not very vocal in expressing this anticlerical sentiment. But wherever the eremitic movement included many lay people in its ranks, the question naturally arose whether they, too, had the right to preach and to hear confessions. From what these preachers themselves said, one gets the impression that they regarded the question as beside the point. But the bishops were, of course, of a different opinion. They insisted that every

17. C. Higounet, *La Grange de Vaulerent* (Paris, 1965). For England, cf. C. Platt, *The Monastic Grange in Medieval England* (London, 1969) and bibliography there.

preacher request permission from the local bishop before operating in his diocese. At times the lay status of a preacher escaped the bishop's attention. This happened, for instance, in the case of Henry of Lausanne, who was active when the Gregorian reform movement had come to an end. His lay status, it would seem, is the primary reason that he changed from a reformer into a heretic.

4. ASSIMILATION TO THE URBAN POPULATION

IN THE Roman Empire Christianity was clearly an urban religion. Christianizing the countryside proved to be a much slower process. The English word "pagan" is derived from Latin *paganus,* which meant "country dweller." With the fall of the empire, at least in the West, cities and towns lost their social importance, and the Germanic peoples had no affinity whatever with town life. The cities did not disappear completely. Where they survived they often served as episcopal residences.

The revival of the cities in the later Middle Ages posed new problems to the church, especially with regard to the monetary economy. Though this was never confirmed by a church council, the church had taken a stand against the charging of interest. With the rise of a monetary economy this opposition was now expressed more explicitly.

Questions surrounding the charging of interest were not the only problems that the revival of urban life presented for the church. Wealth and property changed so drastically that the ideal of poverty, which had been emphasized in the eremitic movement, demanded a more radical expression. The protest against wealth, particularly in the church, did not always follow the path of orthodoxy. In fact, the church's suspicious attitude sometimes invited those who voiced this protest to depart from orthodoxy. Some of the laity were increasingly articulate, especially in cities that had risen to prominence, and saw the church as lording it over them, which also played a role in the rise of heresies. The emancipated urban population focused on participation in government, and not only in the affairs of their own city. At times the struggles on the part of the urban laity for political and ecclesiastical emancipation were almost inseparable, especially in cities with bishops, where local government was in the hands of the church.

The main obstacle to emancipation of the laity was their illiteracy. This was gradually changing. But even when they learned to read, they remained illiterate in the eyes of the clergy, since their knowledge was limited to the vernacular and did not include ability to write. Writing in the vernacular was generally a matter of translating and presupposed substantial knowledge of Latin. There was widespread interest in translations of the Scriptures, or at least of portions of it. This the church opposed vehemently. Nevertheless, the Scriptures were distributed. Direct translations were especially popular among heretics. Lay people who remained in the church, and who wanted to stay there, produced biblical paraphrases, Bibles in verse, and Bible histories. A comparison of the development of the vernacular in the northern Netherlands with other parts of the country shows the relationship between these literary initiatives and urban development: The North was at least a century behind not only because its language was more different from Latin, but also because cities developed there later.

All these problems and the more open manifestations of non-Christian practices did not usually occur in isolation from each other, but were rather linked together or joined with other tensions experienced by faith and church in the new urban setting. This became apparent, for example, in the emergence of movements which promoted voluntary poverty as a reaction to new forms of wealth and exploitation. According to some, the religious aspects of these movements served only as a cloak for social problems that could not present themselves at face value in a society that still felt the yoke of the "original sin of belief."

THE WALDENSIANS, who ultimately left the church, offer a striking example of religious and social causes working together. Their movement was started by Peter Waldo (†1206/7), a wealthy merchant from Lyon. He owed part of his wealth to lending money against interest, which was forbidden to Christians. On a Sunday in 1173 or 1174, so the story goes, he heard a jongleur, a minstrel, telling the story of St. Alexis, a repentant son of a rich man who fled his parents' home on the eve of his marriage. The saint opted for a life of poverty and many years later returned home as a beggar. There he was welcomed, though he remained unrecognized. Having heard this story, Waldo consulted a theologian and then decided to sell his possessions, give away his money, and begin living a perfect life (*vita perfecta*). He commissioned two clergymen to make a translation of the Gospels, some Old Testament writings, and some sayings of the Fathers.

He chose these texts because he regarded reading from them as part of the perfect life that the Christian should lead in the footsteps of the apostles.

There are some discrepancies between this conversion story and Waldo's contract with the translators, which still exists. The element of poverty has often been overemphasized, especially by social historians. From the start Waldo realized that the church's main deficiency with regard to the common people was lack of preaching. The itinerant preachers shared that conviction. Waldo wanted to remedy that deficiency, but canon law provided but little room for lay initiatives. His earliest followers trained themselves to preach and, where they were allowed, mounted the pulpit in churches beginning in 1176.

To better institutionalize these preaching activities, Waldo and some of his companions traveled to Rome in 1179, when the Third Lateran Council was in session.[18] They did not receive official sanction, but were allowed to preach when invited by the clergy. But they were not always welcomed. Many clergy were afraid of the anticlericalism developing among the urban masses in response to the shortcomings of the clergy and their dominant role in the church. This combination of religious and social discontent explains to a large extent the success of the lay preachers. Some of Waldo's followers lost their preaching privileges after expressing themselves too strongly. But that was not the breaking point between the movement and the church.

In fact, no break with the church occurred in Waldo's lifetime. The movement's teaching remained free from heresy. Some of his followers rejected prayer for the dead with the argument that good works were the decisive prerequisites for salvation. But there was no break with the church because Waldo did not want to rebel against ecclesiastical authority and in no way intended to bring reform to church or society through his decision for poverty. Many in the church appreciated both Waldo and the work of the Waldensians. But the archbishop of Lyon intentionally provoked a conflict, no longer allowing the Waldensians to preach in his diocese or to stay in Lyon.

In 1210 the breach became final, partly because some of Waldo's followers went beyond what he himself wanted. An important factor was that women came to be accepted into the movement and gained a share

18. Cf. R. B. Brooke, *The Coming of the Friars* (London/New York, 1975), 72; cf. 151f. for the text of Walter Map's biased account of the interrogation of the Waldensians at the Council.

in the preaching activity. The break brought internal conflict. Some of the Waldensians pulled out of the movement, and this part of the "poor men of Lyon," as the Waldensians were called, remained in the church as the "poor Catholics."

The Waldensian movement had, no doubt, a social aspect, but this factor can be exaggerated. Medieval revolts against the established authorities were not directed toward social reform, an ideal that did not yet exist. The aim was simply to acquire the position and wealth of those rebelled against and usually to redress concrete grievances, though there might be some idea of a return to a vaguely defined golden era of the past. At any rate, the Waldensian movement cannot be compared with such short-lived revolts.

Another social expectation of those days focused on earthly bliss — in the dream of a millennium during which heaven would fill the earth. But again it would be a mistake to associate the Waldensians with such an idea. Medieval millenarian dreams were rooted in the official eschatology of the church, but the church viewed its own presence on earth as the realization of the biblical prophecies of a millennium. The more vociferous millenarian eschatologies were less significant in the Middle Ages than would appear from the overemphasis they have received from some historians. They found their most concrete expression in the images of Jerusalem operative among the crusaders and later in the influential ideas of the Calabrian abbot Joachim of Fiore (†1202), who looked for the coming of the rule of the Spirit in the rise of monasticism.[19] But revolutionary eschatological movements like those later created by some Anabaptists were unheard of in the Middle Ages. For that reason it would be wrong to identify the Waldensians, who throughout their long history remained committed to their religious aims, with the more socially inspired revolts that occurred when the Waldensians were first active.

❧   ❧

THE CATHARI (or Albigensians) must be assessed differently. They first appeared in Western Europe in the twelfth century in a number of urban centers, being noted first in the Rhineland around 1143. It is probable that their movement originated in the Balkans. It resembled the theology of

19. B. McGinn, *Visions of the End: Apocalyptic Traditions in the Middle Ages* (New York, 1979), 126-41.

the Bogomiles and was also akin to ancient Manichaeism. Both Catharism and Manichaeism presupposed an evil power operating independently from the power of good. Matter, both groups said, belongs to the realm of evil, while the spiritual was of the realm of the good.

The Cathars distinguished in their own ranks between the *perfecti* and mere followers. Because they regarded the material world as evil, they rejected sex and marriage as unsuitable for *perfecti*. Animals were not to be eaten, since they owed their existence to sexual intercourse. The Cathars rejected baptism, except by the Spirit, and the Eucharist. They held that forgiveness of sins was possible only through a ritual of laying on of hands, the *consolamentum,* which was extended to those joining the ranks of the *perfecti* and to the dying. The Cathars used the Lord's Prayer and accepted the New Testament, though their interpretation of the latter was directed against the ecclesiastical hierarchy.

The Cathar movement came to be localized in southern France, where it grew to such importance that the church waged war against it (the Albigensian Crusade, 1209-29).[20] When warfare failed to have the desired result, a special inquisition was established that began a meticulous search in the Languedoc region, where most of the Cathari were concentrated.

Why was Catharism so popular in Languedoc? Dualistic natural religion was common in the medieval world, and was christianized to varying degrees. A striking example is the purification ritual for a woman who had given birth. But in Catharism dualism was more important. It has, therefore, been suggested that Catharism expressed a deeply rooted discontent with newer ideas that were surfacing in medieval society. But this suggestion is in need of more evidence, since the Cathar movement, which had support from all classes, was too complex a phenomenon to be explained from one point of view. Political issues must have played a role, given the involvement of so many of the nobility of the region. Moreover, Languedoc had known a strong anticlerical sentiment since the preaching of Peter of Bruys and Henry of Lausanne in the first half of the twelfth century. Geographical isolation may also have been of some influence. But it is unlikely that Catharism can be reduced to a social heresy rooted in the discontent of one particular class.

20. J. Sumption, *The Albigensian Crusade* (Boston, 1978).

❧   ❧

HISTORIANS' VIEWS of heresies of the past do not depend just on ideological predispositions or preferences for particular social systems. Their disputes regarding the heretics date back as far as the Reformation. Catholics, with their affinity for the medieval church, have defended the persecution of heretics. Protestants have often come to regard the heretics as precursors of the Reformation.

In both camps heretics have been viewed in ahistorical detachment from the times and circumstances in which they lived. Peter Waldo was judged apart from other developments in regard to voluntary poverty; possible connections between Franciscan ideals and developments outside the church have sometimes been disregarded. All these currents of thought of that time, whether their adherents stayed in the church, left it freely, or were forced to leave, were part of the same social environment, which went beyond matters of religion. They were part of the movement of emancipation in which city-dwellers demanded a role in government from local rulers and insisted on sharing in the privilege of literacy, even if they were restricted to the vernacular.

One religious and ecclesiastical consequence of this drive toward emancipation was that lay people were obtaining firsthand knowledge of the gospel and were adjusting their lifestyles accordingly. They, too, began to speak of imitating Christ and his apostles, with a strong emphasis on poverty and preaching, as had participants in the eremitic movement.

At first church authorities reacted negatively. Waldo remained unsuccessful, though he and most of his followers wanted nothing more than to call sinners to repentance, the pious to perseverance, and the clergy to commitment to their duties. The clergy may have felt threatened in regard to their social privileges by all this, but the primary explanation of the rise of anticlericalism would have to be the intangible nature of these movements: They were outside the church structures and uncontrollable when they slid toward heresy. This the church authorities saw as a grave danger, the more so because of the extensive use of the vernacular. Significantly enough there was far less ecclesiastical concern about the beliefs and superstitions of the laity at large, who were the target of the preaching activities of these movements.

The effect in church and religion of the emancipation of city-dwellers could not be ignored forever by the ecclesiastical authorities. Pope Innocent III (1198-1216) understood that the church had to accommodate this lay movement. He restored permission to preach to the Poor Catholics, the followers of Waldo who had reconciled themselves with the church. One of the constitutions of the Fourth Lateran Council, held during his pontificate, dealt with the need for a stronger emphasis on popular preaching.[21] His many canonizations of saints are evidence of his conscious effort to align the church with society. He seems to have contemplated using the Poor Catholics in his attempts to give more attention to the efforts of the laity to gain a deeper religious experience. But because he saw a better possibility, the Poor Catholics did not receive that role.

THIS POSSIBILITY presented itself in Francis of Assisi, the son of a rich merchant. His father and many others believed that he was merely infatuated with poverty. But when it became clear that his choice of poverty, which he often praised as his bride, was not a temporary whim, an open separation between father and son ensued. The local bishop took an interest in this religiously motivated fool, who interpreted literally a divine commission to rebuild the church, and so began to repair decaying country chapels with donated materials. When others joined him in ever increasing numbers, Francis himself barely realized the need to institutionalize the movement that had grown up around him. For this he needed papal permission and for that purpose the bishop sent him to Rome.

The rule that Francis initially presented was only what the Gospels prescribed as the perfect way of life. That, perhaps, was his good fortune. The general tendency was to allow no new rules for orders, and this restriction was legislated during the Lateran Council. The rules that existed, it was thought, were adequate. What Francis presented could not, however, be put in any existing category.

A later story about the visit of *Il Poverello* — as Francis was often called — to the pope in 1210 was captured in a fresco by Giotto on the wall of the church of Assisi. According to this story, Pope Innocent III dreamed that he was in most prestigious basilica in Rome, that of St. John Lateran. The building was about to collapse, but this was prevented by an unseemly beggar who supported the pillars with his hands. When Francis visited the pope the following day, Innocent recognized him as that beggar.

21. Constitution 10: *De praedicatoribus instituendis = COD,* 239f.

This story is part of the legend that soon was woven around the appearance of Francis. In a different way his canonization also contributed to the legend. He was canonized in 1228, only two years after his death. The pope made this decision without the usual investigations that precede a canonization, perhaps in a deliberate effort to foster the growth of the legend. The results were that the bare facts about Francis, which could have provided more historical certainty about his person and intentions, were never collected. The drafting of the rule of the order at the pope's insistence was also part of the weaving of the legend. The rule was needed to institutionalize the movement, though it eclipsed the earlier rule, which retained its informal character but never received official approval. This earlier *regula non bullata* nevertheless remains fundamental for reconstructing Francis's intentions. And when the measures taken at that time by the commune of Assisi to exclude the poor and the strangers are taken into consideration, it becomes clear that social protest played a much more pronounced role in his work than is usually recognized.[22]

ONE OF THE CHURCH BUILDINGS renovated by Francis was the monastery of San Damiano, which he reserved for living quarters for women who joined his movement. Clara di Offreducio, a young woman from a noble family, was placed in charge of the women. She and her associates wanted to follow the same rule that guided Francis and his followers — a rule that was, as mentioned above, accepted but not officially approved. The local bishop took exception to this and demanded that the women follow the rule of St. Benedict and live in strict enclosure. He also wanted them to own property, even though Innocent III had granted the Poor Clares, as they came to be called, the privilege of living in poverty. In 1227 this bishop was elected pope as Gregory IX. Though he almost immediately proceeded to canonize Francis, he refused to rescind his decision regarding the Clares. Clara was heavily disappointed, but did not rebel. Later, after the death of Gregory in 1241, she approached his successor, Innocent IV, who restored the privilege of poverty. But the strictly enclosed life of the Clares was maintained.

Recent studies of the position of women in medieval society vary considerably in their perception of the place of women in these religious

22. D. Flood, *Frère François et le mouvement franciscain* (Paris, 1983).

renewal movements. Since women received their liberty only in heretical movements, it is suggested that they must have played a significant role in such movements. Elsewhere in society, it is asserted, and in the realm of religion and church, women had limited roles other than procreation. According to this view the rapid growth of convents in the twelfth and especially in the thirteenth century must be explained on the basis of a surplus of women, resulting from loss of men to the crusades and to stricter observance of clerical celibacy.

Opposed to this view is the theory that emphasizes the strong desire of women to participate in religious renewal. Women, like men, felt inspired by the New Testament and wanted to put into practice what they read. But the church did not allow them to travel around, begging and preaching, and kept them far from anything related to sacerdotal functions. This explains why female participation was concentrated on life in the convents, the growth of which was not simply the result of a surplus of women. Female participation in the heretical movements declined rapidly after initial enthusiasm. In regard to the substantial increase in the number of convents, we must take into account that there were at the start far fewer convents than monasteries for men.

❧   ❧

BUT DISCUSSION of these historiographical issues can be fruitful only when society as a whole is considered. As soon as the church was willing to accept the activities of the reconciled followers of Waldo, they were forced to accept a division of their group. Besides the orders of men and women who entered the religious life, there was a third order for those who remained in the world but were looking for a larger share in the experience of religion than the church normally granted to laity. This manner of life was to be related to the other orders, especially the male order, which supervised the religious activities of the lay people. This supervision resulted in the establishment of separate communities for female members of the third order, which were called tertiary houses.

Thus new communities for women came into existence alongside those already existing and belonging to the older orders, such as the Cistercians and Premonstratensians. The female tertiaries were drawn more heavily from urban society, and there was no requirement, as there was in some of the older monastic communities, that the women belong to noble families of some importance. The sisters of the tertiary houses had more freedom and greater opportunities to be involved in society than those in the houses of the second order, where before long bars were installed to keep the nuns secluded from the world.

Although many tertiary houses were established, not many women were attracted to a religious life that required that they leave the world. The Beguine communities offered the opportunity of a religious project in the context of normal life. The Beguines lived a communal life with no officially recognized rule. For that reason they were suspect and were considered an easy mark for heretical ideas. They owed their name to this mistrust: It was a corrupted form of *Albigensians* and at first only a term of abuse. Episcopal synods in the early fourteenth century repeatedly accused the Beguines of heresy and immorality. In 1310 a Beguine of Paris was burned at the stake as a heretic, and in 1311 the Beguines were outlawed by the Council of Vienne. Subsequently many Beguine houses became tertiary communities with ties to the different mendicant orders — the Augustinian hermits, the Dominicans, and the Franciscans.[23]

THE MENDICANT — or "begging" — orders with the most members were the Dominicans and the Franciscans, or the Preaching Friars and the Minorites, as they were officially called. These two orders soon spread throughout Western Europe. Their male tertiaries, who could move in society with greater freedom, at first largely consisted of members of already existing penitential fraternities — again lay movements within the church. Their special focus was penance and self-mortification.

Initially there was little difference in the mendicant orders between laity and clergy, especially among the Franciscans. Francis himself was never ordained and only with difficulty learned some Latin. But soon these orders were strongly clericalized, partly because of the tasks they took on. They specialized in combating heresy, notably in southern France, where the papal Inquisition had been established for the same purpose. They also focused their attention on proclamation of the faith, but on a different level than the popular preachers. They held disputations with Jews and some of the mendicants engaged, with that purpose in mind, in specialized

23. K. Elm, "Die Stellung der Frau in Ordenswesen, Semireligiosentum und Häresie zur Zeit des heiligen Elisabeth," in *Sankt Elisabeth, Fürstin, Dienerin, Heilige* (Sigmaringen, 1981), 7-28.

study of the Scriptures and of the Hebrew language. They were also involved in scholarly work at universities. Several Dominicans and Franciscans taught theology.

Thomas Aquinas (†1274), a Dominican, succeeded in harmonizing Christian dogma and theology with ideas that were coming into Western Europe from elsewhere. Acceptance of these ideas implied an exchange of the philosophy of Plato for that of Aristotle, whose concept of reality was vastly different. Plato saw reality as a reflection of the "Ideas," while Aristotle held the Ideas to be abstractions of earthly reality. This scientific revolution opened the way, at least in principle, for secularized thinking and for a manner of experiencing reality that no longer looked for a sacral explanation for everything that was not understood. The state was also viewed in a more positive light, and no longer was its subjection to the church a philosophical certainty, at least in the context of Thomas's teachings. But church authorities continued for some time to be troubled by this alignment of Christian dogma with fundamentally new insights and continued to argue against it.

Where the Dominicans emphasized scholarship without neglecting popular preaching, in the case of the Franciscans the situation was reversed. The churches they built were structures intended for preaching. Their task was to assist bishops in preaching, though they did not fall under the jurisdiction of the bishops.

To facilitate their preaching, both Dominicans and Franciscans received instruction from their orders and were provided with preaching *exempla,* stories to be used in sermons to enable them to hold the attention of their audiences. This literary genre originated in the twelfth century with the Cistercians and took on a life of its own in *exempla* collections.

Franciscans differed from Dominicans in their efforts concerning personal piety. They promoted several Christ-centered devotions, such as the stations of the cross, the crèche, and contemplation of Mary's joys and sorrows. They also played a role in the introduction of the rosary. The Franciscans also cared for pilgrims arriving in Jerusalem, while they urged people in Western Europe to make this pilgrimage.

5. THE FOURTEENTH AND FIFTEENTH CENTURIES

EARLY IN THE fourteenth century the growth of the medicant orders stagnated. From 1320 on no new communities were established. The

Preaching Friars and the Minorites, as well as the Augustinian hermits and the Carmelites, relied on donations for their daily subsistence. In order not to spoil the market, so to speak, each house had its own territory in which the mendicant brothers made their regular rounds of begging. With time there was simply no place to establish new communities. Materialism no doubt also played a role. Mendicant orders were well aware of the value of material things. That may be inferred from complaints of secular clergy about the greed of these monks, though these complaints were, of course, at least partly inspired by declines in their own incomes.

For a considerable time a controversy had already been raging among the Franciscans about the degree of poverty to be observed in daily life and provisions. Those who were more radically inclined, the Spiritual Franciscans, went to extremes. The moderates, who were in the majority, accused the Spirituals of insincerity since in spite of their frugality they continued to reap the benefits of property put in the names of third parties. Since some Spirituals wanted to see their striving for perfection adopted as the general rule for the whole church, this internal controversy led to conflicts with ecclesiastical authorities.

The writings of Pietro Olivi were a particular bone of contention for most Minorites. Olivi was an important theologian belonging to the most militant group of Spiritual Franciscans, which had its center in Narbonne. After his death in 1298 he was venerated as a saint by some and condemned as a heretic by others. His teachings were believed to resemble those of the Brethren of the Free Spirit, which were a liberalized interpretation of official dogma, rather than outright heresy, though the Brethen were accused of heresy.[24] Olivi was similarly accused, because of his originality as a theologian. His writings also demonstrated the affinity between the Spiritual Franciscans and the apocalyptic vision of Joachim of Fiore, who had by then been condemned. Joachim had announced the establishment of the rule of the Spirit on earth as a result of monastic activity, and the Spiritual Franciscans had more or less adopted the task implied by this vision.

Papal intervention was inevitable in the increasingly sharp conflict among the Minorites. The intolerance of the Spirituals partly explains why this intervention went against them. Olivi foresaw the danger. Pope Celestine V had in 1294 allowed the Spirituals to separate from their order and to continue as an order of hermits. But Celestine, who had lived as

24. Cf. R. E. Lerner, *The Heresy of the Free Spirit in the Later Middle Ages* (Berkeley, 1972).

a recluse before his election to the papacy, soon abdicated because he was not equal to the task. When Pope Boniface VIII was elected, he withdrew the privileges that Celestine had granted.

Olivi opposed this move with theological arguments. In his *Quaestiones de perfectione evangelica* ("Questions regarding evangelic perfection") he included a chapter on obedience, in which he also discussed the validity of papal authority. He dealt in this context with, among other things, the scope of papal authority from the point of view of the infallibility it was supposed to possess, which Olivi accepted in the sense that papal decisions, including privileges like those extended to the Spirituals, could not be revoked. Such an interpretation, however, implied a limitation of papal sovereignty by predecessors' decisions.[25]

So ambitious popes, such as Boniface and, later, John XXII (1316-24), had from the start little appreciation for the Spirituals. When the Spirituals rebelled openly, John forced them to submit and brought those who persisted in rebellion before the secular courts. Some of them were subsequently condemned to the stake.

These papal actions raised new questions concerning the character and scope of papal authority. Intellectual enemies of that authority were able to make themselves felt in society with the support of Emperor Louis of Bavaria. In their writings they rejected the direct claims to secular authority made by popes of the time. Between 1318 and 1324 Marsilius of Padua wrote his *Defensor Pacis,* in which he accused the pope of disturbing the peace through such claims. William of Ockham had philosophical objections against the popes' claim to represent Christ on earth. And the conciliar theory was gaining in popularity. According to its proponents papal authority in the church is superseded by that of a general council of the church.[26] This idea was shaped largely by the growing desire at all levels of society to share more fully in government in all its forms.

❦   ❦

THE DISPUTE OVER papal authority was not the only crisis Christendom had to face. In many ways the fourteenth century was an age of crisis in

25. Cf. B. Tierney, *Origins of Papal Infallibility, 1150-1350: A Study of Infallibility, Sovereignty and Tradition in the Middle Ages* (Leiden, 1972).

26. *Idem, Foundations of the Conciliar Theory: The Contribution of the Medieval Canonists from Gratian to the Great Schism* (1955; repr. Cambridge, 1968).

general. The century began full of promise, with Boniface declaring 1300 a holy year. All pilgrims to Rome who visited any of several designated churches received a jubilee indulgence, providing full absolution of all punishment for sin. For the city of Rome this holy year seemed the beginning of better times.[27] The city's population was still largely dependent on income from agrarian sources and was still quite poor. Pilgrims would supplement this income. After the last crusader stronghold had fallen in 1298, ecclesiastical Rome sought to fill the place formerly occupied by Jerusalem.

But the fourteenth century turned out to be the darkest period for medieval Rome. The pontificate of Boniface ended in such conflict with Philip the Fair of France that it seemed advisable to select a Frenchman as the next pope. This French pope did not go to Rome, but, after some time, settled in Avignon, where the papal court remained for seventy years. The return to Rome in 1379 brought no improvement, since it led to the Western Schism, with two and then three rival popes concurrently in Rome, Avignon, and, at the end, in Pisa. Only later did Rome benefit from the income from pilgrims and become a prestigious city.

But before it did, the jubilee indulgences took root and ordinary indulgences came to be inflated. 1350 was proclaimed another holy year. The plague that swept through Europe at that time encouraged many to avail themselves of this "means of deliverance." Those who acquired this indulgence were assured of avoiding purgatory and going straight to heaven at the moment of death, after they made a contrite confession.

The development of the system of indulgences offers some insights into the despondent feelings of that century. But there were more concrete reasons for the inflation of the system of indulgences. The disastrous economic decline of Rome caused its many sanctuaries, in particular the large basilicas, to lose substantial parts of their income, including rent from land and houses. The need for other sources of income led to increased sale of indulgences. The number of days of penance that could be compensated for by a visit to such a sanctuary was drastically increased. When popular belief began to interpret the time periods associated with indulgences as direct remission of the corresponding number of days one would have to suffer in purgatory, this inflation also spread to other sanctuaries. Increasing the value of indulgences needed papal approval.

27. R. Brentano, *Rome before Avignon: A Social History of Thirteenth-Century Rome* (London, 1974).

Petitions to that effect were submitted to the papal court, and a special department, directed by a *datarius,* was created to deal with requests regarding privileges and dispensations. The information we possess about the requests and supplications processed by this person, but in final analysis decided on by the pope, dates mostly from the fifteenth century. The papal court kept meticulous account of its income.

The interest in certain shrines and the indulgences they provided were typical aspects of religious life in the fourteenth century, aspects of what has been called the privatization of religion. The social crisis played a major role in that the need for devotional practices increased sharply. Privatization was also encouraged by the church's institutional crisis. The faithful were no longer sure what they could expect from the church leadership, not only from the central authority, which lost the interest of many, especially during the nearly forty-year schism at the end of the century, but also the bishops.

Already before the Avignon period, Rome had begun to reserve appointment of bishops and other dignitaries to itself. Over time, papal reservation was extended and became the basis for traffic in ecclesiastical offices. As a result the princes regained some of their influence on episcopal appointments. It became normal practice, however, for all new appointees to make some kind of payment, usually the income generated by the office in one year, known, therefore, as the *annate.* The income of recipients of offices was sometimes multiplied by giving vacant offices to someone already serving as a bishop, who thus received the opportunity for further promotion. The system allowed for men to accumulate offices without residency obligations, such as canonates and parish priesthoods. Hunters of benefices, that is, of income from endowed offices, and of prebends, stipends attached to certain offices, were strongly criticized. These non-resident clergy left the work connected with such offices to underpaid vicars. The system was detrimental to pastoral care and was a major factor in the decline in appreciation for the church as an institution of salvation, which contributed further to the privatization of religion. Privatization was an important characteristic of religion in the fourteenth century among both laity and clergy.

❧   ❧

LOCAL SHRINES provided a suitable climate for more private religious experience. The shrines encouraged specialization of the saints who were approached in prayer — often prayer for healing. There was a saint for every illness. But privatization of religion for lay people was broader than just that. It also came to involve detachment of celebration of the Eucharist from the Mass. The number of eucharistic miracles increased, often in connection with alleged desecrations of the sacred host. Supposed miracle hosts were often venerated, and churches where they were preserved came to function as shrines and were visited by many. The situation resembled that of the places where the cult of the saints prospered. Often such a shrine was visited to honor a pledge made after some answer to prayer — a *quid pro quo* one took on oneself. At least this is what we may glean from the miracle books of several shrines.

The privatization of religion was also noticeable in the veneration of more recent figures as saints. At that particular time papal canonizations were difficult to obtain. Nonetheless, those whom the faithful regarded as saints were venerated and depicted as such. Often such veneration had the approval of a local bishop. The holiness of such unofficial saints was of a different kind, or was, at least, described differently by hagiographers. They excelled in works of penance, self-chastisement, special devotion to Mary, and intense focus on the sufferings of Christ. Though they did not live in monasteries, their mortifications were more extreme than those of monks. Their lives in the world led them not to greater forms of virtue but to greater religious ecstasy. The hagiographers took this different type of sainthood into account: Saints were no longer people to be imitated, but people to be admired for their unusual holiness.[28]

The privatization of religion among the laity was not limited to these devotional practices. Many joined religious brotherhoods, which increased rapidly in number in spite of the usual obligations of membership, which were typically weekly presence at Mass, generous almsgiving, and participation in processions on special days. Likewise, there was a rapid increase in the number of penitents, those who were eager to perform acts of penance and mortification without leaving the world for a monastic life. Most prominent were the third orders of the Preaching Friars, the Minorites, and the Augustinian hermits. Popular sentiments regarding anxiety and fear of death were clearly discernible in devotional practices, but such thoughts were not their sole motivation. The religious fraternities closely resembled the monasteries in spirituality and were fervently involved with the substance of the Christian religion.

28. R. Kieckhefer, *Unquiet Souls: Fourteenth-Century Saints and their Religious Milieu* (Chicago, 1984), 14f.

This involvement led to, among other things, interest in theology. This was met with great reluctance on the part of the church, especially in regard to those who belonged to circles of the lay religious over whom the church had little or no control, namely, the Beguines who remained independent and their male counterparts, the Beghards. The privatization that these groups represented carried with it the suspicion of mystical free-thinking.[29]

Mysticism in general was subject to this kind of suspicion. With some mystics the manner in which a person contemplating God could be absorbed into the divine took on pantheistic traits, as was the case with the Dominican friar Meister Eckhart.[30] Unmediated contemplation and absorption into the divine, to which we will return, was another form of privatization. Mystics had little use for church or society. Their disregard for the official church was also apparent in their preference for the vernacular in writings of theological and mystical direction. Because it was difficult to control, use of the vernacular often led to accusations of heresy. Heresy was difficult to pinpoint; it was a matter of mentality rather than doctrine. Therefore, references were made to the heresy of the free Spirit. That serious mistakes were possible became tragically apparent in the burning of the Beguine Margaret of Porete in 1310. Her work *Mirror of Simple Souls* (originally written in French) brought on her condemnation, but was later widely distributed and highly appreciated.[31]

The church's reactions to the life of the lay religious convey the impression that these groups received more criticism for the privatization of their religion than did the laity in general. But the religious practices of ordinary lay people came in for criticism as well. Nonetheless, it must be admitted that the church proved remarkably lenient with regard to, for example, the demonizing of saints, of saints, that is, who, due to the power ascribed to them, were venerated in magical ways. The privatization of the message of religion contributed to an increase in superstitious practices. Many argue that the apparent growth of superstition in the later Middle Ages must be attributed to the greater availability of data for that period

29. Cf. Lerner, 35-60.

30. Lerner, 182-86; K. Ruh (ed.), *Abendländische Mystik im Mittelalter* (Stuttgart, 1986), 1-115.

31. F. Oakley, *The Western Church in the Later Middle Ages* (Ithaca, NY/London, 1979), 176. On Margaret see Lerner, 68-78, 200-207. For the text of the *Mirror* see P. Verdeyen and R. Guarnieri, *Speculum simplicium animarum — le mirouer des simples âmes* (*CCCM* 68; Turnhout, 1986).

than for the earlier Middle Ages — that this growth is, in fact, a mere illusion. No doubt this is partly true. But superstitious practices did actually have some increase, and this was due to the privatization of religion and to the greater tolerance on the part of the ecclesiastical authorities.

❦   ❦

THE RECOGNIZED religious orders also experienced this privatization. There it was not combated so much since it did not pose a threat to ecclesiastical authority. It was, however, a result of the crisis in church and society. Privatization expressed itself in monasteries in withdrawal from any sense of social responsibility.

This is particularly evident in the remarkable growth of the Carthusian order in the fourteenth century. Establishing a Carthusian monastery was a costly business. The monks' eremitic life required special provisions for their housing. A wealthy founder was a prerequisite. Some of the names of these founders are known: Among them was Willem van Duvenvoorde in the Netherlands, who had amassed his possessions in dubious ways. His name and those of others indicate not only that the sponsors had come to possess wealth, but also that they needed to perform acts of penance for the manner in which it had been accumulated.

The relationship between these monasteries and their founders explains why the monasteries were, contrary to earlier custom, built near towns. This was, for instance, the case with the Certosa (the Carthusian house) built near Florence. And we should also mention the astonishing Certosa near Pavia. The building of this monumental monastery, now a tourist attraction, was begun in 1392, as an act of penance for a murder committed by Galeazzo Visconti, the founder of the duchy of Milan.

The recruitment of monks for the monasteries is a clear witness to the renascence of private religion. The intensity of the Carthusians' mode of life made it suitable only for a few. Nonetheless, between 1307 and 1392 fourteen Carthusian houses were founded in the Netherlands, the last one in Amsterdam. If each community consisted of about twenty monks and three lay brothers, the order must have had some three hundred members in the Netherlands at the end of the century.

Some of the Carthusian recruits were already clerics or monks who came to choose the more ascetic life, thereby withdrawing from an active life in the service of the church. The quality of their libraries indicates that these monks must have been well educated. Though few of their books are preserved, the titles are often known from surviving catalogues. Many of the Carthusians had studied at universities before entering the monastery — theology in particular. This study prepared them for careers in the church that they apparently did not want. They must have had personal motives for that decision, but the social circumstances and the situation in the church were no doubt significant factors, along with the complicated situation in the ecclesiastical hierarchy. Of course, there is no direct proof for these assumptions, but the experience of Gerhard Groote, who came to be the founder of the Brethren of the Common Life, offers a telling indication: He, too, seemed predestined for a career in the church, but after his conversion in 1372 he initially withdrew, for a two-year period, to the Carthusian house of Monnikshuizen near Arnhem.

A SIGNIFICANT ASPECT of the privatized religious experience of that time was — in retrospect, of course — the revival of popular mysticism. This, too, was in a sense the result of the lack of confidence in the church on the part of the faithful. Internal problems prevented the church from adequately presenting itself as an institution of salvation. But this mysticism was rooted in the traditions of the church, and its history goes back to the twelfth century. It was heavily dependent on the mystical writings of Bernard of Clairvaux and William of Saint-Thierry. But these men had not written in the vernacular. The new use of the vernacular points to broader changes in religious life: Mysticism was originally intended for those who had left the world to follow a religious calling, but it had come to be practiced by people who remained in the world, as a means of setting themselves free from that world.

It is reasonable to assume that only few were involved with mysticism in this way. Mystical writings were, of course, distributed only in handwritten copies, and few people were sufficiently educated to read them, even in the vernacular. *The Life of Jesus,* written in Latin by Ludolf of Saxony, a Dominican who became a Carthusian in 1340, was translated into many languages. It became quite popular, but only over a long period of time.

It remains remarkable that many mystics wrote directly in the vernacular. They must have had a thorough command of Latin, since they wrote about subjects that so far had only been treated in that language. They used the vernacular only because their writings had found ready acceptance with that segment of the population which read only the vernacular, not Latin. For that reason fourteenth-century mysticism may justifiably be called *popular* mysticism.

This form of mysticism found its clearest expression in the Southern Netherlands. Jan van Ruysbroeck (†1381) was its most important representative, but not the only one. His predecessors included Beatrice of Nazareth (†1268), Hadewijch (who died before 1275), and an anonymous priest who wrote a life of Christ in verse. Others followed in van Ruysbroeck's steps. Best known is Jan van Leeuwen, the cook at the Groenendaal monastery near Brussels, where van Ruysbroeck lived from 1343 on.

But van Ruysbroeck overshadowed all others, both with his theological knowledge and his ability to put his mystical experience into words — explaining how one can progress to contemplative love for God. The titles of Ruysbroeck's writings reflect his own experiences: The Spiritual Wedding *(Die Gheestelike Brulocht),* The Glittering Stone *(Vanden Blinckenden Steen),* and A Mirror of Eternal Salvation *(Een Spiegel der Eewigher Salicheit).* But his statement in *Die Gheestelike Brulocht* is possibly even more revealing: "When the barrel is ready, it is filled with costly liquor. There is no nobler barrel than the loving soul and no more wholesome liquid than God's grace. . . ."[32]

❧   ❧

THE CRISIS of church authority deepened in the course of the fourteenth century. It led not only to privatization of religion, by which the faithful evaded what was problematical about the hierarchy's claims to authority, but also to sharp criticism of that authority. This was already apparent during the pontificate of John XXII in the first half of that century.

This criticism was repeated later in the century with more radical theological arguments, formulated in particular by the English theologian John Wycliffe (†1384). Wycliffe was teaching at the University of Oxford, where he was held in high regard. He had powerful protectors at the English court and moved freely in those circles. His theological engagement at times led him to deal with political questions, but his main interest was the church as he knew it from his own experience in society. He clearly perceived the church's structural defects and corruptions and considered

32. *Jan van Ruusbroec: leven en werken* I (2nd ed.; Antwerp/Malines, 1944), 147. On van Ruysbroeck see Oakley, 276-85.

it inappropriate to cover these over with a cloak of love for the sake of the church's mission. His personal life was devout and ascetic. His one weakness was his love for publicity and his insistence on staying in the limelight. The protection he enjoyed had something to do with that. He could afford to create a disturbance, as he did before 1378 with his radical proposal to secularize all church property. He also proclaimed his conviction that the church had no right to impose disciplinary punishments. Papal condemnations were sure to come. They reached him in 1378, but his status allowed him to defy them. After the beginning of the Western Schism in the next year he had more to fear from English bishops than from any pope.

Two of Wycliffe's most important writings were published in 1378. The first dealt with the Bible and suggested that any ecclesiastically sanctioned commentary on Scripture was superfluous. Rather than trying to understand the Scriptures by consulting the writings of the Fathers, one should understand the Fathers on the basis of Scripture. Nothing can be added to the Scriptures and there can be no question of a development or extension of gospel teaching.

In the second of these works Wycliffe wrote about the church. He rejected the common notion of the church as being represented by the pope and the cardinals, who must be obeyed by all. He resisted this paralyzing clericalization and objected to the concept of a church as an institution directed by the pope. The church, he argued, was a community not of believers but of the predestined, so that only God knows who belongs to his church. Christians may even wonder whether a pope belongs to it. That question can only be answered on the basis of one criterion: the Scriptures. In Wycliffe's opinion the church had no distinct salvific function. Salvation is dependent on grace, through which a person is predestined to salvation. The value of the sacraments depends on the predestination of the minister of the sacraments. Moreover, the sacraments are not necessary for salvation. One may reach God without recourse to the hierarchical church. The mystical writers shared this opinion to some extent, but did not challenge the church's salvific role.

With these ideas Wycliffe deviated completely from church teaching regarding the relationship of humanity to God and about the church's task of leading the human person to God. Naturally they evoked resistance and condemnation. In the course of time Wycliffe could no longer count on open support from his protectors, as they did not want to compromise themselves. He had to leave the university, but remained safe from personal attack. His closest sympathizers were given opportunities to rectify their relationships to the church hierarchy, which was of some importance to their church careers. Wycliffe himself became more and more isolated and died a lonely death. Since he had not been excommunicated, he did receive a church burial. But after he had been condemned as a heretic at the Council of Constance, his body was exhumed and burned and his ashes were dispersed.

In spite of all this Wycliffe had followers in England after his death. They included few intellectuals, and the group showed little doctrinal cohesion. The majority were more interested in his anticlericalism and his opposition to Rome than in his views regarding the Bible and the church. These Lollards, as they were called, were primarily a popular movement waging a political campaign against obligatory auricular confession, invocation of saints, and mandatory pilgrimages. The Inquisition did persecute the Lollards, but the group met its end through decline of interest rather than through persecution. Their movement simply had too little substance.[33]

❧   ❧

But the ideas of Wycliffe did have other aftereffects, particularly in Bohemia. At the time of the Western Schism in 1379, the University of Paris sided with the pope in Avignon, while Bohemia remained loyal to the pope in Rome. Bohemian students in Paris fled to Oxford, where they learned of Wycliffe's ideas. They introduced these ideas into their own country, where they found ready response. The church occupied an important place in Bohemian society and had numerous clergy, many of them of dubious standing. Visiting taverns and brothels was a regular pastime of the lower clergy. The higher clergy often had concubines and accumulated prebends, leaving the work involved to underpaid vicars. The theological education of most priests was limited and few were able to differentiate true doctrine from heresy.

This sad state of affairs in the church had led to reaction and had given rise to an active reform movement, which had adherents especially among Czech students and teachers of theology at the University of Prague, which had been founded in 1347. As at other universities, the criticism of the church did not stay within the confines of orthodoxy. During the

33. On John Wyclif and the Lollards see M. Lambert, *Medieval Heresy: Popular Movements from Bogomil to Hus* (London, 1977), 217-71.

Schism it was easier to oppose papal authority, and many supported the view that papal authority ought to be subject to that of a general church council. One could even dare to characterize the pope that one did not recognize (normally the one at Avignon) as the antichrist. The climate was thus at least favorable for Wycliffe's ideas.

Jan Hus was among those who belonged to the reform movement in Bohemia. Born in 1370, he had at an early age entered the University of Prague to study theology, where he joined the reform movement. Before 1409 about fifty percent of the students and teachers of theology there were German. In that year the Council of Pisa elected a third pope and declared that the popes of Avignon and Rome were to be deposed. The pope of Pisa was recognized by the king of Bohemia, who demanded the same response from the university. The Germans left the university, accusing the Czechs of following Wycliffe's ideas. Since the Czechs had rejected the pope of Rome, this accusation against them found ready acceptance in Rome. The fact that the Czechs now had to prove their worth without the German presence also helped Wycliffe's ideas to receive even more attention.

All this brought Hus into discredit. As a preacher and advocate of church reform he had acquired considerable prestige, especially outside the university. But his position in the university had become weaker, even though he accepted Wycliffe's views only in part and with many reservations. The reason for his weakened position lay elsewhere.

The pope elected at Pisa died soon afterward, and his successor, who took the name John XXIII, gradually compromised himself. He instituted an indulgence in order to raise money. He was then deposed at the Council of Constance, which began in 1414. This council not only endeavored to end the Schism but also to restore orthodoxy. Thus it firmly opposed the teachings of Wycliffe, whose remains were exhumed and burned.[34] Hus was accused of adhering to such ideas and was summoned to the council to give account of himself.

At the request of Emperor Sigismund, who had convened the council, Hus received a safe-conduct from the council fathers. But the outcome was a foregone conclusion. Though Hus expected a fair hearing and was prepared to go to Constance even without the safe-conduct, he

---

34. E. C. Tatnall, "The Condemnation of John Wyclif at the Council of Constanz," in *Councils and Assemblies,* ed. C. J. Cunning and D. Baker (Cambridge, 1971), 209-18.

was quickly imprisoned. The predetermined aim of his trial was to bolster the reputation of the condemnation of Wycliffe. Two prominent Parisian theologians taking part in the proceedings had earlier subscribed to the conciliar theory, but now eagerly seized this opportunity to display their orthodoxy. The most damaging testimony was to come from a Czech theologian who had been removed from the University of Prague by the king of Bohemia and who blamed Hus for this action.

Hus's naïveté was evident when he was allowed to speak in the cathedral. When he did, he referred to the church as the community of the predestined, and thus strengthened the suspicion against him. His careful written and spoken comments on the errors of Wycliffe, even where he rejected them totally, had the same effect. To the judges this meant that Hus had reservations about their condemnation of Wycliffe and thereby, in their opinion, that he was confirming the accusations against himself. He was condemned as a heretic on July 6, 1415 after a three-day cross-examination. Because the emperor withdrew his protection, Hus was handed over to the secular authorities, who burned him at the stake the same day.[35]

The tribunal might have operated more judiciously and might have given more careful thought to Hus's answers had the judges been conscious of what the condemnation would unleash. The Czech people were highly sympathetic toward Hus and saw what the council inflicted on him as a national injustice. A popular uprising against German domination followed, which evolved into a protracted war of religion. Its many incidents of violence were justified as acts of faith. Attempts at reconciliation were repeatedly unsuccessful and the compromise finally achieved in the sixteenth century, which among other things gave the laity permission to take the cup during the Eucharist, was acceptable to only some Hussites.[36]

❧   ❧

TWO ASPECTS of the fifteenth century stand out: continuing decline in spirituality (together with widespread ignorance of the content of Christian doctrine) and attempts at restoration rather than reform.

There were many complaints at the time of moral and spiritual

---

35. On Hus see Oakley, 295-312; F. Seibt, *Hussitenstudien: Personen, Ereignisse, Ideen einer frühen Revolution* (Munich, 1987), 229-40: "Hus in Konstanz."
36. Cf. Lambert, 288-334.

decline. Writers emphasized clerics' moral shortcomings and neglect of their duties and pleaded for a restoration of older patterns of church appointments. These complaints seem credible in the light of what followed: the Reformation. But these writings resembled the moral complaints of all ages. They have received too much credit from Catholic historians who, thinking they thus support the cause of ecumenism, have argued that the Reformation found its justifiable origin in this moral decay.[37] But the question remains whether moral decay was more serious in the fifteenth century than before.

Other data lead to a more positive interpretation, which does not, however, apply to all aspects of church life. The top of the ecclesiastical hierarchy remained an important hindrance on the road to restoration and renewal. The Council of Constance had laid plans for church reform, of both head and members. It was thus decided to hold reform councils on a regular basis. But the next council, held in Basel (1432-35), was to be the last for the time being, since at that council a conflict erupted between pope and council. The pope, now only one since Constance had ended the Schism, did not concur with a situation wherein the council placed itself above him by initiating a reform among the curia.

The zeal for reform on the part of the council fathers entailed material problems for the curia, as its members would lose much of their usual income. The Schism had already seriously impoverished them. Plans to rescind the system of granting church offices against payment of annates would hurt them further, as would plans to reestablish residency requirements, since the members of the curia themselves held multiple titles. Consequently these abuses remained in place. The cardinals came over time to live more opulently, thus contributing to further increase in these abuses.

Many in the church were disillusioned. The first popes after the Schism lacked authority to reform the curia, and their successors clearly had other priorities: They needed to put things right in the Papal States and to guarantee safety for pilgrimages to Rome. The popes tried to remedy the situation by appointing family members to administrative posts, but this nepotism was less harmful than has often been suggested. The curia increasingly consisted of members of aristocratic families that battled among themselves to gain or hold power. To maintain themselves in the

37. A well-known example of such a judgment is J. Lortz, *Die Reformation in Deutschland* (6th ed.; Freiburg im Breslau, 1982), 149.

midst of these intrigues, the popes developed a policy of making treaties with the surrounding Italian city-states. All this paralyzed their administrative power, which they needed if they were to function as leaders of the church.

As a result of this malaise, attempts at reform could only be partial. In one particular case, that of Savonarola in Florence at the end of the century, reform was opposed, because his plans stood in the way of papal political aims in Italy.[38] Reform movements with more chance of success — those that were more balanced in nature — were similar to each other and may be referred to under the single term of "observantism." Their aim was to return the monasteries and orders to strict compliance with older rules and customs and to end the practice of allowing monks, through the system of prebends, to have private incomes. Gerhard Groote had already, after his conversion, opposed such abuses, as it made communal life in a monastery impossible. For the mendicant orders observantism implied a stricter obedience to the rules concerning poverty. The number of monks and nuns in many communities had been decimated by the bubonic plague, and in the recruitment of new members the rules had been somewhat ignored.

These attempts at restoration did not go unchallenged. But in many cases they yielded remarkable results. In several countries the mendicants were able to establish new monasteries, though they met strong opposition as well. For instance, the adherents of observantism among the Augustinian friars in Germany encountered obstinate resistance.[39] The movement known as the Devotio Moderna, no doubt a first manifestation of this revived desire for a stricter mode of life, was related to observantism. There were also links with other initiatives for a restoration of church and religion. In the old orders congregations were started on a more or less national level, bringing monastic life to new prosperity. This occurred among the Benedictines in the congregation of Bursfeld in Germany and that of Saint-Justin in Italy.[40] The Cistercians experienced a similar revival in Spain.

These national congregations were also related to other programs

---

38. D. Weinstein, *Savonarola and Florence: Prophecy and Patriotism in the Renaissance* (Princeton, 1970).

39. H. Zschoch, *Klosterreform und monastische Spiritualität im 15. Jahrhundert* (Tübingen, 1988).

40. B. Collett, *Italian Benedictine Scholars and the Reformation* (Oxford, 1985).

of reform, such as those championed by Cardinal Nicholas of Cusa (†1464) in Germany and by Cardinal Ximenes (†1517) in Spain, whose reform was continued in the Counter-Reformation. The Counter-Reformation, a reform movement launched after the Reformation, is totally misunderstood if it is portrayed as just a late reaction to the Reformation. It was primarily a continuation of reforms already undertaken, or at least begun, in the fifteenth century. The Devotio Moderna was also part of this reform. The most important difference is that the Counter-Reformation was supported by Rome and thus was much better coordinated.

The Reformation must not be seen as a reaction to the whole of religion and church life in the late Middle Ages, in particular in the fifteenth century. It merely concerned certain aspects, such as abuses in popular veneration of saints and the administration of the sacraments and the failure of church authority. This authority was traditionally more tolerant toward aberrations in popular belief than toward attempts at renewal. In dealing with new ideas, the ecciesiastical authorities were usually more worried about the purity of the faith or at least about the manner in which the faith had traditionally been defined. The Reformation directed itself most strongly and most radically against these abuses in popular belief and corruptions in church rule.

Other matters related to the Reformers' opposition, such as the interest of the princes in former church properties, have perhaps combined with the emotions involved to lead to a degree of historical bias. The intrinsic merit of authentic attempts at reform in the fifteenth century have been widely misunderstood and have usually been mentioned too little in histories both of the Counter-Reformation and of post-Reformation Protestant reforms, which might also benefit from continued study of religion and church in the Middle Ages.

II

Against Misunderstanding
the Medieval Mentality[1]

⁊⁊   ⁊⁊

IN HIS WIDELY ACCLAIMED *Church History* the twelfth-century historian
Orderic Vitalis (†1141), a monk of the Norman Benedictine monastery of
Saint-Evroul, at times offers rather curious information.[2] The eighth book,
for instance, contains some remarkable statements about Fulk IV, who was
count of Anjou at the end of the eleventh century (1067/8-1109). With
other chroniclers of his time, Orderic mentions the marriage of Count
Fulk to Bertrada of Montfort.[3] His union with this young bride in 1088
was his fourth marriage, or possibly his fifth. It lasted only four years
because Bertrada allowed herself to be abducted by Philip I of France, who
repudiated his wife in Bertrada's favor. But this notorious event was of less
interest to Orderic than the fact that Fulk had deformed feet and had
shoes made with long toe caps to hide his deformity. He thus introduced

---

1. This chapter is a slightly revised version of my inaugural lecture at the Vrije
Universiteit in Amsterdam and was published earlier in Dutch as "*Oratio pro domo.* Tegen
een misverstaan der middeleeuwen."

2. *HE.* About this medieval author cf. also M. Chibnall, *The World of Orderic
Vitalis* (Oxford, 1984).

3. L. Delisle, "Examen critique des Historiens qui ont parlé du divorce de Philippe
Ier, roi de France, avec la reine Berthe et de son mariage avec Bertrada de Monfort, Comtesse
d'Anjou," *Recueil des Historiens des Gaules et de la France,* 16 (1878; repr. Paris, 1968), xxx-cxiv.
On Fulk IV, see O. Guillot, *Le comté d'Anjou et son entourage au XIe siècle,* I (Paris, 1972),
III-26.

a new fashion, much to the displeasure of Orderic, who therefore characterized the count as an infamous, reprehensible person.

The lifestyle of Fulk IV did indeed give cause for a negative response. But why did Orderic place it in this context? It was no literary clumsiness on his part to mention this criticism in his discussion of the new fashion. To him this new fashion was just as reprehensible as the behavior of the count. Changes in fashion were eagerly adopted by frivolous people who loved anything new *(amatoribus novitatum)*. What virtuous people in those days *(olim)* saw as most despicable, these *moderni* found attractive, behaving as if they had distinguished themselves in a remarkable way. Orderic could hardly stop talking about this fashion and the behavior of these *moderni*. He also mentioned the long toe caps at the court of the English king William Rufus, which were modeled after ram's horns (whence the king's nickname of "Cornard"), and the fact that this frivolity was aped by a considerable part of the nobility as if it represented an exceptional example of honesty and virtue.

Placing this fashionable behavior in a wider context, Orderic subsequently characterized it as a questionable form of alternative lifestyle:

> At that time, effeminates set the fashion in many parts of the world: foul catamites, doomed to eternal fire, unrestrainedly pursued their revels and shamelessly gave themselves up to the filth of sodomy. They rejected the traditions of honest men, ridiculed the counsel of priests, and persisted in their barbarous way of life and style of dress. They parted their hair from the crown of the head to the forehead, grew long and luxurious locks like women, and loved to deck themselves in long, over-tight shirts and tunics. Some of them frivolled away their time, spending it as they chose without regard for the law of God or the customs of their ancestors. They devoted their nights to feasts and drinking-bouts, idle chatter, dice, games of chance, and other sports, and they slept all day.[4]

Such statements — and some of the stronger expressions have been omitted — might serve as a bridge to our days, at least for those who are still troubled by the alternative behavior patterns of the younger generation. But the historian who attempts such a comparison will be apt to forget that the first duty in interpreting statements from the past is to place these in the social context in which they were first made. Moreover,

4. *HE* VIII.10 (IV, 189).

such a historian should recognize that words that have remained in common parlance through the ages may have undergone shifts in meaning. In the statement quoted above *moderni* may well have a meaning that it does not have today. So we should try to determine of whom Orderic spoke when he used this term.

ୢ୧ ୢ୧

I HAVE FOUND that this is not a superfluous question and I would like to take it a little further. There are apparent similarities between what Orderic says about the *moderni* and some present-day negative judgments about the lifestyle of some young people, along with their clothing and hairstyles. But the context of Orderic's statement makes it clear that he was not just referring to young people. He was not dealing with things that were just beginning to appear as he was approaching old age and was writing his eighth book, matters, in other words, that arose just in the thirties of the twelfth century.

According to Orderic's report the fashionable alternative lifestyle that he so unremittingly opposes had been in style since his own early youth. He mentions the years in which Pope Gregory VII and William Rufus died (1085 and 1100) as particular moments when the virtuous moral precepts of the ancestors *(antiquorum patrum)* had been completely abolished in the West. Elsewhere in his book he identifies the calamities of 1089, when Archbisop Lanfranc of Canterbury died, as divine punishments for the desecration of divine law. This desecration consisted in the fact that knights had departed in clothing and hairstyles from the customs of the ancestors and in the way that this was soon imitated by citizens and peasants, that is, by almost everyone.[5] These *moderni,* those whom Orderic blamed for these fads, were therefore not the younger generation but a major part of the general population, which for almost half a century had dared to stray from tradition.

Because of his loathing for this departure from tradition, Orderic's use of the term *moderni* is quite negative. But elsewhere he uses the same word to refer to the recent past. He reports, for instance, that Richard of Fourneaux, who has just died, was *moderno tempore* abbot of the monastery of Preaux. But usually Orderic uses the term in the less complimentary sense or in reference to more positive matters that he does not agree with.

5. *HE* VIII.22 (IV, 269).

He has, therefore, but little use for the "modern" monastic institutions that departed from the Cluniac customs. He calls the monks of these institutions "neophytes." Even there the term "modern" concerns matters that could already claim some history. The monastery of Cîteaux was since its founding in 1098 foremost in the departure from and rejection of tradition. Orderic mentions that it has already been in existence for thirty-seven years and that "within that short period" it has established affiliations with sixty-five abbeys. This lapse of time was insufficient to make Orderic relinquish his designation *moderni*.

He accuses these monastic *moderni* of pride. They have renounced the black hood and habit, worn for ages by monks and canons as a sign of humility, to show their superior righteousness and to distinguish themselves from other monks by their unusual clothing. Orderic is, of course, a little more careful in his criticism of these *moderni* than in his denunciation of the alternative lifestyle of the laity. But even here he expresses himself rather bluntly. His remarks about the monastic renewal of the Cistercians, who pretended to return to the way of life of the early monks, may serve as an example:

> Many noble warriors and profound philosophers have flocked to them on account of the novelty of their practices, and have willingly embraced the unaccustomed rigor of their life. . . . Among the good men are some hypocrites, who, clothed in white or other distinctive habits, have deceived men and made a great show to the masses. Many seek to be numbered with the true servants of God by their outward observance, not their virtue; their numbers disgust those who see them and make true monks seem less worthy in the faulty judgment of men.[6]

In his bias Orderic thus turns against modern teachers, those who prefer new ways over traditional customs and who continue to scold other monks as worldly and condemn them as violators of the rule:

> I shall not abuse them, out of respect for their zeal and asceticism; nevertheless, I do not think them better than the early Fathers, whose word is proved.[7]

In these polemical passages against the Cistercians and others who were striving for monastic reform, Orderic does not contrast his use of the

6. *HE* VIII.26 (IV, 327).
7. *HE* VIII.27 (IV, 333-35).

word *moderni* with the terms *antiqui* or *antiqui patres,* as he does in his protest against the "modern" laity. This difference is understandable. The monastic reformers of the early twelfth century did not at all regard themselves as *moderni,* but insisted that they, as renewers, followed in the steps of the *antiqui* of monasticism. The first period of the abbey of Clairvaux — the place around which this renewal crystallized — was compared with the *aurea saecula,* the golden era that had characterized the beginnings of monasticism.[8] On the other hand, Bernard of Clairvaux accused the monks of Cluny of disloyalty to their past abbots and to the earliest days of monasticism, a disloyalty he regarded as of recent origin.[9]

Because of this complication — *moderni* who present themselves as *antiqui* — Orderic does not appeal to the *antiqui patres,* at least not through a use of that term. He refers only to *prisci* and *priores* and to *maiores patres.* The *moderni* have departed from the ways of such people, and Orderic regards the claim that this renewal was sought to fulfill the ideal of the beginnings of monasticism as a mere pretense. This prevented him from appealing to 'the *antiqui* in his discussions with them. The Cluniacs — Orderic included — regarded themselves, nonetheless, as the true successors of the *antiquitas* and as the defenders of monastic traditions they were being attacked by these *moderni.* Orderic used the term *moderni* as a negative description in connection with the recent past, at least insofar as it exhibited signs of decay. These signs were defined as deviations from the original past, from *antiquitas.*

꿏 꿏

AMONG CHRISTIANS *antiquitas* had not always been considered the ideal standard. In late antiquity the pagans had lauded *antiquitas* and contrasted it with recent calamities, for which Christians were held responsible. Christians quickly reacted by calling to mind the disasters of an even more distant past while emphasizing the blessings of the present. They contrasted *antiquitas* with the *tempora christiana.*[10] This was done in particular by Augustine and his younger contemporary, the Spaniard Orosius.

But less than two centuries later, at the end of the sixth century,

---

8. *Vita prima sancti Bernardi* I.33 (*PL* CLXXXV, 247).
9. See chapter V below.
10. W. Freund, *Modernus und andere Zeitbegriffe des Mittelalters* (Cologne/Graz, 1957), 17-24.

Cassiodorus pleaded as a Christian for the restoration of *antiquitas* as he saw its cultural attainments being lost. He used the term *modernus* in the sense of "contemporary." But the distinction between Christian and classical antiquity was obscured in his concept of *antiquitas*. His plea for *antiquitas* was inspired by his concern for the literary heritage of the Church Fathers, which could only be saved if knowledge of Latin survived. And thus the cultural compromise between Jerusalem and Athens arrived at by the Fathers was reaffirmed by Cassiodorus and handed on to the Middle Ages.

In the Latin West the two concepts of *antiqui* and *moderni* reemerge from the eighth century onward, beginning with the Venerable Bede. For him *antiquitas* denoted, for the most part, ancient Christianity. He called the present *tempus modernum,* a time that was viewed as different, at least in historical retrospect. Comparisons of the present with a past that one had not personally experienced commonly favored the latter. So it was natural that the term *modernus* came to be used less frequently in a neutral sense and more often with a negative meaning.[11] The assessment of present experiences did, of course, influence this shift in meaning. The way in which a person is involved in the present results in inability to make this assessment objectively.

Appreciation for *antiquitas* — as a designation for a past that one has not personally experienced — went beyond reasonable proportions. It was idealized as the golden age. Appreciation for the old and suspicion of change were seen as biblically founded: "Guard what has been entrusted to you," Paul had written, and he had condemned all who dared to preach "another gospel."[12] Opposition to renewal was everywhere. Different forms of exegesis were treated with mistrust, since they lacked the authority of the Church Fathers. New forms of asceticism and liturgical changes likewise evoked suspicion. Linguistic changes and revisions of Latin orthography were also found objectionable. Legal injunctions could include only what had been accepted in the past or what was believed to have been accepted. In all respects the concern was expressed that the present should not manifest any discontinuity with *antiquitas.* Wherever such a break was thought to exist, this situation had to be remedied. Renewals were welcomed only if they were a return to *antiquitas.*

When *antiquitas* was remained rather vague. The time of the origin

11. W. Hartmann, *"Modernus* und *antiquus,"* in *Antiqui und Moderni,* ed. A. Zimmermann (Studia Mediaevalia; Berlin/New York, 1974), 21-39.

12. 1 Timothy 6:20; Galatians 1:7; cf. Proverbs 22:28.

was considered normative, but it came eventually to include all generations preceding the more recent past, which had been personally experienced or was known through living witnesses. The past generations were the *maiores*, the "superior" ancestors. Later generations were not to regard themselves as on equal footing with the *maiores*. If they did see farther or more clearly than earlier generations, this resulted — according to a well-known statement of Bernard of Chartres from the beginning of the twelfth century — from the fact that the later generations were like "dwarves standing on the shoulders of giants."[13]

Nevertheless, it appears that in the twelfth century the term *moderni* was already undergoing a shift in meaning.[14] Some, particularly among the philosophers who were introducing Scholasticism, already dared to call themselves *moderni*. For them the distinction between *antiqui* and *moderni* referred to a difference of opinion among contemporaries. Both groups remained focused on the past; their difference of opinion had to do with the authority of the philosophers and Fathers of the past. Since Abelard had introduced his dialectical method, philosophers had mastered the art of recognizing differences and even contradictions in the ideas of these authorities. In those circles, then, the dissimilarity between *antiqui* and *moderni* became a difference in how the teachers of the past, of *antiquitas*, were appreciated. For Abelard and his supporters or opponents this concerned first of all an appreciation for the significance of Plato for Christian theology and philosophy. During the transition to the thirteenth century this difference between *moderni* and *antiqui* increasingly involved a choice between Platonic and Aristotelian thought.

Differences in method and emotional cast were, of course, also important factors. The emotional aspect repeatedly emerges in the protests of the *antiqui*, as, for instance, in the famous complaint of Steven of Tournai (†1203) about changes in theological education:

The word of flesh and blood quarrels irreverently over the incarnation of the Word. The indivisible Trinity is cut in three and dissected so that there are as many heresies as theologians, as many scandals as lecture halls, and as many blasphemies as church squares.[15]

13. For this expression, cf. M.-D. Chenu, *Nature, Man and Society in the Twelfth Century* (Chicago/London, 1968), 326 and nn. 42f.

14. E. Gössmann, *"Antiqui* und *Moderni,"* in Zimmermann, ed., 40-57.

15. Letter 251 (*PL* CCXI, 516). H. Denifle, *Cartularium universitatis Parisiensis* I (Paris, 1889), 47f.

But in spite of this, both groups remained preoccupied with the past. The line of demarcation between *antiqui* and *moderni* was determined by whether or not one followed the traditional choice.

⅔ ⅔

BUT THE SHIFT in the meaning of the term *moderni* during the Middle Ages is not our main theme. It merely introduces us to the dual understanding of the past that we saw in Orderic. We need to remember that a differentiation between a more distant past and a more recent past that continues to be a factor in the present is not unique to the Middle Ages. Even today that distinction is made, at least by historians. To others only the recent past seems to matter, and the more distant past is of little interest except as it provides an opportunity to project current social models and to make that part of our ancestry into a set of useful human examples.

Yet, there is some similarity between then and now: Today we often find this same negative view of the recent past that was so common in the Middle Ages. But there the similarity, in first analysis, ends. Today the recent past is most often condemned because it seems to hinder the future development that is envisaged. In those days the recent past was judged negatively because it deviated from *antiquitas* — as it was imagined to have been. In both cases the recent past is denounced as contrary to what is considered ideal. But the ideas that in those days formed the basis for criticizing the *moderni*, those of the recent past, did not directly relate to the future. The ideal then was a projection into a much more distant past. Reforms were considered by their supporters as a return to *antiquitas*.

On the other hand, there are reports from the Middle Ages of a more positive evaluation of the recent, personally experienced, past. Repeatedly it is mentioned with satisfaction that antiquity had been equaled or superseded in the present. This appreciation does not signify just a turning against a more distant past. *Antiquitas* was retained as the norm. But the present was not to be ignored, when in one's own past antiquity had been equaled or superseded. This understanding finds expression in the common practice of praising a contemporary as "a new Constantine," "a new Charlemagne," "another Augustine," and even as *alter Christus*.[16]

Appreciation for the recent past as a manifestation of resistance against *antiquitas* was not totally absent in the twelfth and thirteenth

16. Gössmann, 46.

century. I am referring to the protest of a social group that was part of the rather small student population: the somewhat boisterous crowd of wandering students who no longer wanted to study the classical authors, especially since as members of the clergy they were not allowed to enjoy the more tangible joys of the present. This protest was expressed in the *Carmina Burana,* satirical verses that are still appreciated today.[17]

The most articulate presentation of this protest against *antiquitas* is found in the works of the Oxford clergyman Walter Map (†1210), who is supposed to have authored part of this anonymous poetry and may certainly be considered as belonging to this milieu. His *De Nugis Curialium* (Trifles of Courtiers) has remained well known. There he criticizes society with biting humor, speaking of a remarkable miracle: "The dead live and the living are buried," that is, "In foolish comedies we celebrate with truncated verses the divine nobility of the Charleses and the Pippins, but about the emperors of our day no one speaks." Elsewhere Map states how each era is dissatisfied with its *modernitas,* the period during which we remember the main events as if they had just happened, which is a century long, since some people live one hundred years, while others have heard what happened from their parents and grandparents, and so feel that they experienced those events personally. For that reason he supposed his writing would only be appreciated by the most distant posterity, when it would at last have acquired the authority of *antiquitas.*[18]

Criticism of the recent past was especially present, as we saw with Orderic, when tradition had to be defended against reforms that claimed to be based on the ideal of the Beginning. Such criticism is found among the Cluniacs in the work of Peter the Venerable, who was abbot of Cluny beginning in 1122 — after his predecessor had been dismissed for attempts at renewal. Peter's task was to restore the old order. Ten years after he became abbot he sent an evaluation of his own times to one of his most inflexible supporters, Matthew of Albano, who had just been made a cardinal. Alluding to Jerome's statement that many monsters are born into this world, Peter wrote that past times were happier since they remained infertile for such a long time. As a result they were not put to shame by rotten fetuses. But he considered his own time deplorable since it had given birth to hideous offspring with unnatural fertility.[19]

17. Cf. Chenu, 317f.
18. *De Nugis Curialium: Courtiers' Trifles,* ed. and tr. M. R. James (Oxford, 1914), 203, 158f.; rev. ed. by C. N. I. Brooke and R. A. B. Mynors (Oxford, 1983).
19. Letter 47 (Constable, I, 144).

But tradition was the guide for the present even for Bernard of Clairvaux, Peter's most significant opponent. Bernard had not only supported but had also perhaps actively provoked Cluny's attempts at reform with his polemical writings. Tradition coincided with *antiquitas,* as something not to be rediscovered, but to be retained. Therefore, Bernard's first argument against introducing a liturgical festival to celebrate the Immaculate Conception of Mary was that it deviated from the teachings of the Fathers and thus claimed a wisdom superior to theirs.[20] On the other hand, he was in favor of returning to the ideal of the Beginning. In a letter to Pope Eugenius III, in which he took the liberty to make some critical remarks about the greed of the Roman curia, he included this lamentation: "Who will grant me, before I die, to see God's Church as she was in the days of old?"[21]

❧   ❧

THIS TIE TO TRADITIONS that had been in force from time immemorial and therefore had to continue found its primary origin in the closed character of medieval society. Emphasis on tradition — normally the means by which a closed society protects its veneration of the ancestors — acquired in this new form also a theological meaning when during the Carolingian period the separate Germanic tribal units were replaced by one new all-comprising collectivity, that of Christendom. The specific way in which Christianity interpreted its ties with Jewish monotheism and its understanding of history on the basis of its faith in the incarnation of God worked as the point of departure for this theological development.

For the Christian, the passing of time is not thought of primarily in terms of a cyclic process, but rather in terms of a final event, for both the individual and society. Humanity and the human world are en route toward God. In the "post-Christian" world this belief was secularized into faith in progress. Christians of today see the concrete forms by which the existence en route of the Christian and of the world were understood in the Middle Ages and before the Enlightenment as expressions of a faith rooted in an outdated theological interpretation. People today know from experience how theological interpretations must be seen in their historical contexts. But in the Middle Ages the theological interpretation was universally accepted as incontrovertible and included, for instance, belief in purgatory and limbo.

20. Letter 174 (*SBO* VII.388; James, 289 [letter 215]).
21. Letter 238, 6 (*SBO* VIII.118; James, 279 [letter 205]).

Therefore, the way in which history was understood, resting as it did on the current theological interpretation, enjoyed absolute validity. History had to serve the needs of the medieval theological interpretation of humanity and the human world as being en route. History presented a concrete picture of that human situation, and the theological interpretation had its center in eschatological expectation of the rapidly approaching end of time. The medieval view of history was linked to this expectation, and history was therefore recounted from this eschatological perspective, which was also applied to the present and the future. A historical account was only considered reliable when it was set within the eschatological framework that was theologically acceptable at the time.[22]

This theological understanding was built on the method of allegorical interpretation, which had been developed in Christian antiquity and applied by Augustine and Gregory the Great particularly to the story of creation in the book of Genesis.[23] According to this interpretation, adopted by many medieval authors from Isidore of Seville,[24] the six days during which God created the universe and the world were symbols of both the stages of human life and the eras of world history, which were seen as closely connected. Old age, the stage prior to death, was identified with the sixth day of creation, and the corresponding era of history was also viewed as a time of senescence. This last era of history began with the birth of Christ and would end with the end of the world, when Christ would return. Medieval writers believed that they were living in this time of senescence, that the end of all things was at hand, and that the world around them showed signs of aging. In their search for signs of the end, many *calculatores* even tried to establish the exact year in which the end would come — something that even today, after the Enlightenment, continues to occupy intellectual minds. Even in the modern era some have thought the end would come in the year 2000.

Since medieval writers lived in the final era, the era of old age, they

22. H. Grundmann, "Die Grundzüge der mittelalterlichen Geschichtsanschauungen," *Archiv für Kulturgeschichte* 24 (1934), 326-36; repr. in *idem, Ausgewählte Aufsätze* I (Stuttgart, 1976).

23. By Augustine in *De catechizandis rudibus* XXII.39 (*PL* XL, 338f.); by Gregory in *Homiliae in Evangelia* I.1f. (*PL* LXXVI, 1154f.). The latter applied the allegory of the six days to the parable of the master who hired workers for his vineyard (Matt. 20:1-7) and makes the six periods of time symbolized by the six days of creation coincident with the six hours of the day in which the workers were taken into service.

24. *Etymologiarum* V.XXXVIII.5, ed. W. M. Lindsay, I (1911; repr. London, 1971).

believed that the world was manifesting the same problems that tended to accompany old age in human life. The world was weaker than in the previous era. The use of such terms must, of course, be understood as literary expressions, but it is significant to find this idea persisting. A poet at the Carolingian court wrote that in former times people had greater bodily strength and better use of their senses because of the youthfulness the world still possessed at that time.[25] Then around 1124 William of Saint-Thierry used the same image when, because of old age, he planned to step down as abbot of Saint-Thierry. When the example of King David, who in extreme old age continued to rule from his bed, was pointed out to him, William argued that in David's time the foolishness of an aging world had not yet progressed to the point that grey-haired men who had served all their lives were deprived of the honor due them.[26]

While these thoughts of doom prevailed, we must also note the joyful surprise at signs of revival that seemed to indicate that the destruction of the world might be averted or at least delayed. This explains the sometimes joyful discovery that at times *antiquitas* could be equaled or even surpassed. Recognition of signs of revival may be found from the earliest Middle Ages on. A synod in Tours paid the compliment to Queen Radegunde (†587) that she had with her zeal revitalized the aging world that was approaching its end and that the radiance of her love had given warmth to what had almost died from coldness. Alcuin, who spoke of us "insignificant people of the end of the world," paid a similar compliment to Charlemagne: The whole church should be grateful to God for giving to Christendom in the final — and also most dangerous — period of the world's history such a devout, prudent, and righteous leader and protector.[27]

The danger to which Alcuin alluded was, of course, that of the coming of the antichrist, which had been heralded by signs of decay. The idea that the end of time and the coming of the antichrist could be delayed by moral renewal in the present, that is, by a return to *antiquitas,* found acceptance throughout the Middle Ages. More than five centuries after Gregory of Tours, Cardinal Matthew of Albano, the defender of the Cluniac way of life, who has already been mentioned, used the same image, though in an ironic sense. He sent a letter of protest to a number of abbots

25. Dungal Scott, Letter 1; *MGH Epistolae* IV, 577, lines 10f.
26. *Meditatio* XI (*PL* CLXXX, 239c).
27. Gregory of Tours, *The History of the Franks* IX.39, tr. L. Thorpe (Harmondsworth, 1974), 527. Alcuin's Letters, 23 and 123 (*MGH Epistolae* IV.61, 176).

in the archbishopric of Reims who wanted to introduce a stricter rule in their monasteries and included this riposte:

> Blessed be God. The antichrist is on his way, as is written: "Scarceness precedes his coming." But God has provided in these miserable times people of quality and has placed you as bright shining lights and gleaming stars to chase away the darkness that envelops the monastic life in your region in a dense cloud.[28]

The irony of this statement is that Matthew, who in the same letter sharply protests against the reform plans of these abbots, must have seen in their intentions a sign of the antichrist's imminence rather than of his expulsion.

❧   ❧

EXPECTATION OF THE ANTICHRIST — a central theme in medieval eschatology — was not exclusively or even primarily linked to the interpretation of the sixth day as the era beginning with the birth of Christ. More important in this respect was the division of history into four world empires. Following the Church Fathers, medieval theologians based this division on Daniel's vision of the statue with clay feet and the explanation of the vision in the biblical text. In their comments on Daniel, as with other eschatological texts in the Bible, medieval writers were often carried away by desire to anchor this eschatological perspective in history. This resulted in, among other things, the conviction that Rome was the fourth and last empire and was to be followed by the time of antichrist. Augustine had emphatically disassociated himself from this view, in contrast to Jerome, who in this case went beyond a purely spiritual-religious interpretation.

But the political events of 476, when the Germanic king Odoacer deposed Romulus Augustulus, the last Western Roman emperor, and the subsequent takeover by the Ostrogothic king Theodoric the Great, did not lead to eschatological tensions. For those living at that time these events did not yet represent a break with the past. Cassiodorus, a member of the Roman senate and a high civil servant under Theodoric, considered the prophecies of Daniel as still unfulfilled.[29] In the Merovingian Empire, at

---

28. Latin text in *William, Abbot of St. Thierry: A Colloquium at the Abbey of St. Thierry*, ed. J. Carfantan (Cistercian Studies 94; Kalamazoo, MI, 1987), 65f., lines 8-12.

29. D. Verhelst, "La préhistoire des conceptions d'Adson concernant l'Antichrist," *Recherches de Théologie ancienne et médiévale* 40 (1973), 76.

roughly the same time, the Gallo-Roman bishop Gregory of Tours insisted that the Franks had not destroyed the Roman Empire, but had, rather, renewed it. He considered King Clovis a new Constantine. For that reason he modeled his description of Clovis's conversion on that of the conversion of the first Christian emperor.[30]

Eschatological tensions are, however, evident in the writings of Pope Gregory the Great. He experienced what Italy suffered when the Byzantine emperor Justinian recaptured the region. But in the midst of the apprehension caused by the siege of Rome, he limited himself to commentary on the biblical stories of the fall of Samaria and of Nineveh, which he understood in reference to his own times. Sharing in the loyalty of the official church to the Augustinian interpretation of eschatological Bible passages, he abstained from any comment on the book of Daniel. Yet, he did not completely neglect the antichrist. He believed that everyone who lives in iniquity already bears the antichrist within,[31] and he saw moral decline as a sign foreshadowing the antichrist — an ever-recurring theme in the Middle Ages. The compliment to Queen Radegunde, alluded to above, that her revival of morality would delay the destruction of the world, indicates that Gregory the Great did not develop a totally new view of the antichrist.

It is important to ask how this explanation of the coming of the antichrist was worked out in medieval society. Did the expectation that the antichrist would appear as a result of human conduct influence medieval behavior? Were the moral laws of the church obeyed out of eschatological fear? What results did this have for the ways in which society functioned? The realization that human moral conduct could hasten or delay the calamities of the end probably affected those who accepted this view only to a limited degree. But this fear might easily have led to moralizing criticism of the "misconduct" of others.

Our questions are related to the fact that this aspect of medieval eschatological thinking has received considerably less attention than what has often been called "the pursuit of the millennium," the dream of Christ's thousand-year rule on earth at the time of the end. This millenarianism has excited historians because of the clamorous and spectacular way it was repeatedly presented in the Middle Ages. It proved attractive in those days, not only because of the way in which it was presented, but also because

30. *The History of the Franks,* II.31.144.
31. *Moralia* XXXVIII.15 (*PL* LXXVI, 484f.).

it did not burden human personal conduct with responsibilities. It also fitted more easily in a world that usually saw threats as coming from otherworldly powers.[32]

We have already mentioned the tendency of the Church Fathers to give the eschatological visions of the Bible concrete historical meanings. The first Christians lived with the expectation of an imminent return of the Lord as a historical reality, and this sort of expectation persisted for centuries. This tendency to view things in terms of concrete historical realities was stimulated by the politically uncertain future of the Roman Empire. Many Christians were concerned for the empire's chances of survival, since soon after Constantine many came to view the empire as the social framework within which the church would continue to exist until the end of time.

This view contributed to the empire's survival in imagination when it had already perished in reality. It was not until the collapse of the Carolingian Empire and the concurrent invasions of the Vikings and the Magyars that people came to experience considerable anxiety concerning the political and social chances of survival of Western European society. Due to its limited horizon, this society naturally understood itself as the whole world, and fear for its own demise could therefore easily lead to the conviction that the time of the end had arrived. The nature of these threats, notably the fact that they came from the outside, helped, in the context of this eschatological anxiety, to rekindle interest in this-worldly, that is, millenarian, expectations regarding the end.

※   ※

IN THIS LIGHT we are hardly surprised by the further elaboration of the figure of the antichrist in the tenth century within a millenarian expectation of the end. We owe the one detailed treatise that we possess to Abbot Adso of Montier-en-Dèr (†992). Going back to Greek and Byzantine legends, he postulated the appearance of a last emperor prior to the coming of the antichrist. After a long rule, during which the pagans would be converted by force and the Jews would be baptized, this emperor — who was to be the greatest of all — would go to Jerusalem, where he would lay down his imperial insignia and return his empire to God the Father. At

32. Cf. N. Cohn, *The Pursuit of the Millennium* (rev. ed.; Oxford, 1970).

that moment the antichrist would appear, but he would be overpowered and killed by the archangel Michael on the Mount of Olives.[33]

Although the official church disassociated itself from these this-worldly eschatological expectations, they were immensely popular, even though it is impossible to measure their exact influence. At times they were used as political propaganda, especially with regard to the identity of the person who might be the last emperor. Charlemagne and Otto I, to whose sister Gerberga Adso's *De Antichristo* was addressed, were suggested, as were Emperor Henry IV, King Louis VII, and Frederick Barbarossa. The inclusion of the last two names in this list had to do with the crusades, in which eschatological expectations also played an important role. But in this case this-worldly expectations about the end time coincided with heavenly hopes of salvation, since Jerusalem was not only an earthly city but also a biblical symbol for expectation of heavenly salvation. This convergence in turn determined to some extent the way in which the antichrist was portrayed.

Guibert of Nogent's chronicle of the First Crusade provides a striking example. He gave the appeal of Pope Urban II in 1095 (even though he did not have direct access to the pope's text) this very twofold meaning. Urban argued, according to Guibert, that the antichrist would manifest himself in Jerusalem. And since it was hardly likely that the antichrist — as his name indicates — would fight the heathen and the Jews, Christians had to go to Jerusalem. There they were to restore the mother church of christendom, and in so doing they would resist the unbelief of the antichrist and his followers.[34]

It is unlikely that Guibert was completely able to ignore the view that Christians could resist the antichrist by their moral conduct. The ideas referred to above do not shed any further light on this aspect, but his other writings show a strong emphasis on the heavenly salvation of each individual person. But just as it is impossible to ascertain the extent of the influence of millenarian expectations of salvation, it is likewise futile to speculate about the continuing influence of this religious and moral understanding of the antichrist. But there is some indirect information. It is found in the degree to which people were acquainted with the ideas of Gregory the Great concerning the antichrist.

---

33. Adso Dervensis, *De Ortu et tempore Antichristi,* ed. D. Verhelst (*CCCM* 45; Turnhout, 1976).

34. Cf. E. Peters, *The First Crusade* (Sources of Medieval History; Philadelphia, 1974), 11-15.

❧   ❧

THE IDEA REFERRED TO ABOVE that a revival of faith and Christian love would delay the appearance of the antichrist is one such indication, as are the few instances in which heretics are labeled precursors or heralds of the antichrist. But there is clearer evidence. Gregory spoke of other religious phenomena as forebodings of the antichrist: if the church were to be deprived of its signs of virtue, if the gift of prophecy were to be darkened, if the charisma of healing were to cease, if the virtue of voluntary abstinence were to be undermined, and if miracles were to cease. He listed these signs in his commentary on Job 41:22b (verse 13b in the Vulgate: "Scarcity precedes his appearing"). Gregory applied this text about Leviathan, a monster described in symbolic terms, to the coming of the antichrist.[35]

This comment of Gregory appears to have become part of the literary-eschatological parlance of the medieval church. Cardinal Matthew of Albano appealed to it in his backhanded compliment of the abbots in the archbishopric of Reims: Their opposition to abuses was to be viewed as a sign that God still had men of high quality at his disposal in a time so near to the coming of the antichrist — when scarcity was a sign of his soon appearing. We find even clearer traces of Gregory's ideas in the writings of Orderic Vitalis. His statement about the coming of the anti-christ was also closely related to a number of allusions to this theme made two centuries earlier — in the troubled tenth century — by Odo of Cluny (†942). In his introduction to the fifth volume of his history Orderic wrote:

> Now is the time when the love of many waxes cold and iniquity abounds, miracles, which are the proofs of holiness, grow rare — whilst crimes and sorrowful complaints are multiplied all over the world. The altercations of prelates and bloody wars of princes provide more material for the historian's pen than the treatises of theologians or the fasts and prophecies of ascetics. The time of Antichrist draws near, preceded, as God made known to the blessed Job, by a drying up of miracles and a growing frenzy of vices in those who give themselves up to fleshly lusts.[36]

---

35. *Moralia* XXXIV.III.7 (*PL* LXXVI, 721).
36. *HE* V.1 (III, 9). About Odo of Cluny, cf. the preface to his *Life of Gerald of Aurillac* and his *Sermon on St. Benedict* (*PL* CXXXIII, 641, 722).

These and similar statements indicate that we are dealing here with a traditional portrayal of the antichrist. Therefore it would be worthwhile to give further study to the influence of the religious-eschatological belief that human moral failure must be regarded as a sign of the coming of the antichrist. Such study might help us gain a better idea of the determining factors in the interactions of different groups in medieval society. A connection between such eschatological views and the theme of contempt for the world, which was broadly accepted in the later Middle Ages, seems clear.

Insofar as this religiously oriented eschatology did not lapse into the "pursuit of the millennium," into speculations regarding a thousand-year reign, it considered the religious and moral shortcomings of humankind as hastening the antichrist's coming. These shortcomings were known from one's own experience of the past. They did not belong to the idealized *antiquitas,* but to the era that had followed the *antiquitas,* which was still influencing the present. Therefore, the recent past was regarded as the time of scarcity, as the time that heralded the appearance of the antichrist. Another characteristic of this scarcity, apart from the decrease in spiritual gifts, was moral decay, the cessation of efforts to rein in the carnal passions. Those who allowed the recent past to deviate from *antiquitas* were to blame for the soon coming of the antichrist.

꙳   ꙳

WE HAVE NOW COME full circle to the question of the meaning *moderni* had for Orderic Vitalis. He used it of those whose conduct presented an eschatological menace. The meaning of the term must therefore be found in eschatological expectation in the generally accepted spiritual and religious sense. Even though *moderni* acquired another connotation, Orderic's usage of the word reflected what was already familiar to many. Nontraditional practices and ideas carried for many an eschatological menace, because they interfered with the traditions of their world. This menace was, as Walter Map writes, the reason why every age always rejects its own recent past, its own *modernitas.*

But apart from all this there may well be some literary hyperbole. And we should also recognize that we know only the opinions of the literate elite, though those opinions showed a remarkable continuity and were able to penetrate the thought patterns of the common people. Moreover, it must not be forgotten that this elite, that is to say, the clergy, had assigned to itself the task of preaching to the people and that this preaching included the transmission of these eschatological ideas. Social protest against this elite was usually limited to occasions when the clergy had failed in its task of proclamation or in its eschatologically determined conduct in daily life.

But we must also realize that this elite wrote not only to express this eschatological fear but also to mitigate that fear. Another popular eschatological theme concerned the time that would follow the sixth day. Augustine had already provided a model for this. In the last book of his *De Civitate Dei* he speaks of the seventh day as a sabbath without evening, therefore an *eighth* day lasting for all eternity, the day of the Lord. This day for the eternal rest of soul and body is prefigured by Sunday, which is sanctified by Christ's resurrection.[37] This heavenly expectation of salvation was an essential aspect of religious eschatology. From this standpoint millenarian views were illegitimate, since they looked forward to a permanent this-worldly salvation.

In the context of this religious eschatology the recent past was understood as an interim period, as the beginning of the transition that separates *antiquitas* from the bliss to follow the time of the antichrist. Every generation saw the recent past, therefore, in a negative light. Human moral failures, especially of the clergy, made this interim into a sign of the coming of the antichrist. This eschatological interpretation of the recent past is the basis on which we divide history into periods, at any rate the basis for our term "Middle Ages." This term, as well as the negative evaluation that has long been attached to it, goes back to the way in which the recent past was evaluated in the Middle Ages. Both the name and the evaluation were assigned to the recent past as the eschatological frightening interim period.

THIS CONCLUSION has not been drawn hastily. It fits in with what has long been known about the origin of the term "Middle Ages." We know that Nicholas of Cusa (†1464), unlike others of his time, preferred the term *media tempestas* (interim era) for the post-apostolic age. He was also opposed to an eschatological understanding of this term.[38] Moreover, the French equivalent seems to have been used as a term for the recent past. Huizinga mentions

---

37. XXII.30 = *Concerning the City of God, against the Pagans,* tr. H. Bettenson (Harmondsworth, 1972), 1087-90.

38. P. Lehmann, "Mittelalter und Küchenlatein," *Erforschung des Mittelalters* I (1941; repr. Stuttgart, 1959), 52f.

that in the first half of the fifteenth century the time that one could remember was called the *temps moyen*.[39] Finally, we know that Petrarch (†1374) resolutely identified *antiquitas* as the period of classical antiquity and saw the subsequent centuries as a time of darkness. His expectation that this darkness would come to an end in his time suggests that he understood it as an interim.[40] And there is a much earlier representative of the view of the interim as a time of decline: Walter von der Vogelweide († after 1210) believed that the period of decline, which he himself was experiencing, had begun with Constantine the Great, whose "donation" to the pope had brought about the decline of the church of Rome.[41]

But it is of little importance to determine exactly when the eschatological emphasis took root and this rather vague demarcation of an interim period began. Those erudite persons who freed themselves from the way in which history was usually understood in the Middle Ages, who left behind the familiar eschatological view of history, could and did move to a chronological demarcation of the interim period. Given the distinction between *antiquitas* and the ensuing eschatological interim, one would be forced to decide when the earlier time ended and the other began. But historical accounts that simply wanted to affirm that the recent past was the beginning of the end did not come to such a decision. In such accounts the interim period, this *tempestas media*, was merely the most recent past as it was moving forward.

The interim period after *antiquitas* was not only a period of decline for Petrarch and others who wanted to establish its boundaries. The term "Dark Ages" finds its origin in the medieval period itself, as L. Varga has shown. It is based on the eschatological view of the recent past.[42] People spoke of a dark time because of the sins of humankind, in particular of Christians, and especially of the clergy — so that clergymen, sometimes individual clerics, were often sharply criticized. The idea that the time in which one lived heralded the coming of the antichrist inevitably led to a condemnation of sins. Spontaneous irritation inspired such criticism, but it was also supposed that resisting these modern symptoms of falsehood could delay the antichrist's coming.

39. "Temps moien dit de memoire d'omme." J. Huizinga, "Een schakel in de ontwikkeling van de term middeleeuwen," *Verzamelde werken* IV (Haarlem, 1949), 433-40.
40. T. E. Mommsen, "Petrarch's Conception of the 'Dark Ages,'" in *Medieval and Renaissance Studies,* ed. E. F. Riche (Ithaca, 1959), 106-29.
41. *Lieder und Sprüche Walter von der Vogelweide,* ed. V. Michels (Halle, 1924), 128.
42. *Das Schlagwort vom Finsteren Mittelalter* (Vienna, 1932), 5-35.

As we have noted, this eschatological conviction discouraged any exact demarcation of the interim period. In particular those who, like Bernard of Clairvaux, rejected all attempts to tie this religious eschatology to any concrete historical reality regarded this contemporary darkness as without chronological boundaries. A striking example of this is found in one of Bernard's sermons on the Song of Solomon:

> This world has its nights — not few in number. I say the world has its nights, but it is almost all night, and always plunged in complete darkness. The faithlessness *[perfidia]* of the Jews, the ignorance of pagans, the perversity of heretics, even the shameless and degraded behavior of Catholics — these all are nights. For surely it is night when the things which belong to the Spirit of God are not perceived?[43]

❧   ❧

TO DEPART from this eschatological point of view must have involved a drastic social process. This change in perspective took place gradually during the disintegration of late medieval society, even though there were some earlier attempts. In this process of emancipation, of distancing oneself, those who truly succeeded in freeing themselves from the medieval eschatological view connected, or even identified, their new position again with their understanding of *antiquitas*. The Renaissance became an identification with classical antiquity and in part also with Christian antiquity. The Reformation focused completely on the early church as the ideal. Freedom from the idea of a rather vague and ever shifting interim period came by determining the temporal limits of the interim. But this presupposed that a new reality was beginning in the present and would be realized in the future; it presupposed, in other words, a new ideal of the future. The new reality inevitably coincided with the idealized conception of *antiquitas*. For there are no alternatives when one searches for the ideal.

This process of growing away from the medieval way of understanding reality was only partly completed. Those who championed this development retained, nonetheless, many ties with older ways of experiencing reality and kept many nonrational presuppositions concerning matters that later proved to belong to the earthly human realm. An example

43. *Sermo in Cantu* LXXXV.10 = *Sermons on the Song of Songs* IV (Kalamazoo, MI, 1980), 106.

is the continuance of medieval prejudice against Jews. But the Counter-Reformation, Rome's attempt to reposition itself when confronted with the changes that were happening, opted again fully for the medieval traditions, although with some distortions. Nevertheless, from then on the term "Middle Ages" was generally accepted, at least from the moment that schoolbooks began to distinguish antiquity, the Middle Ages, and the modern era.

Thereafter, endorsement or rejection of the Middle Ages remained an important aspect of the disagreement between Rome and Protestants, particularly with regard to ways in which faith was translated into daily life and into theological rationalizations that were kept alive only by Rome. In this context evaluation of the Middle Ages became a rather emotional matter. There was clearly a continuation of the medieval mentality. But for the emancipated the period remained filled with the same darkness that had formerly been seen as characteristic of the eschatological interim. But for those who remained faithful to the medieval sacral views of reality, the Middle Ages became the normative ideal that equaled or even replaced *antiquitas*.

The polarizing climax of these conflicting interpretations did not come until the nineteenth century, after the traditional contrast between the Middle Ages and the modern era had been made largely irrelevant by the Enlightenment. The Enlightenment no longer respected nonrational presuppositions, which were still current even among those who had been emancipated from the medieval mentality. These presuppositions were implicit in, for instance, acceptance of the divine right of kings and rejection of historical criticism of the Bible or the results of natural science. But the Enlightenment critical approach did not stop when essential matters of faith were at issue. But then neither was the distinction between essential and nonessential matters of faith maintained in the reaction following the Enlightenment, when once again pleas were made for an attitude of faith. Romanticism again cherished nonrational presuppositions with regard to earthly realities.

But Romanticism did more, at least where it touched on religion. It focused anew on the Middle Ages, demanded that that era be rehabilitated, and set it up as the ideal that was to inspire a new Christian Europe. In order to return to a genuinely Christian culture, it was considered necessary to go back to those times. Support for this view brought many back to the church of Rome. Rome had conserved medieval Christian culture, which was itself experiencing a revival in countless new ideologies.

It possessed the authentic culture of Christianity, it was said, valid for any time and place. This reappraisal of the value of Christianity for society was first introduced by René Chateaubriand in his *Genie du Christianisme*, published in Paris in 1802. But he did not include the Middle Ages in his reappraisal. That had to await the booklet *Christendom or Europe*, which had been written about 1799 by Novalis (†1801) and which on its publication in 1826 caused a strong revival of interest in the Middle Ages and led many of its readers back to Rome. This Rome-oriented revival of the Middle Ages did, of course, further increase the emotional prejudice against the Middle Ages that elsewhere was still very much alive.[44]

It is true that Romanticism significantly stimulated the study of the Middle Ages, and this study led to greater openness. But this remained, for a time, limited to only a few. What was more significant was the projection of nationalistic feelings onto the Middle Ages, which created new misunderstandings with regard to this era of history,[45] bringing on, for instance, the emotions surrounding the incident commonly referred to as the "journey to Canossa." In this emotionally laden atmosphere old controversies and prejudices, which contributed greatly to perpetuating the divisions in Christianity, remained alive. A striking illustration of the intensity of these differences of opinion is found in the sarcastic apologetic of a German Catholic priest at the end of the nineteenth century:

> Our ancestors were for centuries the victims of Pelagian delusions and a dozen other heresies . . . and so did not in the least exert themselves to regain the so-called lost truth. Often they persisted in feeling at home with the evil geniuses of the papacy, of hostility toward the truth, of disbelief, and of contempt for humankind. They lived foolishly and carelessly, it is claimed, in pagan self-righteousness and legalism, giving not a thought to raising themselves to real human dignity. The crude religious sensuality with which they sought after human and divine matters led to a terrible dualism, to a bizarre mixture of divine and human, a blend of paganism, Judaism, and undiluted superstition that one could simply call idolatry — a renewed heathenism, pure magic and sorcery. By praying to "that so-called Madonna" and to the saints, they became more stubborn in their criminal ridicule of the Holy of

---

44. Cf. the satirical writing of Heinrich Heine from 1835: *The Romantic School* (New York, 1882).

45. Fr. Schneider, ed., *Universalstaat oder Nationalstaat und Ende des ersten deutschen Reiches* (Innsbruck, 1934).

Holies. Christ was forgotten and lost, and the piety of those days could produce only impious hymns, prayers, and litanies.[46]

⁊⟡   ⁊⟡

MUCH HAS CHANGED since then. On both sides understanding and appreciation of the Middle Ages — and the extent to which such claims were true — has increased. Accusation and apology have disappeared. The progress of social change has increased the distance between the Middle Ages and our time to such a degree that that era is now generally regarded as unique, as a civilization *sui generis.* But this has new consequences for the study of that time. Meticulous investigation of medieval institutions resulting in scrupulous distinctions with regard to social and legal rules and divisions is no longer adequate. To outline the precise differences between the feudal nobility and the gentry and to give a detailed description of the different kinds of medieval towns no longer adequately answers the questions that are being raised about our medieval past, even though this traditional approach to research continues to offer invaluable insights when answers to these new questions are sought.

Following the newer social sciences, such as structural sociology, social psychology, and cultural anthropology, historians are now asking of the Middle Ages how people thought and acted in their social networks. What power or weakness characterized that society in its relationship to constructed realities and to the social consequences of human endeavor? In brief, historians want to gain insight into the different factors that shaped people as individuals and as groups. Their questions concern not just socio-economic factors, but also what helped to define these factors, namely, the medieval way of experiencing reality. This is a new kind of historiography, although it has had some precursors. It is usually referred to as the "history of mentality." In this rather general characterization it can easily present itself as an attractive renewal of medieval studies, which has become dusty with the passage of time.

But study of the "history of mentality" may easily lead to another misunderstanding of the Middle Ages, since it gives the historian the opportunity for an almost unnoticed return to an emotionally determined

---

46. A. M. Weiss, *Apologie des Christentums* III (Freiburg im Breisgau, 1879), 587-89, quoted by H. Rost, *Die Wahrheit über das Mittelalter nach protestantischen Urteilen* (Leipzig, 1924), 13, n. 1.

approach to the era. The mentality of an era is the result of a complex of presuppositions that are accepted as self-evident by the different groups in a society. If people truly share a common way of thinking, leaving to one side the variants corresponding to the particular communal nexus to which individuals belong, then they cannot distance themselves from the presuppositions of this shared mentality, as long as they remain within their group. People are normally defenseless against their own society's ways of thinking.

The mentality of medieval society, insofar as it had stable characteristics during a period of almost ten centuries, must have been formed by a considerable number of presuppositions that were generally accepted by major groups. As a coherent whole, it has been superseded and has disappeared. But aspects of this medieval mentality may still to some extent be found among the presuppositions of some smaller groups of today. In our pluralistic world we can refer to this phenomenon as the "contemporaneity of what is not contemporary." Whatever we may think, we must accept that what one person regards as a manifestation of medieval mentality may still be part of the ideas and presuppositions of another person, who will regard it as contemporary. This difference of opinion affects many areas, including religion, morality, politics, and ideologies.

Because of this diversity of opinion, which can be called *modern* or *merely medieval,* depending on one's own mentality, the history of the medieval mentality can easily get bogged down in emotional controversies about differences among a variety of *contemporary* social norms and values. Some will run the risk of being regarded as deadlocked and frustrated atavists, while others will be accused of polemical projections of personal ideas that they try, in a polarizing manner, to elevate to general rules. In brief, the Middle Ages become a field for tournaments in which the nature of our *present-day* mentality is fought over, but without the courtliness of former times. If the history of mentality can only be practiced in such a way, it might be better to leave the dust on medieval studies.

The research topics for a history of the medieval mentality must be chosen with great care if the historian is to escape the problem of projection. Moreover, the inevitable differences of opinion about countless aspects of the medieval mentality can result in a theoretical approach that remains highly superficial, precisely because the historian wants to avoid such differences. But there are some general features of medieval society that are quite widely accepted as characterizing its mentality. We can mention, for instance, the binding authority of tradition, the dualistic approach to spirit and matter, the corporate society, which asked — or rather demanded — conformity from the individual, the sacral experience of reality, which supplemented personal powerlessness by presuppositions of otherworldly power, and the experience of time in its eschatological finality in accordance with biblical allegory.

This last aspect is mentioned because this experience of time constitutes the most distinct aspect of the mentality of the Middle Ages. It is farther removed from our present way of experiencing reality than any other aspect of the medieval mentality. Moreover, it differs from the experience of time in classical antiquity by its unique character of finality. The way in which time was experienced in the Middle Ages is therefore the most suitable point of departure for a study of the history of the mentality of that era. It can protect us against emotional and controversial definitions of the medieval way of thinking, which only cover up and find nothing new and which impede, rather than advance, the study of the medieval past. For the sake of advancing the discipline of medieval studies as it attempts to align itself with modern approaches in the social sciences, I have emphatically wanted to address myself to this matter of methodology. In all this the empirical must prevail above models that have been constructed in accordance with modern presuppositions.

III

Jerusalem in the West[1]

❧   ❧

In 1122 Pons of Melgueil, the powerful abbot of Cluny, was forced by Pope Callistus II to lay down his office and dignity. His opponents within his monastery and his order had accused him of mismanagement before the pope, saying that his policies were characterized by inconsistent and imprudent decision making, wasting of resources, and arrogance. The abbot had thereby, they said, harmed the monastery and had brought the way of life *(ordo)* of the Cluniacs into disrepute. Almost all, the accusers claimed, had rebelled against the abbot. We will describe below how this conflict, which led to a schism in Cluny, was eventually resolved.[2] Here we want to focus on the solution that Abbot Pons chose in this controversy, which seemed polarized beyond any possibility of reconciliation.

Pons decided to travel from Rome to Jerusalem. We are told that he made his journey in the company of twelve monks, an indication that he traveled in his capacity as abbot. Monks were not allowed to travel to Jerusalem without the explicit permission of their superiors, in this instance the pope. Callistus gave his permission on the condition that Pons quit his office. But it seems that the abbot paid little attention to these conditions, considering the group that accompanied him and his claim to his

---

1. This chapter is based partly on "Jérusalem dans l'occident médiéval," in *Mélanges offerts à René Crozet,* ed. P. Gallais and Y.-J. Riou (Poitiers, 1966), I, 259-71.
2. See chapter V below.

79

position after his return. Pons clearly attached great importance to making the journey at that particular moment, since the problems that it created did not deter him.

One gets the impression, in fact, that he made his decision as a spontaneous reaction to his discovery in Rome that the conflict at Cluny was beyond any solution. He made it clear that he did not intend to give up his office, at least not permanently. His decision to go to Jerusalem must be understood in this light: The pilgrimage was the only way he could escape from an impossible situation.

Such a choice was often made. In 1124 a severe winter destroyed the harvest in the northeastern part of France, where the Cistercian monastery of Morimond was located. But the abbot, Arnold of Cologne, refused to request or accept help from other monasteries of his order, particularly from Clairvaux, which had been founded on the same day as Morimond in 1115. Arnold saw the two monasteries as rivals and felt that Morimond had to equal or even surpass Clairvaux in its expansion. Each of the two monasteries had established three daughter institutions up to 1124, when Morimond tried to take the lead by founding another. But in the circumstances brought on by the crop failure, this proved too heavy a strain, and Morimond was threatened with ruin. Abbot Arnold decided at that point to travel with his monks to Jerusalem. But this plan, which did not receive official approval, failed. Only with help from Clairvaux was Morimond able to weather the crisis.

Jerusalem was thus regarded as the fitting destination for people with serious and insoluble problems.

ꙮ   ꙮ

DID THIS PLAY a motivating role for those who responded to Pope Urban II's appeal in November 1095, which launched the First Crusade? Did they consider Jerusalem as a last resort for problems that otherwise would have remained insoluble?

This question, as intriguing as it is, only introduces the broader question of the significance of Jerusalem for the West. But the initial question is audacious in that it makes discussion of the crusades among historians even more complicated than it already is. That discussion usually begins with the question of religious versus economic motivations for supporting or participating in the crusades. Such a distinction of motivations is made particularly in regard to the original purpose of the First

Crusade and the reason that so many were willing to fight in it, which is usually held to have been more religious than for the later crusades.

Historians have repeatedly asked whether Pope Urban already had the liberation of Jerusalem as a goal when he made his appeal in Clermont or sought only to assist the Byzantine emperor Alexius I, who had asked Urban for help in his struggle against the Turks. But now we are asking how those who responded to the pope's appeal understood that appeal. Can a possible difference between the pope's original aims and the crusaders' motives for signing up for the journey be explained by the significance Jerusalem had for the West, specifically its significance as a destination for those who found themselves in insoluble difficulties?

The tendency to give greater weight to religious motives for joining the First Crusade than for joining the later crusades is such that an author who stresses economic factors still recognizes that they played less of a role in the eleventh century than later and that the importance of the crusades with regard to trade was not as clear for the Italian cities as it was to be after the Crusader States had been established.[3] But we do know that some of the leaders of armies — even before they left for the First Crusade — intended to acquire power and establish new states in the Middle East, while the knights who accompanied them counted on being rewarded with fiefs for their service.

In this connection historians usually refer to the situation of the Burgundian knights. Frequently they were the younger sons of holders of small fiefs who left their inheritances undivided, passing the whole to their oldest sons in order to prevent the family holding from becoming totally unprofitable by further partitioning.[4] For that reason some of these knights, those who did not object to a celibate life, became monks. But this alternative was less appealing for those knights who still thought of fighting as their life's work — and their almost daily pastime. For them the crusade offered a solution, in particular by providing them an economic base.

But this economic motivation appears less important in light of the fact that going to Jerusalem was viewed as the last resort in escaping any

3. E. Werner, "Die Kreuzzugsidee im Mittelalter," *Wissenschaftliches Zeitschrift der Karl Marx Universität Leipzig* 5 (1957/58), 135-49.

4. Cf. G. Duby, "Les 'jeunes' dans la société aristocratique dans la France du Nord-Ouest au XIIe siècle," in *Hommes et structures du moyen âge* (Paris/The Hague, 1973), 213-25.

insurmountable difficulty. We may well ask whether the knights would have signed up for this expedition, in spite of the slogan that it was God's will, if it were only aimed at assisting the Byzantine emperor in reconquering land lost to the Turks in the 1070s. Jerusalem was, in fact, not part of that lost territory: The city had already passed into Muslim hands in 614.

It must be admitted that the material prospects would have been less promising for the participants if their only aim was reconquering recently lost territory, but this would also have been much less risky. Joining an expedition to Jerusalem, into the heart of Muslim territory, would be much more precarious. Such a venture would only be undertaken if more than an economic motivation were at stake. There was still ample opportunity at home in the Latin West for those who wanted to fight, and, indeed, the pope intended with his appeal to end such fighting: He called specifically those who were guilty of disturbing the peace to this holy war.

But the destination remains a matter of great importance, insofar as the knights' decision to participate involved more than the economic situation. With Jerusalem as the goal the decision to go may also be viewed as a last resort in a totally desperate situation. But this explanation is only acceptable if we can more clearly pinpoint the religious significance of Jerusalem in the imagination of the West.

Many for whom Urban's appeal was not intended — poor workers who were hardly managing to stay alive — responded to the appeal. They often heard about it from itinerant preachers, among whom Peter of Amiens — Peter the Hermit — was the most prominent. For them this appeal may well, in the form in which they heard it, have pointed to a solution to their despair. In those years their chances for survival were marginal. In 1042-70 an epidemic of gangrene *(la maladie des ardents)* claimed countless victims, especially among the poor, and again after 1090 this illness spread rapidly. The lives of such people was always threatened by crop failures and floods.

If in that society Jerusalem was viewed as the last resort in utter despair, this segment of the population would have been aware of that. But such people were usually lacking in the means and the freedom to make such a journey. Jerusalem remained out of reach. But in late 1095 and early 1096 they heard from preachers about the possibility of going to Jerusalem by joining the crusade. Their interest in the journey makes it highly probable that the pope's appeal was almost immediately understood as referring to a reconquering of Jerusalem — or that it was creatively interpreted in that way — though in reality the purpose was to help Byzantium.

Many of these members of the army of the poor were totally unfit to participate in such a military expedition, and they made but few preparations. They did not want to lose much time prior to their departure, and they showed more haste than the other armies. They expected to be in Jerusalem soon. Often they had no idea about the distance to be covered, and each town on the way was immediately hailed as the goal of the journey. It was not participating in a holy war but going to Jerusalem that motivated them.

As has been already been stated, there have been different views about the pope's appeal. Was his only initial concern to assist Byzantium, or did he from the very first have the deliverance of Jerusalem in mind? Only the sources can tell us. But the text of the sermon preached by Urban II to the council fathers in Clermont has not been preserved. Accounts from contemporary authors of histories of the crusades do not always agree. The decisions, or canons, of the council have also been preserved, but their textual history is rather chaotic, depending entirely on the notes of different council fathers.

The notes made by Lambert, bishop of Arras, are the only ones that mention a council decision about a journey to Jerusalem, and they do, in fact, seem to indicate that it was decided to liberate Jerusalem. The second canon of the *Liber Lamberti* reads: "All those who through piety, and not for fame or money, go to Jerusalem to free God's Church can consider this journey as a penance for the punishment of sins."[5] This may lead us to the conclusion that from the beginning the pope clearly preached the holy war to free Jerusalem.

The problem remains that this decision is absent from the other lists of canons. And if it had indeed been decided to liberate Jerusalem, this would certainly have been sufficiently important to have been recorded. The historian Orderic Vitalis, who wrote before 1135, does record in his account of the council how the pope launched an appeal to liberate Jerusalem, without, however, mentioning this in his list of council decisions.[6] According to the eyewitness report of the council by Fulcher of Chartres, the pope — without referring to Jerusalem — promised the par-

5. R. Somerville, *The Councils of Urban II* I (Annuarium Historiae Conciliorum, Supplement 1; Amsterdam, 1972), 74.
6. *HE* IX.2 (V, 10-18).

ticipants: "All men going there who die untimely deaths, whether on the journey by land or by sea or while fighting the pagans, will immediately have their sins remitted. I am entitled to grant this to those about to go by the gift of God."[7]

Accounts of the Council of Clermont from other chroniclers of the First Crusade suggest that the pope did speak of Jerusalem, but in different ways.[8] Fulcher wrote this part of his history of the crusade earlier than the other chroniclers. It is at least doubtful whether these later chroniclers even attended the council, in spite of their own assertions that they did. And their accounts of the pope's sermon clearly interpret it on the basis of their knowledge about what actually happened during the crusade.

Fulcher supposedly had the text of the council canons at his disposal when he composed his account. But some have conjectured that he did not mention Jerusalem on purpose. He participated in the crusade in the army of Baldwin of Boulogne, who established, prior to the siege and conquest of Jerusalem, the crusader state of Edessa and thus changed the destination of his army during the crusade. Fulcher would have been disavowing Baldwin's accomplishment had he mentioned that the council from the outset had decided on Jerusalem as the goal of the crusade. But the title of his work, which has been transmitted in various forms, consistently refers to the accomplishments of the Franks with respect to Jerusalem. Moreover, Fulcher is probably the least gullible of the chroniclers of this crusade. But in any case the precise focus of the pope's appeal remains uncertain.[9]

The remaining sources that may help to shed further light on this point are three letters of Urban II, written in December 1095 and September and October 1096. In the first letter the pope announces to the faithful in Flanders the decision of the council to prepare an expedition that would depart on August 15 of the following year:

7. As translated in L. Riley-Smith and J. S. C. Riley-Smith, *The Crusades, Idea and Reality* (Documents of Medieval History, 4; London, 1981), 41.

8. Cf. *The First Crusade: The Chronicle of Fulcher of Chartres and Other Source Materials*, ed. E. Peters (Philadelphia, 1971), 1-14.

9. Cf. H. E. J. Cowdrey, "Pope Urban's Preaching of the First Crusade," *History* 55 (1970), 177-88. Cowdrey concludes that the pope summoned the council for the liberation of Jerusalem. See also D. C. Munro, "The Speech of Pope Urban II at Clermont," *American Historical Review* 2 (1906), 231-42. In the second volume of A. Becker, *Papst Urban II* (Stuttgart, 1988), the author, who also addresses the circumstances of this pope's appeal to a holy war, does not make clear his opinion of what Urban II said at Clermont about the liberation of Jerusalem.

Your brotherhood, we believe, has long since learned from many accounts that a barbaric fury has deplorably afflicted and laid waste the churches of God in the regions of the Orient. More than this, blasphemous to say, it has even grasped in intolerable servitude its churches and the Holy City of Christ, glorified by his passion and resurrection. Grieving with pious concern at this calamity, we visited the regions of Gaul and devoted ourselves largely to urging the princes of the land and their subjects to free the churches of the East. We solemnly enjoined upon them at the council of Auvergne (the accomplishment of) such an undertaking, as a preparation for the remission of all their sins.[10]

This last aspect — pardon for sins — is also found in the second canon of the *Liber Lamberti* and in Fulcher's account. We may presume that it reflects a council decision. But if the decision was made in the form in which it was recorded by Lambert, why then did the pope not communicate it in the same way? Moreover, why did he remain vague about the destination of the journey? In his other two letters, written in the autumn of 1096, this ambiguity is absent: Both refer to a journey to Jerusalem for the purpose of liberating the church there.[11] But in the meantime the uncertainty had been removed, since the army of the poor was already en route to Jerusalem under the leadership of Peter the Hermit.

We may thus conjecture that Pope Urban had at first no clear plan for assisting Byzantium and that he based the further development of a plan on the responses he received from the different segments of Christendom. One reason for offering help was the oppression of the churches by the Turks. In this connection Urban very soon — if not from the very beginning — cited Jerusalem as an example of the oppressed church, possibly because of the particular appeal of this example. It proved to be so alluring, in fact, that those who supported the papal initiative began to speak of liberating Jerusalem. Then the pope also began to refer to Jerusalem as the destination of this rescue mission. This probably constituted a change in the manner in which he granted the request of Emperor Alexius. The emperor had to be satisfied with this turn of events — which must have been difficult for him — when the Western armies arrived in Byzantium.

10. A. C. Krey, *The First Crusade: The Accounts of Eye-Witnesses and Participants* (1921; repr. Gloucester, MA, 1958), 42f., quoted by Peters, 15f.
11. Cf. Riley-Smith, 38f.

The assistance given to Byzantium was therefore determined only to the least extent by what the pope had envisaged in his contact with Alexius and by what he expressed in his first appeal — and far more by the significance already attributed to Jerusalem in the imagination of the Latin West. We have already mentioned that some went to Jerusalem as a last resort when all else had failed. But the significance of Jerusalem was multifaceted, and through the centuries a notion had evolved that had become the common property of Latin Christendom.

The complexity of that idea of Jerusalem is already apparent in how it could be extended in the context of the crusades. The New Testament text: "Jerusalem will be trampled on by the Gentiles, until the times of the Gentiles are fulfilled" (Luke 21:24) was directly applicable. The Christian armies traveling to Jerusalem saw it as their task to ensure that the times of the Gentiles were fulfilled — by attaching Jerusalem to the "city of God" on earth, which Latin Christians identified with themselves.

One concrete consequence of the First Crusade was that for many Jerusalem began to have more material importance. As a result the way in which the ideal significance of Jerusalem was expressed deteriorated to a large extent into propaganda for other matters that the crusades involved. The symbol, the point of reference that Jerusalem embodied for the West, was thus subject to wear and tear.

But this propagandistic abuse never totally obliterated the symbol. At the beginning of the thirteenth century the Fourth Crusade ended with the conquest and plundering of Constantinople and the founding of a Latin empire, more or less on the model of the other crusader states. The first result of this was that now crusades could be undertaken which did not involve Jerusalem at all — such as the crusade against the Albigensians. But another result was the initiation of the "Children's Crusade" (1211). This crusade did not end well for its participants, but it was undertaken with the conviction that the kingdom of heaven, and thus Jerusalem, belongs to the children.

꙰   ꙰

THE SIGNIFICANCE attributed to Jerusalem in the West survived the crusades: Pilgrimage to Jerusalem, which was carried out before the crusades, was revived. For many pilgrims the journey to Jerusalem and the sojourn there were an experience that called for a literary account. The custom of writing such accounts continued until the end of the seventeenth century. It is striking how little the break between Rome and the Protestant churches is reflected in the pilgrimages and in the accounts of pilgrimage. Through the centuries Jerusalem retained its significance as a point of reference, and it remained irreplaceable as place of pilgrimage. But how this significance was understood by Christendom remains difficult to assess, perhaps due to the richness and diversity of data, which requires a selective use of the sources.

Jerusalem was known in the West first of all through the Scriptures. But even in the Bible the name "Jerusalem" has many meanings. Paul in his letter to the Galatians distinguishes between the Jerusalem that presently exists as a historical reality and the heavenly Jerusalem. The first "is in slavery with her children." The other Jerusalem is free and is "our mother" (4:24-26). The epistle to the Hebrews refers to this heavenly Jerusalem as "the city of the living God" (12:22).

The further elaboration of these meanings became a specific theme in medieval biblical exegesis. If the name "Zion," which is often used for the earthly Jerusalem, is included, exegetes had more than a hundred texts to deal with that directly mention Jerusalem. They could add a far greater number of texts or pericopes that in some way refer to Jerusalem, and they also had a flood of patristic commentaries to quote or elaborate on.

Walafrid Strabo (†824), for instance, discerned three historical cities on the same site that gave their names to Jerusalem. First was Salem, built by Shem, the son of Noah. Then there was the town inhabited by the Jebusites, who gave it the name Jebus. Finally, there was the city of Solomon, to which he gave the name Jebusolyma, and this was the city later destroyed by the Romans. Walafrid made these observations in a sermon "On the Destruction of Jerusalem," which went on to say: "In an allegorical sense Jerusalem is understood as the contemplation of peace, that is to say, as the holy church. For the Jerusalem above can only accommodate those who have come to experience peace through faith in Christ."[12]

This allegorical interpretation, based on the etymological presupposition that "city of Salem" is to be interpreted as "city of peace," was widespread. According to Augustine, Jerusalem, according to this interpretation, referred to "our eternal mother in heaven."[13] She has brought us into this world and is the mother of the saints, "some of whom live as

12. *De subversione Jerusalem* (*PL* CXIV, 973).
13. *De Genesi ad litteram* XXVIII.36 (*PL* XXXIV, 438).

pilgrims in exile but most of whom live in heaven. For those who dwell in heaven, she is characterized by the bliss of angels. For those here on earth, she is the hopeful expectation of the righteous."[14]

Augustine contrasts Jerusalem, the city of eternal peace, with Babylon, the city of earthly, temporal peace and of confusion. Babylon was often used as a symbol for earthly corruption. Early Christians used its name to refer to Rome (e.g., 1 Pet. 5:13). Augustine even places some of the inhabitants of Jerusalem, the city of eternal peace, in Babylon. There they remain in captivity because of their sins. He thereby attempts to explain that human sinfulness prevents people from sharing in eternal peace, even though they long to take part in it. As a result, both cities — Jerusalem and Babylon — though spiritually separated from each other, have in the passing of the centuries become physically connected because of human sinfulness.[15]

This tropological interpretation of Jerusalem as the city of peace, already current before Augustine, became a *topos* (a commonplace) in medieval exegesis. The contrast between the citizens of Jerusalem dwelling in heaven and those still in exile acquired a new dimension in monastic spirituality. Religion could be experienced in either the world or the monastery. The conversion that led people to the monastery (leaving aside other motives for the moment) was regarded as entry into the heavenly Jerusalem. This, in turn, led to the argument that monks did not have to make a pilgrimage to the earthly Jerusalem. The monastery was Jerusalem, and many monasteries in fact adopted that name. For instance, when the Gerkes-klooster in Frisia was adopted as a daughter institution by the Cistercian abbey of Klaarkamp in about 1240, it received the name Jerusalem.

This exegesis also included a more far-reaching interpretation: Jerusalem became the place of the salvation to be ushered in at the end of time. Just as there were several historical, more or less literal, interpretations of the name Jerusalem, so also allegorical interpretation had both moral and mystical dimensions, as we have seen. And the eschatological dimension played a role of no less importance. It was largely based on what the book of Revelation, especially chapter 21, says about the Jerusalem that descends from heaven. For many this notion provided the main motive for a pilgrimage to the earthly Jerusalem: There the heavenly Jerusalem was within reach.

---

14. *Enarratio in Psalmum 149* (*PL* XXXVII, 1952).
15. *Enarratio in Psalmum 136* (*PL* XXXVII, 1761).

When drawing these distinctions between the different allegorical interpretations of Jerusalem, it must be remembered that they were not kept separate: They were set side-by-side in a dynamic unity that put many allegorical possibilities into play. Medieval biblical exegesis in general was characterized by the allegorical approach, but when applied to Jerusalem this approach had a peculiar effect:

> In the name "Jerusalem" the whole history of Israel is already summarized. It contains the full content of the Old Testament and, through this, of the whole church of Christ, of the complete soul of the Christian, and of the whole city of God. . . . Thus the interpretation given to it covers in principle the full explanation of the Christian mystery. For that reason it is hardly astonishing that the Christian tradition, on the invitation of Scripture itself, so rapidly attached itself to Jerusalem.

This is the view of an expert in the biblical exegesis of the Fathers and of the medieval authors.[16]

THE SYMBOLICAL IDENTIFICATION of the heavenly Jerusalem with the church of the saints never resulted in a direct and complete reverse identification of the church on earth with the Jerusalem here below. The church on earth, viewed as the hopeful expectation of the righteous, was symbolized by Zion, the dim mirror in which the image of the church in its present form may be discerned. Jerusalem, the blessed city, was the mystical designation for the church. And there were other expressions associated with this designation.

Medieval exegesis received the image of Zion as a symbol for the church on earth from Augustine and Gregory the Great. The destruction of the earthly Jerusalem by the Romans forty years after Christ's death was also emphasized; even the number forty was interpreted symbolically. Since Christ himself had foretold the city's destruction, it was easily explained as a punishment for Jewish unbelief. This view was based on a text from the Gospel of Luke: "They will not leave within you [Jerusalem] one stone upon another; because you did not recognize the time of your visitation from God" (19:44). According to this interpretation the Jerusalem on earth

16. H. de Lubac, *Exégèse médiévale*, I/2 (Paris, 1949), 645.

89

was cursed — a view that was held quite generally in Christian antiquity. Jerome (†420) remarked that Jerusalem was often called "cursed soil,"[17] though he himself rejected that view. But, following Augustine and Gregory, several Carolingian authors had just such a negative view of the city, including Alcuin, Bishop Haimo of Halberstadt, and Walafrid Strabo.

This distinction between the chosen and the cursed Jerusalem could not prevent the holy places of the earthly city, sanctified by what is reported about them in the Bible, from evoking religious sentiments in Christians. These feelings manifested themselves in particular from the time of Emperor Constantine the Great (†337). He gave the name "Jerusalem" to the pagan settlement of Aelia Capitolina, which had been founded in 135 on the site of the destroyed city. Prompted by his mother Helena, the first Christian "archaeologist," and influenced by Bishop Macarius of Jerusalem during the Council of Nicaea (325), the emperor decided to build shrines in Jerusalem, namely, the basilicas of the Holy Sepulchre and of the Mount of Olives. But even earlier those holy places had been venerated by Christians and had drawn the attention of ecclesiastical authors. This veneration must have gone back in local tradition to the time of the apostles.[18]

The oldest, but not the most remarkable, witness to western involvement in this veneration is the travelogue of a pilgrim from Bordeaux (330). It soon became fashionable, also in the West, to visit Jerusalem and the Holy Land. At least eighteen travelogues have been preserved from the mid-fourth to late eighth centuries.

Jerome became the most eloquent champion of pilgrimage to Jerusalem. In 386 he left Rome for Jerusalem and until his death lived as a hermit in Bethlehem. But Jerome set some limits for pilgrimage. Alluding to several biblical texts, he wrote, "It is not commendable simply to have been in Jerusalem, but to have lived there in the right way. One should not praise the city that killed its prophets or draw profit from it, but rather praise the city that the streams have made glad."[19] On the other hand, he called the faithful to come to the places "where the feet of the Lord have stood." He protested vehemently against the term "cursed soil" and asked: "How can one curse this place, if one blesses the places where Peter and Paul shed their blood? . . . If we venerate the graves of the martyrs, who

17. "Maledictam terram nominant." Letter 46.8 (*PL* XXII, 488).
18. H. Vincent and F.-M. Abel, *Jérusalem: Recherches de topographie, d'archéologie et d'histoire* II/4: *Jerusalem nouvelle* (Paris, 1926), 894-902.
19. Letter 58.2 (*PL* XXII, 581).

would then dare to scorn the monument where Christ was buried?"[20] When he left Rome (where he had offended too many people) for the Holy Land, Jerome was followed by widows and virgins who belonged to the highest Roman aristocracy. They began the establishment of religious and charitable institutions, which came to determine for centuries the picture that people had of Jerusalem and its surroundings.

JERUSALEM'S FAME in the West was to a large extent due to relics originating from the Holy Land. In the West these relics became objects of veneration and thus stimulated interest in Jerusalem both locally and more generally. The *Scala santa,* the stairway in front of Pilate's house, which Christ climbed to be interrogated by the governor, was in Rome from 326 on. There were also relics of more dubious origin.

Most of the relics came to the West from Constantinople, where a large number of them had been brought from Jerusalem by Empress Athenaïs-Eudochia in the fifth century. With her help some of the chains that had bound Peter in his imprisonment came to Rome for the sanctuary of St. Peter in Chains. The relics were widely dispersed in the West. In the sixth century the city of Milan acquired the relics of the three Magi, which in 1161 were then taken as war booty to Cologne. Charlemagne received from the Byzantine emperor the garment worn by the Holy Virgin when the Holy Spirit overshadowed her. In 861 Charles the Bald sent this garment to the cathedral of Chartres. There the relic survived several church fires and is still in the cathedral. In Spain, already in the fifth century, relics were obtained of the first martyr, St. Stephen. These also eventually became part of the collection of Athenaïs-Eudochia and were also venerated in the eleventh century in Bordeaux. At that time relics were not remains of saints' bodies, but did include *brandaria,* objects that had to do with their graves or tombs.

When the crusaders plundered Constantinople at the beginning of the thirteenth century, the many relics from Jerusalem kept there were among the favorite objects of booty. The desire for relics from the Holy Land continued through the Middle Ages. After the conquest of Jerusalem in 1099 the crusaders began a long-lasting search of Palestine for relics and brought to France in the course of the twelfth century the relics of the

20. Letter 46.8f. (*PL* XXII, 488f.).

apostle Thaddeus, of the sinful woman St. Pelagia, of Sergius and Bacchus, and of Cosmas and Damian. The hair of the Holy Virgin was obtained and the sudarium of Christ was given in about 1239 to the Cistercian abbey of Cadouin by Simon of Montfort.[21] The scourging post to which Christ had been bound, which was already venerated at Jerusalem in the fourth century, was brought to Rome after the conquest of Damietta in 1219. Since the beginning of the twelfth century, Christ's seamless tunic has been venerated at Trier. Legend has it that Empress Helena gave it to the city.

The relics did not always reach the West through ordinary channels.[22] In this connection we might mention such remarkable places as the abbey of Fécamp in Normandy, where the precious blood of Christ was kept, and the Italian town of Loreto, where the house of Mary in Nazareth could be seen. The abbey of Fécamp had been founded around 660 as a convent for nuns. After the Viking invasions it was rebuilt as a Benedictine abbey, which then came to be associated with Cluny. The story was told that the monastery had been built on that particular site because a relic of the precious blood had been found there. The blood had been collected when Christ was hanging on the cross and preserved in a small container. When the Muslims occupied the Holy Land, this container was floated over the sea and washed ashore in Normandy. There it was discovered because the vegetation on that particular spot was much higher than elsewhere. An abbey was then built on the site, which became a shrine for pilgrims to venerate the blood.[23]

A legend relates how the house in which Mary was born, conceived of the Holy Spirit, educated her son, and died was transported by angels from Nazareth to Loreto. The origin of that legend can be identified with some certainty: A large basilica for Mary had been constructed over a Marian chapel in Loreto, just as in Nazareth a basilica stood on the site of Mary's home. Many pilgrims came to Loreto to venerate Mary. In the thirteenth century the legend emerged that the old chapel had been Mary's home in Nazareth. Miracles and answers to prayer, as well as papal letters of indulgence, gave credibility to that legend until the beginning of the twentieth century.

From the eleventh century on relics of James the son of Zebedee

21. J.-M. Maubourguet, *Le suaire de Cadouin* (Paris, 1928).

22. Cf. P. J. Geary, *Furta Sacra: Thefts of Relics in the Central Middle Ages* (Princeton, 1978).

23. Cf. *Lexikon des Mittelalters* (Munich/Zurich, 1989) IV, 323f.

and Mary Magdalene were venerated in Santiago de Compostella and Vézelay respectively. The relics were human remains that had been found in both places. How they had come to where they were found was not explained, but the eleventh-century author of *Miracula sanctae Mariae Magdalenae* had little difficulty with the question: For God all things are possible. Compostella continued to be a favored destination for pilgrims and enhanced its reputation by gathering a collection of relics from the Holy Land. Perhaps Vézelay ought to have done the same. It lost its pilgrims in the thirteenth century when it was claimed that there were relics of Mary Magdalene at St. Maximinus in Provence.[24]

Such veneration of the saints — long accepted by the church because of the pious intent of those practicing it — was frequently challenged in later years. But this criticism often isolated the veneration too much from other phenomena. Veneration of these saints at the shrines should be seen in the context of interest in Jerusalem, which manifested itself in the West in a variety of ways. Even though the cults of these saints began to some extent to live a life of their own in popular religion, they belonged, nonetheless, to the periphery of a new spirituality — the imitation of the human Christ — which developed, under the influence of the ever growing interest in Jerusalem, from the early eleventh century on.

❧   ❧

THIS SPIRITUALITY was related in part to two forms of devotion that were connected with relics and that originated in the Holy Land: devotion to the Holy Cross and to the Holy Sepulchre. The cross was discovered in the time of Constantine the Great and was transported to Constantinople during the reign of Emperor Heraclius (†641), probably to keep it out of Muslim hands, though Heraclius sent part of it back to Jerusalem. This made it possible to obtain splinters of the cross in both places. Robert the Pious (†1031) acquired a major piece of the cross from Constantinople, and at about the same time Fulk Nerra, the count of Anjou, carried a relic of it with him as he returned from his second pilgrimage to Jerusalem. The story of Thibald of Montmorency shows what people were willing to

24. Many of the documents on the cult of Mary Magdalene are collected in M. Faillon, *Monuments inédits sur l'Apostolat de Sainte Marie-Madeleine en Provence* (2 vols.; Paris, 1865). See also *Monumenta Vizeliacensia: Textes relatifs à l'histoire de l'abbaye de Vézelay*, ed. R. B. C. Huygens (*CCCM* 42; Turnhout, 1976). Cf. V. Saxer, *Le culte de sainte Marie Madeleine en occident des origines à la fin du moyen âge* (2 vols.; Auxerre/Paris, 1959).

sacrifice for a piece of the cross: To ensure that he would not lose his piece of the cross to bandits on his way back home from a pilgrimage, he is said to have hidden it in an incision in his thigh, which may be why he died on the journey.

Related to the veneration of relics of the cross was veneration of the nails used to fasten Christ to it. The nail kept in Rome in the church of Santa Croce in Gerusalemme is supposed to have arrived in the West at an early date. More problematic is the authenticity of the other thirty nails venerated in a number of places in the West, except perhaps the one at Trier, which is also said to have originally been part of the collection of Empress Helena.

The crown of thorns presents a similar situation. Several churches possessed thorns that supposedly were part of this crown, but they have been shown to be from two different kinds of thornbushes. The crown itself went to Constantinople, where Baldwin II, the Latin emperor, pawned it to Venetian merchants. Louis IX bought the relic from them and subsequently had La Sainte-Chapelle built in Paris for it. Individual thorns of this crown are also reported to have found their way elsewhere.

Even more important became devotion to the Holy Sepulchre. This cult did not primarily focus on the death or resurrection of Christ and had nothing to do with the heavenly Jerusalem. It was totally directed to the rock in which Christ's tomb had been hewn. It was tangibly present in the earthly Jerusalem and thus provided a stimulus for pilgrimages. Apart from the grotto in Bethlehem, this was the only place that had, in a very physical way, been touched by Christ during his life on earth. But the sepulchre was different from the grotto, since there Christ had been both dead and alive. And it had in common with the cross that it had been sanctified by his blood.

In the West the Holy Sepulchre was often copied or imitated, though in a number of ways. The oldest imitations were the crypts in Romanesque churches, which date back to the Carolingian era.[25] Since the crypt symbolized the Holy Sepulchre, it often contained relics of saints, who were thereby reunited with Christ. But in the eleventh century in the West the desire developed to possess the sepulchre in a more tangible way. Fulk Nerra carried a piece of the rock of the tomb back from one of his pilgrimages and donated it to the abbey of Beaulieu, where subsequently

25. C. Heitz, *Recherches sur les rapports entre architecture et liturgie à l'époque carolingienne* (Paris, 1963).

a "church of the sepulchre" was built.[26] St. Meinwerk, the bishop of Paderborn (†1036), sent an abbot to Jerusalem to take precise measurements of the Church of the Sepulchre in Jerusalem and then had a copy constructed in his episcopal see.

Devotion to the Holy Sepulchre was directed less toward the Lord's passion and more toward his resurrection. It expressed triumph and joy. This explains the importance of lamps that had burned in the Holy Sepulchre and were then brought from Jerusalem in the eleventh and twelfth centuries. These lamps contributed to a considerable increase in the number of churches devoted to the Holy Sepulchre. But they could only qualify as relics if they had been lighted in the sepulchre on Easter Saturday from the Easter fire.

In the thirteenth century devotion to the Holy Sepulchre acquired a mystical dimension that was, however, to have greater popularity in later times. This mystical dimension was related to the increasing devotion to the Eucharist — outside the Mass — which manifested itself in miracles of the sacred host (and in other ways). Pope Urban IV instituted the feast of Corpus Christi in 1246. Pressure to do so had been exerted from the Netherlands, but for the pope himself the main importance of the feast lay in the fact that the tabernacle, venerated in this devotion as the place where the Eucharist remained except during the Mass, symbolized the Holy Sepulchre. For there in the sepulchre the body of the Lord had rested for three days. Later in places where the sacred host had been desecrated churches were established and dedicated to the Holy Sepulchre, often largely financed by local Jews, since they were accused of the desecration.

ESCHATOLOGY ALSO PLAYED a role in the way in which Jerusalem was allegorically understood and experienced. Pilgrims were sometimes motivated by the hope of experiencing the realization of the apocalyptic vision in the book of Revelation — of actually being there when the heavenly Jerusalem descended. For there was a widespread conviction that the heavenly city would descend on the site of the earthly Jerusalem. This belief was based on two verses from the book of Ezekiel: "This is Jerusalem; I have set her in the center of the nations, with countries all around her" (5:5), ". . . the people who were gathered from the nations . . . who live

26. *Lexikon des Mittelalters* I, 1757.

at the center of the earth" (38:12). "Center" in these texts was *umbilicus,* "navel," in the Latin Vulgate. This word was taken literally and led to the conviction that Jerusalem was at the navel of the world. There the heavenly Jerusalem would descend. For the Lord, the Psalmist says, works his salvation in the midst of the earth (74:12).

This cosmological concept of salvation was of Jewish origin. Its introduction into western Christianity must be attributed to Hegesippus, a second-century Christian anti-heretical writer and convert from Judaism. A rather free Latin translation of the works of Flavius Josephus is attributed to Hegesippus.[27] Jerome picked up Hegesippus's views in his commentary on Ezekiel,[28] and, we should remember, Jerome's commentaries were diligently copied and studied until the late Middle Ages.

This concept of Jerusalem as the navel of the world is also found in several ancient descriptions of the city by pilgrims from the West. One such account was dictated around 680 to Adman, the abbot of the Scottish monastery of St. Columban, by a Gallican bishop whose ship had suffered shipwreck during its return voyage from Jerusalem. This account tells of a tall pillar in the center of Jerusalem, erected where a young man returned to life when the Holy Cross was placed on his body. The pillar was positioned so that it cast no shadow at noon on the summer solstice.[29] This story was undeniable confirmation that through Christ's passion and resurrection Jerusalem was both the center of the world and the navel of the earth and was often repeated. It is found, for instance, in a sermon on the sepulchre of the Lord by Peter the Venerable, the twelfth-century abbot of Cluny, in which he also stresses the importance of the empty tomb for the truth of the Christian faith, since it proves that Christ is not there as a dead body, but rules in the heavens as the living God.[30]

The eschatological interpretation of Jerusalem evoked in many the desire to travel to Jerusalem. But many pilgrims also wanted to stay in the city. They did not want to return to their former, often hopeless, situations. They even longed to die on the way to Jerusalem or in the city — in order to arrive in the heavenly city. Radulfus Glaber (†1050) has the pilgrim Lethbald pray to Christ along such lines:

27. *De excidio urbis Hierosolymitaniae* (*PL* XV, 2178).
28. *Commentariorum in Ezechielem* 2.5 (*PL* XXV, 52). On Jerome's influence see the last section of chapter X, pp. 315f. below.
29. *Jerusalem Pilgrims before the Crusades,* tr. J. Wilkinson (Warminster, 1977), 99.
30. *Sermo in laudem sepulchri Christi* (*PL* CLXXXIX, 979).

I pray to You, infinite Goodness, to grant me, if my soul must leave my body during this year, that I do not depart from here, but that this may happen to me while I behold the site of your ascension. Because I believe that, just as I followed your example by bringing my body to this place, so also my soul will follow you soundly, safely, and joyfully to paradise.

This prayer was answered the same day.[31] Those who had to be more patient for death could stay in Jerusalem's monasteries and in its *hospitia*, the number of which increased dramatically in the eleventh century.

Eschatological expectation concerning Jerusalem was also connected with the idea that the end of the world was near. In the biography of St. Altman we are told of a pilgrimage group in 1064 whose participants, all belonging to the nobility, were motivated by this eschatological expectation. The author suggests that they were misled by popular opinion.[32] Radulfus Glaber mentions the same expectation among the common people, referring to a great multitude, as had never been seen before, that traveled to Jerusalem in 1033, one thousand years after Christ's death. This event he took as a sign of the coming of the antichrist, who was to show himself at the end of time.[33]

Officially, the church always held itself aloof from such views. Basing itself on the interpretations given by St. Augustine, it understood the thousand-year rule of the saints as the period of the church's present existence on earth, from its founding until judgment day. History was usually divided into six periods paralleling the six days of creation. The sixth day had begun at Christ's birth and would continue until the end of time. In this scheme the antichrist was supposed to be near (see chapter II above). Or history could be divided into four world empires, in which case the antichrist could be expected when the empire that the Franks inherited from the Romans collapsed.

Expectation of the antichrist was a hotly debated subject in Christian literature of late antiquity and the early Middle Ages. An indigenous Latin tradition gradually developed. Authors such as Gregory the Great, Isidore of Seville (†636), and the Venerable Bede (†735) gave the topic considerable attention, without attempting to calculate how much time remained until the critical moment. From 800 on the coming of the

31. *Histoires*, IV.188 (Paris, 1886, pp. 106f.).
32. *Vita Altmanni* 4 (*MGH Scriptores*, XII, 230).
33. *Histoires*, IV.18 (106).

antichrist was, at least in Spain, linked to the presence of Islam. Elsewhere, other major calamities led to study of the apocalyptic writings, resulting in developments in scriptural commentary in the Carolingian era.

As long as confidence in the Roman Empire, as renewed by the Carolingians, persisted, panic was averted. But panic broke out when the Carolingian Empire disintegrated. Many signs now seemed to herald the coming of the antichrist. In his writings against the Jews, Agobard, the bishop of Lyon (†840), mentions the antichrist's coming repeatedly. He suggests that everything known about the antichrist be gathered, and he added a new element to the antichrist legend, that of the last emperor, whose reign would precede antichrist's appearance. With this appeal and this new interpretation, which he, in fact, borrowed from Byzantine sources, Agobard paved the way for the treatise that Adso of Montier-en-Dèr would write a century later.[34]

Jerusalem occupied a central place in this transformed sense of expectancy. There the last emperor would take up his residency, the antichrist would manifest himself, and the thousand-year reign that would follow his imprisonment would begin. Jerusalem would remain the center of the messianic kingdom. For the book of Revelation makes it clear that it was also in Jerusalem that the downfall of this final empire would take place:

> When the thousand years are ended, Satan will be released from his prison and will come out to deceive the nations at the four corners of the earth, Gog and Magog, in order to gather them for battle; they are as numerous as the sands of the sea. They marched up over the breadth of the earth and surrounded the camp of the saints and the beloved city. (20:7-9)

The beloved city was, of course, Jerusalem.

The eschatological view of Jerusalem was in no way limited to this chiliastic view. It was often mixed with a mystical understanding of the city, which was also expressed in many pilgrim accounts. Jerusalem not only differed from other places of pilgrimage in that many wrote accounts of their journeys to the city, but also in the nature of the devotions to which the city inspired the pilgrims. In Jerusalem pilgrims were continuously exposed to Christian salvation history. Some of the accounts record that pilgrims read Scripture passages associated with the journey, particularly the pilgrim Psalms or passages that had to do with places along the

34. *De ortu et tempore Antichristi (CCCM 45; Turnhout, 1976).*

way. And in Jerusalem they listened at those places where the biblical events had occurred to a deacon reading relevant passages, including Old Testament prophecies.

⁂   ⁂

A PILGRIMAGE MADE from devout motives was an imitation of Christ. Dangers and adversities encountered on the way were accepted as a participation in his passion. The robbers into whose hands one could fall were likened to the soldiers who stripped Christ and divided his clothing among them.

Such comparisons are particularly found in the written Lives of the saints. It was an essential part of the story if one whose holiness was described and whose canonization was sought had made a pilgrimage to Jerusalem. Such a pilgrimage was proof that the saint had exercised the virtues of asceticism and perseverance. In this respect the saints were compared to Old Testament figures: The patience of Abbot Poppo of Stavelot, which according to his hagiographer had equaled martyrdom, was likened to that of Job. The pilgrimage of another abbot was compared with Abraham's departure from Ur of the Chaldees.[35] Of course, these saints also did special works of penance on the way. St. Gerlach (†1170), the hermit from South Limburg, traveled barefoot and wore a hair shirt under his outer garments.[36]

The pilgrim to Jerusalem would visit the holy places and then end his itinerary by bathing in the Jordan River. In this he also followed Christ's example. But he also cleansed himself at home before he even set out on his journey. This was expressly commanded in the book of Revelation: "But nothing unclean will enter it [Jerusalem], nor anyone who practices abomination or falsehood, but only those who are written in the Lamb's book of life" (21:27). So before beginning the trip the pilgrim was obliged to return any goods he had wrongfully acquired.

To start out on a pilgrimage to Jerusalem required repentance and was, in a sense, on a par with entering a monastery. It was thus a decision for voluntary poverty, which was to play an increasingly important role in the piety of *imitatio Christi* from the twelfth century on. It is frequently said in saints' Lives that they gave away all their possessions before departing for Jerusalem.

35. *Acta Sanctorum* 25 Jan. (II.639), 22 May (V.179).
36. *Acta Sanctorum* 5 Jan. (I.307).

99

The pilgrim who cleansed himself prior to his departure had then to maintain his purity. For that reason women were dissuaded from going to Jerusalem. Though they had been among the earliest visitors to the Holy Land, they rarely went in the Middle Ages, except as participants in the Second Crusade, if that can be considered a pilgrimage. Bernard of Clairvaux did promote that crusade as a pilgrimage, as a year of special grace in which one could do penance for one's sins, but he later blamed its failure on the sins of the crusaders.

So women were excluded from the pilgrimages. St. Hildegonde was dressed as a man when she visited Jerusalem in 1188 — at least according to her prudent hagiographer.[37] In the thirteenth century the bishop of Acre gave boots and a horse to a woman (who had made the pilgrimage barefoot and with chains around her body) — in order that she might return forthwith.[38] St. Hrosnate (†1217) was released from her pilgrim's vow on the condition that she take an even higher vow and establish a monastery.[39]

Pilgrimages by women also became the subject of negative propaganda. We learn from the Life of St. Altman — which mentions the collective pilgrimage of 1064-65 — about an abbess, an attractive woman, who was among the participants. She took part against all advice and on the way was, in the presence of the other pilgrims, raped by the heathen, which resulted in her death.[40] Similar stories are told elsewhere, for instance, in the chronicle of Bernold, a monk of the monastery of St. Blasius in the Black Forest. Such stories were told in order to dissuade women from taking part in these journeys, since they thus risked losing their virtue or leading their male companions astray.[41]

❧   ❧

SIMILAR ARGUMENTS were made against pilgrimages by monks and hermits. At first, for a monk to make the pilgrimage was not seen as a problem, as long as the monk's abbot gave his permission. But when it had become an accepted idea that monks could reach Jerusalem, so to speak, through their life in the monastery, traveling to the earthly Jerusalem became less

---

37. *Acta Sanctorum* 20 April (II.783).
38. Reported by Thomas of Cantimpré in his supplement to the Life of Mary of Oignies; *Acta Sanctorum* 23 June (IV.673).
39. *Acta Sanctorum* 14 July (III.805).
40. *Vita Altmanni* 4 (*MGH Scriptores*, XII, 230).
41. In the year 1096 (*MGH Scriptores*, V, 464).

acceptable. We see this repeatedly in the sources. Lampert of Hersfeld tells in his monastic chronicle how on his return from pilgrimage he was afraid to see his abbot, since he had left without the abbot's blessing.[42] We are told about the difficulties of other monks in gaining permission. Some had to give up their travel plans altogether. Sometimes God intervened to stop them: Peter Damian (†1072) tells of a monk who broke his leg when kicked by a horse as he was planning to make the journey against the wishes of his abbot and thus to break his vow of *stabilitas* (permanence). Damian adds: "Breaking his leg taught him how he would have sinned by breaking his vow."[43]

In the eleventh century responding to a monastic calling was already regarded as of higher value than going to Jerusalem. Anselm of Canterbury (†1109) was definitely opposed to pilgrimages by monks. He wrote, "It is not permitted to wander without rule and [for an abbot] to send monks to Jerusalem or to go personally. This leads to shame and doom."[44] Bernard of Clairvaux also spoke against pilgrimages by monks, for instance in the crisis concerning Morimond, mentioned near the beginning of this chapter. He believed that the Holy Land was not in need of monks to pray but of soldiers to fight.[45] Likewise the general chapters of the Cistercian order did not allow pilgrimages by monks.[46] The Cistercian monk Caesarius of Heisterbach († ca. 1240), commenting on Jesus' words "take up their cross daily" (Luke 9:23), emphasized the word *daily:* "Christ does not say 'for one or two years' but 'daily.' Many become worse as a result of pilgrimage and delight even more in their former sins. For monks who live according to the rule, life is a taking up of the cross in its entirety, in the sense that obedience crucifies them in each of their members."[47]

In a letter written by Elving, a monk of Corbie, to Master Isembold, we find a more meditative argument against literal pilgrimage to Jerusalem, one that is typical of monastic spirituality. Isembold has asked for advice

42. *Annales Hersfeldenses,* ed. O. Holder-Egger (Hanover, 1894); *MGH Usu Scholarum,* 74f.).

43. *Vita Romualdi,* ed. G. Tabacco (Rome, 1957), 38.

44. Letter 195 = *Opera omnia,* ed. F. S. Schmitt (Edinburgh, 1968) IV, 85; cf. also letters 75 and 410.

45. Letter 359 (*SBO* VIII, 304f.).

46. Cf. A. H. Bredero, *Études sur la "Vita prima" de Saint Bernard* (Rome, 1960), 67, n. 3.

47. *Dialogus Miraculorum* I.6, ed. J. Strange (1851; repr. Ridgewood, NJ, 1966) I, 12.

about his plan to join the Second Crusade, which was to begin in 1147. Elving believes that monastic life can fully take the place of such a pilgrimage:

> With Abraham you have left your country by giving up your earthly possessions. You have left the place of your birth by renouncing all wickedness and by turning your back on the devil, who was your first father. . . . Your calling is the Jerusalem above, which is our mother. The Jerusalem here below may be likened to human intercourse with animals.[48]

Alluding to the conquest of that Jerusalem by the crusaders, Elving further remarks that the believer should not consider blessed a person who succeeds in approaching the dilapidated walls of Jerusalem, walls reddened by much human blood. He ends his argument by stressing the importance of hastening to the new Jerusalem, built from living stones around the cornerstone, Jesus Christ.

To what extent Jerusalem was regarded in the twelfth century as a spiritual symbol of eternal bliss is evident in poetry of the time. Among the authors of such poems is the Cluniac monk Bernard of Morlass, whose *Urbs Sion aurea* is still found in many hymnals ("Jerusalem the golden, with milk and honey blest . . .").[49] This yearning for the heavenly city also existed outside monastic circles, for example, in the hymn for the sabbath written by the controversial philosopher and theologian Peter Abelard (†1141), remarkable for its sonorous first line: *O Quanta Qualia Sunt Illa Sabbata.*[50]

> How mighty are the Sabbaths,
>   How mighty and how deep,
> That the high courts of Heaven
>   To everlasting keep.
> What peace unto the weary,
>   What pride unto the strong,

---

48. *MGH Scriptores*, V, 13f.

49. For the Latin text see F. Raby, *A History of Christian-Latin Poetry in the Middle Ages* (1927; repr. Oxford, 1953), 315-19. The hymn is found translated in, e.g., *The Hymnal 1982* of the Episcopal Church (number 624). On Bernard of Morlass (= "of Cluny"), see *Lexikon des Mittelalters* I, 2001f.

50. *Mediaeval Latin Lyrics*, tr. Helen Waddell (1933; repr. Harmondsworth, 1962), 174-77.

When God in Whom are all things
   Shall be all things to men.

Jerusalem is the city
   Of everlasting Peace,
A peace that is surpassing
   And utter blessedness;
Where finds the dreamer waking
   Truth beyond dreaming far,
Nor is the heart's possessing
   Less than the heart's desire.

. . . .

But ours, with minds uplifted
   Unto the heights of God,
With our whole heart's desiring,
   To take the homeward road,
And the long exile over,
   Captive in Babylon,
Again unto Jerusalem
   To win at last return.

It should not surprise us, then, that in monastic spirituality the heavenly Jerusalem was the symbol *par excellence* of the final destiny of the human person — which could be attained in this life in a monastery. Bernard of Clairvaux, who in a passionate manner renewed monastic spirituality, gives this allegorical explanation: The monk is already a citizen of the heavenly city since he belongs, by virtue of his contemplative life, to those who closely follow the Lord as he triumphantly enters the heavenly Jerusalem. For Bernard Jerusalem was the symbol of the eternal bliss that one enters through a spiritual and monastic conversion. He put his monastery in Clairvaux on a par with Jerusalem.[51] He states this in no uncertain terms in one of his letters: Clairvaux "is the Jerusalem united to the one in heaven by whole-hearted devotion, by conformity of life, and by a certain spiritual affinity."[52]

---

51. Cf. A. H. Bredero, "Saint Bernard and the Historians," in *Saint Bernard of Clairvaux,* ed. B. Pennington (Cistercian Studies, 28; Kalamazoo, 1977), 59f.; idem. *Bernardus van Clairvaux. Tussen cultus en historia* (Kampen, 1993), 297-305.

52. Letter 64.2 (*SBO* VII, 158; James, 91 [letter 67.2]).

This symbolism received a farfetched but creative elaboration from one of Bernard's literary disciples, his rather pompous secretary Nicholas of Clairvaux. Nicholas wrote a sermon about the twelve gates of the heavenly city mentioned in the book of Revelation: three facing east, three facing north, three facing west, and three facing south (21:13). According to Nicholas these gates symbolize the four Christian virtues. On the east one enters through Innocence, on the north through Compassion, on the south through Justice, and on the west — and here the influence of the pilgrimages on monastic spirituality is manifest — through Penance.[53]

53. *PL* CLXXXIV, 1117-22. On the sermons of this author, cf. "Les collections de sermons de Nicolas de Clairvaux," *Recueil* I, 47-82.

IV

The Bishops' Peace of God: A Turning Point in Medieval Society?[1]

❧ ❧

HISTORY TEXTBOOKS usually cite three reasons that inspired Pope Urban II to launch his first official appeal for the First Crusade at the end of the Council of Clermont-Ferrand in 1095: to assist Byzantium, to liberate the holy places from occupation by the "infidel," and to reduce the frequent fighting among members of the knighthood, who apparently could not be controlled by any civil authority. Of these reasons the first is undeniably correct. The emperor of Byzantium had asked for the pope's assistance against Islam, which increasingly threatened his empire. The pope believed that a favorable answer to this request might provide an attractive opportunity for ending the schism between the Greek church and the Latin church, which had existed since 1054.

It is more difficult to determine to what extent the pope launched his appeal with the specific aim of liberating the holy places. It is clear that Urban's call received widespread response because of the desire to take these places away from the "infidel," but whether this aspect was included in the pope's initial appeal remains an open question. As I mentioned in the previous chapter, the text of his sermon has not been preserved. Furthermore, the greater the distance in time the writing of the various accounts is from the actual events, the more likely those accounts are to

1. This study was published in Dutch first in L. de Blois and A. H. Bredero, ed., *Kerk en vrede in oudheid en middeleeuwen* (Kampen, 1980), 95-122.

emphasize liberation of the holy places as a motivation for the pope's appeal.

It is even more difficult to assess the pope's distress about the continuing disturbances of the peace in the Latin Christian world. How was this concern related to his call for a crusade? It has been supposed that the pope wanted peace, or at least that he wanted to keep the knights from fighting in the Latin West, since he needed a good army to fight against Islam. This did play a role in the later crusades, which were sometimes preceded by prohibitions of tournaments.

But circumstances at the time of the First Crusade differed greatly from those of the later crusades. This is apparent just from the fact that no king participated in the First Crusade. In 1095 the need for peace was still largely considered a problem of authority. Throughout the eleventh century it had been a matter of ecclesiastical concern, and the church had sought solutions for it. This ecclesiastical focus is, for instance, apparent in the introduction to a letter sent in 1075 by Pope Gregory VII to Duke Geisa of Hungary, "If it is part of our task to defend the rights of all, to bring peace and to establish unity, then reason and common interest demand even more that we sow seeds of love among the great of the earth, since their love or hate for each other infects many."[2]

Urban II likewise showed his concern for peace, as can be seen from solutions that he pursued, even after 1095. But one of the decisions of the Council of Clermont-Ferrand already bears witness to this concern. The first canon in a list of council decisions stipulated that monks, priests, and women should enjoy peace, or, in other words, be treated peacefully. This was the "Peace of God." This obligation was not applied with respect to other victims of violence, at least not from sunrise on Monday until sundown on Wednesday — though the "*Truce* of God" did seek to prohibit fighting altogether every Thursday through Sunday. But those who treated others unjustly during the rest of the week were guilty of a breach of the peace and were to be tried and punished. William of Malmesbury, a twelfth-century historian, says that according to the stipulations of the council, the Truce of God did not cover just Thursday through Sunday but also all the days from the beginning of Advent through the eighth day of Epiphany (January 13) and from Septuagesima Sunday (three weeks before the beginning of Lent) through the eighth day of Pentecost.[3] And

2. E. Caspar, *Das Register Gregors VII* I (1920; repr. Berlin, 1967), 230 (II, 70).
3. Mansi XX, 814f. Cf. R. Somerville, *The Councils of Urban II* I (Amsterdam, 1972).

in fact the Council only repeated what many councils in the eleventh century had already decreed.

But these observations about the decisions of Clermont-Ferrand do not immediately clarify what kind of connection existed between the Peace and Truce of God, on the one hand, and the pope's call to a holy war, on the other hand. There may be some indirect evidence in a decision made for the first time in 1054 at a council in Narbonne: There it was decreed that no Christian was allowed to kill a fellow Christian, since whoever kills a Christian sheds Christ's blood.[4] No decision was being made to prohibit fighting in general, nor was such a decision made during earlier councils or later at the Council of Clermont-Ferrand. Fighting and engaging in war were only subjected to certain restrictions. When these restrictions went so far as to say that violence could not be used against other Christians, knights had to find other objects for their aggression, at least if they wanted to take these precepts seriously. So we may expect that the ecclesiastical authorities who devised these limitations on warfare must have thought that waging war against the "infidel" contributed to peace in the Latin Christian world.

This solution to violence, redirection of it toward outsiders, was thought of already in the middle of the eleventh century. From the beginning, combat against invading armies of Vikings, Magyars, and Muslims was more or less considered holy war, to which the church had repeatedly called the faithful. This was also the case with the struggle against Islam in Spain. In 1063 Pope Alexander II even announced an indulgence to provide participants in this conflict with the prospect of remission of the consequences of sin.[5] The indulgence was announced as an army was being gathered in the south of France to go to Spain. The connection between a search for peace in the Latin Christian world and a call to a holy war against non-Christians was also present at the Council of Clermont-Ferrand: Its second decision determined that the journey provided full absolution for those who were willing to go to Jerusalem, provided they went not for honor or money, but dedicated to the deliverance of God's church.

❧   ❧

THESE INTRODUCTORY REMARKS about the efforts of the medieval church to obtain and maintain peace show that a knowledge of the social circumstances

---

4. Canon 1 = Mansi XIX, 827.
5. N. Paulus, *Geschichte des Ablasses im Mittelalter* (Paderborn, 1922) I, 195f.

that provide the context of historical events is a prerequisite for correct understanding of that history. But to get that knowledge is far from simple. Little is known of the concrete events by which the church's direct involvement with the peace problem first manifested itself. And the church's precise intentions also remain vague. Did the church want primarily to safeguard its own interests, to protect the clergy and secure its own property? Did it defend the weak only in an attempt to further its own interests, or did it strive for social change in order to bring peace to society? Above all, what criteria do we have for manifestations of a Peace of God movement? It is doubtful whether the synod convened in about 990 by the archbishop of Narbonne was a manifestation of this movement, since the record tells us only that the synod intended measures against members of the nobility *(viri nobiles)* who had attacked religious people and church property. But the Synod of Charroux, convened in 989, can be regarded as a manifestation of the Peace of God movement. There the common people — peasants and other poor people — were also given protection, and cattle stealing was condemned.

It is difficult to distinguish the line of development of the Peace of God movement. The Council of Charroux is usually regarded as its beginning, but its decision was based on the authority of earlier synods. The chain of constitutions on which that council drew does not make things any clearer, since the earlier synods showed a similar ambiguity in measures that were intended to keep in check laypeople *(seculares)* who committed acts of violence. We are told that the Council of Vienne in 892 limited its concern to protecting the clergy, but the Council of Fines in 881 also addressed the problem of violence against the poor. Perhaps the greatest amount of information is provided by a decision, more or less in the form of a prayer, reached during an episcopal synod in Metz in 888:

> The bishops who have been mentioned have urgently been requested to pray for their lord, King Arnulf, and to keep a three-day fast in the near future. We will pray to God with litanies and intense self-mortification that he will cause us to turn to him with heart and soul, that he will open our hearts for his law and stipulations, and that he will give us peace. May it also please our Redeemer to liberate the oppressed and to restore to safety those who are in danger. May we by so doing receive forgiveness here and now and live in the life hereafter in a peace that will continue without end.[6]

6. Canon 13 = Mansi XVIII, 82.

Where was the boundary between what led up to the Peace of God movement and what may be regarded as a clear manifestation of the movement? During the ninth century and most of the tenth century the bishops left immediate responsibility for peace and safety to secular rulers. Usually the Peace of God is identified only with instances when the clergy took direct action going beyond pious words and standing up for more than just their own safety and that of church property.

The difficulty of drawing an exact boundary around the Peace of God also concerns the distinction between Peace of God *(pax Dei)* and the Truce of God *(treuga Dei)*. Often both existed side by side, and by the end of the eleventh century the conditions of a Truce of God were regarded as a Peace of God. But from the beginning a Peace of God was an ideal that was envisaged but could not be translated into social reality: It was considered desirable to protect the defenseless against violence, but war was still permitted. A Truce of God was an attempt to approach this ideal, since it consisted of measures intended to lessen and interrupt the stream of acts of violence by imposing a truce on certain days. The Peace of God manifested itself as a mass movement with large gatherings and was characterized by intense religious feeling. This was, in accordance with the spirit of the times, expressed in the collection and veneration of relics. It was not until the Council of Toulouges-Rousillon in 1027 that the Truce of God and the Peace of God are claimed to have converged.

But the decision reached during that council did still have two aspects. It prohibited attacks on enemies from the ninth hour on Saturday until the first hour on Monday out of respect for Sunday. And it prohibited attacks on unarmed priests and monks, on anyone on his way to church or returning from church, or on anyone in female company — and on church buildings and other buildings less than 45 meters from churches. Nonetheless, the convergence of the Truce of God and the Peace of God is apparent in the last sentence of the document: "This treaty or truce *(pactum sive treugam)* has been agreed on . . . because the law of God and the whole Christian religion has been virtually destroyed, and, as has been written, iniquity abounds and love for neighbor has vanished."[7]

This first instance of a convergence of a Peace of God with a Truce of God that can be retrieved from the sources does not prove that the Truce of God originated only as a sequel to the Peace of God. In a sense, in fact, the

---

7. Mansi XIX, 483. This sentence refers to certain bishops, archpriests, deacons, and canons as well as a number of saints and a crowd of the faithful, both men and women.

Truce is much older. It had long been a custom to observe holy days and holy seasons, though the church had never absolutely prohibited fighting during those periods. When around 860 the Bulgarians put a question about this problem to Pope Nicholas I, his answer was: "During a war there should be no fighting on holy days and during periods of fasting, unless it is necessary to fight for the defense of the country or for other reasons. It would be tempting God to trust the Lord and remain idle."[8] But the desire for strict Sunday observance from the ninth hour on Saturday to the first hour on Monday dates from Christian antiquity, in the West as in the East. Exhortations to that effect and curses on those who disregarded these exhortations were published in letters that claimed to have fallen from heaven, having been written by Christ himself. The church invariably rejected the authenticity of these letters, but in the context of the Peace of God movement such propaganda for strict observance of holy seasons was widely used since it was seen as a way to limit fighting.

The origin of the relationship between the Truce of God and the Peace of God remains a mystery. Already before the eleventh century there was a Truce of God in the county of Barcelona, but it is uncertain whether it was declared in connection with a Peace of God movement. But it is highly probable that the convergence of the two changed the character of the Truce of God: Soon it went beyond Sunday observance. We have already noticed how the duration of the Truce of God was increased. From the twentieth day prior to the beginning of a Peace period it was also prohibited to build a fortress or a stronghold that could be used to deny access to a bridge. For such constructions indicated that a breach of the peace might be imminent. With regard to the relationship between the Peace of God and the Truce of God, it may also be suggested that the Peace of God movement was partly inspired by the more or less dormant popular belief in the necessity of a change in behavior on holy days if divine punishment was to be avoided. This popular belief provided the Peace of God movement with the possibility of giving more concrete form to its attempts to establish peace in a world in which fighting remained a widely accepted occupation.

❧   ❧

THERE ARE STILL OTHER QUESTIONS we need to ask about the Peace of God movement. Why did the bishops play such an important role? Why

8. Letter 96.24 (*PL* CXIX, 993).

did the movement occur in the eleventh century and not a century earlier or later? Other questions concerning the contemporary context of the movement will be asked later, but now we will concern ourselves with a question of a different kind: What were the movement's aim and motivating social ideology? This question goes well beyond the explicit intentions of the different councils and the truces they declared. Their immediate intentions are sufficiently clear. In fact, the Peace of God movement was quite pragmatic in its strategies, both in regard to the persons and times that defined situations in which the peace was to be observed and in regard to sanctions against violators of the peace.

This pragmatic approach resulted in a diversity of conditions for the various truces. Ivo of Chartres remarked in about 1100 that in case of a breach of the peace the verdict had to be in accord with the agreements and stipulations settled on in the particular diocese, according to written documents or the memory of trustworthy people. For a Truce of God was not the result of generally accepted laws but was based on the authority of the bishop and the churches, since it was set in motion for the common good in an assembly of the whole town or region.[9]

The question of the social significance of the Peace of God movement became particularly relevant at the end of the nineteenth century and the beginning of the twentieth when an international peace movement attempted to counter the threat of war, which, due to a strongly developed system of military alliances, involved nearly all the nations of Europe. The urgency of the moment thus increased scholarly interest in the eleventh-century Peace of God movement. But this study suffered from its own preoccupations and was strongly colored by the aims of the *modern* peace movement. A Peace of God or a Truce of God, the *pactum pacis,* was interpreted as a social treaty intended to prevent crimes of war and to limit the calamities of war, as if in the eleventh century such humanitarian goals were already thought of and promoted. It was too easily forgotten that advocates of peace in the Middle Ages had no qualms about taking up arms against violators of the peace or about waging war against the "infidel."

The only resistance to the Peace of God movement on the part of anyone who wanted peace came in 1032 from Gerard, bishop of Cambrai. He believed that breaches of the peace should be dealt with not by bishops but by secular rulers. This way of thinking reflected attitudes in the German

---

9. Letter 90 (*PL* CLXII, 111). Cf. R. Sprandel, *Ivo von Chartres und seine Stellung in der Kirchengeschichte* (Stuttgart, 1962), 150.

Empire, of which Cambrai was a part. Bishop Gerard was, moreover, afraid of changes in the relationships among the three orders of society: those who fight, those who pray, and those who farm. He believed that the divinely ordained order of society was more important than the limited ideal of peace held by his French colleagues.[10] Such a position was hardly shocking at the time. Indeed, combat was regarded as just as sacred as peace, as long it was waged in the right manner, against the right foe, and in the right place.

In this connection we recall that at the beginning of the twelfth century Guibert of Nogent described the crusades as acts of God performed by men: His revision of an anonymous account of the First Crusade was entitled *Gesta Dei per Francos* — "God's Acts through the Frankish People." Fighting for the Peace of God, when necessary, was, in fact, regarded in the same light.

That is clear from references to the movement in contemporary chronicles, in saints' Lives, in miracle stories, and in sermons. We will include the texts of three such stories to elucidate further our understanding of the Peace of God. They illustrate how this movement was experienced, lead us back to the context in which it occurred, and raise again the question of its importance in historical perspective. To what extent did this temporary movement have a continuing influence? Can it be viewed as marking an important turning point in social change? Did society approach matters of peace and security differently after the Peace of God movement?

☙ ☙

A TEXT CONCERNING the Peace of God that does not yet mention a Truce of God is found in the fourth volume of the *Historiae* of Radulfus Glaber, a Cluniac monk who wrote around 1040. He describes the beginning of the movement as follows:

> In the year 1000 after the Lord's passion, when the famine, to which we have referred, had ended, and the heavy rains became less frequent, heaven once again put on a joyful face. The clouds disappeared and favorable winds began to blow. Once again creation showed its respect for God's goodness and compassion and thus visibly manifested the Creator's generosity. The whole earth blossomed again and gave an abundance of fruit, which made all scarcity disappear.

10. G. Duby, *Les trois ordres ou l'imaginaire du féodalisme* (Paris, 1978), 35-61.

At that moment bishops, abbots, and others who had consecrated themselves to the religious life, began to gather the people together and to hold councils. They brought to these assemblies the bodies of saints and numerous reliquaries. This was first done in Aquitaine, which served as an example for all dioceses — first in the provinces of Arles and Lyon, then in the kingdom of Burgundy, and even in the remote regions of Frankish realm — of how councils could be convened in designated places by the prelates and princes of the realm to reestablish the peace and to confirm the faith. When the people heard of this, they all went willingly to these gatherings: the great, the middling, and the poor *(maximi, mediocres ac minimi),* all prepared to obey whatever the shepherds of the church might prescribe. A voice from heaven to humankind could not have improved this result. For all were still anxious because of the recent calamities and afraid that they would not be able to harvest the fertile abundance that had manifested itself.[11]

The following text is from the section of the *Miracula* of St. Benedict written by the monk Andrew of Fleury around 1043.

In the year 1038 after the Lord's incarnation, on August 8, the sun was darkened at noon and for two hours hid its rays. The next day this phenomenon repeated itself during the whole day, while the sun flared up red as blood. Precisely at that time Aimo, the bishop of Bourges, wanted to institute a peace in his diocese to be sworn under oath. With the approval of the bishops of his ecclesiastical province and supported by the counsel of his suffragan bishops, he placed all persons of fifteen years and older under a law that obliged them to resist all who would defile this covenant. Neither was anyone to enter into any agreement that would interfere with episcopal property. If necessary, they were to combat these disturbers of the peace with arms. Even the ministers of the sacraments were not exempt from this duty: When necessary, they, too, were to march with the others against desecrators of the sworn peace, carrying the banners of the Lord's sanctuary with them. They were to tear down fortresses and in so doing, with divine help, frighten all the rebels so that they would flee and leave the gates open when they heard that the faithful were approaching, because of the terror God would instill in them. You should have seen how these people, bound together by their oath like a new people of Israel, raged

11. *Histoires* IV/5 (Paris, 1886), 14; M. Prou, ed., *Raoul Glaber: Les cinqs livres de ses Histoires* (Paris, 1886), 103f.

against the multitude of those who had ignored God and with what tenacity they continued to repel them in order to force them to turn from their false covenant to justice.

In this connection it seems worthwhile to mention the other conditions of this covenant, which was confirmed under oath by the archbishop together with the other bishops: "I, Aimo, archbishop of Bourges by the grace of God, promise in the presence of God and his saints, and gladly confirm, that I will do the following with zeal and without deception or hypocrisy: Without no hesitation I will combat all those who have taken church property, who incite others to plunder, who oppress monks, nuns, and members of the clergy, and who endanger the mother church, until they come to their senses. I will not be misled by enticing gifts, nor will I be moved by sympathy for family or friends, nor by any consideration that would place me outside the realm of justice. But I promise to oppose those who disobey such stipulations and to remain firm in every respect, until the persuasiveness of those who neglect their duties will be overcome." After the archbishop had sworn these words on the relics of St. Stephen, the first Christian martyr, he admonished the others to do likewise. They obeyed with one accord, all (as has been mentioned) who were fifteen years or older. They declared to which diocese or parish they belonged and made their promise with a similar confirmation.[12]

The third text is from the *Miracula* of Adalhard, who was abbot of the monastery of Corbie in the diocese of Amiens from 775 to 826. After his death he was venerated as a saint, and his relics came to be of great importance in the Peace of God movement in Amiens. The *Miracula* and *Life* of Adalhard were supposedly written by Gerard, the abbot of Saint-Saveur near Bordeaux, who was a monk at Corbie between 1080 and 1095. The text indicates that Adalhard was deeply involved in the Peace of God movement. There is, in fact, much similarity between the account of his life and the account that was later written of Gerard's life.

The quotation below from the *Life* of Adalhard tells of an experience of Gerard himself when he was a youth, probably before he entered Corbie. He dates it in about 1040, but it actually occurred some ten years earlier. But here, as before, we are not concerned with what exactly happened as much as with the testimony to those events, since it indicates how such events were experienced and interpreted.

12. *Miracula* 1f.; E. de Certain, ed., *Les miracles de Saint Benoît* (Paris, 1858), 191-93.

In those days Corbie experienced much discomfort, but the Frankish Empire was plagued by yet greater calamity. The most important church of Corbie, St. Peter's, had been set on fire out of diabolical jealousy, while almost all of Gaul was ravaged by famine. The Frankish Kingdom was ruled by King Robert [the Pious], while Abbot Richard ruled Corbie in the name of Christ. Both had prosperous reigns, apart from the fact that one was confronted with this fire and the other had to deal with a bitter seven-year famine. The famine killed so many people that it seemed as if the Fates were cutting the threads of life not with scissors but with a sword. This deadly disaster, which also struck severely elsewhere, ravaged above all the region of Amiens.

Constrained by this emergency, the people there decided to avail themselves as quickly as possibly of refuge by seeking the favor of God, whom they had repeatedly insulted by their evil deeds. They realized that they had called forth heaven's revenge by their negligence in serving peace, which the Lord loves and commands us to love. For the people of Gaul possess, more than those of other nations, an innate tendency to indulge in unrestrained warfare. But why should that be so? There is no need to want to die in war, because people are already dying in great numbers by the swords of hunger and pestilence. The world cannot bear the wrath of the Most High Judge. The people will have to follow the counsel once given to the inhabitants of Nineveh. Where peace and justice live together, people rejoice over the return of the rule of Saturn. For the desperate there remains but one thing to advise: Let them stave off the wrath of the Most High Judge by enlisting the help of the saints. That is why relics are in demand and why people gather around relics brought from surrounding places. And there an inviolable covenant of peace is confirmed.

For that reason the people from Amiens and Corbie gathered with their patron saints and concluded a total peace, that is to say, a peace for all the days of the week. They all promised God that they would return to Amiens each year during the feast of St. Firminus to reconfirm this covenant. They committed themselves to this by a promise and again confirmed it with an oath. This renewed promise stated that they would not, if conflict should arise from some disagreement, demand their right by means of looting or arson until a peace trial could take place in the presence of the bishop and the count on the appointed day.[13]

13. *Liber primus miraculorum s. Adalhardi* IV, 7f. (*PL* CXLVII, 1066f.)

❧   ❧

BEFORE SKETCHING the political, social, and economic circumstances — the social context — of the Peace of God movement, we must examine the mentality that lay behind the movement according to the texts quoted above. These texts clearly indicate that the struggle for peace was fundamentally linked to a transmundane experience of reality. Much of what happened in the world remained unintelligible and was experienced with a sense of helplessness. Such events were attributed to otherworldly, sacral powers. These powers had to be approached and reconciled if one wanted to escape their threats and enjoy the benefits that they controlled.

In this sacral experience of earthly events that could not be accounted for merely on the basis of the visible world, the absence of peace was like other calamities, such as famine and epidemics, from which society suffered. Such calamities left people helpless. Sanctions could be imposed on violators of the peace, but they were of little effect, since they were generally based on merely moral grounds. This probably further strengthened the sense that the absence of peace was a punishment for human shortcomings with regard to otherworldly powers, particularly God. Conversely, a return of peace was a sign of God's willingness to offer people reconciliation in spite of their misdeeds, and it was experienced, therefore, in a manner analogous to a disappearance of famine or a return of good harvests. People knew that there was often a direct relationship between war and famine, since a harvest could easily be stolen or destroyed by war. But the most essential relationship between the two was that both were expressions of God's wrath on wrongful behavior.

Human shortcomings had, above all, an eschatological meaning: They indicated the nearness of the antichrist and of the destruction of the world, which would be brought on by human sin. The scarcity that was to precede the antichrist's coming (Job 41:13) was not of food but of miracles and of love for neighbors. This view of the absence of peace is found in a passage about the Peace and Truce of God declared at Toulouges-Rousillon in 1027 "because the law of God and the whole Christian religion has been virtually destroyed, and, as has been written, iniquity abounds and love for neighbor has vanished."[14] This relationship between calamity and sin is mentioned again and again in connection with the antichrist's

14. Cf. Mansi XIX, 483. On this eschatological expectation, see chapter II above.

appearance, it was what motivated the convening of that council and its declaration of a Truce of God, and it is often encountered in texts dealing with wars and other disasters (see chapter II above).

It is often said that since the sources that inform us of this mentality were all written by clergy, they show a significant bias. But this can be misleading, since it suggests that laypeople thought otherwise and were more solidly grounded in earthly reality. Such a view seems plausible, since literacy was monopolized by the clergy, but it represents, finally, a gross misunderstanding. Laypeople experienced everyday reality in the same sacral way as the clergy, though with the difference that for them the magical aspect of the sacral experience of reality must have been even more pronounced, since they were less influenced by what was written. Their interpretations did not have to find a direct basis in Scripture, as was the case with the clergy. It has also been suggested that sources from the later Middle Ages show a greater degree of superstition than sources from the earlier centuries, including the period dealt with in this chapter. One possible explanation could be that in the later centuries literacy was no longer the exclusive monopoly of the clergy.

࿔   ࿔

THE SOCIETY in which the Peace of God movement grew up saw, in the course of a few centuries, enormous changes, but it continued to have an elite whose behavior was largely determined by the business of war. This elite included both a military caste and a landowning nobility, though these two groups largely coincided, particularly in West Frankia. Therefore our point of departure in understanding the relationship between this elite and the other two estates, the clergy and farmers, is the convergence of military activity and land ownership.

The military elite's relationship with the clergy was largely determined by the fact that most of the clergy came from this elite. In actual fact, the clergy served the military elite, and church property was to a considerable extent exploited by this elite. The system of proprietary monasteries existed from the days of Charles Martel and allowed the military elite to take most of the income for itself. To safeguard this income the members of the elite favored celibacy for priests and for members of religious orders. Naturally they had a strong voice in the appointment of church officials, including abbots and bishops.

In the tenth century the first attempts were made to reverse this system of proprietary churches. When it was founded, the monastery of Cluny was placed under the authority of St. Peter, and thus it fell under the immediate authority of the pope. But the reform movement later initiated by Cluny, which would restrict lay authority over the monasteries, did not become effective until well into the eleventh century, notably during the abbacy of Hugh of Semur (1049-1109). And even then the influence of the military elite on the clergy continued. The nobles protected the churches and monasteries and thus retained power over them, especially as the need for protection increased.

But this was not all. For centuries the monasteries had been cult centers for the nobility. From the time of their conversion to Christianity, the nobles had in the monasteries a way to continue worshiping their ancestors, who were buried at the monasteries, while the monastic communities secured the nobles' eternal salvation through prayer and penance, assuring them remission of the punishment due to sins for which they themselves had not done penance during their lives. Many monasteries were founded specifically for this task and continued to perform it. And for that reason many noblemen, especially as they approached death, continued to bestow favors on churches and monasteries. A document from Cluny from around 1000 says: "As water extinguishes a fire, so donations to the church extinguish sin."[15]

We can see how greatly this benefited the churches from an often quoted statement of Radulfus Glaber:

At the beginning of the year 1003, church buildings were being restored over almost the whole world, but especially in Italy and Gaul. Though most of these buildings were in reasonable state and showed few defects, each "clan" of worshippers of Christ, out of jealousy toward other communities, decided to build a church that would be even more worthy. The world seemed to rediscover its freedom and to shed its age, and therefore dressed itself everywhere in a white garment of new churches. In brief, in that time the faithful everywhere exchanged their church buildings for better ones — in episcopal sees, in monasteries dedicated to various saints, and among the smaller oratories in the villages.[16]

15. A. Bruel and A. Bernard, *Recueil des Chartes de Cluny* III (Paris, 1884), 595, no. 2522.

16. *Histoires* III.13.115-17.

Most likely this program of church rebuilding was not funded only by those in spiritual need. Furthermore, we can doubt whether it happened with the speed that Radulfus Glaber describes.

Indeed, donations by members of the military nobility could cause problems. Sons of donors were asked for their approval in the hope that they would not, at some later date, try to reclaim such donations. When the possessions of a church or monastery had been confirmed by means of a papal privilege, those who wanted to reclaim their gifts could be threatened with excommunication. But the relationship between the military nobility and the clergy was not limited to balancing spiritual need with material assistance. Children who did not opt for the military profession could find a place among the monks in the monasteries. Moreover, the higher clergy was recruited from among noblemen's sons.

The relationship between the peasants and the military elite was quite different. For the peasants it was rather oppressive, as most of them were not free. Usually they had for generations lived on small parcels of land over which they had but little control. They had no legal standing, and public laws did not apply to them. They were, instead, subject to the determinations of their lords.

Marriages among serfs of the same community were subject to severe restrictions: The church stipulated that a blood relationship to the sixth degree was an impediment to marriage, though this rule was largely disregarded among the Germanic tribes and clans. But the nobles tended to regard the marriage of a serf with someone of a different community with disfavor, since this could bring about a situation where the descendant of a serf might be able to escape bondage, which would result in a devaluation of the land and a decline in income. Therefore, the noble landowners arranged the marriages of their serfs — and many serfs remained unmarried. A similar problem existed with regard to inheritance: If children born outside the serfdom of a particular community inherited a plot of land from one of the community's serfs, such an event could result in loss of the land to the noble.

The peasants, both free and serfs, were poor. They depended on the crops of their small plots and also had to work on the demesnes, from which the nobles derived their income. The nobles had to be free for military service. Usually the peasants were not able to receive any cash income from their plots, even though the land began to yield more as a result of new agricultural techniques, including use of the horse collar, the heavy plow, the three-field system of crop rotation, and manure. But at first the market trade was of little importance and demesnes still ran according to the laws of a closed economy. Better harvests did, however, lead to increased population growth, since infant mortality could be reduced. Here perhaps we also see a concrete result of the christianization of the people, more than in the other developments we have mentioned: One can assume that Christianization led to the gradual disappearance of abandonment of unwanted children. But it must be remembered that progress in actualizing moral precepts could be made only if certain material conditions were met. Therefore, that infants were abandoned less often cannot be considered in isolation from the totality of social changes occurring at the time.

❧   ❧

BUT THE STRUCTURAL relationships between the military elite and the other two orders of society were not the basis for the rise of the Peace of God movement. Undoubtedly this elite caused discontent among the other two orders by exploiting them in the service of their own military activities. But this discontent gave the bishops neither an opening nor a rationale for intervening directly to preserve or restore peace and justice. Such intervention, which developed into the peace movement, must rather be explained on the basis of social changes experienced by the military elite. These changes, often referred to as the feudalization of society, occurred when the authority of the king proved inadequate to guarantee the external defense of the realm and the maintenance of internal peace and justice.

As the West Frankish kingdom disintegrated toward the end of the Carolingian era, the task of defense fell to the regional lords. These regional rulers also claimed the royal privileges of having an army, meting out punishment, securing the peace in the land, and administering justice to the people. But even their authority came to be severely fragmented. This process of disintegration first occurred in western Frankia in the late tenth and early eleventh centuries. The German Empire would experience a similar disintegration later. Disintegration led to complete anarchy, and the blood feud could once again be revived and accepted as legal.

During the Carolingian era the Germanic tribal laws had remained in force. Their most important aim was to solve conflicts peacefully and to punish crimes instead of letting them be answered by feuds. Enforcing these laws was one of the main purposes of government. But as the administrative system was fragmented, feuding as a means of justice was revived. This led to totally irregular acts of violence by and among members of the military elite. The booty from these exploits enabled these men to have private armies. In the escalation of unrestrained violence the defenseless, those who possessed no arms, were the first victims: the clergy, peasants, women, traders (some of them Jews), and pilgrims. Their lives and possessions were no longer safe.

The bishops reacted with the Peace of God movement against this situation and, naturally, received much support. The movement did not seek a general peace. It recognized the feud as a way of settling legal conflicts, and, therefore, also private warfare. But it sought a drastic decrease in the acts of violence that accompanied these wars by offering protection to persons and things that had nothing to do with the fighting and by restricting the times during which war could be waged.

Georges Duby points to an ideology that developed from the beginning within the Peace of God movement. The church, he says, justified its intervention in politics by means of this ideology. Duby concludes:

> The development of the "Peace of God" ideology went hand in hand with the last phases of feudalization. It was expressed for the first time shortly before the year 1000 in southern Gaul, the region where the collapse of royal authority had come about earliest. By slow degrees this ideology acquired a measure of consistency, though it spread through the whole of Latin Christendom in various guises. Its principles were quite straightforward: God had deputed to anointed kings the task of maintaining peace and justice; kings were no longer capable of so doing; God therefore took back His power of command into His own hands and vested it in those of His servants, the bishops, with the support of local princes.[17]

But it seems questionable whether this kind of thinking was dominant already at the beginning of the movement. I believe it is doubtful that there even existed an ideology, a political justification of these initiatives, in the first phase of the movement. It was clearly a matter of pragmatic action without concern for theoretical conception.

This is particularly evident in Aquitaine, where the movement began, notably in the region where the royal authority disappeared completely and where authority soon also escaped the territorial princes. Duke William V of Aquitaine, surnamed Fier-à-Bras, was present at the

---

17. *The Early Growth of the European Economy* (London and Ithaca, 1974), 162f.

first peace synod. It is not completely certain that he convened the Council of Charroux in 989, but we do know with certainty that he did issue the call for the councils held between 1000 and 1014 in Limoges and Poitiers. These synods did not yet link the Truce of God to the Peace of God, since enforcement of the peace could be entrusted to the authority of the duke. But when he died and was succeeded by his sons, who could no longer guarantee peace to the duchy, later synods issued rules regarding a Truce. So in Aquitaine the Peace of God movement began as a support for the authority of the duke, but when that authority was dissipated, the bishops bolstered the Peace of God by declaring a Truce of God.

The collecting of saints' relics also suited the essentially pragmatic character of the movement. In the thinking of the time, which was characterized by a sacral, otherworldly experience of reality, relics radiated the power of the saints. Venerating relics and, if possible, touching them in order to receive that power gave protection against all threats to life and brought deliverance from fear. Veneration of relics was widespread, but usually required journeying to widely scattered shrines to benefit from the protective power of the saints in all its diversity. Gathering relics was therefore an effective way to assemble large crowds. The peace councils needed massive support, and this suggested the use of collections of relics. But this method of bringing together crowds represented no cynical opportunism, since the organizers shared the common understanding of relics. Even the monks of Cluny aided the temporary transfer of relics.[18]

At the most it might be suggested that these gatherings were sometimes utilized to promote the cults of particular saints. The peace council sermons of Adhemar of Chabannes give reason to believe that he emphasized St. Martial, who was buried in Limoges and venerated there, in an effort to promote his cult.[19] The account of the Peace of God in the *Miracula* of Adalhard was likewise propaganda for veneration of Martial. According to the author, one could not find reconciliation with God except by calling on this saint.

---

18. The *Liber Tramitis,* in which are described the monastic customs of Cluny from the first half of the eleventh century, contains a chapter that indicates circumstantially how relics were conveyed in procession to the place where they had to be deposited. *Liber Tramitis aevi Odilonis abbatis* XXVII.168 (*CCM* X [1980], 240-42).

19. *Sermones tres in concilio Lemovicensi (PL* CXLI, 115-24). Cf. *Translatio et miracula S. Viviani* III (Analecta Bollandiana 8; 1889), 263.

ਠੇ   ਠੇ

THE IDEOLOGY that, according to Duby, developed in the Peace of God movement from the beginning actually began to play a role only when the movement entered another phase and spread to other parts of France. The authority of the regional rulers did not erode to the same extent everywhere as it did in Aquitaine, which in the twelfth century was still considered a land without a king, duke, or prince. In Normandy and Flanders the territorial rulers often did exercise their authority and accepted a shared responsibility with the bishops for the enforcement of the Truce of God. They even profited from the peace movement, using it to strengthen their power over their vassals. In these regions episcopal initiatives to hold assemblies for a Peace of God depended on the cooperation of these rulers. The rulers did not allow the bishops to do as they pleased, and, naturally, questions were raised about the right of the bishops to take such initiatives. The bishops were forced to defend this right, and their arguments may have developed into the ideology described by Duby. In any case, one thing is clear: The ideology originated where the bishops faced resistance to their involvement with the peace movement. This was never an issue in Aquitaine with its power vacuum after the death of Duke William V.

Furthermore, another ideology gained currency in the Peace of God movement. The earliest signs of its presence are seen in the Council of Narbonne in 1054, that is, when the Gregorian reform had already begun. At that council it was decreed that Christians were not allowed to kill fellow Christians. The thought behind this precept originated in Carolingian times, when, in an effort to foster the unity of the empire, the bond of an overarching unity of all tribes in Christendom was promoted. This aim can be identified in the conditions of surrender that Charlemagne forced on the Saxons in 775-90: They were to put aside their pagan tribal customs and adopt those of the christianized Germanic tribes. Any infringement would be punishable by death, even if someone out of contempt for the Christians ate meat during Lent.[20]

What Charlemagne envisaged was realized in the course of a few

20. *Capitulatio de partibus Saxoniae* 5 (*MGH Capitularia* I, 68). For this problem, cf. J. van Laarhoven, "*Christianitas* et réforme grégorienne," *Studi Gregoriani* 6 (1959-61), 1-98.

centuries. This new collectivity, Christendom, emerges already in an agreement of 862 between Louis the German, Charles the Bald, and the son of Lothar. The first two accused the last not only of having failed with respect to their blood relationship and their God-given consecrated authority, but also with regard to the community of Christians.[21] Later Pope John VIII (872-82) appealed to this unbreakable unity as a factor in the defense of Western Europe against invasions by non-Christian peoples. This idea was taken up by the Ottonian emperors in their struggles against the Magyars. In Western Frankia the need for resistance against the Normans initially provided an argument for the collectivity of Christendom, but the Normans settled and were converted. The traditional basis for this ideology seemed thus to have disappeared, but it had already grown to the extent that it could develop further into the Peace of God movement.

It was, in fact, in the period of the Peace of God that Christendom as a collectivity began to show a sharper profile. The Gregorian Reform was, of course, a factor in this process, as it brought centralization and uniformity to the church. At the same time Christendom distinguished itself more clearly from those who were outside its collectivity. Increasing exclusivism was accompanied by growing intolerance. This exclusivism did not restrict itself to calling the attention of the military upper class to warlike tribes outside the church and to those who broke the peace. From the eleventh century on there was also increased opposition to other groups that were outside the collectivity or that had moved away from it, namely, Jews and heretics. The ideology of a closed Christendom did not have its origin in the Peace of God movement, but was successfully integrated into it and thus facilitated the transformation of the peace movement into the crusades, though we should be careful not to reduce the crusades to an extension of the Peace of God movement.

What more can we say about this movement as a turning point in medieval society? In what has been discussed so far, it has remained unclear how it functioned as such a turning point. The Peace of God movement cannot be portrayed as anticipating the future of medieval society, with its greater agricultural prosperity. At most it may be supposed that better harvests stimulated irritation over acts of violence, against which the Peace of God movement was a reaction. Neither is there any definite relationship between the nascent reform movements in the church, which sought to

---

21. The Latin text of the treaty notes: "communem christianum." *Hludowici, Karoli et Hlotarii conventus apud Saponarias* 5 (*MGH Capitularia* II/2, 161).

reduce the number of proprietary churches, and the bishops' opposition to private wars and to escalation of those wars.

Finally, it might be noted — with reference to the significance of the veneration of relics during the Peace of God councils — that this movement also did not have any relationship to the religious changes that manifested themselves in the twelfth century in a new spirituality and a transition in religious art from Romanesque to Gothic, that is, the reorientation of Christianity toward the incarnate Son of God known as the "imitation of Christ." This reorientation caused the presence of human good and evil to receive more emphasis, so that saints and demons lost something of their dominant place in the perception of otherworldly reality.

And even with regard to war itself the peace movement did not have all that much significance. Wars continued to be fought, and the military profession kept its social status and importance — as long as war was waged in a chivalrous manner and was not delegated to mercenaries, who were more effective, that is, more brutal.[22] Restrictions on when fighting was permitted came to be ignored. Duby describes the Battle of Bouvines in 1214, which pitted the king of England against the king of France and the German emperor and in which armies of many regional rulers participated, as "The *Sunday* of Bouvines."[23]

❧   ❧

ONE ASPECT that has not been mentioned is the institutionalization of the goals of this movement, that is, the transition from the Peace of God movement to the Peace of God. This institutionalization may be found, beginning at the end of the eleventh century, in both ecclesiastical and secular contexts. Ecclesiastical institutionalization was mainly a matter of codification, whereby the Peace of God temporarily received its place in canon law. This process of codification began during church councils in the last decennia of the eleventh century. There the most important provisions of the Truce of God, as they had been formulated during the heavily attended peace councils, were repeated, and the Peace of God was often explicitly identified with the Truce of God. The provisions were accom-

22. G. Duby, "Guerre et société dans l'Europe féodale," in V. Branca, ed., *Concetto, storia, miti e immagini del medio evo* (Florence, 1972), 449-82.

23. *Le dimanche de Bouvines* (Paris, 1973).

panied by spiritual sanctions against those who broke the peace and against those who were excluded from the church — and, in fact, from society at large.

One of these codifications may be found in the *Panormia,* the third and last collection of legal texts produced by Ivo of Chartres shortly before 1100. The text indicates that this is a papal codification, that is to say, a statement about the Peace of God promulgated during a council in the presence of the pope and possibly under his direct supervision:

> We declare that priests, clerics, monks, pilgrims, departing and return-ing merchants, and peasants with their plow oxen, seed grain, and sheep are to live in continuous peace. The Truce of God, which extends from sundown on the fourth day of the week until the second day [of the next week], between Advent and the eighth day of Epiphany, and from Septuagesima until the eighth day of Pentecost, must be observed in its integrity as we have prescribed. No bishop will, except in a life or death situation, release a violator of the peace from the anathema that his violation brings on him before he has been subjected to an apostolic investigation and has accepted whatever he has been ordered to do. If such a person dies, he will not receive a Christian burial — even if on his repentant request the last rites are not refused. Someone who has dared to violate the Peace of God and has not made satisfaction will after three warnings be excommunicated by the bishop, and the bishop will notify the neighboring bishops in writing. Bishops are not to accept someone who has been excommunicated into their com-munities, but are to respect the written judgment. Whoever dares to disobey this rule, is in danger of losing his ordination. And since "a three-fold cord is not quickly broken" (Ecclesiastes 4:12), we command the bishops to assist in word and deed the maintenance of the peace and not to disregard such matters out of sympathy or hate for anyone. Bishops who show fear in the pursuit of this work fail in the duties connected with the dignity of their office.[24]

This provision is also found in a shorter form among the decisions taken during the Lenten synod convened in 1093 in Troia in Apulia by Pope Urban II.[25] We do not know whether Urban announced this decree

24. *Panormia* VII.147 (*PL* CLXI, 1343). Cf. A. Grabois, "De la treve de Dieu à la paix du roi," in *Mélanges offerts à René Crozet,* ed. P. Gallais and Y.-J. Riou (Poitiers, 1966), 586 and n. 13.
25. Mansi XX, 716.

in this form during any other council. He may well have done so during the Council of Clermont-Ferrand, for the scattered notes about the decisions of that council constitute an incomplete account.[26] In any event it seems likely that Ivo of Chartres recorded such a decree made by Urban. When Ivo wrote the *Panormia* points in that direction, as does the early history of Urban II. As prior of Cluny Urban was, already before the council, well acquainted with the subject of the Peace of God. It is unknown whether his predecessors Gregory VII and Victor III, both Italians, were so directly involved with the peace issue, since it primarily concerned France. Moreover, the text seems to indicate that it was only drafted after an important part of the Gregorian reform program — the establishment of papal authority over the bishops — had been realized.

But during the first general council of the Latin church, the First Lateran Council of 1123, this peace resolution was not repeated. Only that "which has been decided by our predecessors, the popes of Rome," was reaffirmed.[27] But during the councils of Clermont-Ferrand of 1130 and Reims of 1131, both presided over by Innocent II, who had come to France in an attempt to find support for his struggle against the anti-pope Anacletus, a peace provision was taken up. It was basically similar to what Ivo of Chartres had recorded in his *Panormia*. The subsections of the provision were more clearly distinguished and the stipulation regarding the refusal of Christian burial was extended to those who died during tournaments.[28]

During the Second Lateran Council, convened by Innocent in 1139 after the papal schism of Anacletus had been ended, the decisions of the councils of Clermont-Ferrand and Reims were repeated.[29] They were again reaffirmed at the Third Lateran Council in 1179,[30] but by that time the codification of peace provisions had lost much of its meaning. During the council held in 1149 in Reims and presided over by Eugenius III, the text of the peace provision drawn from the *Panormia* had already undergone substantial change. What had been said about the safety of priests, clergy, monks (including *conversi* or lay brothers), pilgrims, and peasants was repeated, as was the precept prohibiting tournaments. But a truce period was no longer mentioned, and there was a new rule that a bishop faced

---

26. Cf. R. Somerville, "The Council of Clermont (1095) and Latin Christian Society," *Archivum Historiae Pontificum* 12 (1974), 55-90.

27. Canon 15 = *COD* 193.

28. Mansi XXI, 439 (canons 8 and 9), 460 (canons 10, 11, and 12).

29. Canons 11, 12, and 14 = *COD* 199.

30. Canons 20, 21, and 22 = *COD* 221f.

with a breach of the peace — that is, with violence against persons who did not belong to the military — was to bring the culprit before his ecclesiastical tribunal.[31]

A more significant indication of the loss of meaning of this codification of peace by the church is found in the *Decretum* of Gratian, which was completed in 1144. In this collection of church canons, which came to have a great amount of prestige in the church, hardly any attention is given to the Peace of God. Gratian reiterates the earlier decrees in an abbreviated form, in particular that of Clermont-Ferrand in 1130, but ties them to the general duties of the bishops with regard to peace. He does not even mention observance of sacred periods during which all fighting is forbidden.[32] It could be argued that he was just not very interested in the Peace of God, but the reason for this lack of interest is the lessened importance of the Peace of God for the church as a whole. The stipulation, accepted in Reims in 1149, that the bishop had to bring a violator of the peace before his tribunal was borrowed from what was already common practice in secular courts. We have already mentioned that rulers strengthened their authority by means of the Peace of God. They were charged with the enforcement of peace decrees and with their tribunals they decided the fate of the violators, even though for this they still depended on the authority of church dignitaries with whom they continued to conclude Peace of God agreements.[33]

In a sense the administration of justice in these matters of peace by the princes became easier when Louis VI (1108-37) attempted to regain royal authority in the crown domains and in the kingdom as a whole. Louis did not shy away from fierce conflict with recalcitrant vassals and also resorted to the Peace of God decisions, to which he demanded strict obedience. To what extent obedience to the conditions of the Peace of God was realized remains unclear, but the result can be inferred from the actions of the next king, Louis VII.

In 1155 this Louis declared a *Landfriede,* a nationwide peace, which was accepted by the many regional rulers subject to him, who then arranged for peace tribunals in their own territories. The duke of Burgundy and the counts of Flanders, Nevers, Troyes, and Soissons are mentioned

31. Mansi XXI, 716 (canons 11 and 12).

32. H. Hoffmann, *Gottesfriede und Treuga Dei* (Stuttgart, 1964), 232f.

33. An early example is offered by the Council of St. Omars, called in 1099 by Count Robert II of Flanders (Mansi XX, 969-72).

by name. This *Landfriede,* which was to remain in effect for ten years, was declared at a council in Soissons. It guaranteed peace and safety to the persons and property of the clergy, peasants, merchants, and all who were prepared to accept the jurisdiction of those who were to enforce the peace. The term "Covenant of God" was no longer used, and the role of the clergy had become marginal. Archbishops and abbots were allowed to promise, in the presence of their holy relics and the full council, that they on their part would do everything to further the peace.[34]

Here we have come to the real consequence of the Peace of God movement and of the Peace of God as an institution and can now see in what way the movement marked an important social change. The Peace of God opposed acts of violence and gave legal status to a system of justice that answered them with punishment. It facilitated the emergence of the *seigneurie banale,* a system where the holder of a lordship was responsible for administering justice. (The jurisdiction of a seigneurial lord was usually restricted to lesser crimes, while the authority to judge capital crimes remained the privilege of territorial rulers. Over time it became possible in such matters of high justice to appeal to the crown.) A judicial system tied to the authority of the seigneurial lord restricted freedom but increased security, because a violator of the peace would be called to account for his deeds. He had not just harmed the interests of others but had also infringed the public order.

The punishments meted out also changed, partly due to the revival of Roman law. The wergild system of Germanic tribal law no longer sufficed, but the wergilds and the income they brought to the lord no longer dominated the lord's judicial activity. Protection of others had become important for him, because of the rapid increase in the economic strength of the merchants and the peasants. Through the Peace of God this new legal system spread to other parts of Europe and functioned as a guarantee of public safety that had been lacking for centuries. The *Landfriede* and the royal peace identified many crimes with violation of the peace, and thus a penal code developed that provided medieval society with a legal system, at least in those regions where rulers were not at war with each other. For, as was mentioned earlier, the Peace of God did not bring an end to war.

34. *Recueil des Historiens des Gaules et des Francs* XIV (Paris, 1806), 387f.

V

Cistercians and Cluniacs[1]

᪥   ᪥

AN EDUCATED Cistercian monk in the first half of the twelfth century and consequently belonging to the order's first generation, if asked about the Cistercians' relation to the old monasticism, would probably have answered that his order was its continuation, or at any rate that the Cistercians had cut their links with Benedictine monasticism as traditionally practiced in those days, because it deviated too much from the old monasticism. An indication for such an answer is already provided by the earliest account of the origin and the beginnings of the Cistercian order, the *Exordium parvum.* The monks who left the Molesme monastery to found "the new monastery," the original name given to Cîteaux, reached their decision as a result of frequent conversations among themselves about the neglect of the rule of Blessed Benedict, the spiritual ancestor of the monks. They lamented the fact, and were saddened by it, that other monks who in solemn profession had promised to keep this rule, did not observe it at all, and thus were consciously guilty of perjury.

The earliest Cistercians wanted to combat abuses in contemporary monasticism through a return to the old (i.e., original) precepts of St. Benedict and to forego all changes, mitigations, or extensions to which

---

1. This chapter was published as "The Early Cistercians and the Old Monasticism" in *The End of Strife,* ed. D. M. Loades (Edinburgh, 1984), 180-99, and appears here with changes and more complete notes.

this rule had been subjected as a result of ensuing customs, which had obtained the force of law within traditional Benedictine monasticism. With respect to this they considered themselves reformers, who moreover were especially interested in the last chapter of Benedict's rule, a chapter considered by some as a later addition. In it the rule is described as a rule for beginners, and those who are in a hurry to reach the full unfolding of monastic life are referred to the doctrine of the holy fathers, the exercise of which leads mankind to the summit of perfection.[2] These holy fathers are the monastic predecessors of St. Benedict, and on account of the attention paid by the early Cistercians to these "desert fathers" their monasteries have at times been described as the "deserts of the twelfth century."[3] When founding their monasteries, they behaved as Eremites who wanted to flee from the world completely; they sought loneliness under extremely difficult circumstances and made inhospitable regions habitable.

Naturally, this representation of things contained a certain element of fantasy. In their own opinion the Cistercians were returning to the old monasticism, but in reality their thoughts and conduct were the product of a contemporary situation, which was held to be identical with that of the old monasticism. They stuck to this figment of their imagination even in situations that did not fit the conditions which they themselves had proposed with regard to the founding of new monasteries and which had been incorporated as a precept in their oldest *statuta,* namely that monasteries would not be built in towns, fortified places, or existing domains, but only in places far removed from human company. In by no means all cases was this completely true. In spite of this, a monastic chronicle sometimes related, as in the case of Silvanes, in what barren waste the respective abbey had been founded.[4] Moreover, the oldest Cistercian *consuetudines,* the *Ecclesiastica Officia,* show that a Cistercian monastery with its material provisions was by no means a primitive community in those early days.[5]

From what has been said so far it should be clear that in this context "old monasticism" means something different from what the early Cister-

2. *RSB* 73.
3. E. Gilson, *The Mystical Theology of Saint Bernard* (2nd ed.; New York, 1955), 31.
4. C. H. Berman, "The Foundation and Early History of the Monastery of Silvanes: The Economic Reality," in *Cistercian Ideals and Reality,* ed. J. R. Sommerfeldt (Cistercian Studies, 60; Kalamazoo, 1978), 280-318.
5. B. K. Lackner, "Early Cistercian Life as Described in the *Ecclesiastica Officia,*" in Sommerfeldt, 62-79.

cians understood by it, at least from the perspective of historical reality. We must inquire into the relation between the young Cistercian order and the traditional Benedictine monasticism which had developed since the Carolingian era and had taken shape in various monastic associations or orders such as Brogne, La Chaise-Dieu, Gorze, Hirsau, and Cluny. All of these were monastic associations which themselves had attempted a reform of Benedictine monasticism more or less on the lines of the reformatory measures submitted for approval to the synod of Aachen by Benedict of Aniane. Our information about this relationship is restricted, namely to the relationship between the Cistercians and the Cluniacs. Their monasteries were situated close to each other, especially in the early days of the Cistercian order, which was then limited in its expansion to France. The extension of both orders into Germany led to a rivalry between them, particularly between the Cistercians and the monks of the congregation of Hirsau, who were described as Cluniacs because they derived their *consuetudines* from Cluny.

To a large extent, this rivalry, which was an important characteristic of the relationship between the Cistercians and the Cluniacs, stemmed from the spectacular growth of the Cistercian order. The main facts of this growth are generally known. In 1098 Cîteaux was founded. In the years 1112-15 this abbey founded its first four daughter abbeys: La Ferté, Pontigny, Clairvaux, and Morimond. Forty years later, in 1153 when Bernard of Clairvaux died, the order numbered 335 monasteries for men. Clairvaux and Morimond had taken the lion's share in this expansion. There were at this time at most only twenty convents for nuns; thus the prime of this branch of the order does not belong to the period discussed here.

❦   ❦

THE GROWTH of the Cistercian order was a complex matter in those early days. The credit for this growth has been largely given to Bernard of Clairvaux. He indeed involved himself frequently in the takeover of existing abbeys or the acquisition of donations of land on which a new foundation could be started.[6] But at least equal importance must be attached to the fact that in those days Benedictine monasticism underwent a change, a crisis according to some, because a different observance of the

6. A. H. Bredero, "Saint Bernard and the Historians," in *Saint Bernard of Clairvaux,* ed. B. Pennington (Kalamazoo, 1977), 53-58.

rule forced itself upon the monks as a result of changes in contemporary society — an observance different from what was customary in the long-established monasteries.

These social changes, which stimulated the desire for a different observance of the rule of Benedict, were partly of an economic nature. The old abbeys got into financial trouble because an important part of their income, the tithes of landed property not belonging to these monasteries, began to decrease. This was partly due to an increase in population on the domains, giving rise to a more intensive consumption of agricultural produce. This decline of income was also partly a result of the advent of a market economy, which was made possible through an increase in the circulation of money. It became more attractive to sell surpluses of produce for money than to donate them to monasteries. The decline in income did not automatically result in a reduction in an abbey's cost and expenditure. The circulation of money, moreover, opened the possibility of borrowing money. The monks made use of this practice too freely, because on the one hand they did not comprehend the structural character of the decline of their income, and because on the other they lacked experience in the paying of interest. On the whole, however, this did not become a serious problem for the Cistercians. Their strict rule of life restored to its pristine place of honor the prescript of manual labor. This manual labor was made productive in the reclamation of land and the cultivation of the fields. Whereas the old Benedictine monasteries were mostly situated on hills (although Cluny was an exception to this rule), the Cistercians consciously chose the valleys, where they harnessed the watercourses and adapted them to the needs of their monasteries. This in turn frequently resulted in secular initiatives for the foundation of Cistercian abbeys. These abbeys were often looked upon as incentives for the development of an agrarian society.

The Cistercians did not consider tithes to be a legitimate income for monks, for neither the rule nor the Life of Benedict mentioned them. This also meant that they rejected the obligation to pay tithes to a third party, an obligation sometimes attached to property donated to them. Moreover, their recruiting methods differed somewhat from those customary in the traditional Benedictine monasteries. No one was allowed admittance to a community under the age of fifteen (eighteen), and the novitiate of one year's duration prescribed by the rule, but often ignored in the Cluniac monasteries, was strictly adhered to. The Cistercians also developed the institution of the lay brothers or "conversi," although the idea for it had not come from them. During the week these lay brothers remained in the country houses, the granges, and were present in the abbey only on Sundays to participate in the liturgy. Thus a distinction developed between choir monks and working brothers, as a result of which the difference between the choir monks of the traditional monasteries and those of Cistercian abbeys was in fact less sharp than was often imagined.

The point on which the differences between Cistercians and Cluniacs were maintained longest, and about which no mention at all was made in the polemical writings exchanged between the orders, was the organization of these orders. Cluny had developed from a monastery into an order because to this monastery had been entrusted other monasteries by their owners at the time, often lay persons, in order that the Cluniac way of life might provide them with the leaven of renewal. On the occasion of such a takeover, Cluny had usually sent a number of monks to join such a community. As a result of this, such an abbey became — unless older privilege prevented it — a priory belonging to the order of Cluny. Anyone entering that priory made his profession in the presence of the abbot of Cluny. Consequently, the latter became abbot of all monasteries affiliated to Cluny, and by their bond with him these monasteries formed an order. In his supervisory duties the abbot of Cluny was naturally assisted by others, whom he recruited carefully. But he was personally responsible for the policy of the order and of its monasteries. For that reason he would undertake many journeys of visitation and was considered to be the abbot general.

Things were quite different with the Cistercians. The order did not have an abbot general, but it did have a general chapter, which was convened once a year and in which in principle all abbots had to participate. True enough, the first four daughter abbeys of Cîteaux possessed special rights within the order — rights obtained only later by Morimond, although it had been founded simultaneously with Clairvaux, for which reason it vied with Clairvaux in the founding of daughter abbeys. But even in respect to their behavior vis-à-vis their daughter abbeys, recourse could be had to the general chapter. One of the great advantages of instituting a general chapter was that moral decadence and crises in Cistercian monasteries could be tackled much more efficiently, while on the other hand there was no tendency of individual abbeys toward independence from Cîteaux. In Cluny, on the contrary, this tendency toward independence within various monasteries, or the movement toward the restoration of the free election of abbots, was often the cause of internal crises, while the person who had to solve this problem, the abbot of Cluny himself, was at the same time by his function its institutional cause.

Finally, the Cistercians and the traditional Benedictines differed from each other in something which to us may appear trivial but which in those days was considered essential, especially because of the symbolic explanation given to it. It was moreover a difference which tended to be conspicuous at all times, for it had to do with dress. From earliest times the Benedictines wore a black habit, while the Cistercians opted for a habit of undyed wool which therefore had a greyish-white color. The latter was chosen because the Cistercians wished to dress more soberly than was usual in the existing monasteries. The difference in color, which in the *Exordium parvum* was not actually mentioned, easily led to animosity between the two orders because of the meaning ascribed to it. This is clear, for example, from the argument with which Rupert of Deutz, himself a Benedictine abbot (†1129), transformed his preference for the black monastic dress into a value judgment, referring to Song of Songs 1:5: *Nigra sum sed formosa:* "I am black but beautiful."[7]

Among the Cluniacs this difference of color was by no means incidental. Peter the Venerable, abbot of Cluny, in a letter written to Bernard of Clairvaux in 1127 or 1128, accused the Cistercians of pride because of their choice of a white habit. The ancient fathers, so he assured them, had dressed in black out of humility, but the Cistercians evidently thought themselves better than their predecessors. But at the same time Peter was also willing to give a positive interpretation of this color. The white habit signified that the Cistercians found their happiness in poverty, their joy in sorrow, and their cheerfulness in grief.[8] In later letters to Bernard of Clairvaux the abbot of Cluny returned to this difference in color. In doing so he drew special attention to the fact that it contributed to misunderstanding between the two orders.[9] From the perspective of the Cistercians, this difference in color was discussed only in an anti-Cluniac polemical document which appeared after the death of Bernard of Clairvaux: the *Dialogus duorum monachorum.* Here it was argued that the life of a monk approaches the life of an angel, and that consequently the monk also ought to wear the dress of an angel, thus a white habit.[10]

Finally, there was considerable negative comment on the Cistercians

7. *PL* CLXX, 511f. The biblical text reads "black *and* beautiful" in the New Revised Standard Version. "Black *but* beautiful" reflects the Latin text.

8. Letter 28 (Constable I, 58). Concerning the interpretations of these colors see Constable II, 116.

9. Letters III, 150 (Constable I, 290, 367-71).

10. III.46, ll. 931-35; R. B. C. Huygens, ed., *Le moine Idung et ses deux ouvrages* (Spoleto, 1980), 180f.

among the traditional Benedictines, as well as outside the order of Cluny itself. Orderic Vitalis, a monk of the Abbey Evroul in Normandy and author of an *Historia Ecclesiastica,* written about 1135, gave his verdict as follows:

> Many noble warriors and profound philosophers have flocked to them on account of the novelty of their practices. . . . Among the good men are some hypocrites who, clothed in white or other distinctive habits, have deceived men and made a great show to the masses. Many seek to be numbered with the true servants of God by their outward observance, not their virtue; their numbers disgust those who see them and make true monks seem less worthy in the faulty judgement of men.[11]

❧   ❧

THIS NEGATIVE REACTION to the Cistercians from within traditional Benedictine monasticism was caused by a concrete point of friction which had occurred between Cistercians and Cluniacs and which had inevitably led to rivalry between the two orders; at least this was the obvious explanation of the many writers who commented on it. The point of friction par excellence that could occur between monasteries, namely the arrival of monks wishing to exchange their monastery and order for another, occurred between Cîteaux and Cluny as well. This problem had already been anticipated in the rule of St. Benedict, for it declares that an abbot must be wary of accepting permanently into his monastery a monk from an abbey, even though an abbey with which he is familiar, without permission or letters of recommendation from the monk's abbot.[12] At the same time, however, it was customary for an abbot to consent to the departure of a monk from his abbey when the latter wished to exchange his way of life for a stricter one.

This was the basis for the privilege, which Cluny received from Pope Urban II in 1097, of accepting monks from another monastery. The abbot of Cluny did not have to take into account the objections or complaints of the abbey from which the monk in question originated, at least if the latter made the change *pro vitae melioratione.* The reason for this privilege is evident. Cluny had great merits on behalf of the reform

11. *HE* VIII.26 (Chibnall IV, 326f.).
12. *RSB* 61.

of Benedictine monasticism, and many abbeys indeed had joined this movement *pro vitae melioratione.* But other abbeys had stayed out of the Cluniac movement, probably against the wishes of some of their monks. Naturally, several of those monks then opted for Cluny on their own account, but they did not always obtain the cooperation of their abbot. Urban II, who before his election as pope had been great prior at Cluny, possessed firsthand knowledge of this problem. This is probably why he granted Cluny this privilege, which deviated from the rule of Benedict.

The Cistercians at first observed this prescript of the rule; this at least is the impression one gets from the letters of Bernard of Clairvaux dealing with monks joining the Cistercians from other abbeys. Repeatedly, Bernard sent back a monk if it appeared that the latter's abbot did not approve. The letters in question belong, admittedly, to the first period of Bernard's abbacy. But according to his treatise, *De praecepto et dispensatione* (On Precepts and Dispensations from Them), which he wrote in 1142, Bernard had become even more cautious in accepting monks from Bene-dictine abbeys. He had written this treatise in answer to questions from some Benedictine monks and sent it to them through their abbot. In it he also dealt with the motives which might lead a monk to cease to observe the vow of *stabilitas loci* which the rule demanded of him and to go to a different abbey.

Bernard naturally maintained that no monk could join another abbey without the consent of his abbot. Besides, the only valid argument for a change of order of abbey was the choice of a stricter way of life than the one customary in the abbey where one was residing. Bernard illustrated his exposé with the example of a Cluniac monk who wished to leave his order because he had chosen the poverty of Cîteaux instead of the Cluniac way of life. To the above-mentioned conditions which would allow such a change of monastery to take place, Bernard added some commentary. One should not condemn a person leaving his monastery for this reason, but neither should one condemn someone who in such circumstances decided against leaving his monastery so as not to scandalize his brethren.[13] From the example given and the commentary added to it we may conclude that the abbot of Clairvaux had some experience with Cluniac monks joining the Cistercians. In other ways as well, it is clear that here he was dealing with a delicate problem. Of the approximately 335 monasteries

---

13. *On Precept and Dispensation* XVI.44-46 = *The Works of Bernard of Clairvaux* I: *Treatises* (Washington, 1974) I, 139f.

which belonged to the Cistercian order in 1153, a number were already in existence before joining the order. At times monasteries joined the order separately, as was the case with Canons Regular; then again, they did so as a group of abbeys, as in the case of the congregation of Savigny. However, the number of Benedictine abbeys or priories taken over by the Cistercians was very small, and among them there was not even one Cluniac monastery. In Cluny, the monks who opted for the poverty of Cîteaux had to face the problems which Bernard outlined in his treatise.

Bernard's view on the stricter way of life which gave a monk the right to leave a Cluniac monastery for one belonging to the Cistercians — with the proviso already mentioned — also makes clear that in the opinion of the Cistercians the privilege granted to Cluny of accepting monks without the consent of their own abbot could not possibly apply to monks of their own order, for a Cistercian leaving for Cluny could not have made a choice *pro vitae melioratione*. Bernard had to deal with this problem as well while a young abbot, and in a rather exceptional way at that. According to what is known, Bernard did not want to resign himself to one of his monks' leaving for Cluny. The case is generally known and concerns a relative of Bernard's, Robert of Châtillon, who had entered Clairvaux as a young man but had previously been promised by his parents to Cluny. This state of affairs was not accepted by Cluny. During one of Bernard's absences from his monastery, the great prior of Cluny visited the monk in question and persuaded him to leave Clairvaux for Cluny. Robert's residence at Clairvaux was against the promise made by his parents, and apparently Cluny was not prepared to tolerate such a breach of promise.

The reaction of the abbot of Clairvaux to this intervention became widely known. He sent Robert a letter, which according to the *Life* of Bernard he dictated in the open air. When a thunderstorm burst he continued the dictation, and the falling rain is supposed to have spared the parchment. About the contents of this "letter in the rain," however, the *Life* of Bernard remains silent. Nevertheless, some light can be shed on the matter. Bernard called the prior who had lured Robert away a "wolf in sheep's clothing," preaching to the young monk a new gospel in which drunkenness was recommended and sobriety condemned, and voluntary poverty labeled as misery, while fasting, vigilance, and silence were called foolishness. Naturally, Bernard also protested against a Cluniac appeal to Rome, where this course was supposed to have been legalized. In this letter Bernard compared himself with the woman whose child was stolen by another woman who had smothered her own child in her sleep. But Bernard could not count on the wisdom of a Solomon to redress this injustice. He also asked himself what kind of love the Cluniacs fostered for the salvation of this monk, if in its cause they had to destroy the salvation of Bernard himself.

The text of the passage following this question deserves to be quoted:

> Ah! would that these men might save you apart from me. Would that if I die, you, at least, may live! But how can this be? Does salvation rest rather in soft raiment and high living than in frugal fare and moderate clothing? If warm and comfortable furs, if fine and precious cloth, if long sleeves and ample hoods, if dainty coverlets and soft woollen shirts make a saint, why do I delay and not follow you at once? But these things are comforts for the weak, not the arms of fighting men. They who wear soft raiment are in kings' houses. Wine and white bread, honey-wine and pittances, benefit the body not the soul. The soul is not fattened out of frying pans! Many monks in Egypt served God for a long time without fish. Pepper, ginger, cummin, sage, and all the thousand other spices may please the palate, but they inflame lust. And would you make my safety depend on such things?[14]

The monks in Egypt mentioned here are the ancient desert monks to whom Bernard considered the Cistercians to be related, and with whom he contrasted the Cluniacs. This shows that Bernard used the incident with Cluny concerning the monk Robert to attack the Cluniac way of life. The incident was nothing more than the occasion to do this, for if his main purpose had been to get Robert back to Clairvaux, such a public indictment of the Cluniac way of life would hardly have been the most appropriate means to achieve it. That Bernard made use of the incident for this controversy becomes quite clear if one knows that a short time afterward he repeated the same polemical stand in his *Apologia*. This polemical treatise Bernard wrote at the request of a Benedictine abbot, William of St.-Thierry, to whom he sent this criticism of the Cluniac way of life officially. In it he repeated the reproaches which he had already uttered in his letter to Robert. But also he denounced other matters, like the pomp and splendor with which the Cluniac abbots surrounded themselves during their journeys and also the luxury shown in the building of

14. Letter I, 1.1. Cf. James, 7f.

monasteries and churches. It was especially because of this last point that this *Apologia* continued to be widely read during the late Middle Ages. In the fourteenth century Geert Groote referred to it in a pamphlet in which he attacked the plans to build a tower next to the cathedral at Utrecht.

⅔   ⅔

BUT THE POLEMICAL WRITINGS of Bernard of Clairvaux mentioned above do raise some questions. Everyone agrees that the letter to Robert was not meant for him personally, but must rather be considered a pamphlet used by Bernard to attack Cluny. Some such outburst by Bernard was understandable as long as it was generally thought that the pamphlet was written before 1122, the year in which the then abbot of Cluny, Pons de Melgueil, was forced by Rome to abdicate. This abdication was explained as a consequence of the abbot's rule, which was considered to have been a period of lawlessness and was supposed to have done serious harm to the spiritual life at Cluny. But the letter to Robert cannot be linked with this situation of decadence, at least not as a criticism of the way of life at Cluny as it was thought to have been under Abbot Pons. Indeed, it has been proved that this letter was written as late as the end of 1124, only a short time before Bernard wrote his *Apologia* in 1125.

Thus we must conclude that Bernard attacked the way of life at Cluny during the tenure of its new abbot, Peter the Venerable, otherwise known as a reformer of the Cluniac way of life. At the moment when Bernard denounced the abuses at Cluny, this new abbot was meeting considerable opposition in his monastery and his new order from followers of his deposed predecessor. Pons had first made a journey to Jerusalem, a customary reaction in that period on the occasion of a social impasse, and could be seen as an act of eschatologically determined resignation in the face of problems with which one could no longer cope.[15] In 1124, Pons returned from Jerusalem and took up residence in northern Italy in a small monastery of Eremites, belonging to the jurisdiction of Cluny. Subsequently his followers at Cluny renewed contact with him, and in the course of 1126, during an absence of his successor, Pons returned to Cluny. His followers welcomed him back as their abbot. It is said that this was accompanied by acts of violence committed by the lay population living around Cluny, who had also chosen Pons's side. But there are also indica-

15. See chapter III above.

tions that violence was used only when followers of Peter the Venerable attempted to regain control of the abbey. At any rate, Pons's position at Cluny became untenable, because Rome refused to accept him once more as abbot. A papal legate was sent, and subsequently procedures were conducted against him in Rome, after which he remained in an ecclesiastical prison in that city until his death soon afterward.

Between these events and the anti-Cluniac writings of Bernard, in my opinion, we must accept the existence of a direct link. In his *Apologia,* the abbot of Clairvaux made clear among other things that he did not write because the change of monks from one abbey to another was such a tremendous problem for him, and he also made clear that he was intervening in an internal problem of Cluny itself. Concerning the first point Bernard wrote:

> Some monks I have known, who have come to us from other communities and observances, who have knocked and gained admittance, have scandalized their brothers by their thoughtless departure, and have been no advantage to us, upsetting us by their wretched conduct. They scorned what they had, and foolishly coveted what was beyond them. However, by the due outcome of it all, God has made known how worthless they were. Fecklessly they let go of what recklessly they had snatched at, and they returned discredited to the place they had left with so little forethought. The fact is that they had sought our cloisters more because they were dissatisfied with your order, than from any desire of ours. What sort of monks they were was revealed by their flitting back and forth, from you to us, and from us to you, a scandal to us and to you and to every decent man.[16]

The difference of opinion implied in these two writings of Bernard must not be directly interpreted as an expression of rivalry between the two orders. He considered them too different from each other to merit comparison.

❧   ❧

WHAT HE WROTE ABOUT Cluny was not meant to compare Cluny with Cîteaux in order to condemn it. Rather, he wrote because he condemned certain developments at Cluny and wanted to oppose them. This intention

---

16. *Apology to William* XI.31 (cf. *The Works of Bernard of Clairvaux* I, 68f.).

he had already made clear in the first part of the *Apologia*. There Bernard reprimanded the Cistercians who wanted to belittle the order of Cluny. By way of conclusion of this reprimand of his fellow Cistercians, he observes that at this point his treatise could have been brought to an end. But the attack on Cluny had yet to start. Its opening words make clear that it was not meant to be an attack by the Cistercians as such against Cluny, but as an intervention in the internal affairs of that order. This conclusion becomes all the more cogent if we connect this treatise with what happened at Cluny shortly afterward and with the subsequent reply of Peter the Venerable to the reproaches Bernard had leveled in his *Apologia* against the way of life at Cluny.

The opening words of Bernard's so-called attack on Cluny are as follows:

> Because I have been unsparing with our own monks, it may appear as though I am condoning a number of elements in your Order, which are not to your liking, I know, and which are, in fact, avoided by all good monks. Though such abuses are in the order, I hope they are not of the order. No order can have room for disorder, and whatever is disorderly cannot belong to an order. Hence my objections must be regarded as helping to promote the order, rather than as pulling it down. It is not for belonging to the order that I rebuke them, but for their vices. So it is that I have no fear that those who really love the order will be upset by what I am going to say. Quite the contrary, they will probably be grateful that I condemn the things which they themselves detest. If anyone is angry with me, this only proves that he has no real love for the order, since he will not condemn the vices that are ruining it. To him I reply, in the words of St. Gregory, that "it is better for scandal to arise than for truth to be abandoned."[17]

The Latin word for "offense" or "scandal" used here by Bernard is *scandalum*. A literal translation of this word is in order here, because Cluny had indeed to face a scandal, namely, the occasion of Pons's return. The current opinion on this event is mainly dependent on a report by Peter the Venerable. However, the latter was clearly a party in the conflict. In 1127 or 1128, he answered Bernard's reproaches with a long letter in which he defended all the existing customs at Cluny, providing them with his commentary. He even defended things that had not been mentioned in

17. Ibid. VII.15 (I, 51f.).

the *Apologia* nor in the letter to Robert. This letter was moreover sent by Peter the Venerable to all Cluniac priors.[18] This makes us presume that this letter was just as much addressed to his own Cluniac order, particularly because Peter the Venerable officially addressed this very long treatise to someone he did not yet know but who had interfered in the internal problems of his order.

If one reads the above-mentioned passage from the *Apologia* against the background of the conflict that subsequently arose at Cluny and which Peter the Venerable afterward had to settle, one can only understand it as the opening stage of the intervention Bernard permitted himself in an internal controversy at Cluny. This controversy became an open conflict when Abbot Pons returned there and Peter the Venerable became deeply involved because his leadership was being questioned. This leadership was under attack from the followers of Pons, but when they had lost their cause Peter the Venerable had to take charge once more. For this purpose he wrote a defense of the existing way of life at Cluny because his leadership concerned the maintenance of that way of life, from which many had wished to deviate. Bernard had chosen their side, first in his letter to Robert and subsequently much more clearly in his *Apologia*. This circumstance then provided Peter the Venerable with the opportunity to settle the internal conflict at Cluny, which had led to scandal on account of Abbot Pons's return, particularly because it had come about in a veiled and discreet manner. Peter could now pretend not to have to settle conflicts within the order, but simply to answer objections that had been brought against Cluny from outside.

This interpretation of what happened at Cluny in the years 1124-26/27 also calls for a revision of the reason why Pons de Melgueil abdicated as abbot there. Generally the cause is sought outside Cluny, though the pope acted on complaints against Pons from within the order. Even more surprising is the supposition that the general crisis experienced by monasticism in the transition from the eleventh to the twelfth centuries could have left Cluny completely untouched. This crisis led to new interpretations of the rule of St. Benedict which people wished to observe once more in an authentic way, stripped of the customs which had gradually overtaken it. It is just unthinkable that in Cluny, where these customs had developed to such a degree, no discussion should have concerned this problem or that there should have been at most question of the preference of a few

18. Constable I, 206.

Cluniac monks for a stricter monastic way of life as reason why they chose another abbey or another order. Such a discussion must have undoubtedly taken place at Cluny, and the letter which Peter the Venerable addressed to Bernard of Clairvaux in 1127 or 1128, as well as to all priors of his order, served as a final chapter in this discussion.

The aforementioned crisis at Cluny was a result of this discussion, and the manner in which it was conducted between champions and opponents of change in the monastic way of life resulted in the two camps ending up diametrically and implacably opposed to each other. Abbot Pons also took sides in this discussion, favoring those who advocated change. His choice was probably partly determined by the fact that the current way of life at Cluny had resulted in economic problems, but he did not allow himself to be led exclusively by economic considerations. Indeed, even though during the later years of his tenure his community lived in poverty, no cuts were made in the daily distributions of food to the poor, a situation later denounced by Peter the Venerable as mismanagement.

※   ※

PETER THE Venerable was not initially involved in the controversy about the monastic way of life, at least not directly. He was chosen as the new abbot by Pons's opponents after the premature death of the latter's successor. Only then did Peter the Venerable come to Cluny, where as a young abbot he had embarked on the course advocated by Pons's opponents, namely the return to the traditional way of life. This task the young abbot adhered to religiously during the first years of his abbacy. So much is clear from the letter he addressed to Bernard of Clairvaux, ostensibly in answer to Bernard's letter to Robert and to the *Apologia*. In his letter Pons made clear to the priors of the Cluniac monasteries that all existing customs remained in force. The arguments he used to buttress this statement amounted principally to this: that these customs had to remain unaltered because they had originated during the time of Abbot Hugo, Pons's predecessor (who meanwhile had been canonized).

Gradually, however, it must have dawned on Peter the Venerable that even at Cluny some changes were necessary and that reforms in the way of life were needed. From a report by Orderic Vitalis, it appears that Peter's efforts to achieve this, which he started in 1132, met with opposition. Moreover, the *Statuta,* which he promulgated in connection with these changes, begins with an elaborate defense of the changing and restoration of customs as such.[19] The reforms Peter the Venerable introduced were carefully formulated. He limited himself mainly to the shortening of liturgical usages and acts. But in addition, he emphasized existing precepts concerning the abstention from meat, fasting, silence, and the use of furs and cloaks — precepts taken from the rule, by which current customs were pushed into the background. Thus there is quite a distance between the point of view held by Peter the Venerable in his early years, that is, in the above-mentioned letter to Bernard, and in his later *Statuta,* however carefully he formulated them. What really aroused Peter's indignation in later days appears quite clearly in a letter which he sent to all Cluniac priors. In it he wrote, in addition to other reproaches:

> . . . our brethren, belonging to a holy order and predestined for heaven, monks bearing the name of Cluny, continue the whole year round in God-forsaken and shameless manner with the consumption of meat. They do not do so secretly, but openly and publicly, and thus proclaim, according to a word of the prophet, their sins which emulate those of Sodom.[20]

For a more accurate assessment of the relation of Cîteaux to the old monasticism, it is important to know what happened at Cluny when Pons was forced to abdicate and Peter the Venerable began his tenure, because with his letter to Robert and his *Apologia* Bernard intervened in this internal conflict about conservatism and renewal. It is not easy to bring those events to light because we depend on nothing more than indirect information, for Peter the Venerable tried meticulously to wipe out all traces of these events for posterity. Though he later embarked to a certain degree on the same course that Pons had wished to follow, Peter always made it appear as if his task as a reformer consisted in restoring order after the lawlessness during the regime of his predecessor. In this he ignored the fact that slowly he had had to change his own abbatial policy considerably, probably because the customs — from which he, too, had deviated — were more dear to him than they had been to the reformers who had earlier received Abbot Pons's support. Thus the contradiction contained in Peter the Venerable's policy does not become too conspicuous. But it does show itself quite clearly if one compares the uncompromising attitude taken up by Matthieu d'Albano, Pons's strongest opponent within

19. Ed. G. Constable, *CCM* VI (Siegburg, 1975), 39f.
20. Letter 161, written between 1145 and 1156 (Constable I, 388f.; II, 206).

Cluny and at first a close collaborator of Peter the Venerable regarding efforts at reform by Benedictine abbots at Reims,[21] with the efforts then being made by Peter the Venerable at Cluny to achieve reforms in spite of everything. Nevertheless, Peter the Venerable later wrote Matthieu d'Albano's hagiography, in which Matthieu's implacable opposition to Pons de Melgueil is reckoned among his greatest merits.[22]

It seems equally hard to recover clear data regarding the intention of Bernard of Clairvaux in his polemical writings in respect to Cluny. Was he indeed involved in the internal conflict there? An indication that he was is offered by two letters which the abbot of Clairvaux sent to the Cardinal-legate Peter in the summer of 1126. The latter had been sent by Rome to start an investigation into the events at Cluny, namely, into the drama that took place following the return of Abbot Pons. From the first letter it appears that the cardinal-legate would have liked to speak to Pons, but the abbot declined the request. He thought that he should stay as much as possible in his monastery — a somewhat remarkable argument if one looks at Bernard's constant traveling. The cardinal-legate then seems to have inquired about what the abbot had written. Bernard also felt compelled to evade the issue. At the end of a long treatise, the abbot wrote that his writings were not very important and did not deserve the cardinal's attention. He then summarized them, concluding: "I have also written for the benefit of a friend an *Apologia* which is concerned with the observances of Cluny and ourselves, the Cistercians. I have written a few letters to various friends. . . ."[23] On the basis of these letters, in which Bernard gives evasive answers to the person who had to investigate the dramatic events which took place at Cluny, is it hazardous to conclude that the abbot of Clairvaux thought it advisable, after the facts, to draw a veil also over the way he had intervened in the internal controversy at Cluny through these polemical writings?

BERNARD'S INTENTION IN COMPOSING these writings becomes clearer if we consider what induced him to start on them. It was a daring thing at

---

21. Latin text in *William, Abbot of St. Thierry,* ed. J. Carfantan (Kalamazoo, 1987), 65-82.

22. *De Miraculis* II.4-23; ed. D. Bouthillier (*CCCM* 83; Turnhout, 1988), 103-39.

23. Cf. James 54 (Letter 19, 5).

that moment for Cistercians to pit their strength against Cluny. From Bernard's own declarations it appears that he did not want to make special propaganda for Cîteaux; moreover, the text of these writings shows that his main preoccupation was to contrast the life which the Cluniacs should lead with the way of life which was in fact customary there when Peter the Venerable began his tenure. An explanation for Bernard's intervention in this matter is offered by his relation to the Benedictine abbot William of St.-Thierry, a man who had a deep influence on him. William asked Bernard to write the *Apologia,* which the latter considered as *scriptitare* and therefore as a rewriting (i.e., of the letter to Robert). Consequently, William asked Bernard to do his work again, namely to replace this letter with another text, because it had not become sufficiently clear that the objections against Cluny, voiced in the letter, concerned only those who had abandoned the life which should ideally be lived there.

Abbot William is better known from his writings than from his life, which on the whole has been insufficiently studied. We cannot fill this lacuna here either, but we can safely maintain that William long devoted himself to the introduction of reforms within the old Benedictine monasticism. By this he caused a good deal of annoyance to the Cluniacs. While Peter the Venerable later reached a relationship with Bernard of Clairvaux which he describes as friendship, he consistently ignored William of St.-Thierry and even avoided him explicitly. Cluny entered into a communion of prayer with St.-Thierry only when William had abdicated as abbot of St.-Thierry and retired to a Cistercian monastery.[24] Apparently they were not willing to forgive William his influence on Bernard of Clairvaux regarding Bernard's intervention at Cluny. How great William's influence on Bernard was is clear, for that matter, also from other things, for example, the fact that Bernard later, at the instigation of his friend, also attacked the opinions of Peter Abelard.[25] It appears, moreover, from the first book of the *Vita prima Bernardi,* which the former abbot of St.-Thierry wrote during Bernard's lifetime, that William knew Bernard well. But it is striking that in a later conflict between traditional Cluniac opinions and reformatory tendencies within the old monasticism, led by the abbots in the archdiocese of Reims and headed by William of St.-Thierry, Bernard took no sides. He let William fight this battle all by

24. Rheims City Library ms. 349 (obituary martyrology of St.-Thierry), folio 19 verso.

25. See chapter VIII below.

himself, a battle against the most implacable opponent of Pons de Melgueil, Matthieu d'Albano.[26]

That brings us finally to the question of what Bernard's intervention in the controversy at Cluny meant in relation to the Cistercians' attitude vis-à-vis the old monasticism. What Bernard tried to achieve, under orders from William of St.-Thierry, was not accomplished. The reform-minded camp at Cluny suffered a definitive defeat through the events accompanying the return of Pons, and Bernard himself suffered a loss of his good name. In general, Bernard's intentions were probably badly understood, both among the Cluniacs and elsewhere. At least, that is the impression one gets from the "answer of the old monasticism to the manifesto of Bernard of Clairvaux," written in England. Its probable author, Hugo of Amiens, may have written his response in consultation with Matthieu d'Albano, with whom he was at least in contact.

%%   %%

IT IS REMARKABLE that Bernard afterward abstained from all criticism of Cluny, even on the occasion of conflicts that arose between the two orders about political and material interests.[27] Nor did he intervene in connection with the reform movement of the Benedictine abbots in the archdiocese of Reims. He expressed his approval in general terms but did not assist at their meeting, to which he had been invited, leaving William of St.-Thierry, as mentioned above, to reply on his own to Matthieu d'Albano's attacks on these reform projects. More important in this connection is probably the fact that Bernard in his letters to Peter the Venerable nowhere acceded to the latter's repeated request to collaborate in reducing the animosity between Cluniacs and Cistercians, which according to the abbot of Cluny manifested itself at every meeting between monks of both orders.[28]

It is furthermore quite remarkable that from the perspective of the Cistercians nothing more was written against Cluny after Bernard had written the letter to Robert and the *Apologia*. Only after the death of the

26. A. H. Bredero, "William of Saint Thierry on the Crossroads of the Monastic Currents of His Time," in Carfantan, ed., 113-37.

27. Cf. G. Constable, *Cluniac Studies* (London, 1980), chapters VIII and X.

28. A. H. Bredero, "Saint Bernard in His Relations to Peter the Venerable," in *Bernardus Magister: Papers Presented at the Nonacentenary Celebration of the Birth of Saint Bernard of Clairvaux,* ed. J. R. Sommerfeld (Kalamazoo, 1992), 315-47.

abbot of Clairvaux did the *Dialogus duorum monachorum* appear, between 1155 and 1157. From this document one can conclude that the Cistercians had developed a strong aversion for Cluny, which, however, was no longer being expressed in writing during Bernard's lifetime. One explanation is that in the region where this *Dialogus* originated the rapid growth of the Cistercian order had come to a standstill; by contrast, the number of abbeys belonging to Hirsau was rapidly increasing, and these abbeys were there considered as belonging to Cluny. Consequently, we probably cannot take this text as completely representative of the Cistercian order. But what it unjustly states, namely that Molesme (where at the time the foundation of Cîteaux was being prepared) was a Cluniac abbey which therefore rebelled against its order, agrees to a certain extent with what is said about Molesme in the *Exordium magnum,* a text at the time much more representative of this order.

This Cistercian text, written at Clairvaux at the end of the twelfth century and dealing among other things with the beginning of this order, also links the rise of Cîteaux with the decline of Cluny.[29] This representation of things clearly deviates from what had earlier been narrated by the *Exordium parvum* and the *Exordium Cisterciense.* There we read only this: that the founders of Cîteaux had separated themselves from the community of Molesme because of the decay of traditional monasticism, which nonetheless continued to show itself in this young community. So we may conclude that the aversion for Cluny, expressed in the *Dialogus duorum monachorum,* had been increased more in general in the Cistercian order.[30]

This animosity apparently developed gradually among Cistercians against Cluniac monasticism, which was considered to be representative of the old monasticism and which indeed fulfilled this role to an important degree. Here the polemical writings of Bernard, with which he had intervened in a controversy at Cluny, came to perform an important function. From the manuscript tradition we know that especially the *Apologia* spread very widely. On the contrary, a work like the *Dialogus duorum monachorum* hardly spread at all. True enough, it contained many quotations from Bernard's polemics with Cluny, but from a literary point of view it bore no comparison with what had been written by the abbot of Clairvaux.

29. *Exordium Magnum,* II.9, ed. B. Grieser (Rome, 1961), 59-60.
30. A. H. Bredero, *Cluny et Citeaux au douzieme siècle. L'histoire d'une controverse monastique* (Maarssen/Lille, 1985).

The reproaches he had uttered against the traditional Cluny were contained in a text that could not be equaled. This probably explains in part why no further polemical writings from the Cistercians against Cluny appeared, not to mention the fact that Bernard did not want a continuation of this polemic. But in the opinion of the Cistercians themselves, what could be said against the Cluniacs had already been said by Bernard in such a way that nothing needed to be added to it. It was sufficient to read these texts. But in all this, the Cistercians did not realize that the abbot of Clairvaux had written this polemic with an apparently different intention from that with which people read it afterward.

VI

Saints and Sainthood[1]

❧   ❧

1. INTRODUCTION

IN NO PERIOD during the Christian era have the saints received more attention than during the Middle Ages. Historians disagree about the place of the saints in medieval society. But whatever their place in society was, the medieval saints have caused considerable controversy among those who have in later times looked back on those centuries. These controversies began already in the sixteenth century. During the Reformation statues of saints were destroyed, their names were eliminated from the calendar, and this "idolatrous cult" was renounced. The Counter-Reformation preserved veneration of the saints with the argument that a person is entitled to intercession by them in his or her relationship with God and is able to attain holiness by following their example.

Some champions of veneration of the saints went beyond this. They did not limit themselves to publishing pious texts, which today we might entitle "daily devotions with the saints," but also produced historical studies designed to separate fiction about the saints from fact. This required, first of all, the publication of all the different versions of all the

---

1. The first two sections of this chapter appeared first in the Dutch predecessor of this book, the second having been given as a lecture in 1981. The third section is a revision of a review article, "De heiligheid van Bernard van Clairvaux," *Bijdragen* 39 (1978), 310-21.

Lives of saints, as far as we know of them. This resulted in a monumental work, which now consists of the sixty-seven folio volumes of the *Acta Sanctorum,* in which these *Vitae* and the accompanying *miracula,* together with accounts of the elevation and translation of the saints' relics and accounts of canonizations were published in the order in which the saints' days appear in the liturgical year.

In many ways this publication is already outdated, though it remains indispensable for our knowledge of many of the saints. We now possess better editions of many of the texts that appear in the *Acta Sanctorum,* additional documentation, and above all better, or at least more up-to-date, commentaries. The credit for all this is to a large degree due to the same group of people who furnished us with the folio series, the generations of specialized Jesuit scholars usually referred to as the Bollandists. The progress in this field is due mainly to the present generation of Bollandists and their immediate predecessors. Study of medieval veneration of saints, which seems so popular at present, profits immensely from their work.

The point of departure for many of these studies is no longer — at least not exclusively — the discipline of church history, which for centuries was responsible for this research. Other methods are now used, and there is close cooperation with scholars who are not historians but sociologists, cultural anthropologists, or folklorists. Apart from the philological skills needed for understanding of the texts — which is often lacking in our time — study of the lives and veneration of the saints has developed from a church-dominated discipline into a field of study within the humanities. This does have some disadvantages where the shift is too radical, since knowledge of liturgy is essential if such research is not to deteriorate into amateurism.

The main goals of these studies for many scholars of today are understanding of the medieval person in the context of the society of that era, understanding of the mentality of the time as it expressed itself in faith and superstition, and understanding of the way people related to the powers and forces that superseded their human capacities. Modern researchers are far from unanimous in their interpretations of these matters, because their own presuppositions play an important role. Some are inclined to see the veneration of saints in isolation from the Christian faith because they do not see the phenomenon of saints as a credible reality. Others are inclined to relate the cult of the saints intimately to the Christian faith and to view it primarily as an expression of that faith. Both groups may learn from each other.

One remarkable example is the progress in interpretation of the saints' Lives. A *Vita* is no longer seen as a source that tells us exactly what happened. In the past this view led many to disregard such sources or to study them solely with the aim of branding them as obvious frauds. Now the consensus is that these texts do contain many implausibilities, but historians have learned to ask what lies behind these implausibilities.

An example of this change in approach is seen in a paper read a few years ago by F. W. N. Hugenholtz in the abbey of Egmond and dealing with St. Aldelbert, the patron saint of the monastery and of its medieval predecessor.[2] The two *Vitae* of Adelbert date from the tenth and the twelfth centuries. In both texts Adelbert remains a somewhat vague individual, and there has been much discussion of which text may be considered reliable, since they seem to deal with two completely different saints. Hugenholtz looks at both texts chiefly within the context of the times in which they were written and compares the roles in relation to the abbey that the saint plays in the two texts. His conclusions are both surprising and convincing:

In the tenth-century text Adelbert is portrayed as a saint whose accomplishments were so enormous in God's eyes that he was given the power to work many miracles of healing and salvation. These accomplishments gave the newly established abbey publicity, fame, and, possibly, added income. Little is said about Adelbert himself.

This biographical reticence is also seen in the later *Vita*, which differs from the older text mainly in its choice of miracle accounts: Almost all of its miracles are recent as the text is written. Since the monastery now has property and is a well-established institution, the saint demonstrates his power on the abbey's behalf in totally different ways than he does in the tenth-century accounts. He now protects the abbey and its property against the evil people around it and against floods and serves as the guide in the construction of a new church. Because the needs of the monastery have changed, the saint's role has changed.

The manuscript tradition of the earlier *Vita* is much more abundant than that of the later one. This makes it clear that the need for the twelfth-century *Vita* was not that of pilgrims. So the monks of Egmond had some other reason to write it than the simple need to adapt the

---

2. "Adelbert in twee gedaanten," *Benedictijns Tijdschrift* 45 (1984), 47-56; G. N. M. Vis, "Sint Adelbert en andere structuren," in *Heiligenlevens, annalen en kronieken* (Hilversum, 1990), 35-54.

presentation of the saint to a changed situation. In the earlier *Vita* popular veneration is focused on a well dug with the aid of the saint's intervention. But the well, which is where Adelbert was originally buried, was not located on the abbey grounds. His remains were later moved to the abbey, and therefore the well does not receive further attention in the later *Vita*. The later text focuses emphatically on the remains of the saint, which the faithful can now venerate at the abbey itself. Therefore we may suppose that the monks wrote the new *Vita* in order to gain a larger share of the revenues brought to Egmont by pilgrims.

Hugenholtz's approach to these two *Vitae* has the advantage of not attributing ideas or intentions to medieval people that were unknown at the time. There is often a strong temptation to do so when interpreting forms of veneration of saints. Often this leads to the hasty conclusion that a saint's cult had little or no intimate relationship with the medieval church, especially if it is studied in isolation from its context and if the study fails to consider the broader medieval setting in which these matters must primarily be seen.

Stimulus for such isolated study is found in late medieval veneration of the saints, which ignored the authority of the highest ecclesiastical institutions, which by that time had acquired the exclusive right to determine whether a person whom people wanted to venerate qualified for "the honor of the altars." The late medieval period does show an increasing rift between popular belief and ecclesiastical authority. But this does not imply that there was no longer any relationship between popular belief and church teachings concerning sainthood and the significance of the saints for the faithful.

The deeper meaning of veneration of saints also demands attention and is insufficiently understood if we look only at the magical aspects of veneration of saints, which we find in particular in what might be called "hagiotherapy." In curative powers every saint was regarded as a specialist. Every ailment or disability had its own saint. But we still need to ask whether the saints that were venerated without Rome's approval were regarded as no longer belonging to the church. Was veneration of them neglected in church liturgy?

This question demands extensive and laborious study and cannot be fully addressed here. But we do want to touch on one aspect of that question, namely, ecclesiastical control over the veneration of saints. This control developed gradually, until, in the twelfth century, it had become the sole privilege of the pope. By that time the tradition of veneration of saints was already established and was to continue in the church. That Rome, having gained control over veneration of saints, later lost it to a considerable extent, was probably due less to an increase in religious expression outside the church than to wrongful exercise of the right of control. This relationship between church authority and veneration of saints is discussed further in the next major section of this chapter (see below, pp. 158ff.).

⟡   ⟡

MEDIEVAL SAINTS provide historians with many different challenges. The question arises whether their sainthood had significance only for that time or still has some meaning today. In answering this question we are not just dealing with purely legendary saints, whose life stories are fragmentary or even consist primarily of clichés and stereotypes. We are rather dealing with people living in medieval society who came to be recognized as saints, though they did not present themselves as such — Francis and Bernard, for instance. The medieval definition of sainthood was not humanly oriented but looked to God. His grace, it was said, elected a person to sainthood, and that election began before birth and was manifested by what God effected through that person. Of course the saint also distinguished himself or herself by exercising virtue, perhaps even in heroic ways. But since sainthood had to be recognized by ecclesiastical authorities, hagiographies were adapted to the standard norms for sanctity.

The historian who studies a saint of the Middle Ages whose *Vita* presents the saint not as he or she really was but in accordance with the criteria of the canonization process has a fascinating task in rediscovering the human person in that saint. In the course of research the historian will have to ask how much of a saint that person really was. But what place should be assigned to ecclesiastically recognized sainthood in this evaluation? There are two extremes from which to choose: The historian can from the beginning think in terms of the saint's sainthood, since it has been recognized by ecclesiastical authority. The historian's judgment of any act of that person can thus be based on that premise of sainthood and can exclude any further evaluation of the person. The other extreme would be to ignore the sainthood of the subject of study altogether and even to dispute its validity.

This question is not at all purely theoretical. In the actual practice of historical research of medieval saints both approaches have been exercised. But both result in serious problems. If we ignore the sainthood of a medieval

155

person, we disregard the value that was attached to that person in the world in which he or she lived. In order to justify this approach, the researcher will often be inclined to look for impure motives behind the acts of the saint in order to negate the sanctity attributed to him or her. The other point of departure is just as objectionable, since it continues a cultic approach, which has portrayed this person as a saint already for centuries. It thus gives this ahistorical method a pseudo-scholarly appearance.

The latter approach was very common in the nineteenth century, particularly in France — a country which has had a substantial number of saints. In a supposedly historical biography the *Vita* account, which would contain some amount of historical data — was simply repeated and supplemented with other historical and geographical facts. The account was thus supposed to have evolved into a scholarly biography. Hagiography occupied a large place in historical publications of the nineteenth century. Interest in this approach came largely out of reaction to treatment of medieval saints during the Enlightenment, when historically significant saints were systematically reviled.

The Enlightenment approach is no longer current in scholarly publications, but the shift away from it has resulted in an impasse in the writing of scholarly biographies of medieval saints. To mention a clear example: There have been many new publications about Bernard of Clair-vaux since Vacandard wrote his *Vie de saint Bernard* at the end of the last century — a work in which he already tried to avoid such pseudo-scholarly hagiography.[3] But more recent attempts to rewrite Bernard's biography have proven to be restatements of Vacandard's work, even though he was not able to distance himself completely from a cultic approach.

Even today we find remnants of this cultic approach in the work of historians. Or we see amalgamations of cultic and historical approaches, sometimes at congresses honoring the centenaries of particular saints' deaths or births.

Such congresses began to be held in the nineteenth century. They seem to have arisen as a substitute for liturgical commemoration of the saints, which was losing much of its splendor. Many saints belonged to the religious orders, which now have a less important or at least different

3. *Vie de Saint Bernard* (2 vols.; 1895; repr. Paris, until 1928).

place in society. The decline of liturgy at centennial celebrations is, in fact, somewhat compensated by the commemorative congresses and colloquiums and by the accompanying publications. This was the case in 1980, which was proclaimed the year of St. Benedict, the spiritual father of Europe. In 1985, 750 years after the death of Elizabeth of Thuringia, a major exhibition was held in Marburg, where she died, and a collection of historical articles, many of them excellent, was published. But to what extent is this scholarship and to what extent is it cult?

Nineteen eighty-four offered several such commemorative events. Eight hundred fifty years earlier Norbert of Xanten, the founder of the Premonstratensian order, had died as bishop of Magdeburg. Historians paid tribute in a collection of articles. In Grenoble, Bruno of Cologne was commemorated, together with the order he founded, because he had established the Grand Chartreuse nine centuries before. An international congress and a manuscript exhibition were held, and the delegates to the congress attended a massive celebration of the Eucharist held according to the Carthusian rites. In the Netherlands interest in Gerhard Groote and the Devotio Moderna, which he founded, was revived by commemoration of his death 600 years earlier. In 1985 an international congress on "The Gregorian Reform and Europe" was held in Salerno in southern Italy, where nine centuries earlier Pope Gregory VII had been buried. There was a church ceremony and even a papal visit in connection with the congress.

It is not my intention to say anything against these commemorative events. But they underline the question of how the historian who wants to study a saint should approach the saint's sainthood. The third main section of this chapter will focus particularly on St. Bernard of Clairvaux, the dominant figure in the first half of the twelfth century. In 1953, 800 years after Bernard's death, an almost unending series of publications, of very unequal quality, appeared about him. In many of them, though they dealt with him as a historical person and with his significance in history, the question of his identity as a saint was clearly at issue and received controversial answers.

Since then this question has not lost its currency. It has come to be focused particularly on how much we can know about Bernard's actual sanctity and on how important this aspect should be in historical discussion of him. The general opinion has been — and many still adhere to this view — that God chose and sanctified Bernard even before his birth and that his human accomplishments and failures are therefore of only marginal importance. Diametrically opposed to this position is the view, which I will defend, that Bernard's sainthood, which largely escapes human observation, can be considered as an additional factor in study of him, not as essential. We can study to what degree he developed — with all his human qualities and defects — into a saint.

In the mid-1970s Dom Jean Leclercq, who in earlier publications had given priority to the sainthood of this Cistercian abbot in his evaluations of Bernard as a historical figure, once again dealt with this question and tried to shift somewhat toward the other camp, but without abandoning the priority of Bernard's sainthood. It must be emphasized that Leclercq is a foremost scholar of this medieval saint and therefore deserves the attention of all who want to study Bernard. I have given him this attention in the extensive review article presented below as the third main section of this chapter.

2. VENERATION OF SAINTS AND THE AUTHORITY OF THE CHURCH

IN DECEMBER 1963, during the third session of the Second Vatican Council, the Constitution on the Sacred Liturgy was accepted. Chapter five of this document deals with the liturgical year, and the last part of the chapter deals with veneration of saints.[4] The cult of the saints is sanctioned there in accordance with church tradition. This includes veneration of authentic relics and of images, but one restriction was made: Feasts of saints may not occupy a more important place in the liturgy than the regular celebrations of the mysteries of salvation. Probably to prevent this from happening, it was added that feasts of saints who were venerated only locally or nationally or who were of significance only to a specific religious community were to be deleted from the general liturgical calendar. This stipulation almost seems to reverse canonizations of earlier times; some speak of "decanonizations." The Constitution does not mention any of these deleted saints by name, but the rule applies, for instance, to St. Christopher, the patron saint of travelers, and St. Nicholas, the bishop of Myra who gained greater fame from a secularized cult than from the legend of his sanctity.[5]

4. Art. III = *COD* 839.
5. C. W. Jones, *Saint Nicholas of Myra, Bari, and Manhattan: Biography of a Legend* (Chicago, 1978).

Exactly four centuries earlier, in December 1563, the fathers assembled at the twenty-fifth session of the Council of Trent discussed invocation and veneration of saints and relics and images of saints. Their decree, longer than that of Vatican II, was primarily a defense of invocation and veneration. According to the teachings of the church the saints reign together with Christ and offer their prayers to God on behalf of humankind. Therefore it is good and profitable, the decree stated, to plead with them in order to receive God's favors through Jesus Christ.[6] Veneration of relics was defended with the argument that the bodies of the saints are living members of Christ and temples of the Holy Spirit. Those who taught that veneration of those bodies by the faithful was futile were condemned. But the faithful were to be instructed that the fruit of veneration is not merely blessings and rewards. The saints' miracles and salutary examples are given to the faithful so that they may thank God and in their daily conduct follow that example and may more fervently pray to God.

Abuses in the veneration of saints resulting from ignorance, superstition, or financial greed were criticized at Trent, as were gluttonous feasts and drinking bouts in connection with saints' feasts and visits to relics. Secular images were barred from church buildings. Unusual statues were not to be erected without approval from the bishop, who also had to approve new miracles and new relics, if there were plans to start a cult around them. In case of any conflict the bishop was to consult with his archbishop and fellow bishops so as to avoid undesirable decisions. The council decree prudently maintained the practices associated with veneration of saints as they had been prescribed and accepted by church authorities throughout the Middle Ages, without, however, referring directly to any particular decisions or pronouncements except those of the Second Council of Nicea, held in 787.[7]

It appears from existing council pronouncements that the Fourth Lateran Council, held in 1215, was in fact the only medieval general council to deal with veneration of saints. There is no indication that the subject was even discussed at the other councils. The interest of the Fourth Lateran Council was limited and was focused entirely on veneration of relics. It prohibited exhibition, veneration, and sale of old relics not kept in a reliquary. This stipulation was to prevent fraud with relics. No one was allowed to initiate veneration of new relics without papal approval. This

6. *COD* 774-76.
7. *COD* 137, ll. 8-25.

constitution of the council (number 62) did not address veneration of saints as such, but rather only matters in which the faithful could be deceived.[8]

On this basis one might conclude that the church did little during the Middle Ages to regulate veneration of saints and relics. But procedures for canonization were in fact established by the ecclesiastical authorities, even though this is not mentioned in council decisions. The gradual evolution of these procedures followed the development of veneration of saints as a whole, at least insofar as veneration took place in the context of the church's liturgy. No matter what popular devotions originated outside the church, the desire for ecclesiastical recognition — so that the cult of a particular saint might be embedded in the liturgy and so that his or her relics might be venerated in a church as those of a recognized saint — was the most prominent characteristic of medieval veneration of saints. Many Christians repeatedly did their utmost to procure such recognition for their saints, as is evident from the many documents about canonizations that have been preserved and from the many *Vitae* of saints written for just that purpose of winning ecclesiastical approval.

At a rather early date the church began to exert control over veneration of saints, but it was not always the same church agency that exerted this authority from time to time. The oldest known precept with regard to this subject was issued in 401 by an African council in Carthage. It specified that fictitious martyrs and those whose sanctity was uncertain were not to be honored.[9] This principle has been repeated through the ages and from the sixth century on has been included in collections of ecclesiastical canons. Charlemagne issued the same rule in 789 in his *Admonitio Generalis,* addressed to the clergy of his empire.[10]

As we have noted, there was during the Middle Ages considerable difference in the levels of authority from which these pronouncements concerning veneration of saints originated. But these differences do not reflect simple arbitrariness. They had to do both with the ways in which veneration of saints changed and with developments in the church's authority structures. If both lines of development are taken into consideration — which is not usually the case — it becomes clear that the gulf between liturgical commemoration of saints and veneration of saints in popular

---

8. *COD* 263f.

9. Canon XV (*PL* LXXXIV, 212). Cf. E. W. Kemp, *Canonization and Authority in the Western Church* (Oxford, 1948), 15.

10. Kemp, 25, 36.

belief was not solely the result of the privatization of religion that was occurring at that time (see above, pp. 40-44). It was also closely related to the increasing role of papal authority in the canonization process — the only control mechanism for the veneration of saints at that time. Papal control in this area was very gradually extended and was not just the result of a policy of the curia to strengthen papal authority in the church and papal power in the world.

It is not easy to determine how these two factors, developments in the veneration of saints and in the church's authority structures, interacted, since we have to consider a number of additional complications. One is that the decision regarding the veneration of saints reached during the African council differed in meaning from what Charlemagne included in his *Admonitio Generalis*. The decision of 401 was rooted in a concern that the same cult that had developed near the tombs of martyrs might be duplicated at the graves of others whose sanctity was less certain. But in Carolingian times this concern was replaced by fear that human remains be mistakenly identified as relics of a saint. Furthermore, at first Charlemagne did not quite understand the nature of the problem and thought that he was dealing with sacrificial rites, invocations, and conjurations of pagan origin, which would evoke the anger rather than the compassion of the saints venerated in such ways.

Another complication arises from the shift in the meaning of the word *sanctus* ("holy, saint"). The tombs that were venerated in the fifth century were those of martyrs, those who had been recognized as such by the local churches to which they had belonged or for some other reason were commemorated for their martyrdom. Martyrs were registered in the *martyrologia* of churches and were liturgically commemorated, each on the day on which he or she had been killed and had entered eternal bliss. Churches exchanged *martyrologia* in an attempt to bring more uniformity to the cult of the martyrs.

But the development of the cult of the martyrs met a complication in the restriction of the meaning of *sanctus*. The word was originally used of any dead person who continued to be remembered as devout. But after the fifth century *sanctus* was reserved for authentic saints. From then on martyrs were not the only saints who were admitted. The *sancti* commemorated in a particular monastery, such as the deceased members of the particular community, could be listed not only in that monastery's *martyrologium,* but also in *martyrologia* of other places. This resulted in a rapid increase in the number of saints whose names were known.

There was at first no way of keeping this increase in check, and this was true also with regard to relics of the saints in Gaul and to some extent beyond the Rhine. There was an enormous demand for relics because new shrines were being built continuously. Together with other treasures these relics could be bought in Italy, where Christianity could boast a longer past. It was often claimed that relics had been obtained supernaturally (see above, pp. 92f.). The *Vita* of St. Remaclus, the bishop of Maastricht († after 670), tells us, for instance, how he traveled to Rome in connection with the founding of the monasteries of Stavelot and Malmedy. In Rome he prayed and fasted until he could return with relics of St. Peter. We are told that Chrodegangus of Metz (†776) stole the relics of St. Gorgonius in Rome, being assisted by the saint so that his pursuers had to flee because of fog and thunder, while he was able to continue his journey in the sunshine with the treasured relics.

Not all relics were obtained in Italy. St. Meinolf († ca. 857) founded the Böddeke convent at a location shown to him in a vision. This saved him money, since at the same spot many relics were found; at least that is what his *Vita* tells us. The relics may have been of dubious origin, though the same would have been true if the relics had been bought in Italy. There the deals were also sometimes made under less than supernatural circumstances. We know that Deusdonit, a deacon in Rome who was in charge of the tombs, on request and against payment, robbed graves and furnished relics authenticated by an accompanying *Vita*.

We also meet suspicion of the authenticity of saints themselves in Carolingian times. A council held in Frankfurt in 794 prohibited the veneration and invocation of new saints. Only those who had been chosen on the basis of martyrdom or virtuous life were to be venerated in the churches. The *Capitularies* of Thionville, issued by Charlemagne in 805-6, contained a new directive: No new saint without a reliable tradition could be venerated without episcopal approval.

Eight years later, at the Council of Mainz, Charlemagne forbade the translation (removal) of saints' bodies to new locations without prior consultation with the relevant prince or bishop and without approval of a holy synod.[11] This addition to what had been decreed in the *Capitularies* of Thionville was a prerequisite for any actual control over initiatives for new cults, since control of the relics of newly discovered saints would by itself not solve the problems of the veneration of inauthentic saints. The

11. *MGH Concilia* II, 272.

rule that no new cult be established without approval could easily be evaded if physical remains could be translated without the consent of ecclesiastical or secular authorities, who were willing to enforce the new rule. The bishop or prince had to give permission, not only for the elevation of any new saint, that is, for exhumation of the saint's remains, but also for the translation of those remains, which would establish a new cult in the particular diocese. When such permission was given, it amounted, in principle, to episcopal canonization.

꛰   ꛰

LATER EVENTS drastically reduced the actual effect of these stipulations. The disintegration of the Carolingian Empire ruled out approval by secular rulers. Unapproved translations of relics became frequent with the Viking, Magyar, and Muslim invasions. Because of the troubled times many monks fled their monasteries and in their exodus carried off — if possible — their monasteries' relics, with or without the appropriate *Vitae*. Sometimes these relics began a long sojourn, as in the case of those of St. Phillibert. In the seventh century this saint had preached the gospel in the Vendée. After he died, his body was kept in Noirmoutiers, a monastery that he founded. When the monks were forced to leave the monastery in 837, they took the relics of their saint with them. After a temporary stay in at least five different monasteries, these relics were finally moved, thirty-nine years later, to the abbey of Tournus, north of Mâcon, where they still are.

Such forced moves caused many *Vitae* to be completely or partially lost. Because of their value for the relics, the *Vitae* would be rewritten. This contributed to a strong revival of hagiography in the tenth century. Moreover, even some *Vitae* that had not been lost were rewritten, partly because they now had to meet new requirements — since the functions of particular saints had changed and political and economic circumstances had changed. For instance, a monastery with a claim on a piece of property could give the claim sacral power by establishing a link between the property and the life of the community's holy founder.

This rewriting of *Vitae* caused a great number of legends to grow up around saints' lives. And some of the biographies were entirely fictitious. If, for instance, a grave was found in the ruins of a destroyed monastery, it could be identified as that of a fabricated saint.

It is impossible to determine how often such things occurred. But from what we have said so far it will be clear that there was a great demand for saints and their protection. This demand and specifically the demand for relics, which were thought to possess the power of the saints, explains the enormous number of thefts of human remains that happened in the ninth through the eleventh centuries.[12] In 860 the body of Saint Foy was stolen by a monk of Conques from Agen. The account of this theft says that it was carried out for the sake of the health of people in the area of the monastery and for the deliverance of many. A similar argument is found in regard to the eleventh-century account of the translation of St. Valentine's head to the abbey of Jumièges in France. One of the abbey's monks had stolen it in Rome.

In spite of these more or less frequent abuses, it is certain that some did in fact obey the Carolingian directives regarding the exhumation and translation of saints' remains. The small amount of information that we possess seems to indicate that this was the case in monasteries that had been won for the reform of religious life that began in Carolingian times, even though there are examples to the contrary. An example of such adherence to the rules is found in the account of the translation of the relics of St. Eugenius, a Spanish bishop of early date. They were kept in Saint-Denis, an old and famous monastery near Paris, from which many other relics were distributed. The reformist abbot Gerard of Brogne (†959) succeeded in obtaining them for his monastery and took them with him. But he interrupted his journey to request the approval of the bishop of Liège in order to legalize the introduction of the cult of this saint in his diocese. He received the requested permission.

The passage that tells us of this detail was not incorporated into the account of the translation just to mention the stipulation, but because of what happened later. When the Brogne monastery developed into a popular place of pilgrimage because of the relics of St. Eugenius and thus unfavorably affected pilgrimages to other sanctuaries, the victims complained to the bishop. He then wanted to rescind his approval. But before he came to a decision, he was struck by a fatal illness. He regarded this as a sign from heaven and charged the representative of the plaintiffs with rehabilitating the relics of St. Eugenius. Subsequently the bishop regained his health.[13]

Although the rules governing the episcopal right of canonization remained valid and at times even operative, they were not elaborated

12. P. J. Geary, *Furta Sacra* (Princeton, 1978).
13. *Translatio Sancti Eugenii* (Analecta Bollandiana, 3; 1884), 29-57.

further in canon law. The decisions of the African council and the Council of Mainz were repeated in the canon law collections of Burchard of Worms (†1025) and Ivo of Chartres (†1117) and in the *Decretum* of Gratian, which was completed in 1143. In the second half of the twelfth century the decisions of the Council of Mainz were even interpreted in a way that was unfavorable for the bishops. The council statement referred to "prince and bishops," and this was now given the meaning of *pope* and bishops. Canonization thus became practically impossible without papal involvement. But it seems strange that in the preceding period no precise rule was established regarding episcopal authority to canonize, since recorded events indicate that episcopal canonization had by the tenth and eleventh century become an established procedure.

The nature of the procedure that was followed in episcopal canonization offers an explanation for this. It had much less to do with legal assent to the cult of the new saint than with the bishop's participation in the cult. He did not communicate his approval in a letter, but was present at the elevation of the saint. The remains were then solemnly placed in an altar, which was usually erected over the saint's grave. Often the bishop was accompanied by his colleagues from surrounding dioceses. This meant that episcopal canonization was first of all a cultic matter.

The situation was different when the bishop had to intervene in conflicts regarding the authenticity of relics. Such conflicts could flare up when translations of relics took place, requiring the bishop to judge between two competing sanctuaries, each of which wanted to establish a monopoly for its relics or to break the other's monopoly. We have already encountered this in the translation of the relics of St. Eugenius by Gerard of Brogne. We meet something similar in the account of the translation of St. Landulf and his companions to the abbey of St. Bavo in Ghent.

Landulf and his companions had been buried on property owned by the monastery but not at the abbey itself. A cult had developed around their graves and had the approval of the bishop of Liège. Because of his sanction, a translation of their relics to the abbey was possible. But this was opposed by the monks of the abbey of St. Blandina, also in Ghent. They claimed the relics were fraudulent and insisted that they be subjected to an ordeal by fire. But new miracles were happening near the remains, which had in the meantime been translated to the abbey, and the monks of St. Bavo themselves turned to the bishop. He put the controversy on the agenda of a synod, where the view of the monks of St. Bavo was accepted. The bishop ordered that a report be made of the authentic miracles of Landulf and renewed his approval for the cult.[14] This report more clearly showed the canonical authority of the bishop, but without any direct link to his right of canonization.

Bishops also used their jurisdiction in regard to veneration of saints to strengthen their prestige by canonizing their predecessors in the episcopal office. In earlier centuries abbots had arranged for the canonization of the founders of their monasteries, and this had enhanced the prestige of the abbeys. It seemed that in the tenth century it was the dioceses' turn. Shortly after 900 Bishop Rainon of Angers, for instance, arranged for the translation of the relics of one of his predecessors, St. Mauril. Mauril had supposedly been a disciple of St. Ambrose, the fourth-century bishop of Milan revered as a church father. Prior to this, Bishop Rainon had arranged for a *Vita* of Mauril, the authorship of which was ascribed to Venantius Fortunatus († ca. 600), an author of *Vitae* of much earlier date.

This case was hardly unique. We know of translations and canonizations in at least ten other dioceses of bishops of much farther back in history. This was done to reinforce the living bishop's authority, even in relation to his own metropolitan. The canonization of an ancient predecessor allowed a bishop to call on the antiquity of his see and to lay hold of the sacral power of a sainted predecessor. There are even some examples of canonizations of completely legendary predecessors, presented as disciples of the apostles.

In Trier, a city dating back to Roman times, for instance, the remains of Bishop Celsus, who had supposedly died there in 150, were found in 980. Celsus, it was claimed, had been a disciple of Bishop Eucherius, who was also venerated in Trier as a saint and was said to have been a disciple of the apostle Peter. In the diocese of Toul an even more direct link with St. Peter was established. There an early bishop, Mansuetus († ca. 375), was furnished with a *Vita*, written at the request of Bishop Gerard of Toul by Adso of Montier-en-Dèr (†992), a well-known author of the time, according to which Mansuetus had been a disciple of St. Peter.

A similar pious fraud may have occurred in the diocese of Metz, though the facts are less certain. According to an old legend mentioned in the eighth century by Paulus Diaconus in a short treatise *(libellus)* about the episcopal succession in Metz, the first bishop, Clement, had been a disciple of St. Peter. Two of his own disciples had succeeded him, and they,

14. *Ex adventu et elevatione S. Landoaldi sociorumque eius* = MGH Scriptores XV, 2, 601-7.

in turn, were succeeded by a Bishop Patiens, who came from the East and claimed to have been a disciple of the aged apostle St. John. The story was corroborated by the miraculous fact that Patiens, though a Greek, was able to understand the language of the inhabitants of Metz.

We do not know where this story originated. There is only one *Vita* of Patiens, by an unknown author, and the account of the rediscovery of his remains — his relics — is missing. The text of this *Vita* cannot be older than the eighth century and we may reasonably assume that it dates from no later than the tenth century, since it fits in with the attempts of bishops of the time to use their authority to canonize to initiate cults of their predecessors and, in so doing, to enhance their prestige as bishops.

THE FIRST DOCUMENTED papal canonization dates from the same time, from the end of the tenth century. But it would be presumptuous to suggest that it occurred as a reaction to the attempts of some of the bishops mentioned above. Papal authority in the church was not strong at that time, and there was no question yet of strengthening it. Nevertheless, studies of the development of papal authority to canonize saints link this development with the aspiration for greater papal power. But this aspiration began only in the mid-eleventh century, when the reform that was affecting the church elsewhere also touched Rome. In later times there definitely was such a relationship between the increased involvement of popes in canonizations and the growth of papal authority. But initially papal canonizations did not constitute a break with the still current procedure of episcopal canonization.

That first papal canonization took place in 993, when Bishop Ulrich of Augsburg (†973) was canonized by Pope John XV. This took place during the Roman synod of that year, which was held in the Lateran palace, the papal residence at that time. According to the report of the part of the synod that dealt with this canonization — the only account that has been preserved — Bishop Liotulf of Augsburg took the full initiative. He asked for the floor and requested permission to read the book containing the *Vita* and miracles of Ulrich, which he had in his hands, to those present. And he asked them to agree to the veneration of Ulrich as a saint.

The report sent by John XV in a letter to all archbishops, bishops, and abbots in France and Germany also contained the decision reached in Rome, together with the arguments on which it was based. It was stated that the presence of the Holy Spirit had been undeniable, as the Scriptures indicate, "Where two or three are gathered in my name, I am there among them" (Matthew 18:20). On the basis of this awareness, after hearing the account of Ulrich's life and miracles, the synod decided that he was to be venerated with the most pious affection and the most loyal devotion. The letter ended with a curse aimed at those who would oppose what had been determined by papal authority in the matter of this privilege.[15]

Obviously the form of this canonization decision reflected that of canonizations by bishops, which also resulted from petitions by those who worked zealously for recognition of particular cults. In cases where a bishop took the initiative, the decision was made during a synod and was transmitted to the other bishops in attendance. Such decisions were inspired by the Spirit just as much as a synod presided over by a pope. The elements of the procedure followed during a papal synod — request, information, proclamation — were also customary in the episcopal procedure. The difference is that the papal canonization ended in a proclamation, while the episcopal canonization was followed by solemn elevation or translation. These procedures also followed a papal canonization, of course, but the pope was, as a rule, not involved in them.

An exception to this rule was a canonization by Pope Leo IX. As bishop of Toul before he was appointed pope in 1049 by Emperor Henry III, Leo had commissioned Bishop Gerard, whom we accused of pious fraud above, to write the *Vita* of Mansuetus, Leo's fourth-century predecessor in Toul. This commission implied that Leo was already making preparations for Mansuetus's canonization. But the canonization had not yet taken place when Leo became pope. In February 1050, during Leo's first papal synod, the canonization bull was promulgated and in October of that year Leo was present at Mansuetus's elevation and consecrated the altar containing his relics.

At that moment Pope Leo IX was still also bishop of Toul. That may be why he participated in the actual initiation of the cult, which made the canonization of this saint public. Without cultic initiation a canonization did not lead to liturgical veneration and thus remained incomplete. Initiation of a cult was usually the task of the bishop, and it caused problems if he did not cooperate, as was the case with the second papal canonization of which we are informed, that of the hermit Simeon of Padolirone (†1016).

15. Kemp, 56-58.

Simeon's canonization was proclaimed by Pope Benedict VIII in 1020 in a manner that indicated that he viewed this as primarily the task of the bishop. The marquis of Mantua had asked the pope to consent to the building of a church in which the body of this hermit could find a worthy resting place. In effect, the pope was thus being asked to permit a translation of the hermit's remains. The pope was approached because the bishop of Mantua did not want to cooperate. The hermit may have given the bishop trouble, but we have only indirect information on this point. But we do know that the bishops of Mantua continued to procrastinate in this matter and did not consecrate the church, which in the meantime had been built. In the 1060s the pope had to remind the bishop of Mantua of his duty. At the same time he appointed two bishops to assist the bishop of Mantua with the translation.

This canonization shows that bishops' refusals to approve particular canonizations was one reason for the development of papal canonization. In such instances, when there were solid reasons to canonize a person, the pope apparently had to come to the rescue. A quite remarkable example of this is that of the early abbots of the monastery and order of Cluny. Several of them were canonized by the pope. But the implementation of these canonizations created a problem for bishops. Shortly after its founding the abbey was placed under the immediate jurisdiction of the pope and was thus withdrawn from the jurisdiction of the bishop, whose approval was neither expected nor desired.

The abbots of Cluny from its founding in 910 were Berno (†927), Odo (†942), Aymard (†963), Mayeul (Majolus, †992), Odilo (†1048), and Hugh (†1109). Berno and Aymard were not commemorated as saints, and we do not have *Vitae* for them. The other four have been venerated as saints and their sainthood was recognized by the papacy.

We know with certainty only when Hugh was canonized. His successor, Abbot Pons, commissioned the writing of a *Vita*. The canonization followed in 1120, when Pope Callistus II visited the abbey. The elevation of Hugh's remains, which had been buried behind the main altar of the abbey church, did not occur until 1220. The translation of Abbot Mayeul, who had been buried in the abbey church of Souvigny and canonized about 995, was conducted by Pope Urban II in 1097. The elevation of Abbot Odilo, also buried in Souvigny, was carried out by Peter Cardinal Damian in 1065, and a translation was done in 1345 by the archbishop of Bourges, with the knowledge and probably at the request of Pope Clement VI, who had resided as pope in Avignon from 1342.

Clement had begun his ecclesiastical career as a Benedictine monk and had been abbot of Fécamp, which belonged to the Cluniac order.[16]

These saints were venerated differently by the Cluniac monks than they were by the laity. The monks commemorated them in the liturgy, both in the mass and in the lections of the divine office. In popular devotions the accent was on veneration of relics. The length of time it took between the recognition of these men as saints and their elevations or translations caused little problem within the monasteries because of the manner of commemoration there. But that elevation or translation eventually did take place shows that even in the monasteries canonization without veneration of relics was incomplete.

These papal canonizations show that in the eleventh century this method of canonization did not result from a struggle for greater papal power in the church. Gregory VII, the first pope who deliberately tried to extend his authority, did not canonize any saints. It is therefore not surprising that for a considerable time both papal and episcopal canonizations continued. Ambition for power or for recognition of that power was not the primary concern, but rather the desire to canonize the departed and to open the way to veneration of them. This aspect has received too little attention in studies of the development of papal canonizations.

❧   ❧

WHEN EXACTLY canonizations became an exclusive papal prerogative cannot be determined exactly. Pope Alexander III wrote a letter in 1172 that unequivocally stipulates this right. In this letter, addressed to the king of Sweden, the pope remarked that he had heard that someone was venerated as a saint who had been murdered while he was intoxicated. The pope did not appreciate this and commented further that it will not be permitted to venerate this person publicly without prior approval of the church, even if he had performed many signs and miracles.[17] It has long been thought that only from that moment the pope reserved canonization for himself. The pertinent statement is included in the decretals of Pope Gregory IX, which was published in 1234; there it has become the *locus classicus* for papal reservation of the right of canonization. But it does not tell us when

16. A. H. Bredero, "La canonisation de saint Hugues et celle de ses devanciers," in *Le gouvernement d'Hugues de Semur à Cluny* (Cluny, 1990), 149-71.

17. Kemp, 99.

the pope restricted this right to himself.[18] At that time rights had to be justified by appeal to tradition.

How the pope acquired this exclusive right may to a large extent be deduced from study of the procedures followed in papal canonizations. These procedures underwent a change that distinguished papal canonizations from other canonizations. As we mentioned above, there were three elements in papal canonizations: the request for canonization, the documentation used to justify the request, and the proclamation or promulgation made when the request was approved and the canonization announced. The change in procedure affected the stage of documentation. Originally the petitioner furnished ·the required information during a synod attended by the pope by reading the potential saint's *Vita* — an essential document in most canonizations, since it provided the basis for determining the viability of the candidate's cult.

Society changed in the twelfth century. Rationality gained in importance. *Vitae* came to be judged not only with respect to the proposed cult and the virtue and the miraculous power ascribed to the person whose canonization was desired, but also with regard to the truth of what was narrated. So a reading and subsequent discussion of a *Vita* during a synod were no longer the most appropriate procedure. The first time, as far as we know, that this procedure was set aside was at the canonization of Emperor Henry II. Pope Eugenius III (1145-53) proclaimed Henry's sainthood in 1146, but first demanded more documentation. His predecessor, Pope Innocent II (1130-44), had refused a request for the canonization of King Edward the Confessor, since the petitioners represented too restricted a social group, which limited the possibility of gathering documentation. Similarly, Eugenius said that he was deviating from the normal procedure in the case of Henry II so that he could obtain broader documentation.

It is also remarkable that the petitioners of canonizations only learned about the change in procedure through experience. Since Eugenius did not handle any further requests, petitioners remained ignorant of the change. The same was true during the pontificate of Adrian IV (1154-59). The change became apparent only during the pontificate of Alexander III (1159-81) when the canonization of Bernard of Clairvaux was requested in 1163.

18. *Decretales Gregorii IX* III.45.1; *Corpus Iuris Canonici* II, ed. A. E. Friedberg (1879; repr. Graz, 1959), 35. Cf. A. Vauchez, *La sainteté en Occident aux derniers siècles du moyen âge* (Rome, 1981), 35.

Bernard was not canonized until 1174, by which time Alexander had canonized Edward the Confessor (1161), Anselm of Canterbury (1163), and Thomas à Becket (1173). The canonizations of Edward and Anselm were politically inspired. The pope had a sharp conflict with Emperor Barbarossa, who therefore supported an anti-pope. In an effort to persuade King Henry II of England not to side with Barbarossa, or as a reward to him for not doing so, both canonizations, which had earlier been the subject of much discussion, were finalized without any problem. The canonization of Edward was especially important, as it enhanced the sacral status of the English throne. The canonization of Thomas à Becket was a unique case. This bishop had been murdered in 1170 by some English noblemen because of his opposition to the ecclesiastical policies of the king. Thomas was thus a martyr, and his sanctity was beyond doubt. He was canonized even before his *Vita* had been written.

But the canonization of Bernard of Clairvaux (†1153) was a different story altogether. The Cistercians had made early preparations for the request by writing a *Vita;* that work had begun when Bernard was still alive. The bulky document was ready in 1155. It was then a matter of waiting for the opportune moment, which, the Cistercians believed, had come in 1163, when Alexander III — expelled from Rome by Barbarossa — convened a synod in Tours. A request for canonization was made, but it was rejected, which the monks had apparently not expected, though they did find out why it was rejected.

Later, when in 1174 the pope approved another canonization request regarding Bernard, he indicated that he had refused the earlier request because he had too many requests pending at that time. He had considered it inopportune to grant this request while declining others.[19] But the real reason that the first request was turned down was that it was submitted during a synod, where there was little opportunity to gather supporting documentation. The new procedure, which involved hearing witnesses to verify the information that was presented, excluded the older way of requesting canonizations.

This becomes clear when we compare the texts of the *Vitae* presented during the first and second requests. Both versions have been preserved and a close examination of the manuscripts has shown that the

---

19. A. H. Bredero, "The Canonization of Bernard of Clairvaux," in *Saint Bernard of Clairvaux,* ed. B. Pennington (Cistercian Studies, 28; Kalamazoo, 1977), 85f.; idem, *Bernardus van Clairvaux. Tussen cultus en historie* (Kampen, 1993), 59-77.

second version was written shortly after the first request was rejected. It was completed in 1165. The text's swift reworking was the work of Godfrey of Auxerre, a former secretary of Bernard, who had had a major part in the writing of the first *Vita* and had made the arrangements for the first canonization request. Comparison of both versions shows that the second is much less open to verification. Some of the miracles had grown in proportion, and some witnesses who had previously been mentioned were no longer included, even though some were still alive when the revision was made. On the other hand, a vision of one of the monks about Bernard's sainthood was added, but this monk had died in the meantime. In brief, when they submitted the first request the monks learned how the procedure had changed and so were better prepared the second time.

Because of problems in the Cistercian order in which Godfrey of Auxerre was personally involved, the second request was not submitted until 1173 and Godfrey was not allowed to coordinate the request. The request was submitted in Rome, and a detailed investigation followed. But there was yet another problem, which further indicates to what extent the pope had seized the prerogative to make decisions regarding recognition of sainthood. A second person was included with the request for the canonization of Bernard: Malachy, the archbishop of Armagh in Ireland. He had been a friend of Bernard, had spent the last years of his life in Clairvaux, and had been buried in the abbey church. Bernard himself had written Malachy's *Vita* and had considered him a saint.

The reasoning on the part of the petitioners was apparently that if Bernard was to be recognized as a saint, then one who was regarded by him as a saint must *ipso facto* be so. And therefore that person also ought to be canonized. But this view was not accepted and Bernard's canonization was approved on the condition that this additional request be dropped. The canonization of Malachy followed only in 1190 and was not proclaimed as a liturgical saint's day to be observed by the whole church. That distinction was earned only by papal canonization. Episcopal canonizations had always had a limited scope. This was, in fact, one reason that papal canonization was encouraged by those making canonization requests: Papal canonization allowed wider dissemination of a cult.

❧   ❧

MAKING CANONIZATION the exclusive privilege of the pope did not make all abuses in regard to veneration of saints disappear. Nor did the popes suffer from the illusion that it would. This is evident, for instance, from a decision of the Fourth Lateran Council prohibiting veneration of relics not kept in a shrine. Suspicion of fraud with regard to the relics of saints persisted, both in veneration and in the commerce surrounding relics. Perhaps Rome at one time harbored the illusion that stricter requirements for canonizations could reduce the problem. But it cannot have been more than an illusion, for in the end the stricter requirements made the chaotic situation of medieval veneration of saints worse.

The stricter requirements were applied in the last quarter of the twelfth century in Italy, where a papal commission was charged with investigating every request locally. In the thirteenth century this rule was extended to ever more distant regions. Such investigations were especially meaningful when there were witnesses who could give information not only about miracles after the death of the candidate but also about deeds done when the candidate was still alive. That possibility had existed in the cases of Thomas à Becket and Bernard of Clairvaux. In the thirteenth century there was initially a strong preference for canonizing recently departed persons. From 1198, the beginning of the pontificate of Innocent III, to 1268, twenty-three canonizations were proclaimed. In eighteen of those cases there were eyewitnesses to the saints' deeds.

There was more than enough reason in those days to have a special interest in contemporary saints. Society was changing and the church was adapting itself to an urban population. New religious orders were founded and new forms of sainthood developed. Several of these saints have remained popular through the centuries: Francis and Clare of Assisi, Antony of Padua, and Dominic. But the church also needed other contemporary saints, including women. Hildegard of Bingen, Elizabeth of Thuringia, and Hedwig of Silesia are still not completely forgotten.

In spite of the stricter requirements applied in the investigations following a canonization request, papal policy in the first half of the thirteenth century was aimed at canonizing new saints. In this period twenty-four requests for canonization were rejected, eleven times after a second round of investigations had been ordered. At the end of the period 1198-1268, six requests were denied with no investigation. Then the number of denials without investigation rose and the number of canonizations declined. From 1268 to 1431, when papal authority faced a new crisis, eleven saints were canonized and thirteen requests were rejected after investigation (three pending requests were investigated after 1431, all leading to canonization). But thirty-two requests were rejected without investigation in this period.

It became more difficult to submit a request because of the stricter requirements, the length of time involved in the procedures, and the expense related to a request and the ensuing process. The documents for a request became more and more complicated. The petitioner had to bear the expenses of the commission sent by Rome to investigate the claims, and often more than one commission was sent. And those who looked after the interests of the petitioner in Rome also had to be paid. Because an investigation took more and more time and sometimes stagnated for reasons that had nothing to do with the case itself, maintenance of a proctor at Rome became a costly business. All this worked to slow the number of requests.

But the petitioner was never an individual. One of the reasons given for not considering requests was that a group making a request did not adequately represent the different sectors of the population that would supposedly benefit from the canonization. Groups in the church that were too specialized or had too little support had little chance. This led to the organization of pressure groups and lobbies to uphold requests. But even these methods were not automatically successful. Requests taken up for consideration and then deemed acceptable on the basis of the investigators' reports had to suit the policies the papal court was pursuing at the moment with regard to canonizations.

In the first half of the thirteenth century the policies for canonizations were clearly pastoral in intent. Later, such motives, though not fully absent, played a role only to the extent that requests for canonization had a chance if they conformed to the model of sainthood that enjoyed the preference of the curia at the moment. There was some amount of arbitrariness, or, rather, political preferences and animosities. The request for the canonization of the Dominican Raymond of Pennafort (†1275), for instance, was not taken up for consideration because he was Spanish. He was finally canonized in 1603.

Some canonizations resulted from political pressure. Thomas of Cantelupe, bishop of Hereford (†1287), was canonized in 1320 by John XXII in Avignon, even though Thomas was in a state of excommunication when he died. The request remained pending for thirteen years, but was at last approved because of the many miracles at Thomas's tomb, which had made his cult immensely popular in England, but chiefly because of the considerable political pressure Edward I and then Edward II were able to exert at Avignon.

It was also important at that time whether the person for whom a canonization request was made had been a layperson, a secular priest, or a member of an order, whether the person was a man or a woman, and especially whether he or she had shown sympathy for the radicalism of the Franciscan Spirituals. Nationality also played a role. The stay of the popes in Avignon from 1307 to 1379 resulted in four saints for France. Italy and England each received two, and the German Empire and Sweden one each. Four of these ten saints were laypersons, including Bridget of Sweden, the only woman among the ten, and Louis IX of France. One of them, Sebald of Nuremberg, an eleventh-century hermit, was canonized soon after the end of the Western Schism. There was some relationship between this canonization and the role of Emperor Sigismund in ending the Schism. The new pope, Nicholas V, increased the emperor's prestige in his empire with this canonization. Indeed, Sebald became the patron saint of the imperial city of Nuremberg.

Which eucharistic service was to be followed in the liturgy of a particular saint's day was, more than before, determined when the canonization was proclaimed. Specific rubrics had long existed. Martyrs and confessors were distinguished, and both rubrics began with apostles and church fathers. The rubric of the confessors also included bishops, non-bishops, virgins, and women. Almost all new saints belonged in this category and the fact was carefully indicated. At times a special service was instituted, as had happened earlier in the case of Bernard of Clairvaux. But the reason that this happened now depended on an important aspect of canonization policy: limiting the number of saints. Supervision of canonizations had developed into selection of saints.

This development is also evident in the several commentaries of canonists on the decretal by which in 1234 Pope Gregory IX made reservation of canonization for the pope an official part of canon law. This is first seen with the canonist Henry of Segusia (†1271), though later canonists followed him in this. He believed that it was desirable to limit the number of saints in order to prevent a diminishing of the zeal for charity and devotion and a decrease in the prestige of sainthood. He also regarded prevention of popular deception as an argument in favor of papal canonization, since the limited scope of episcopal perspective often led people astray.[20]

---

20. *Tertium Decretalium Librum Commentaria* (Venice, 1581), 172.

❧   ❧

THIS HAS brought us to the question of how the process of papal canon-ization was experienced by people of the time. The Netherlands offers us a clear example. The monastery of Aduard and the Cistercian order wanted to request the canonization of Richard (†1266), a monk who had lived at Aduard for a long time and had died there. But the expense caused them to abandon this project and to limit his commemoration as a saint to the order, which they had done in regard to other deceased members. In 1220, for instance, the Cistercians had requested the canonization of Robert of Molesme, one of the founders of the monastery of Cîteaux. In 1222 the general chapter of the order decided to celebrate his feast in the Cistercian abbeys in the same way that they celebrated the feast of St. Benedict. Rome did not give its official approval, but permitted Robert's feast to be cele-brated within the order.

Many similar solutions were found for the veneration of saints whose canonization was never formally requested, or in cases where a request for canonization had been rejected. These solutions were normally frowned on by Rome, but no measures were taken unless major problems arose. The monastery, order, city, or diocese that venerated such saints worried little if at all about what Rome would say. They had a fair idea of the policy being followed by Rome and knew when a case had no chance to succeed. For that reason they arranged the cults of such saints themselves and had available to them the necessary liturgical possibilities.

As a result there came to be two kinds of saints: those who had been formally canonized and whose public cult was prescribed by Rome, and local saints, who were venerated in the usual way, but without super-vision or recognition by Rome. There were far more local saints than formally canonized saints. This separation remained somewhat hidden, because the Roman liturgy, which prescribed the cult of official saints, was not yet binding on all dioceses. Each diocese kept its own calendar. But in frescoes on church walls, where both kinds of saints were depicted side by side, the difference was often noticeable in the size of the halos.[21]

This distinction between the two, which in later parlance developed into the distinction between saints and blessed, *sancti* and *beati*, was officially accepted in the time of the Counter-Reformation when Pope

21. Vauchez, 101-3.

Urban VIII brought order to the wild profusion of practices by instituting some clear rules. In 1635 he issued a canon that made beatification an official category of canon law.[22] This implied, in fact, the recognition of existing cults of saints that had been approved by a local church and the local civil authorities. When this level had been reached and beatification had been granted, a request for canonization could follow. The refusal of such a request would no longer result in disorder.

Although there was no such formal distinction in the late medieval church, the popes were already applying it during the Western Schism. The different popes tried to rally as much support as they could. They sometimes granted privileges of indulgence to shrines where officially unrecognized saints were venerated, so as to benefit those who went to venerate the relics of such saints. After the Schism had ended, this kind of concession inevitably led to a softening of the process of papal canonization, though it did not yet lessen the gap between recognized saints and unrecognized saints. A liberalization in procedure rather than in requirements did advance the three canonization requests pending from the previous period, all of which ended with canonization. One of these was the canonization of Catherine of Siena, who during the Western Schism had often functioned as the conscience of the Roman pope, and who was therefore not popular in circles of the curia.

The best known of these three pending requests was that of the Augustinian hermit Nicholas of Tolentino. This ascetic priest, who during his life had acquired fame as a great preacher, confessor, and comforting visitor of the sick, was venerated from the moment of his death in 1305 because of the miracles that occurred at his tomb. Already "Nicholas bread," bread blessed by invoking his name and used to heal the sick, was well known. A request for his canonization was submitted in 1325, but little happened. Between 1340 and 1350 a basilica was built over his tomb. During the elevation of his remains, his body bled when those present tried to sever an arm from it. This happened in fact several times. This miracle stimulated his cult even more. But canonization did not follow until 1466.

---

22. Vauchez, 114. In the Anglican Church, which did not abolish the cult of saints but did not follow any further prescription of Rome concerning veneration, there seems to be still some trace of the late medieval differentiation of canonized and noncanonized saints in that there is a great predilection for placing memorials in church buildings for deceased persons of distinction.

꙾   ꙾

THIS LAST EXAMPLE illustrates how popular veneration of saints who had not been officially recognized could remain a local affair. That their sanctity was ignored by the highest authorities in the church did not make much difference. This is further underscored by the solution to this conflicting practice of veneration of saints that the church arrived at later. In other cases we do not find such a sharp contrast as in the case of Nicholas of Tolentino. Therefore, it is not correct to conclude a priori that popular devotion to the saints was something that happened outside the church, much less that it was non-Christian and that the popular belief in saints must be counted among the remnants of paganism.

In any event, people used the possibilities open to them to keep venerating unofficial saints in spite of Rome's attitude. Translations and elevations of saints' bodies occurred, often with the knowledge of the bishops; a practice against which Salimbene of Parma fulminated in his chronicle:

In that same year took place the deceptive miracles of a man from Cremona named Albert, a man who had been a wine carrier, a wine drinker and indeed also a sinner. After this man's death, according to common report, God performed many miracles in Cremona, Parma and Reggio in the Church of St. George and St. John the Baptist; in Parma in the Church of St. Peter, which is near Piazza Nuova. And all wine carriers of Parma congregated in the church, and blessed was that man who could touch them or give them something. Women did the same. And the people formed societies, parish by parish, and marched in procession through the streets to the Church of St. Peter, where the relics of this man Albert were preserved. In their march they carried crosses and standards, and sang as they marched along. And they brought purple cloth, samite, canopies, and much money to the church. Later, the wine carriers divided all these things up among themselves. And when the parish priests saw this, they had Albert painted in their churches so that they would receive better offerings from the people. And at that time, his image was painted not only in the churches, but also on many walls and porticoes of cities, villages and castles. This, however, is expressly against the laws of the Church, for no man's relics are supposed to be held in reverence unless he is first approved of by the Church and written in the catalogue of saints;

in similar manner, a man is not to be depicted as a saint before he has been canonized by the Church. Those bishops, therefore, who allow such abuses to be practiced in their dioceses merit removal from office; that is, they should have the dignities of the episcopal office taken away from them. But there is nobody to correct those errors and abuses.[23]

The liturgies for the feasts of such unofficial saints provided no problem, because eucharistic services existed for the different rubrics of saints. And if there were ever still a difficulty, the feast of All Saints' Day offered a solution: a feast that made it possible to commemorate liturgically all noncanonized saints.

But this does not mean that elements of pagan origin or nature played no role in medieval veneration of saints. To some degree such elements were assimilated, and to some degree they were suppressed. Churches dedicated to St. Sylvester and built in late antiquity and the early Middle Ages were all situated on hills, on the sites of temples to the sun. It may be that the shrine of Mary, set on the highest location in the city of Puy in the Massif Central, was also a substitute for a pagan cult. In this way other saints borrowed functions from pagan deities. The worship of the archangel Michael was supposedly stimulated to replace the cult of Woden.

At times we also find a local cult around a person who was far from holy — the Swedish drunkard mentioned earlier, for instance — or for a nonhuman being, namely, the dog St. Cunefort. And we find mutated cults, as in the cases of St. Ontkommer, who was venerated in the Netherlands, and of the Holy Innocents. All these are instances of a corruption of Christian folk belief that was possible because christianization proved inadequate to prevent them. It is difficult to maintain that such cults, against which the church usually protested, were truly Christian. But they were merely phenomena at the periphery of medieval Christianity. It should be remembered that christianization and dechristianization are often simultaneous processes and can affect the same group.[24]

The role of the saints in hagiotherapy was another marginal phe-

23. J. L. Bair, G. Baglivi, and J. R. Kane, eds., *The Chronicle of Salimbene de Adam* (Medieval and Renaissance Texts and Studies, 40; Binghamton, 1986), 512.

24. For some further introduction to this subject, cf. N. Z. Davis, "Some Tasks and Themes in the Study of Popular Religion," in *The Pursuit of Holiness in Late Medieval and Renaissance Religion,* ed. C. Trinkaus and H. A. Oberman (Leiden, 1974), 307-36.

nomenon. It often involved some saint who had long been venerated and had acquired, because of some association with his or her name or martyr's death, a function as a miracle worker in the struggle against illness. The manner in which such saints were venerated and were asked to provide healing did, at times, resemble the worship of demons. But these saints also had their place in the churches and were commemorated in the liturgy. Moreover, they were remembered as intercessors for humankind before God. The extension of their cults into healing was stimulated by the panic inspired by sickness and other life-threatening problems that was endemic in the later Middle Ages. It is an exaggeration to conclude on that basis that popular veneration of these saints constituted a form of religious experience that was thoroughly alien to the church and to Christian faith. This view cannot be supported by the claim that the popular cults of the saints had moved beyond the boundaries of Christianity as the result of a structural breakdown in the relationship between the people and ecclesiastical authority. The solution to this disturbed relationship, which was realized at the time of the Counter-Reformation, proves the contrary.

3. THE SAINTHOOD OF BERNARD OF CLAIRVAUX

IN HIS BOOK *Nouveau visage de Bernard de Clairvaux,* published in Paris in 1976, Dom Jean Leclercq attempted to throw new light on the complex personality of this medieval monk (1090-1153). As the abbot of Clairvaux, a post Bernard held from the founding of the abbey in 1115 until his death, Bernard was the most important representative of the emerging order of the Cistercians. He also had great social and political influence in a variety of contexts through the first half of the twelfth century. Posterity has venerated him as a saint, especially because of his writings, which have remained well known and have been of major significance for the development of Western Christian spirituality.

But Bernard's place in the history of his own time has proven problematic through the centuries. In the past it was generally believed that we knew him well on the basis of a substantial contemporary *Vita,* which was regarded as historically trustworthy, even though there were differences of opinion regarding interpretation of this document. But since historians began the attempt to recover the more secular aspects of his life, there has come to be an increasing contrast between the cultic image that has long existed and the kind of person he seems to have been in the world of his own time. During the last few decades that contrast has been further sharpened because it has been shown that Bernard's *Vita* was written and subsequently rewritten to support the request for his canonization.

This change has had its emotional aspects. The reconstruction of the historical reality of Bernard is often viewed with suspicion by those who venerate him as a saint and find spiritual enrichment in his writings, which continue to be of great value. But on the other hand many historians find it difficult to maintain the traditional cultic image of Bernard, even when they are prepared to recognize him as a saint.[25] They were and are willing to accept that his sainthood developed gradually, while they criticize the traditional view that, because of his sainthood, Bernard was already before his birth predestined for the role he was to play during his life, as we are told in the *Vita*.

Leclercq's book was a contribution to this ongoing discussion. By introducing a new method of research — a psychohistorical approach — into study of Bernard's writings and his *Vita*, Leclercq attempted to reconcile in Bernard the human being and the saint. But the sources are not alike: The *Vita* was not written by Bernard himself. Nonetheless, using these sources together might be defensible, since the authors of the *Vita* must have been *intimi* of the abbot. This is particularly true of William of Saint-Thierry, who wrote the first book of the *Vita* when the abbot was still alive, and of Godfrey of Auxerre, who was responsible for the last three books and rewrote all five books. Godfrey served many years as Bernard's secretary; it was mainly due to his zeal that the first version of the *Vita* was ready only two years after the abbot's death and was approved by the Cistercian abbots who had known Bernard when he was alive.

Leclercq was assisted in his psychohistorical approach by a psychoanalyst, a psycholinguist, some psychologists, and a medical expert. Through text analysis they attempted to examine Bernard's language mechanisms and thus to discover some of his hidden motivations. Leclercq also used this psychoanalytic approach in, for instance, his *Psychohistorical Essays,* which were republished in 1979 as *Monks and Love in Twelfth-Century France.*

In one of these essays, on aggression and oppression in Bernard, Leclercq compared Bernard's use of language in his more official writings

---

25. Cf. A. H. Bredero, "The Conflicting Interpretations of the Relevance of Bernard of Clairvaux to the History of His Own Time," *Studia Cisterciensia* 1: Cîteaux, 31 (Achel, 1980), 53-81.

with the way he wrote when he was primarily addressing his own community. The author analyzed a number of sermons on the Song of Solomon and the metaphors in them, which are derived from marriage and sexuality. The background for this was an earlier polemic between Leclercq and an author who had, on the basis of the same sermons, reduced Bernard to a sexually frustrated man and had assessed his character and deeds from that point of view. This author thereby devalued Bernard's spiritual heritage — the Christian piety of the centuries that were to follow — typifying it as sexual sublimation.[26]

Leclercq's analysis demonstrated that Bernard's free use of sexual metaphors to illustrate the love relationship between God and the human person in no way indicates any sexual frustration on the part of the abbot of Clairvaux. But however meaningful Leclercq's linguistic analysis may have been in this instance, this does not seem to have extended to his efforts to construct a new face for Bernard and to break the deadlock concerning the interpretation of his historic role — as a human being or as a saint.

The reason for this failure may have been the lack of clarity in his analytical method. He did not justify his methodology, but simply demonstrated it. And it is striking that the conclusions supposedly based on this analysis were often further substantiated on the basis of other texts that were not psycholinguistically examined. It would thus seem that the conclusion of the linguistic analysis was drawn ahead of time, before it was performed, and also that Leclercq's familiarity with the writings of Bernard remained his most important line of approach — even while he applied, assisted by others, a psycholinguistic methodology to passages that were especially intriguing because of their content. It would thus seem that Leclercq made only a limited application of his analytical method.

Leclercq emphasized this himself and stated that the results of his research were neither complete nor definitive. Besides, he subjected only part of Bernard's writings to this method. That is why we focus our attention on the aim of his study rather than on his methodology. Leclercq wrote that its results, which were intended to inform us about Bernard's character as a human being, were to be assessed in the light of the values to which Bernard was devoted. It is possible, Leclercq indicated, to deter-

---

26. W. E. Philips, "The Plight of the Song of Songs," *Journal of the American Academy of Religion* 42 (1974): 82-100; J. Leclercq, "Agressivité et repression chez Bernard de Clairvaux," *Revue d'Histoire de la Spiritualité* 52 (1976), 152-77.

mine to what extent the abbot succeeded in integrating his psychological makeup in the totality of what he tried to achieve during his lifetime in the area of religion and morals. And in this way it should be possible to ascertain to what degree Bernard approached a level of sainthood that matched the level of his values.

The writings of Bernard remained the basis for this inquiry. His historical context was hardly considered. This raises the question to what extent Leclercq's study can possibly contribute to a new evaluation of Bernard. Leclercq did not in any way attempt to reconcile the cultic approach with historical evaluation of Bernard. Rather, he addressed those who accept Bernard as a saint — on the basis of their knowledge of his writings and possibly also because of their affinity with his way of life — with a plea to change their perception of his sainthood.

Therefore, Leclercq's study provides us with a new portrait of Bernard only to a limited degree. It would be more accurate to speak of a few, quite interesting, retouchings of his sainthood, visible to those who are familiar with his cultic image. But such a verdict with regard to this publication would be an injustice to the author. He is intimately acquainted with Bernard's writings, and this study must therefore be seen in the context of what he has written earlier about Bernard and about medieval monasticism, which fashioned the abbot of Clairvaux to such an important degree and on which he himself left such a clear mark.

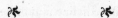

LECLERCQ PUBLISHED *Saint Bernard mystique* in 1948. This earlier book is an anthology of Bernard's writings with an extensive introduction. Leclercq assembled this book as his initial response to a request that he edit a new edition of Bernard's writings, which itself appeared in eight volumes between 1957 and 1977.[27] The request was no doubt prompted by the many articles on monasticism that he had published, in many cases on the basis of texts that Leclercq himself had discovered, and by three books published in 1946, in which he wrote about well-known monks of the eleventh and twelfth centuries, John of Fécamp, Peter the Venerable, and Peter of Celle. In 1948, moreover, he published, assisted by others, the first of six volumes

---

27. *SBO.* This edition has now been completed with a printed wordlist and microfiches: *Thesaurus sancti Bernardi Claraevallensis* (*CC, Thesaurus patrum latinorum;* Turnhout, 1987).

of monastic texts from the same period.[28] Leclercq discovered most of these texts, which were until then unknown, while studying the manuscripts of the writings of Bernard that he used in preparation for the new text edition.

His many subsequent articles continued to appear in a variety of journals, some of them also in preparation for his edition of Bernard's writings. Most of these articles he later republished in four volumes.[29] These studies and publications, along with anthologies of translated writings of Cistercians with introductions and commentaries, are the core of Leclercq's extensive writings. Especially important is Leclercq's synthesis of medieval monastic spirituality, which has appeared in several languages and in which he introduced the concept of monastic humanism, which combines erudition and biblical wisdom in an integrated unity that connects the study of theology closely with the monk's desire for personal perfection.[30] This book thus emphasizes the uniqueness of monastic theology.

Leclercq spoke of this uniqueness also elsewhere, notably in his 1960 study of the hermit-cardinal Peter Damian, who belonged to the eleventh-century Gregorian reform movement, and in his extensive contribution to the second volume of *l'Histoire de la spiritualité chrétien,* which appeared in 1961. He also touched upon this subject in a number of articles, which he revised and published together under the titles *Aux sources de la spiritualité occidentale* (1964) and *Temoins de la spiritualité occidentale* (1965). These articles deal with the sources and witnesses of medieval spirituality as it is seen in Benedictine and Cistercian monasticism.[31]

However incomplete these references to the works of Jean Leclercq might be, they indicate sufficiently that no one in our age has studied the spiritual world of Bernard from so many different angles and as thoroughly as Leclercq did. And no one has had a better knowledge of the many writings of this last church father of Latin Christendom. Leclercq ap-

28. "Textes et études sur la vie des moines au moyen âge," *Analecta Monastica* = *Studia Anselmiana* 20 (1948), 31 (1953), 37 (1955), 41 (1957), 43 (1958), 50 (1962).

29. *Recueil.* These were preceded by another volume, *Études sur Saint Bernard et le text de ses écrits* (Analecta Sacri Ordinis Cisterciensis, 9/1-2; Rome, 1953).

30. The English version is entitled *The Love of Learning and the Desire for God* (1961; repr. New York, 1977). The French title is *L'amour des lettres et le désir de Dieu* (Paris, 1957; rev. ed., 1963).

31. A bibliography of Leclercq's publications of 1938 to 1972 appears in *Bernard of Clairvaux: Studies Presented to Dom Jean Leclercq* (Cistercian Studies, 23; Kalamazoo, 1973), 215-64.

proached Bernard's writings in many different ways: He studied the manuscripts and the history of their transmission, and also their vocabulary and literary genre. And he focused, of course, on their content and on the character of their author. He analyzed, for instance, Bernard's humor and in 1983 wrote a small book about Bernard's views on and attitude toward women, entitled *La femme et les femmes dans l'oeuvre de saint Bernard*.[32]

So, it should not surprise us that Leclercq, who was so intensely involved with Bernard's writings, also wanted to find out what kind of man the writer of these texts was, as this first abbot of Clairvaux continued to intrigue him as an author. It is for that reason that we have paid attention to Leclercq's other writings in these pages about *Le nouveau visage*. This book, which pleads for a new interpretation of Bernard, can only be judged in the context of Leclercq's complete oeuvre. Inspired by what William of Saint-Thierry said in Bernard's *Vita,* namely that those who did not live according to Bernard's spirit should not claim the ability to judge him, we might say that we cannot evaluate *Le nouveau visage* in ignorance of Leclercq's other works and, at the same time, without familiarity with the writings of Bernard himself. Again the question poses itself: Who can equal Leclercq in that respect?

❧   ❧

A QUESTION of a totally different order is posed by Bernard's sainthood and the manner in which it should be approached: cultically or critically and historically? On this point, we may be critical toward Leclercq's analysis, since he almost completely ignored the historical context in which Bernard's writings were written. But such criticism should also take into account what Leclercq wrote in earlier publications about his approach to Bernard as a saint, even though he himself did not refer to these statements. In his preface to *Nouveau visage* he did, however, dispute an older article written by Henry-Bernard de Warren, the title of which was, translated, "The soul of Bernard: the man and the saint."[33] Leclercq commented:

> As the title indicates, [de Warren's] pages deal only with the soul, and never with temperament. Above each paragraph is a heading that

32. Translated into English as *Women and Saint Bernard of Clairvaux* (Cistercian Studies, 104; Kalamazoo, 1989).

33. *Bernard de Clairvaux,* ed. Commission d'Histoire de l'Ordre de Cîteaux (Paris, 1953), 659-77.

mentions a virtue, which is then further expounded. But there are no shortcomings, weaknesses, or sins. Bernard is portrayed as a saint. One might well ask if the man in him has not been forgotten. To the degree that this could be verified, it appeared that the Bernard that was presented never existed.

But in his earliest study, *Saint Bernard mystique,* Leclercq himself opted for a similar approach. He did refer to Bernard's temperament, but this did not lead him to an essentially different standpoint. He only wrote, for example, "His mother had seen him [Bernard] in a dream before his birth as a preacher, but his temperament prepared him for a contemplative life."[34] For Leclercq Bernard was a saint from his early youth, a point of view that implies that Bernard's conduct as a human being is not a crucial aspect for evaluating him.

This orientation also stands out clearly in the conclusion Leclercq reached in this early study:

> Bernard demands admiration. He needs no defense. It suffices just to affirm this. While at times attempts have been made to provide an interpretation on this point, it can never be pretended that it is possible to fully explain the inner mystery of a saint. It was of primary importance just to gather what Bernard had said about himself.

To this conclusion Leclercq attached a significant consequence for historical understanding of Bernard:

> In the case of Bernard a historian will have to deal with the problem of the relationship God maintains between sainthood and temperament. Bernard is a human being: His acts are visible. Scholars entrusted with the task of recording these acts in annals and chronicles sometimes presume to evaluate them. But often they forget this other just as undeniable fact of history: Bernard is a man of God.[35]

In his *Nouveau visage* Leclercq appeared to have given up this view, which demands that we see Bernard primarily in connection with his sainthood, that is, as the favored executor of God's intentions among humankind rather than in terms of his human deeds. In this study Leclercq also wanted to trace the human aspects of Bernard, both in his writings

---

34. *Saint Bernard mystique* (Bruges, 1948), 19.
35. *Saint Bernard mystique,* 236.

and in his *Vita,* in which he was depicted as a saint by his contemporaries. From an earlier study of these texts Leclercq had learned of the existence of several differing redactions of Bernard's writings, and also that Bernard revised his texts himself. Texts that give the reader the impression of having been written spontaneously actually often went through a long process of careful reflection, and at times they conceal a numerological symbolism. Above all, one must take into account the role of the secretary and of the revisions that were, for various reasons, carried out after Bernard's death.

These complications in the transmission of Bernard's writings indicate that Bernard's personality structure cannot be deduced fully from his writings. And for that reason we can understand that Leclercq, with his extensive knowledge of these writings and his familiarity with Bernard's linguistic peculiarities, wanted to search for linguistic means by which to gain further information about Bernard's personality structure.

⚘   ⚘

BUT THE QUESTION remains whether Leclercq sufficiently distanced himself from his original evaluation of Bernard as saint in order to understand his conduct as a human being in the context of his time and of all his social relationships, inside and outside the monastery. Is there not a risk for those who only consider Bernard's writings — which were written in a monastic milieu — of undervaluing his deeds in the world? Should questions about his actions in the world be ignored, especially considering that Bernard has been strongly criticized for those actions, both in his own day and by historians judging in retrospect?

It is because of those actions that many had and have difficulty in accepting him as a saint. There is no need to go to the same extreme as Schiller did and regard Bernard as the greatest spiritual villain in history, even considering the concrete and factual shortcomings that are easily detected in his actions in the world. Many generations have criticized his promotion of the crusades, and his contemporaries suffered through his querulous behavior in connection with episcopal appointments when he disliked candidates or deemed appointees unfavorable to the Cistercian order. Many failed to understand his attitude toward Abelard, whom he opposed because he saw Abelard's scholastic method as a threat to monastic theology. And Bernard was not above dubious practices when he tried to arrange for the founding of new monasteries or the takeover of monasteries by the Cistercians. This kind of conduct was unacceptable to some of his

188

contemporaries and has also given rise to conflicting evaluations by historians. Many have abandoned the cultic starting point that long dominated evaluation of Bernard, precisely because it failed to do justice to his actions in the world beyond the walls of the monastery.

Even in his *Nouveau visage* Leclercq has avoided the kind of historical approach that is willing to deal with objectionable aspects of Bernard's conduct. As I have noted, he focused particularly on Bernard's writings, without feeling the need to pay much attention to the historical context within which a number of these writings can be placed, either in whole or in part, though the task of doing so is not simple. For many texts it is in fact nearly impossible, in part because of the meticulous way in which they were revised. Leclercq has demonstrated this, for instance, with regard to Bernard's letters.[36]

But these obstacles to the identification of context are not present to the same degree in all of Bernard's writings. What Bernard wrote in *De consideratione* about the Second Crusade[37] is clearly related to his embarrassment about the failure of this venture, which he promoted without participating in it. Other passages from this treatise can also be placed in a historical context, such as his devastating critique of the Roman curia, which every generation remembers again. The same can be said about an edifying text in which Bernard deals with the different levels of worth in knowledge,[38] a discussion that has been quoted often since Bossuet. This statement clearly reflects Bernard's contempt for the scholastic approach to scholarship, as he rejects as shameful any scholarship that is sold for money or fame.

Even apart from such passages — and many more could be cited — one must also reckon with Bernard's temporal location in relation to his writings in general. Leclercq has shown too little attention to this. Should we not ask, especially when a psychoanalysis of the texts is attempted, to what extent the opinions expressed by Bernard in his writings must be understood as products of their place in time?

For instance, Bernard's *Praise of the New Knighthood*, addressed to the recently founded Order of the Templars, apparently approves of holy war: "The soldiers of Christ . . . do not know the least fear, neither for

36. "Lettres de S. Bernard: histoire ou littérature?" *Recueil* IV, 125-225.

37. II.I.1-4 = *SBO* III, 410-13; *Five Books of Consideration* (Cistercian Fathers, 37; Kalamazoo, 1976).

38. *Sermones in Cantu* 36.III.3 = *SBO* II, 5f.; *On the Song of Songs* II (Cistercian Fathers, 7; Kalamazoo, 1976), 176.

sin when they kill their enemies nor for the danger that they themselves might perish. This is because to kill someone else for the sake of Christ or to wish to undergo death is not only completely free of sin, but even highly praiseworthy and meritable."[39] We need to ask of such a text whether it simply expresses the mentality of its time.

Leclercq has argued at length that there was serious discontent in the ranks of the Templars rising from the tension between their military tasks and their religious calling. Bernard wrote his treatise, Leclercq says, to answer such objections (*Recueil,* II, 87-99). But what Bernard wrote about killing and being killed in the service of Christ occupies only a minor place in this treatise. Still we must recognize it as a remarkable statement, one that cannot be conveniently ignored in evaluation of a person who became a saint.

In *Nouveau visage* Leclercq mentions *Praise of the New Knighthood* again, now in connection with his linguistic-psychological analysis of the prologues of Bernard's writings. He refers to the prologue of this particular treatise to indicate Bernard's familiarity with military terminology. He wonders whether Bernard simply adapted himself to the mentality of the Templars, or whether we find here traces of the military milieu of Bernard's childhood and early education.[40]

Leclercq thus raises the subject of the influence of the mentality of the time, but limits it to the sphere of language. His book does try to throw light on the human side of Bernard so that we may better understand Bernard's sainthood. But it is unacceptable within this aim to ignore aspects of Bernard's writings that are the products of the mentality of his time. Those parts of Bernard's writings may give too negative a picture of him — if the influence of the spirit of the age is disregarded. Moreover, even when allowance is made for the thinking of his time, we must ask whether, in the pursuit of his ideals of sainthood, Bernard should not have distanced himself from that thinking. It is precisely there that we should find the line of demarcation between an ordinary human being and a saint.

A similar remark is in order with regard to statements in several of Bernard's sermons on the sinfulness of the body and carnal desires.[41]

---

39. III.4 = *SBO* III, 217; *The Works of Bernard of Clairvaux* I: *Treatises* III (Washington, 1974).

40. *Nouveau visage,* 50.

41. Sermon 66, *De diversis* 2 = *SBO* VI, 1, 300f.; *Sermones in Cantu* 30.IX; 82.III.5 = *SBO* I, 216; II, 295 (*On the Song of Songs* II, 122; *Sermons on the Song of Songs* IV [Kalamazoo, 1980], 177); Sermon on St. Martin III = *SBO* V, 401; Sermon 8 on Psalm 90 IV = *SBO* IV, 428f.

Should they be related to the community to which Bernard belonged as a monk, or are they to be understood in the light of patristic tradition in the Latin church? Can they not be interpreted as an expression of the dualism of Bernard's time, in which the difference between good and evil coincides rather with the difference between matter and spirit?

This same question should be asked with regard to Bernard's rather crass remark addressed to itinerant preachers regarding the presence of women among their followers: "To be always in a woman's company without having carnal knowledge of her — is this not a greater miracle than raising the dead?"[42] Bernard's suspicion of women was not exceptional. We need only point to the letter in which Bishop Marbode of Rennes warns the itinerant preacher Robert of Abrissel about the risks he incurs by remaining in contact with the women he has led to conversion.[43] Bernard addressed the same reproof that he addressed to itinerant preachers in a letter written to a bishop, whom he also reproached of other things. Leclercq refers to this letter in his study of the place of women in the writings of Bernard. We do not know for sure who this bishop was, but Leclercq rightly notes that the reproof in the letter is not addressed to the bishop's female companion, but to the prelate himself.[44]

In *Nouveau visage* Leclercq gives attention to Bernard's use of language in writing about women, devoting a separate chapter to "S. Bernard et le féminin," in which he analyzes in particular Bernard's sermons on the Song of Solomon. He points out, among other things, Bernard's "ability to describe a pretty girl." He also tells us that in our own age a reading of these sermons during a service in a monastery caused an uproar because of their erotic imagery, even though an excellent French translation was used. Leclercq suggests that a whole tradition of biblical and patristic language — and of allegory — must have played a role in the way in which the medieval reader and listener understood the erotic language of the Song of Solomon encountered in Bernard's sermons.

Leclercq compares this situation with that of a hymn that can only be appreciated with a fitting accompaniment. Here the accompaniment, so to speak, is lacking for the modern reader. This comment is apt, but can we not assume that our own age's literal approach to these texts was

---

42. *Sermones in Cantu* 65.IV = *SBO* II, 175; *On the Song of Songs* III (Cistercian Fathers, 31; Kalamazoo, 1979), 184.

43. Letter VI = *PL* CLXXI, 1480-86.

44. Letter 538 = *SBO* VIII, 504f.; *Women and Saint Bernard of Clairvaux*, 17.

unthinkable in Bernard's day because matter and spirit were not as closely linked because of his age's dualistic philosophy? The data that Leclercq assembles in this chapter should therefore have been related to their medieval context. That would have resulted in a better understanding of how Bernard could use this erotic imagery when discussing spiritual matters while rejecting actual eroticism in the strongest possible terms: Both actions were in agreement with the spirit of the times, especially in the monastic environment, which was much better known by the outside world than it is today.

⁂   ⁂

A FURTHER SHORTCOMING of Leclercq's book, which also concerns the question of Bernard's sainthood, is in the first chapter, where the author analyzes the contribution of William of Saint-Thierry to Bernard's first *Vita*. Here Leclercq takes issue, to some extent, with my interpretation of William's contribution to the *Vita*.[45] I suggested that the chapters of this *Vita*, written in accordance with the standard models of the medieval hagiographic genre, all contributed to a conscious legendizing of Bernard. Leclercq does not wish to make too much of this legendizing. We are supposed to accept that William knew less and less of Bernard and that his revelations lost their clarity the more he spoke of Bernard. The reason supposedly was that according to William only one who shared Bernard's spiritual way of experiencing reality could hope to truly know Bernard. It was not primarily William's intent to present Bernard as a concrete historical figure carefully situated in the context of time and place. He wanted, rather, to present Bernard as "a mystery to be venerated and admired and to be penetrated by those who had received the grace to do so."[46]

Leclercq's view of William's intentions is incorrect in that it is incomplete. The first book of the first *Vita*, written while Bernard was still alive, can also be read as a tendentious apology, in which William defends Bernard against criticism by his contemporaries. He thus protects Bernard by intentional legendizing and in this way makes him into a saint. Possibly

45. A. H. Bredero, *Études sur la "Vita prima" de Saint Bernard* (Rome, 1960). Cf. also *idem*, "The Canonization of Saint Bernard and the Rewriting of His Life," in *Cistercian Ideals and Reality*, ed. J. R. Sommerfeldt (Cistercian Studies, 60; Kalamazoo, 1978), 80-105; idem, *Bernardus van Clairvaux*, 141-63.

46. *Nouveau visage*, 34.

William himself experienced Bernard as a mystery, since sainthood remains a mystery and is experienced as such as one gains close familiarity with it.

But all this does not erase the fact that William remained silent about substantial matters that might well have evoked the criticism of contemporaries. He did not, for instance, refer to Bernard's polemics against Cluny or to his conflict with Abelard, in which William himself was also involved. This is also the case with Bernard's personal involvement in the acquisition of monasteries for the Cistercian order, in the controversies surrounding episcopal appointments, in his avoidance of friendship with Peter the Venerable, and in his promotion of a new crusade. Contemporaries and later readers looking for more information on these points have had to be satisfied with general excuses, which once again in their own way suggest Bernard's sanctity. For example, William remarks on Bernard's ability, based on a disposition from God that William did not know of and on respect for his holiness, to avoid situations in which he would be forced to be what he did not want to be.[47]

If we subject this text to a linguistic analysis with the intent of seeing its object or its author grow from a man into a saint, this first chapter of *Nouveau visage* clearly falls short. I have already demonstrated that by reading between the lines we may well discover in this first book of the *Vita* that Bernard's contemporaries judged him negatively, just as have later interpreters of Bernard. That he was so judged has been presented by William in an ingenious way, such as, for instance, in the cryptic statement that Bernard never had enemies, since enmity is a mutual phenomenon, and the abbot never hated anyone.[48] It may be objected that this involves an interpretative analysis of the text, while Leclercq limits himself to a linguistic analysis. But in that case, his remarks about William's intentions are irrelevant, since they cannot be based on a linguistic analysis. Leclercq uses linguistic analysis to supplement what he already knows by other means.

❧   ❧

ONE OF THE CHAPTERS in which this linguistic analysis is utilized in greatest depth deals with linguistic mechanisms in ironic use of language. Leclercq explains his methodology at length and pays special attention to words and clauses that are not indispensable elements of the structures of the

47. *Vita prima* I.XIV.69.
48. *Vita prima* I.XIV.71.

sentences they appear in. But applying this principle to writings from the past involves extra complications, since the spontaneity of verbal conduct is largely missing and the emotional or intellectual aspect of a statement is more difficult to detect. But these objections carry less weight when one deals with ironic language, which is abundantly present in the writings of Bernard, for instance in his polemics against Cluny in his *Apology* (1124-25).

Leclercq asks of Bernard's use of language in this polemic whether Bernard exaggerated in his criticisms. He thinks he did not. Bernard did not stoop to sarcasm, and below the surface of a satirical style, which came close to caricature, Cistercians and Cluniacs, who both desired to be true monks, could perceive how Bernard was inspired in his zeal against abuses, which may in part have been imagined, but were in part also very real. Leclercq arrives at this conclusion by an analysis of Bernard's rhetorical questions and of the manner in which Bernard contrasts virtues with vices.

Precisely because of the value of this analysis, it must be regretted that Leclercq does not give any attention to the context of these polemics. It is true that others have often studied this context, but there are more than enough reasons to think that the traditional views are no longer valid. In his *Apology* Bernard did not oppose the Cluniac lifestyle as such, but he did choose sides in a turbulent internal controversy in the order. And, as has been described earlier, this conflict ended unfavorably for the group Bernard supported. He avoided giving the papal legate an account concerning the Cluniac uproar. Moreover, after his intervention there was hardly any further Cistercian polemic against Cluny. It was only after Bernard's death that a Cistercian dared to attack Cluny, using all of Bernard's arguments, but in a totally different context.[49] In order to arrive at a balanced judgment of Bernard as a polemicist using irony, it might have been good to give more attention to the context within which Bernard used his irony.

As was said earlier, Leclercq's book offers some remarkable retreatments in a number of its textual analyses. This is particularly true of the chapter on Bernard as a psychotherapist. One of Leclercq's purposes with this chapter is to find out what Bernard had in mind when he wrote a letter to Ogier, a canon who had long been a friend of Bernard. Leclercq pays considerable attention to a passage in which Bernard compares himself with a tightrope walker who moves with his head down and his feet in the air and is thus devoid of all that is human. This comparison is the

---

49. Idung of Prüfening, *Cistercians and Cluniacs: The Case for Cîteaux. A Dialogue between Two Monks* (Cistercian Fathers, 33; Kalamazoo, 1977), 21-141.

culmination of Bernard's ironic discourse in the letter about himself. Leclercq relates this imagery to, among other things, the criticism Bernard faced because of his role in the condemnation of Abelard at the Council of Sens in 1140. He suggests it might have been an ironic defense against the lack of sympathy he experienced during that council.[50]

There are no solid facts to substantiate this explanation. Moreover, it deals with only one of the reasons for Bernard's self-mockery, which was a subtle answer to Ogier's request that Bernard write a treatise to serve as a guide for Ogier's life as he was retiring from church leadership. Leclercq's explanations illustrate how understatement was understood differently then from now. But they make no effort to detect the almost subconscious linguistic mechanisms. This does not increase the credibility of the methodology that Leclercq advocates in his book.

But we are faced with another, more general, question with regard to Bernard's statements about himself in his writings. If Leclercq wanted to deal with just one of these statements without reference to his linguistic-analytical methodology, why did he choose this particular statement of Bernard about himself? A more extensive treatment of such passages would have strengthened Leclercq's book.

A good example would be the concluding statement in a letter written by Bernard to the prior, also named Bernard, of the Carthusian monastery of Portes.[51] This passage has given rise to many interpretations and suppositions. In it Bernard complains about the duality of his life, between world and monastery, saying that he calls himself a chimera. Many recent discussions based on that statement speak of Bernard as a divided and torn being, one who carried both tradition and renewal within itself, as if that were not a common human trait. Given when this letter was written (1147-50) and that Bernard's letters often merely served to accompany messages that were communicated verbally, his statement may well have been related to his appeal for the Second Crusade, which had already failed, and to the criticism he received as a result. An analysis of the different statements Bernard made about himself in relationship to the situations in which they were made would, therefore, have been appropriate in a study that attempts to elucidate Bernard as a human being.

---

50. Letter 87.XII = *SBO* VII, 231 = James, 135 (letter 90, 12); *Nouveau visage*, 94-107. Cf. also Leclercq, "The Theme of Jesting in St. Bernard and His Contemporaries," *Cistercian Studies* 9 (1974): 7-21.

51. Letter 250.IV = *SBO* VIII, 147 = James, 402 (letter 326); cf. Bredero, *Bernardus van Clairvaux*, 214ff..

This brings us back to the aim of Leclercq's book. The author is interested in Bernard as a human being, but not in detachment from his sainthood. In fact, his primary purpose is not to understand the abbot of Clairvaux in his historical context, but rather to know more about the nature of his sainthood. This intention is very clear in his last chapter, *Psychologie et sainteté*. There Leclercq distinguishes three levels in Bernard: a psychological level, where we can find a number of spontaneous needs arising from his human nature; above this is the level of Christian values, to which Bernard was devoted throughout his life; and between those two levels there was a third, where the abbot tried to integrate these needs and values, that is, to mediate between his human motivations and the motifs that he consistently derived from these values.

Bernard fought for sanctity on this intermediate level, and this he did with success. Leclercq concludes that Bernard achieved an integration between the highest and lowest levels in such a way that humility won over aggression. This is indeed a prerequisite for sainthood, and Leclercq's conclusion must be regarded as authoritative, since he knows both what Bernard wrote about humility and the kind of humility out of which Bernard wrote. In Leclercq's opinion Bernard was a saint because he knew his faults and because he acknowledged his shortcomings while remaining faithful in his service to Christ in spite of his faults. This notion of sainthood is not completely identical with the recognition Bernard received officially in 1174. That is quite understandable, since present-day criteria for the recognition of sainthood do not coincide with those of the twelfth century. But it is less consistent that this interpretation of Bernard's saint-hood does not directly issue from the new insights presented earlier in Leclercq's book.

❧   ❧

As HAS BEEN STATED BEFORE, Leclercq manifested in this book an interest in Bernard as a human being, which is quite different from interest, from a more secularized viewpoint, in Bernard as a historical person. Many only meet Bernard insofar as they study the time in which he lived. And that is where he undoubtedly can be met. But Leclercq learned to know Bernard in the same way as those who approach him from a cultic perspective: He studied Bernard's writings before he studied the time in which Bernard lived. He learned to know Bernard in the spiritual monastic climate in which Bernard wanted to live and did in fact live.

In his study Leclercq did not fundamentally change his view with respect to this point of departure. He only painted a new portrait of Bernard for those who already knew and venerated the abbot as a saint, without having much interest in Bernard as a human being, or, in any case, without asking how Bernard grew into sainthood. What was new in Leclercq's portrait was his portrayal of Bernard's sanctity as an intermediate level between human desire and ambition, on the one hand, and norms tending toward perfection, on the other hand. This new portrait left no room for a sainthood revealed before the saint's birth, as the *Vita* would have it, which ignores the saint's human conduct.

But the picture remained unchanged for those who were not primarily interested in Bernard's sainthood. Leclercq's new methodology did not offer any new perspectives with regard to Bernard as a person, perhaps because it was not sufficiently used, or, perhaps, because it was not applicable. The controversy over how to evaluate Bernard as a human being and as a saint remained unresolved for those who wanted to give priority to the first aspect. We may conclude that this controversy still confirms what William of Saint-Thierry wrote in defense of Bernard, which was that he could not explain what kind of angelic life Bernard already led on earth to someone who was not inspired by the same spirit that moved Bernard.[52] Leclercq made some significant modifications to William's account in the *Vita*, but they, too, are only visible to those who try to understand William's account in the deeper spirit in which he wrote.

---

52. *Vita prima* I.IV.19.

VII

Heresy and Church Reform [1]

❦   ❦

1. THE TRANSITION FROM THE ELEVENTH
TO THE TWELFTH CENTURY

THE ELEVENTH and the twelfth centuries were a period of transition in the history of the Middle Ages. Agricultural profits increased and stimulated the rise of a money economy, a major factor in urban development. There were changes in the way groups in society interacted and in the norms and values that were considered important. The population increased considerably, and the common people enjoyed greater safety as regional principalities filled the vacuum left by the disintegration of the Carolingian state. As a result subjects were ruled more directly than before. Moreover, the urge to fight could now be satisfied outside Western Europe. Society did not yet manifest what would later be characterized as "the birth of the individual." It had acquired a new sense of belonging together: Christendom. For those who were part of it, this all-encompassing collectivity provided a shield against all the mysterious things that threatened humankind. But with the rise of this sense of unity, the social climate deteriorated for those who were excluded from it, specifically Muslims, Jews, and heretics.

---

1. The first section of this chapter was written for this book. The second section is a revision of "Henri de Lausanne: un réformateur devenu hérétique," in *Pascua Mediaevalia: Studies voor Prof. Dr. J. M. De Smet* (Louvain, 1983), 108-23.

Before the eleventh century the last of these groups, heretics, had long gone unnoticed, except perhaps among those who constituted the small literate elite — the clergy and the monks. In that milieu an intellectual heretic might at times manifest himself, as, for example, Gotschalk of Orbais (†869), whose teachings about predestination were condemned by Hincmar, the archbishop of Reims, so that Gotschalk was put in a monastic prison. But popular heresies did not arise until the beginning of the eleventh century. Their emergence was, of course, related to changes in society as a whole. Day-to-day life no longer required all of the laity's time, and they thus became able to look beyond their immediate surroundings. They became more conscious of the society of which they were a part and of their relationships to larger social groups, such as church and Christendom. Some developed their own peculiar opinions about matters such as human existence, faith, clergy, and worship.

Divergent understandings of salvation imported into the Western church from Bulgaria during the eleventh century also played an important role. There the dualistic sect of the Bogomiles had arisen in the tenth century. The Bogomiles borrowed and adapted elements of Christianity that were useful to the development of their dualistic worldview. Monks who preferred a dualistic nature religion above the Christian faith were responsible for this synthesis. Their teachings were in direct opposition to orthodoxy, and they were strict ascetics, rejecting marriage, consumption of animal foods, use of expensive clothing, and the like. They considered their asceticism obligatory, at least for the *perfecti* (the perfect), that is to say, for themselves. They met with considerable response from the Bulgarian peasants, possibly because of the appeal of their dualism, which made both good and evil into absolutes. The peasants were also attracted by the resistance of this sect to the official church, which occupied a dominant place in their agrarian society. But it would be going too far to suggest that the Bulgarian peasants joined the apostles of the priest Bogomile simply to justify revolt against the dominance of church and nobility.[2]

Bogomilism spread along the trade routes to the West, where the church was hardly prepared to deal with this new phenomenon. The early church knew, of course, about heresy, but pastoral care had been concentrated on the continued effects of paganism on religious practice rather than on heresy. When heresy arose, the Fathers were consulted for what they wrote

2. On dualistic currents in eastern Europe and their influence in the West, cf. M. Loos, *Dualist Heresy in the Middle Ages* (Prague, 1974).

about them. Heretics were often given names from Christian antiquity, such as Manichaeans or Arians. Only from the twelfth century on, when heretical sects became more common, were new names created for them.

The influence of Bogomilism is clearly recognizable in twelfth-century Catharism, but is more difficult to detect in the heresies of the eleventh century, since the accounts of the activities of heretics from that time are too ambiguous. The first account dates from about 1000 and was written by Radulfus Glaber (†1050). He relates how Leutard, a peasant from the region of Chalons-sur-Marne, began to preach in that area, interpreting the gospel in his own way. We are told that he began his preaching after some bees had entered his body through his nose, mouth, and ears while he was sleeping outside. When questioned by the local bishop about his prophetic activities, he appeared to be quite incoherent. When the interest of the people faded, Leutard drowned himself in a well.[3] We know a little more about heretical activities in Orleans around 1022. There the heretics belonged to a different social stratum than that of Leutard: Among them were the French queen's confessor and a counselor of the king. But this group considered all material things impure. They rejected marriage, the Eucharist, auricular confession, the ecclesiastical hierarchy, pious works, and prayer. They accepted only the works of the Spirit. They went to the stake with gladness.[4]

Not all heretics were so unrelenting that they had to pay with their lives. In 1025 the bishop of Cambrai-Arras held a disputation with a heretical group that had come from elsewhere. They accepted the New Testament as the sole source of revelation. They also rejected marriage and confession, as well as baptism. Furthermore, they recognized no other saints than the apostles. As a result of this disputation they repudiated their teachings and returned to those of the church.[5] In Turin another group of heretics was less fortunate, since in the midst of their disputation with the bishop the local citizens intervened. The heretics were given the choice of venerating the cross or climbing the stake. Most of them opted for the latter, saying that to do so conformed to their beliefs, since they understood that they were to seek death through martyrdom in order to avoid eternal torment.[6]

3. For the text of his report, see W. L. Wakefield and A. P. Evans, *Heresies of the High Middle Ages* (New York and London, 1969), 72.
4. Wakefield-Evans, 75-81; R. I. Moore, *The Birth of Popular Heresy* (London, 1975), 10-15.
5. Wakefield-Evans, 82-85; Moore, 15-19.
6. Wakefield-Evans, 86-89; Moore, 19-21.

Not only were church leaders ill-acquainted with the problem of heresy, they also found it difficult to decide what to do with those who persisted in heretical beliefs. That uneasiness is apparent in a letter of Bishop Roger of Chalons-sur-Marne to Bishop Wazo of Liège written between 1043 and 1048 and later incorporated into Wazo's *Vita* together with Wazo's response. Roger indicates in his letter that he is not prepared to deliver some heretics brought before him into the hands of the civil government. At the same time he fears that he is forsaking his duty if he does not, since this would make it possible for the corrupting ferment to infect other people. He asks Wazo for advice. Wazo's response refers to the parable in Matthew 13:24-30, 36-43, which states that the weeds and the wheat are not to be separated until the harvest. He believes that his colleague ought to be patient, and concludes:

> We must meanwhile bear in mind that we who are called bishops do not receive at ordination the sword which belongs to the secular power and for that reason we are enjoined by God our Father not to do unto death but rather to quicken unto life. There is, however, another point about the aforesaid schismatics which should be carefully heeded, one of which you are not at all unmindful. They and those associating with them should be deprived of Catholic communion. Let it be officially and publicly announced to all others, so that, heeding the warning of the prophet, they may leave their midst and eschew their most unclean sect, for "He that toucheth pitch shall be defiled with it."[7]

We can find hardly any references to heretics in sources from the second half of the eleventh century. It has been suggested that this had to do with developments within the church. There was a widespread realization that the church needed reform, especially with respect to the conduct of the clergy. The close relationship between the church and feudal society had affected the priesthood negatively. Many priests lived a worldly life, disregarding their obligations of celibacy and the injunction not to bear arms. These abuses had evoked a number of different reactions. The rise of the eremitical ideal, with its adherents and devotees among the different layers of Latin Christendom, can be viewed as one of these reactions. In a sense the rapid increase in the number of monasteries affiliated with

7. Wakefield-Evans, 93. The biblical passage quoted is Sirach 13:1. Cf. also Moore, 24.

Cluny also played a role, since it led to the end of the system of proprietary monasteries, in which abbots was usually appointed by laypersons. But even more important for the success of the reform movement was the support it had with some bishops, notably in Lorraine. From there it gained, from 1046 on, influence in Rome.

There came to be less inclination to turn against the church as the church itself increasingly turned against the clergy whose misconduct had provoked the rise of heresies. We see an example of this development in Cambrai in connection with the policies of Bishop Gerard, who did not join the reform movement. There Ramirhdus, a priest, lost his life on the stake because of heresy. This happened around 1075, when the reform movement was strongly promoted and supported by Rome. Pope Gregory VII (1073-85) rehabilitated the victim posthumously. We are told that his heresy consisted in a persistent refusal to accept the Eucharist from priests who were leading unfit lives. So opponents of the reform movement had accused him of heresy.

But Gregory did not accept the criteria used in this case to identify a heretic. Though Rome had always insisted that the validity of a sacrament could not depend on whether the minister was worthy, at that time Rome was emphasizing a different norm, identifying the buying and selling of spiritual offices as heresy. Since such spiritual offices were associated with consecration by laying on of hands, trafficking in them was a sin against the Holy Spirit. Since heresy was also sin against the Holy Spirit, the advocates of reform argued that buying and selling church offices should be regarded as heresy. But the practice was extremely widespread. (It had come to be called "simony," a term derived from Acts 8:18-24, where the story is told of Simon Magus, who wanted to buy from Peter the power to impart the Spirit to others by the laying on of hands.) Many bishops, abbots, and other members of the clergy, particularly canons, could be labeled as heretics. For it had become customary for lay people who owned churches or monasteries and princes who gave diocese lands in vassalage to appoint the clergy needed for such churches against payment of a fee.

When the reform movement gained momentum in the church, it naturally opposed this lay authority and wanted to stop the investiture of bishops by rulers. This concern was inspired by other abuses that had evolved from this lay investiture. The considerations on which the nobles had based their policies with regard to these spiritual appointments were not always in keeping with the ecclesiastical and spiritual interest of the offices. And often the candidates had inadequate training for the spiritual tasks they were to perform. Princes who appointed spiritual vassals — and at the same time invested them with spiritual authority — accorded a higher priority to the military talents of bishops and abbots than to their understanding of church doctrine. And usually they paid little attention to their moral conduct. The weak point was observance of the vow of celibacy, which was precisely the point from which the reform movement had begun. Interest in the eremitical lifestyle was also a reaction against the problem of violation of celibacy, though there were also other factors involved there. Any improvement regarding the obligation of celibacy could not be expected as long as the higher clergy indulged in a worldly lifestyle, which was itself stimulated by the widespread practice of simony.

It was hard to change this situation because of the role of the German emperor in the church and in Christendom. He was seen as the protector of the pope, who, for his part, crowned the emperor. The emperor had the final word in the election of any new pope. He could also intervene when two popes were elected, resulting in a papal schism, or in revolts against a pope, by either the people in Rome or by influential leaders in the Papal States. The military power of the latter often surpassed that of the popes, so these leaders sometimes backed alternate candidates for the papacy or exacted changes in papal politics to further their own interests. Such problems arose frequently in Rome, and the emperor was expected to solve them. The emperor had done this in northern Italy, where he appointed the bishops as his vassals and invested them with spiritual authority. But the reform movement found much support in the northern Italian towns. A serious difficulty for the reform movement was that the structure of the empire depended to a considerable degree on the appointment of bishops as vassals. The emperor was able to keep his vassals in line as long as many of them were bishops, whose succession was not hereditary but was arranged through the emperor's intervention.

Nonetheless, it was due to Emperor Henry III that the reform movement was able to penetrate Rome. In 1046 Henry put things in Rome in order in a rather drastic manner when three candidates had been contesting the papacy. He deposed the lawful pope and banished him and the two pretenders. Then he appointed as pope a bishop who belonged to the reform movement in Lorraine. Imperial protection and patronage of a papacy favorably inclined toward reform — which would not otherwise have been able to maintain itself in Rome — lasted until Henry's death in 1056. His role had been important enough to make it difficult to do away with imperial authority in the church later on. Besides, many were not convinced that imperial authority in the church was the root of all evil. Pope Gregory VII did have that conviction, especially when Henry IV faced down the church, using the many prerogatives in the church that came with his position. But before that Rome had already decided that the election of a pope ought to be in the hands of the cardinals and that the emperor could only add his approval. Another even earlier result of the renewal of the papacy was the break with the Greek church in 1054, which proved, contrary to what was expected at the time, not to be just temporary.

Under Gregory VII the reform movement, aimed at improving the religious life of the clergy, resulted in a sharp conflict between emperor and papacy over leadership of Christendom. The result was a political earthquake in medieval society. The controversy was called the Investiture Conflict, and in view of the inextricable link between this battle and the reform movement, it has become customary to speak of it as the "Gregorian reform." And Gregory VII did play a major part in the reform.

To implement the reform program the control exercised by civil authority over the church had to be curtailed, and this could only be done if the pope were able to exercise the highest authority. With this in mind Gregory formulated a summary of his prerogatives in Christendom, the *Dictatus papae,* in which he apodictically declared the universality of papal authority over the churches, over the princes, and particularly over the emperor. This was no longer a point for further negotiation. One of the statements asserted that only the pope had the right to issue new laws in emergency situations *(pro necessitate temporum),* that is, when it was considered necessary to deviate from tradition. With this statement Gregory legitimized all the prerogatives he attributed to himself to support his claims of authority in the church and the world — the Christendom of those days.[8]

⅛   ⅛

THE DEVELOPMENTS in church politics that accompanied the Gregorian reforms have made it difficult for historians to know how to assess the reform movement. Interpretation of it depends to a large extent on which elements one emphasizes. It can be viewed as a religious movement,

---

8. Art. 7. Cf. B. Tierney, *The Crisis of Church and State, 1050-1300* (Englewood Cliffs, 1964), 49f.

certainly in terms of its original phase and the support of it by the laity, which was based on their aversion to unworthy clergy. Gregory became the foremost proponent of the movement. The movement is therefore often so closely linked to him that it is seen as part of him instead of his being part of it. But the latter was as much the case as the former. Gregory was not the only one to turn against clerics who put career above calling. Others were able to turn against clerical corruption because of the pope's protection. Local bishops had to face papal sponsorship of local reformers in various ways. Papal support for lay people found expression, for instance, in the controversy in Milan over an episcopal election. Supported by local opposition, the pope resisted the election of a simoniacal archbishop there. Concrete resistance came from a popular militia that by rioting tried — in vain — to get Gregory's candidate seated.

This militia was not an ad hoc force. Its members were recruited from the ranks of the Pataria movement, which since 1056 had agitated against unworthy clerics and, when necessary, did not recoil from violence. It was led by priests and lay people. Because of the armed activities of the Patarenes, one of the movement's lay leaders had received the banner of St. Peter from Pope Alexander II (1061-73), who had formerly been arch-bishop of Milan and had joined the ranks of the reform movement. It is often suggested that the adherents of the movement, with its zeal for a pure church and for a clergy dedicated to the ideal of poverty, were only to be found among the popular masses, and that its fight was therefore a class struggle. But this picture must at least be supplemented with the fact that the Patarene movement also counted many noblemen *(nobiles)* among its followers, while many of the clergy who had received their appointments through simony could rely on the support of the common people. The Patarene movement must be seen primarily as a religious movement in support of church reform, with a strong lay element and a program that could easily raise suspicions of heresy, once Rome believed that the reform movement had achieved its aims.

The Gregorian reform also had a totally different dimension. It established papal authority in the Latin church, provided the basis for a papal theocracy over Christendom, and engendered a process of centrali-zation that gave the whole church the appearance of being Rome's parish. For that reason both praise and blame have been heaped on Gregory VII through the ages. And thus he has remained a controversial figure. He is often seen as the main factor in the reform movement, while the fact that it was also a grassroots movement is more or less ignored. In this connection one might even ask whether the unworthiness of the clergy was the only focus of religious reform. Did not the reform, as a grassroots movement, also oppose the dominance of the clergy in the church, that is, the sacerdotal character that the clergy had acquired since the Carolingian era?

A revolutionary aspect that was undeniably present in the Gregorian reform, while it was focused on renewal, helped the church deal with heretical unrest within Christendom. Heresy was primarily a religious phenomenon, whatever social motivations there may have been. In whatever different ways the fundamental objective of heretics manifested itself, it remained the same: amelioration of the church, regardless of how this was viewed in concrete terms. Almost without exception medieval heretics, the Cathars included, wanted to restore the authentic and original content of the gospel message to its rightful place in the church and to urge Christians to live according to its precepts. Heretics were always interested in a pure understanding of Scripture and of the Apostolic Fathers, the oldest writings of Christendom. The reform of the church that they advocated always pointed to a return to primitive Christianity, to the golden age of the early church. Popular support of heretical movements always came primarily from those who wanted to change their own status in the church, which was in fact led and dominated by priests.

The laity were different from the clergy not only because they were not consecrated, except in marriage, but also because they did not know Latin, the language of the church, and were therefore considered *illiterati*, that is, unlettered. Scripture was for them a closed book, except to the degree that some of its content was depicted in murals and sculptures in churches. The laity had no share in proclaiming the gospel. The fear that they would teach heresy, in spite of their zeal, was an important factor in this exclusion. But that fear was strongly diminished in the struggle of the church of Rome against the established clergy during the Gregorian reform, at least on the part of the popes. This papal attitude was something the bishops had to reckon with, which also helps to explain the absence of heresies.

Where the clergy positively rejected the Gregorian reform, its supporters were in danger of being accused of heresy. This is quite evident in the case of Tanchelm, most likely a priest-monk of either the diocese of Utrecht or the diocese of Thérouanne. He was active in the Flemish coastal region and on the islands of Zeeland, but most of all in Antwerp. In the interest of preaching he went to Rome to plead that a section of the diocese of Utrecht be ceded to the diocese of Thérouanne. His request was granted, an indication that he was seen by Rome as belonging to the reform movement. But the canons of Utrecht, where the reform movement had not yet been accepted, pressed charges against him with the archbishop of Cologne, and probably found other ways of making life difficult for him. Their campaign was facilitated by the fact that Tanchelm, who was finally murdered in 1115, apparently lost his sense of proportion as a result of his success as a popular preacher. This we may deduce from the accusations they brought against him and from what was afterward recounted in the *Vita* of St. Norbert, even if we allow for contemporary prejudices against someone regarded as a heretic.[9]

As far as we know, the murder of Tanchelm was not followed by repercussions from Rome. The situation was changing. At the beginning of the twelfth century Rome began to realize how the Investiture Conflict, which continued to drag on and which demanded so much energy, had begun to endanger the results of the reform movement. Moreover, other matters were being neglected. Episcopal appointments clouded by simony were no longer a matter for worry; it seems that this practice had been fully suppressed. But that very success had consequences for those at the grassroots level who continued to press for reform in the church. The local bishops and their canons sensed in their contacts with Rome an easing of the pressure for reform from that direction. They were therefore able to keep local champions of reform within closer bounds than had been possible during the heyday of Gregorian reform. Not all supporters of reform continued to be considered orthodox in their teaching and to be tolerated by the church. Those whose activities took them outside the now narrower bounds came to face the usual prejudice against heretics.

༈   ༈

THIS PREJUDICE against heretics has been reconstructed in an exceptional way by Herbert Grundmann, who used texts from authors who lived from the twelfth to the fifteenth centuries.[10] Grundmann's point of departure was the assumption that the stereotypical image of the heretic in those texts existed already in the early church. Here our interest is in what

9. On this "rehabilitation" of Tanchelm, cf. M. Lambert, *Medieval Heresy* (London, 1977), 57.

10. "Der Typus des Ketzers im mittelalterlicher Anschauung" (1927) in H. Grundmann, *Ausgewählte Aufsätze* I (Stuttgart, 1976), 311-27.

Grundmann says about the reemergence of heresy at the beginning of the twelfth century, particularly about Henry of Lausanne. To understand the degree to which the stereotypical image had developed by the twelfth century, we need to give some brief attention to the image's origin.

The concept of heresy is as old as the church itself. Leaving aside its occurrence in pre-Christian religions, in which orthopraxy was usually more important than orthodoxy, the problem of heresy originated in the church from the moment it tried to define orthodoxy. In early Christian communities the traditions concerning Jesus' earthly life and his teachings depended on the persons who preached the faith in different regions. The very plurality of traditions must have raised the question of orthodoxy. In the process one particular line of tradition gained the upper hand. Other traditions and views were pushed aside as heterodox and heretical. This pattern of events also explains the distinction that was soon made between canonical and apocryphal writings. Apocryphal writings were suppressed and are therefore usually found on the periphery of ancient Christendom. The establishment of orthodoxy took place in a context of great conflict. Whoever refused to conform was soon labeled a heretic. We can thus understand the prominent place given to refutation of heresies in early Christian literature.

This polemic was present in the Latin church as well as the Greek church and did much to develop the stereotypical image of the heretic. Tertullian, who early wrote *De praescriptione haereticorum* in the third century, found the conduct of heretics devoid of true principles:

> I must not omit an account of the conduct also of the heretics — how frivolous it is, how worldly, how merely human, without seriousness, without authority, without discipline, as suits their creed. To begin with, it is doubtful who is a catechumen, and who a believer; they have all access alike, they hear alike, they pray alike — even heathens, if any such happen to come among them. "That which is holy they will cast to the dogs, and their pearls", although (to be sure) they are not real ones, "they will fling to the swine" [Matthew 7:6]. Simplicity they will have to consist in the overthrow of discipline, attention to which on our part they call brothelry. Peace also they huddle up anyhow will all comers; for it matters not to them, however different be their treatment of subjects, provided only they can conspire together to storm the citadel of the one only Truth. All are puffed up, all offer you knowledge. Their catechumens are perfect before they are full-

taught. The very women of these heretics, how wanton they are! For they are bold enough to teach, to dispute, to enact exorcisms, to undertake cures — it may be even to baptize. Their ordinations are carelessly administered, capricious, changeable. At one time they put *novices* in office; at another time, men who are bound to some secular employment; at another, persons who have apostatized from us, to bind them by vainglory, since they cannot by truth. Nowhere is promotion easier than in the camp of rebels, where the mere fact of being there is a foremost service. And so it comes to pass that to-day one man is their bishop, to-morrow another; to-day he is a deacon who to-morrow is a reader; to-day he is a presbyter who to-morrow is a layman. For even on laymen do they impose the functions of priesthood.[11]

This view was later elaborated, for instance by Augustine, who often wrote against heretics. One of his statements against the Donatists, who divided and paralyzed the church in northern Africa, was used in the Middle Ages to justify violence in the struggle against heretics. Augustine pleaded for coercive measures to force the Donatists to return to the church and to restore unity. For this he appealed to the Gospel of Luke's story of the wedding guests who failed to show up: The host insists on having a full house and so sends his servant out to gather enough guests for the wedding dinner, saying, in the Vulgate, *"Compelle intrare,"* "compel people to come in" (14:23). Augustine based his plea to force the Donatists to conform on this text. He believed the argument was to be used only in exceptional cases, but it later received general validity, since statements by Augustine came to be viewed as incontestable.[12]

Other descriptions of heretics in Augustine's writings or in works attributed to him acquired the same authority. Most suitable among these were characterizations susceptible of leading a life of their own in isolation from the allegorical contexts in which they originally appeared. This was particularly the case when Augustine compared heretics with animals such as foxes, serpents, or bulls, epithets derived from biblical texts. In his exposition of Psalm 69(68):31 Augustine accused the heretics of having the

11. *De praescr. haer.* 41, translation from *The Ante-Nicene Fathers* III (repr. Grand Rapids, 1973), 263.

12. *Contra Gaudentium,* I.25.28. Cf. H. A. Deane, *The Political and Social Ideas of St. Augustine* (New York, 1963), 172-220.

pride of the bull. He also associated their pride with the serpent, which tempts the believer as it once lured Eve and then Adam into the sin of pride.

The image of the foxes was to grow even more autonomously. It was based on two passages: "Catch us the foxes, the little foxes, that ruin the vineyards" (Song of Sol. 2:15) and the account of Samson, who caught three hundred foxes, "turned the foxes tail to tail, and put a torch between each pair of tails," and then sent them into the Philistines' standing grain (Judg. 15:4f.). Augustine likened the foxes' tails to heretics, who leave damnation and fire behind, while their faces offer flattery and deception.

These images of heretics, which could so easily function outside their original contexts, received further elaboration from other early Christian authors, such as Gregory the Great, whose writings were also much read. For him heretics, together with all the unrighteous, were like the antichrist. He also compared them to lepers, with the result that in the Middle Ages heresy was often regarded as a contagious disease.

Patristic writings thus established the view of the heretics that was current in the medieval world. This is also true with respect to the most incriminating image that gained common currency. It, too, was based on a biblical text. Matthew 7:15 speaks of false prophets, those who present themselves in sheep's clothes, but in reality are ravenous wolves. This image was used again and again to illustrate the hypocrisy of heretics in their participation in the life of the church, and to show that their piety was only a matter of appearance. This interpretation of Matthew's verse must have been present in early Christian literature along with the other interpretations of biblical images mentioned above. It was, in any case, derived from earlier writings by the Carolingian abbot Hrabanus Maurus (†856), who used it in his commentary on Matthew: "This must be applied, in particular, to heretics, for they appear to surround themselves with abstinence, chastity, and fasting, while inwardly they are poisonous and deceive the hearts of simple brothers."[13]

Hrabanus wrote his commentary at a time when most people had no direct knowledge of heretics. He was, for his part, just repeating what had been written earlier. In his time his remark was of little consequence, but repetition of his formula would take on new significance when heretics once again manifested themselves in Christendom. From the start it was clear how corrupt were those who, because of the reforms they propagated, came into conflict with ecclesiastical authority. And it was clear how

13. II.7 (3) = *PL* CVII, 845.

hypocritical their activities were and how subversive their doctrines were. Because they were heretics, they were necessarily beset by pride and thus by all the vices that originated in pride. They were, therefore, hypocritical, disobedient, and arrogant. They followed innovations, they bragged, and they gossiped. They hid all these vices under a guise of piety. They pretended to exercise self-mortification and to be devoted to prayer and fasting, but behind closed doors they gave themselves over to orgies. They kept their true actions hidden. We encounter all these charges in the case of Henry of Lausanne.

2. HENRY OF LAUSANNE: FROM REFORMER TO HERETIC

SUCH SUSPICIONS of hypocrisy and corruption had already rested on those who were identified as heretics in the first half of the eleventh century. But then these suspicions disappeared in the second half of that century or were suppressed, because the supporters of church reform were given free play. But when the tide changed, latecomers to the cause of reform once again easily fell under suspicion. When Rome changed its course with regard to the Investiture Conflict after the Concordat of Worms in 1122, local churches could return to their old ways of doing things. And there were even earlier indications that such change was coming.

When Henry of Lausanne first appeared in Le Mans at the beginning of Lent in 1116, he introduced himself to the bishop as a preacher of penance. The bishop, who was about to leave for Rome, gave Henry a license to preach. But on his return the bishop called the popular preacher to order, expelled him from the diocese, and warned his fellow bishops against him. The question arises whether the change in the bishop's attitude was in part the result of his journey to Rome. Had he seen the tide already turning and concluded that local ecclesiastical authorities were free to alter their own course?

It seems to me that this supposition goes too far, considering the bishop involved. We know a bit about him. Hildebert of Lavardin (1056-1133) began his career as a teacher at the cathedral school of Le Mans and in 1096 became bishop there. In 1125 he was elected archbishop of Tours. He is still remembered for his letters and sermons and is also considered one of the best medieval Latin poets. At times he had to defend himself against insinuations that he put his rational views above the authority of tradition. It was a serious accusation, but he was never formally called to account for his views. He administered his diocese with care, had many contacts — also outside his own region — and often participated in synods in Rome. He belonged to the supporters of church reform, notably with regard to the emancipation of the church from the control of the laity and princes. We do not know his attitude to the grassroots reform initiatives, but he cannot have been ignorant of the activities of itinerant preachers and of the problems they posed. In a general way he must therefore have known what he was doing when he permitted Henry to preach in his city and diocese. We must, then, explain his change of mind on the basis of the activities of Henry himself.

We know less about Henry than about Hildebert. None of Henry's writings have survived. There is a report of a disputation between Henry and a monk named William in about 1132. But this report was written by William and we learn about Henry's contribution only through him. Nonetheless, this report is the first information about Henry after his activities in Le Mans. In a treatise written about 1134 against the errors of the heretic Peter of Bruys (†1132), who worked in the south of France, Peter the Venerable, the abbot of Cluny, says that Henry was Peter of Bruys's successor, though the teachings of the two preachers were not the same in all respects. In 1135 we find Henry present at a council in Pisa. He was brought there involuntarily by the bishop of Arles, who had taken him prisoner. In Pisa his teachings were condemned, and he renounced them. Nevertheless, he later continued to preach in southern France. In 1144 Bernard of Clairvaux wrote a letter about this to the count of Toulouse, better known as the count of Saint-Gilles. A year later Bernard undertook a preaching tour through the region where Henry was active in order to repair the damage that Henry had caused. The two did not meet at that time. It is likely that Henry would not have been interested in such an encounter, since it would have meant the end of his freedom. But he did lose his freedom a year later, and the account of how that happened is the last information we have about him.

Historians have wondered whether Henry must be counted among the itinerant preachers who were active in western France in the first decades of the twelfth century. Most have denied this, since these preachers did not leave the church, in spite of the objections that their activities raised. But we can give a more precise answer, because our information about Henry allows us to reconstruct to some extent the development of his views and teachings. What has been recorded about his conduct in Le

Mans does, indeed, point to associations with these popular preachers, at least if we ignore what was said about him to label him as a heretic. Outwardly he resembled these preachers in many ways: an unshaven man with an exhausted look and tired eyes, his hair tied together, barefoot and lightly dressed, even in winter. With no place to call home he was content with a doorway or even slept in a gutter. He and those of his followers who accompanied him looked like penitents, that is to say, preachers of penance, because they carried a cross with them and because he had asked beforehand the bishop's permission to preach.

But Henry arrived on the scene later than those who are known as the itinerant preachers. The beginning of his activities, probably in Le Mans, more or less coincided with the moment when the other such preachers neared the ends of their lives. Robert of Abrissel and Bernard of Tiron died in 1116, Girald of Salles in 1120, and Vitalis of Savigny in 1121. Peter the Hermit, who had preached in support of the First Crusade, had already died in 1115. Chronologically Henry was closest to Norbert of Xanten. Norbert began to preach around 1115, but was considerably older. He, too, was subject to suspicion, even though he had had a career in the church and had in 1113 refused the offer of an episcopal see. He was called to account before a synod in Fritzlar and apparently did not handle himself too well on that occasion. His reputation improved in 1121 when he founded the monastery of Prémontré, which brought an end to his followers' itinerant life.

The itinerancy of the itinerant preachers was criticized chiefly because there were many women among their followers. The questions posed by this could be solved only by placing the women in convents, and the preachers mentioned above all opted for that solution. Even Peter the Hermit founded a convent after his return from the crusade. This method of dealing with female followers was one of the most important ways in which popular preachers who were acceptable to the church were distinguished from those who were labeled heretics. Heretics were accused of always traveling in the company of women. We have quoted in an earlier chapter a well-known statement from a sermon against heretics preached in 1144 by Bernard of Clairvaux: "To be always in a woman's company without having carnal knowledge of her — is this not a greater miracle than raising the dead?"[14]

We do not know if Henry of Lausanne ever attempted to establish

14. *Sermones in Cantu,* 65, IV (*On the Song of Songs* III [Kalamazoo, 1979], 184).

a convent for his female followers. One could argue that he was not able to get to that point since he was forced out of the church after a short period of preaching and so could not have received ecclesiastical permission to establish a convent if he wanted it. But we can also ask whether, after his failure in Le Mans, he still considered himself a member of the church. He probably did, but with the convictions that the church needed fundamental reform and that he was working toward that goal. What he did before Le Mans is also unknown. It is usually supposed that he came from Lausanne, but we do not know whether he also preached there.

From the description of his appearance and clothing we may conclude that Henry was most likely a hermit when he came to Le Mans. He may have been a follower of a popular preacher who had begun to work independently. Since all popular preachers of the time were hermits, that is, not connected to any religious community, it is likely that Henry also had such a background. That he sought the bishop's permission in Le Mans and that he began his preaching there in Lent also point in that direction. Hermits were not only preachers but also penitents.

The main distinction among these hermits was their background. Some had been monks but had left the monastery, sometimes to escape election as abbot. Others were ordained priests who wanted to be involved in pastoral duties no longer. But there were also among the hermits laymen who participated in the hermit's customary activity of preaching to the people, though it was questioned whether they did so legitimately. The hermits themselves, particularly during the period in which they were regarded as the executors of the reform movement in the church, considered this question to be of minor significance. Bernard of Tiron, a priest himself, believed that the preachers had this prerogative because of their ascetic manner of life. Yet the problem was more complicated than that. The preachers' sermons were intended to bring people to repentance. If a sermon was successful, a conversation might follow, culminating in confession. Church law required that confession and absolution — a sacramental act — remain the exclusive prerogative of priests. At times the hermits disobeyed this rule, but not when priests were present.

But even apart from confession, the church did not permit laymen to preach without further qualification. Toward the end of the twelfth century the rules concerning lay preaching were quite strict, and acquiring a license to preach was far from simple. Peter Waldo experienced this when he wanted to preach, and it is particularly clear in Walter Map's satirical story about the appearance of some of Waldo's followers at the Third

Lateran Council in 1179. They came to ask permission to preach but were refused after a theological examination, which was no more than a trap.[15] Earlier in the century the rules were less rigid, which made compromise possible. The sections of the Bible that deal with the mysteries of the faith were reserved for the clergy, but lay hermits were allowed to preach moralizing texts or edifying stories, though we cannot say to what extent this precept was adhered to.

We are left with the question of Henry's status as hermit. Was he a priest, a monk, or a layman? Bernard of Clairvaux called him a runaway monk, one who had studied and had then begun to sell his knowledge of the gospel for money. This statement has remained undisputed until today. But it would seem to me that historians have been misled. For Bernard's statement leaves unexplained why this popular preacher, who in the course of his preaching in Le Mans came into conflict with the local clergy, saw his activities suspended by the bishop. It is true that we do not possess equally full accounts of the conflicts between other popular preachers and the clerical establishment, but there is indirect information that they, too, could be rather harsh in their dealings with the ecclesiastical authorities and turned their fury against them more often than against the sins they were denouncing. This leads us to conclude that the reason that Bishop Hildebert silenced Henry must not be sought exclusively in Henry's conduct and in a policy change on the part of the local church leaders, though we must not forget that Henry began his work as a preacher when the situation had already become less favorable. The grassroots reform movement had already seen its day.

The written report of Henry's activities in Le Mans calls him a heretic, specifically a wolf in sheep's clothing subject to all the typical vices attributed to heretics, though the account does not clarify what was so heretical in his teachings. He felt compassion for prostitutes and arranged many marriages for them. This matchmaking turned out to be catastrophic since the women received no further guidance and continued in their former way of life. In this respect Henry's acts were almost revolutionary, since he ignored the church's prudent insistence on a dowry and a gift to the bride, which would have given such relationships more chance of success. He was also accused of demanding that these women undress before him, of committing adultery with married women, and of seeking sexual satisfaction with boys as well. But these sorts of charges were little

---

15. Wakefield-Evans, 203f.

more than clichés, while Henry's care for prostitutes was the normal practice of other popular preachers.

He was also blamed for inciting rebellion against the clergy, which reflects the usual antisacerdotalism of the hermits of the time. But his success in that regard not only witnesses to his proficiency as a preacher, which was highly praised, but also to popular resentment of the clergy. This resentment was caused not only by the unworthy manner of life of some clergy, but also by the monopoly of the clergy, as the educated class, in church and society, that is, in Christendom. Because of Henry's efforts the people refused to sell to the clergy and treated them as heathen and sinners. This also shows how Henry fitted in with the reform movement "from below," from which Gregory VII had sought support and which he had sanctioned. But in 1116 the days of the herdsman called to be a prophet (Amos 7:14f.) were over.

❦   ❦

HENRY'S THEOLOGICAL VIEWS are not revealed in the account of his activity in Le Mans but are in the account of his disputation with the monk William, which occurred in about 1132. In this discussion Henry stated that his first allegiance was to God and not to humans. God had commissioned him to preach the gospel to all people and to love his neighbor as himself. He based his teaching on the New Testament and not on Jerome, Augustine, or the other Fathers. He also rejected the view that children who die before receiving baptism are lost; according to William this was a denial of original sin. Henry also saw no need for anointing at baptism and held that priests living unworthy lives could not consecrate the eucharistic elements. Marriage, he believed, must be based on the consent of both partners — a point also mentioned as a prerequisite for marriage in Gratian's *Decretum,* which dates from 1143. Henry also denied that the priests of his day should still possess the authority "to bind and to loose." The gospel, he said, gives no indication of a need for confession to a priest and attributes no value to prayers for the dead. Finally, he held that priests and bishops were not to receive money or any other income from church offices, that they were not to display ring, miter, or staff, and that there was no need for churches of wood or stone.[16]

Henry must already have had some of these ideas, such as those

16. For a translation of this account, see Moore, 46-60.

concerning obedience to God alone and his own calling and task, when he arrived in Le Mans sixteen years earlier. Likewise his views about the sacramental disqualification of unworthy priests must already have belonged among his spiritual baggage. No doubt at that early time he already made a rigorous distinction between worthy and unworthy. It is less clear whether he already believed at that time that bishops should forego ring, miter, and staff. He might have been influenced on this point by the notorious criticism launched in 1124 by Bernard of Clairvaux against the Cluniacs. Henry did not condemn these episcopal accoutrements as such, as is clear from the text of his disputation with William. He criticized, rather, the manner in which they were adorned and were covered with precious stones. Henry's opposition to church buildings may also have been inspired by Bernard's criticism. Many protests against lavish church buildings were based on what Bernard wrote in his *Apology*. Finally, Henry's view that confession to a priest is unnecessary may have something to do with his background as a hermit, but may also have been influenced by contemporary theological discussions of this subject.

The influence of the theological debates of the time on Henry's views, as far as they are represented in his debate with William, was not restricted to his rejection of confession. His refusal to accept the authority of the Church Fathers can be placed against the same background. The core of Henry's teaching was not rejection of the Old Testament, but rather his insistence that the authority of the Fathers should not be invoked in interpretation of the New Testament. The first versions of Abelard's controversial treatise *Sic et non* were already circulating when Henry and William held their disputation. It dealt with contradictions among statements of the Fathers, which led Abelard to ask how much authority these statements should be accorded. Henry went further and came to the radical conclusion that the authority of the Fathers ought to be totally rejected. Henry might also have obtained from Abelard his idea that children too young to understand the meaning of faith have no need of baptism. But Abelard formulated his views in a much subtler way, which suggests that — also with regard to issues such as confession and the authority of the Fathers — Henry probably did not have firsthand knowledge of the theological novelties of the time.

Comparing what we know about Henry's teaching during his activities in Le Mans with his views in 1132, we clearly see how his ideas developed, in particular in areas that led him into contradiction of the traditional views of his time. This may indicate that he, in his own views, only gradually drifted out of the church and that he only gradually realized how radical his ideas had become and how his radicalism had broadened in areas of thought that fitted well with his revolutionary nature.

But, as we said before, the official church had no further use for Henry. This was certainly true of Bishop Hildebert. Shortly after Henry's preaching campaign, Hildebert gave two of his clergymen, who for some time had been followers of Henry, a letter in which he declared that they had renounced their errors. This letter was a letter of introduction to other bishops and calls Henry a great snare of the devil and a shield bearer of the antichrist. But at that moment Henry had not yet severed his ties with the church.

When he did break with the church is difficult to determine. The disputation with William probably occurred when Henry still considered himself a member of the church. Otherwise, why would he have bothered to engage in the debate? But it is unclear whether he still felt bound to the church when he went to preach in southern France to people who had earlier listened to Peter of Bruys. There was some difference between the views of these two men. Peter the Venerable indicates in the introduction of his treatise against Peter of Bruys and his followers that he had noticed this difference when reading the account of Henry's disputation with William. This treatise and the account of the disputation do, indeed, point to some differences. Peter of Bruys rejected the Old Testament outright and was much opposed to church buildings, altars, and organ music. He gathered crucifixes for burning, which, according to Peter the Venerable's treatise, proved to be his undoing: His opponents pushed him into a fire kindled to burn crosses. Compared to those of Peter of Bruys, Henry's views were more refined theologically, and he was closer to the teachings of the church.

William wrote his account of his debate with Henry for an un-named bishop. He wanted to give the bishop the opportunity to combat Henry with solid arguments if Henry — referred to as a monster — were to show up in his diocese. William insisted that he wrote his account with great care, but we need not take his word for it. He portrays the debate almost as an interrogation and portrays himself as doing most of the speaking in order to refute at length some of the statements that Henry was allowed to make. This in itself makes the account a somewhat dubious source for Henry's teachings.

Likewise the reports about Henry's attendance at the council in Pisa in 1135 give little information. According to a report included in the chronicle of the bishops of Le Mans, which gives a detailed description of the events of 1116, Henry was declared a heretic and imprisoned. But later — probably against the wishes of the council fathers — he is supposed to have received permission to go to another region, where he had the opportunity to establish a new sect.[17] The other bit of information is found in an account of a journey that Bernard of Clairvaux made in 1145 to southern France to oppose Henry. This account states that Henry renounced his errors in Pisa and was put at the disposal of the abbot of Clairvaux.[18] He sent Henry with a letter to his monastery, with the intent that Henry would become a monk there. But that did not happen, and Henry apparently returned to southern France to continue his preaching. Perhaps his experience in Pisa convinced him that he no longer belonged to the church and forced him into a sectarian mode, so that he acted only out of his own convictions.

The final bit of information about the teachings and person of Henry is found in Bernard's letter to the count of Saint-Gilles in 1144, written in preparation for Bernard's journey to that region:

> We have heard and known of the great evils which the heretic Henry inflicts every day on the Church. He is now busy in your territory, a ravening wolf in the guise of a sheep. But, according to the indication given by our Lord, we can tell what sort of man he is by his fruits. Churches without people, people without priests, priests without the reverence due to them, and Christians without Christ. The churches are regarded as synagogues, the holiness of God's sanctuary is denied, the sacraments are not considered sacred, and holy days are deprived of their solemnities. Men are dying in their sins, and souls are everywhere being hurled before the awesome tribunal unreconciled by repentance, unfortified by Communion. The grace of Baptism is denied, and Christian children are kept away from the life given by Christ.[19]

There is hardly any further information about Henry in this letter. It mentions the same points as we found in William's account. The question remains, of course, where Bernard got his information. He attended the council at Pisa and may have been involved in the case. But

17. Wakefield-Evans, 114f.
18. This was reported by Geoffrey of Auxerre, Bernard's secretary, in a letter to Master Archenfrid, ch. 5 = *PL* CLXXXV, 412.
19. Letter 241 = *SBO* VIII, 125-27 = James, 388 (letter 317).

the abbot was also involved in the major problems for which the council had been called, and these must have taken most of his time. It seems doubtful that Bernard learned more about Henry during this council, considering what else he writes in this letter about Henry as a person:

> Now hear what sort of man he is. He is an apostate who, having abandoned the monastic habit (for he was once a monk), has returned to the world and the filth of the flesh, like a dog to its vomit. Ashamed to live amongst kinsmen and those who know him, or rather not permitted to do so on account of his monstrous crimes, he has girded himself and taken the road to where he is not known, becoming a gyrovague and fugitive on the face of the earth. When he began to seek a living he sold the Gospel (he is an educated man), scattering the word of God for money and preaching so that he might live. If he is able to secure something over and above his keep from simple people or some elderly women, he squanders it in gambling or more shameful ways. Frequently after a day of popular adulation this notable preacher is to be found with prostitutes, sometimes even with married women. Enquire if you like why he left Lausanne, Le Mans, Poitiers, and Bordeaux. There is no way at all of return open to him in any of these places, because of the foul traces he has left behind him.[20]

This letter contains the fullest information about the person of Henry and his activities. But even the region where Henry preached is not completely certain. As indicated before, Lausanne was probably his place of origin, before he became the follower of a hermit-preacher. Poitiers and Bordeaux most likely were part of the area where he was still active in 1144 as the heir of Peter of Bruys. A year later Bernard set out on his preaching tour against Henry's teachings in Bordeaux; he finally ended his tour only in Albi. This correction, if it is such indeed, is of little importance, except as an intimation that the information in this letter may not be as trustworthy as it would seem at first sight. I have already suggested that Bishop Hildebert could take measures against Henry because he was a layman. But that supposition seems to be contradicted by the content of this letter and by the influence of theological novelties of the time on Henry. His disputation with William also suggests that he was an educated man. Would he otherwise have dared to participate in such a debate?

Those who were not intimately acquainted with Henry no doubt

20. Letter 241.2 = James, 389.

regarded him as an educated person. What illiterate layman would engage in such activities as he did? Bernard of Clairvaux must have found it hard to imagine that Henry was merely a lay person. And we should add that Henry himself pretended that he was literate, that he was able to read Latin. Bernard's characterization of Henry in his letter to the count of Saint-Gilles makes Henry resemble Bernard's idea of a heretic as it is found in his three sermons on the Song of Solomon. It is not a true picture. Moreover, one might ask to what extent this sketch may possibly have been the work of one of the abbot's secretaries. Because of his manifold duties and his extensive correspondence, Bernard often gave considerable freedom to his secretaries in the composition of his letters, without always checking what they wrote on his behalf. And to have a letter rewritten on parchment was both costly and cumbersome. Bernard did not authorize his letters with his signature but with a seal, and even affixing the seal was a task of his secretaries. So Bernard's letter offers us no guarantee of Henry's literacy, while the description of Henry as a runaway monk may be reduced to a reminiscence of Bernard of what happened at Pisa: Henry was supposed to become a monk in Clairvaux, but failed to go through with his promise.

As we have mentioned, the account of Henry's debate with William portrays it as an interrogation rather than a real debate. Henry's ideas are given only in outline to provide the opportunity for prolonged and verbose refutation. Would Henry have been content with the role he was assigned if he had been an educated person? His share in the discussions may, of course, have been more extensive. But would such an account have been made, if he had personally been involved with it? It is unlikely that William found it necessary to inform Henry about the written account, but it must be assumed that some notes were taken during the debate. Had Henry been literate, he would no doubt have kept a close eye on what was written down. But the account does not contain any such hint.

It would not in any way have been in Henry's interest for it to become known that he was illiterate. He would have lost any further preaching license, as had happened in Le Mans. His comment on the proposition that one need not necessarily confess to a priest may in fact be an allusion to his own illiteracy: Henry believed one could just as well confess to a peasant or an illiterate person, a term that indicated lay persons, who were considered illiterate because they knew no Latin. Henry must have heard confessions repeatedly and must, in the eremitical tradition, have believed that this could be done by a lay person.

Whether confession to lay persons was permissible was a point of debate among the theologians of the time, but they saw the more general question of whether confession was a prerequisite for absolution as more vital. Some believed that forgiveness without confession was possible; this was hard to disprove, but such statements led to pastoral confusion. One of the sermons of Werner (†1174), a monk of the monastery of St. Blaise, indicates how intensely the connection between confession to a priest and absolution was discussed. Werner's defense of the necessity of confession to a priest rested on a Gospel passage in which lepers are told to go and show themselves to a priest (Luke 5:14). Werner used the lepers as a metaphor for sinners. In his disputation with William, Henry, however, referred to the words of the apostle James, "Confess your sins to one another" (5:16) as the basis for his conviction. That Henry quoted this text is no definite proof that he was literate. The text was probably very popular in eremitical circles and was, no doubt, memorized by Henry. Illiterate people were often adept in the use of their memory.

As for other theological novelties that have left traces in Henry's teachings — for instance, the weakening of the authority of the Fathers in Abelard's shocking work *Sic et non* — Henry may have received such information indirectly through hearsay. The way in which he used this particular idea was far different from what Abelard intended to say about patristic authority: Henry argued that the opinions of the Fathers were of no importance for human salvation, which went considerably beyond Abelard's view. He did the same with regard to infant baptism, which also tends to confirm the supposition that Henry received his information through others. That he did so is quite possible, since he had among his hearers many clergy — and students for the priesthood were already counted as clergy. We know that this was the case in Le Mans, and, considering his success, it must also have been true later. He may well have acquired his information about fashionable theological trends from these clerical followers. This would also explain the imprecise manner in which he incorporated such ideas into his teachings.

❧   ❧

REFUTING THE WITNESSES for the defense does not prove without a doubt that Henry was indeed illiterate and therefore did not belong to the clergy. There are, however, more direct indications of this. We find these in accounts of his activities in Le Mans. In the chronicle of the bishops of Le Mans we are told that during one of his preaching campaigns in the town the canons brought him a letter in which they protested against the way in which he incited the people against them. Henry refused to read the letter. Then one of the canons read it aloud in the presence of the crowd. Henry's only reaction consisted of repeated cries that the accusations being read were lies. In view of the exaggerated nature of other accusations against Henry in this account, this incident loses some of its credibility. But, on the other hand, it does not belong to the part of the account in which Henry is at length accused of immoral behavior and therefore must not automatically be regarded as a mere stereotype and as a case of biased reporting. If the story is true, it is strange that Henry did not take the letter himself in order to refute it while he read it. Such a defense would have been more effective, but would have been possible only if Henry could read. On the other hand, if the story had been intended to unmask Henry as an illiterate who assumed rights that as a layman were beyond his competence, this would have been done in a more explicit way.

Henry's illiteracy is explicitly mentioned in the account of Bishop Hildebert's discussion with Henry after the bishop had returned from Rome and had learned about Henry's activities during his absence. What the bishop had heard gave him ample reason to ask Henry for clarification, if only because of the hostility the bishop experienced when he returned. During this conversation the bishop asked what canonical right Henry had for his preaching; previously Hildebert had not asked such questions, apparently because it did not seem important to him at that time, considering the favorable impression he had of Henry. According to the account, the bishop asked Henry about his *professio* (vow); Henry acknowledged that he did not understand the question. Subsequently Hildebert inquired about his office in the church; Henry answered that he was a deacon. In order to substantiate the truth of Henry's statements, the bishop proposed — and here we perhaps discern the poet in Hildebert — that they sing together the hymn that was part of the matins of that day. Henry then replied that he did not know which hymn was prescribed for that day. The bishop began to sing the hymns in honor of Mary, which were commonly known among the clergy. But Henry did not know the words of those hymns either. And so he was finally obliged to admit the falsehood of his claims of belonging to the clergy and to concede that he had no theological training.

This part of the account of Henry's activities begins with a verse from the Psalms: "Fill their faces with shame, so that they may seek your name, O Lord" (83:16). If this section was meant to be tendentious, then the reason

223

that it began with this verse must also have been tendentious. But if Henry was indeed a lay person, then this section must have been a description of reality. For the bishop the ensuing procedure was quite simple. He did not need to accuse Henry of being a heretic and to prosecute him. That might have been more difficult, since, according to this account, Henry had in Le Mans been guilty of radicalism rather than of concrete heresy, at least according to the norms of the Gregorian reform. It would suffice for Hildebert to expel Henry from his diocese for preaching and for acting as a confessor and as an accuser of the clergy with no authorization.

Finally, there is another indication that Henry was illiterate that tends to confirm our explanation of why he, though he wanted to be a reformer, nevertheless ended as a heretic. As has been mentioned, Hildebert gave a letter of recommendation to two former followers of Henry to show to other bishops so that they might resume their clerical offices in some other diocese. In this letter Hildebert summarized his negative judgment of Henry in one sentence, since it was a short and businesslike letter. We are told that Henry had feigned piety through the way he dressed and literacy through the way he spoke.[21] This remark is somewhat stereotypical, but may in this case have reflected reality, at least with regard to Henry's pretense at being literate.

That Henry was a lay person is probably the main reason that he failed as a reformer and that, when he wanted to persist in his attempts at reform, he drifted further and further from the church. We have left the technical problems aside, such as the dating of William's account and of the treatise of Peter the Venerable. A solution to these problems is at least as important as any other elaboration of our present argument. But what we have specifically emphasized in this context is the tragedy for this lay person, who, when he wanted to work for church renewal in the tradition of the hermits, did not get the opportunity, at least not in the way he anticipated. Another factor in all this was, no doubt, Henry's personality, which remains largely hidden behind the stereotyped image of a heretic. But it does become clear that the church, in spite of the reforms that were taking place, had very little to offer to lay people who wanted a deeper religion and a more profound experience of Christian faith. That was true, in any case, for those who wanted more than just doing penance for their sins and venerating the saints and who wanted to receive the sacraments in other than a purely magical way.

21. Moore, 38.

VIII

Master Peter Abelard (1079-1141):
The Misfortunes of a
Single-Minded Teacher[1]

❧   ❧

ONE OF THE most frequently discussed and translated writings from the first half of the twelfth century is a letter written by Peter Abelard between 1132 and 1136 and addressed to a (possibly fictitious) friend. In this letter Abelard tries to comfort his friend by telling him the sad story of his own misfortunes. Since Petrarch this letter has been known as *Historia calamitatum,* that is, as the story of the calamities that Abelard had experienced.[2] The autobiographical nature of the letter makes it unique in epistolary literature of its time. Some other letters dating from that time do, of course, also contain expressions of personal sentiments or confessions, but they do not give complete life stories.

Autobiographies were not completely unknown at the time, as is evident from what Guibert of Nogent wrote twenty years earlier under the rather transparent title *De vita sua.*[3] Both Guibert and Abelard were influenced by Augustine's *Confessions,* but while Augustine wrote his life story as a praise to God, the two later authors, through writing out of

---

1. This chapter is a revision of my valedictory lecture at the Free University in Amsterdam, October 16, 1986.

2. J. T. Muckle, *The Story of Abelard's Adversities* (Toronto, 1964). Muckle also edited the Latin text: "Abelard's Letter to a Friend (Historia Calamitatum)," *Mediaeval Studies* 12 (1950), 163-213.

3. *Self and Society in Medieval France: The Memoirs of Abbot Guibert of Nogent (1046?-c. 1125),* ed. J. F. Benton (New York, 1970).

Christian motivations, focused more on the stories of their own lives. But they did so in different ways. While Guibert gradually moved away from an autobiographical approach in recounting events that he had experienced but that had not directly affected him, Abelard continued to tell of his own misfortunes. He describes them as a gradual self-purification,[4] but does not place them in any wider social context.

The *Historia calamitatum* is unique among letters in yet another way. The twelfth century knew nothing about postal confidentiality. Usually a letter was intended for more people than the name of the addressee would suggest. Writing materials were too costly and the energy required to prepare them was too great for just one person to benefit from a letter. Often other people had already read a letter before it reached the addressee. The content of letters was usually rather general in nature — though receiving a letter was still an important event — and the addressee often received an additional oral message through the person who delivered the letter. The person who transmitted that message derived credibility and prestige from the letter that he delivered.

Most of Abelard's contemporaries, however, with the possible exception of some friends, remained unaware of this letter, even though it was probably intended as an open letter. Not until a good century later, when the text fell into the hands of Jean de Meung, did it become widely known. De Meung translated the letter and also used the love relationship of Abelard with Heloise, which was mentioned in the letter, in one of his own writings, which was dominated by love themes of antiquity and the Middle Ages. Indeed, de Meung completed the *Roman de la Rose* which had been started by Guillaume de Lorris. Since his day the story of Abelard and Heloise has been regarded, even when detached from the *Historia calamitatum,* as a literary gem.

But there were still other reasons why many showed interest in this text of Abelard. It is not complete in itself. It was when Heloise had read it, almost immediately after Abelard had written it, that she initiated her famous exchange of letters with Abelard. She was at that moment the abbess of a community of nuns that had just moved to a monastery named for the Paraclete, the Holy Spirit as the Comforter of humankind, not far from the city of Troyes. This community flourished under the leadership of Heloise, while the abbess herself was highly regarded by church authorities of the time.

These circumstances did not prevent Heloise from writing to Abelard.

---

4. M. M. McLaughlin, "Abelard as Autobiographer: The Motives and Meaning of his 'Story of Calamities,'" *Speculum* 42 (1967), 463-88.

Her first letter, which in this case was exclusively intended for the addressee, refers without any inhibition to their former love affair and tells Abelard clearly that she continues to relive it in her memory. She also complains that Abelard has not written to her since the affair ended. This letter led to further correspondence, in which Heloise wrote as a woman still in love and Abelard, on the other hand, adopted the role of her spiritual counselor.

Heloise eventually accepted his standpoint and the correspondence ends with three letters in which Abelard writes on the origin of the phenomenon of religious women, saying that their history in the church is as old as that of the monks, in which Heloise asks Abelard to write a rule for Heloise's convent, arguing that the rule of St. Benedict, written for men, is unsuitable for women, and, finally, in which Abelard fulfills this request.[5] All the letters were preserved, probably in a manuscript kept in Heloise's convent. But the fact that the manuscript of the letters dates from the thirteenth century has given rise to doubts concerning their authenticity. It has been asked repeatedly since the beginning of the nineteenth century[6] whether they were, rather, written after the deaths of Abelard and Heloise. One of the problems in this exchange of letters concerns Heloise's complaint that Abelard had never written to her. This is considered improbable since he had assisted her a few years earlier in acquiring the "Paraclete" monastery for her community and had remained in contact through regular visits to the convent. Furthermore, Abelard does not write as a philosopher in these letters and also fails to manifest his philosophical commitment in his *Historia calamitatum*. None of his theological convictions is explicitly mentioned in these writings.

Another argument against the authenticity of the letters arises from Heloise's second letter to Abelard. There she confesses that she is still engrossed in the impure thoughts of their former passion and that her mind is more occupied with such thoughts than with prayer, even during the celebration of the Mass, when prayer must be as pure as possible. It has been repeatedly asked whether such a statement could have been made in the twelfth century by a woman who had devoted herself fully to God, who lived accordingly, and who had assumed major responsibilities.

5. J. T. Muckle, "The Personal Letters between Abelard and Heloise," *Mediaeval Studies* 12 (1950), 163-213; 15 (1953), 47-94; 17 (1955), 240-81; T. P. McLaughin, "Abelard's Rule for Religious Women," *Mediaeval Studies* 18 (1956), 241-92.

6. E.g., P. von Moos, *Mittelalterforschung und Ideologiekritik. Die Gelehrtenstreit um Héloise* (Munich, 1974).

With this question, discussion of the authenticity of these letters is linked to discussion of changes in Western European society in the twelfth century. Does this correspondence, particularly Heloise's letters, give expression to the radical changes that were occurring at that time? Discussion of these sudden changes began in 1927, when C. H. Haskins described the twelfth century as a "renaissance," and continues today.[7]

It appeared that doubts regarding the authenticity of the letters of Abelard and Heloise had dissipated since Étienne Gilson published *Héloïse et Abélard* in 1938.[8] His meticulous textual analyses carried much weight and appeared to have given final proof of the genuineness of the letters. But the controversy was reignited in 1972 during an important international congress on Abelard and Peter the Venerable held in the former abbey of Cluny. There J. F. Benton presented new arguments that these letters could not be older than the thirteenth century, though he could not name anyone in particular who was sufficiently ingenious to be branded as the author of the forgery.[9]

There were emotional reactions during and after the congress, and the polemics started up again.[10] But the discussion did change in character. It now focused more on how much of the content of the letters could be regarded as authentic. Some argued that all the letters were written by Abelard and none by Heloise in view of their linguistic similarities — an argument that is hardly convincing. Others suggested that the *Historia calamitatum* might be authentic, but that all or some of the subsequent correspondence was of later date. Or it is thought that there was an actual exchange of letters, but that they were revised later. Many give some credence to such presuppositions. As a result anyone who refers to these letters as historical feels somewhat insecure.

The increased interest of recent years in the status of women in the past has offered a completely new line of approach to the question of the letters' authenticity. New arguments are now put forward in favor of

7. C. H. Haskins, *The Renaissance of the Twelfth Century* (5th ed.; Cambridge, MA, 1971). Cf. R. L. Benson and G. Constable, ed., *Renaissance and Renewal in the Twelfth Century* (1982; repr. Oxford, 1985).

8. English translation, 1951; repr. Ann Arbor, 1963.

9. J. F. Benton, "Fraud, Fiction and Borrowing in the Correspondence of Abelard and Heloise," in *Pierre Abélard, Pierre le Vénérable. Les courants philosophiques, littéraires et artistiques en Occident au XIIe siècle* (Paris, 1975), 499-506.

10. D. E. Luscombe, "The Letters of Heloise and Abelard since 'Cluny 1972,'" in *Petrus Abaelardus. Person, Werk und Wirkung*, ed. R. Thomas (Trier, 1980), 19-39.

authenticity. Heloise demonstrates with her views of male-female relations how the status of women had changed as part of the broader changes in twelfth-century society. Abelard seems to have accepted this change, at least in principle. In everyday life, however, he still operated with the view of women that had prevailed until then.[11] Naturally, this discussion has not ended. But we should mention that the instigator of these renewed debates has withdrawn some of his objections against the authenticity of the letters.[12]

꙳   ꙳

FOR YET ANOTHER, and totally different, reason the *Historia calamitatum* demands the attention of those who study the changes that occurred in the twelfth century. These changes also concerned to a considerable degree the humanities, philosophy, and theology. The emergence of the scholastic method brought a drastic change in these disciplines. Teaching acquired a central place in them. Abelard had an extremely important, or even pioneering, part in this first phase of Scholasticism. This, of course, also made him a very controversial figure, especially with those who continued to approach these disciplines in more traditional ways and who continued to think of them in terms of Christian spirituality.

Abelard's contribution is apparent in his many writings. These were

11. M. M. McLaughlin, "Peter Abelard and the Dignity of Women: Twelfth-Century 'Feminism' in Theory and Practice," in *Pierre Abélard, Pierre le Vénérable*, 287-333.

12. J. Benton, "A Reconsideration of the Authenticity of the Correspondence of Abelard and Heloise," in *Petrus Abaelardus, Person, Werk und Wirkung*, 41-52; cf. "The Correspondence of Abelard and Heloise," in *Fälschungen im Mittelalter*, 5 = *MGH Schriften* B, 33/V (Hanover, 1988), 95-120. Benton's final conclusion is that the whole correspondence is a literary fiction written by Abelard. The previous opinion from which Benton reluctantly backed down has been defended by the Belgian medievalist H. Silvester in "Die Liebensgeschichte zwischen Abelard und Heloise. Der Anteil der Roman," *Fälschungen im Mittelalter*, 5, 121-65. In response Benton remarks ("The Correspondence of Abelard and Heloise," 98, n. 6):

> To respond appropriately to this learned and challenging article . . . I have decided not to attempt a partial commentary. The heart of our difference, as I see it, turns on the fact that I cannot longer believe, as I did in 1972, that any medieval forger could write an extended work using so many of Abelard's favorite phrases and quotations, and most certainly that a thirteenth-century forger could avoid any clearly demonstrable anachronisms. Not that I believe the *Hist. cal.* accurately recounts "what actually happened," but that I consider all the errors and distortions can be attributed to Abelard himself.

widely distributed, but came to be less popular in the second half of the twelfth century, when the scholastic method had come to be applied along more firmly established lines. In our day his writings have been discovered anew and published in critical editions. In the *Historia calamitatum* Abelard hardly refers to his other writings. He only mentions a treatise that he was forced to burn with his own hands after it was condemned in 1121 at a council in Soissons by a number of bishops under the direction of a papal legate. Abelard emphasizes that he wrote this treatise specifically for his students. The remark is not accidental, since Abelard places all his theological activities in an educational context.

In his scholarly activities education always held a central place. He began his teaching already in 1103, when, at about twenty-four years old, he studied the *artes liberales,* the seven liberal arts, in Paris. Three subjects received the greatest emphasis, the *trivium,* that is, grammar, dialectic, and eloquence or rhetoric. Dialectic was the art of reasoning. Study of rhetoric was mainly aimed at acquiring a familiarity with the writings of Christian and pre-Christian antiquity. One would incorporate relevant passages from these writings into an argument in order to make it more authoritative. In the field of theology this authority was in particular derived from statements by early Christian authors, usually referred to as "the Fathers."

Along with rhetoric the art of reasoning (dialectic) gradually acquired great importance. This was related to the increasing interest in Aristotle's logical treatises. These treatises had long before been translated into Latin by Boethius (†524), but were rediscovered only in the eleventh century.[13] The use of dialectic in accordance with Aristotelian logical notions contributed, for example, to the contemporary discussion of the *universalia,* that is, the universals. Debate was focused particularly on how these universals were related to the concrete objects in which they were embodied. Were the universals derived from the concrete objects, or were they preexistent?

This debate also led to a different treatment and understanding of language, resulting in a dispute between "realists" and "nominalists." The realists believed that the words that they used for universals represented preexisting concepts. The nominalists disagreed, believing that the essential aspects of the universals remained vague and could not be defined *in concreto.* Study of Aristotelian logic thus led to a confusion of tongues in

13. Cf. R. W. Southern, *The Making of the Middle Ages* (1953; repr. London, 1973), 170-82 (ch. IV: "The Tradition of Thought").

philosophy and theology. As a student Abelard was already involved in this controversy. Repeatedly he succeeded in cornering his Parisian teacher, William of Champeaux, who had totally taken the side of the realists. When he wanted to prevent Abelard from attending his lectures, Abelard began to teach himself. Naturally, this led to difficulties. But for the time being Abelard was able to deal with those problems.[14]

A similar situation occurred when Abelard studied theology under Anselm of Laon. Until then theology had consisted solely of interpretation of biblical passages. Even the word *theology* was uncommonly used; the usual terms were *divina pagina* or *sacra pagina* (the divine or the sacred page). The statements of the Fathers provided the norms for biblical exegesis. But Abelard, with his considerable experience in the new approach of the *artes liberales,* in particular of the *trivium,* could not be content with the manner in which Anselm taught theology. Anselm was aware of contradictions between statements of different Fathers about the Scriptures, but this did not lead him to conclude that reason had to play a role in biblical interpretation.

Abelard criticized Anselm's view, but his fellow students did not share in this criticism. Instead, they challenged Abelard to give a lecture in which he would exegete a difficult passage of Scripture with the use of his dialectical method. His lecture received sufficient praise to encourage him to continue. But Anselm forbade Abelard to teach, partly because he might be held responsible for errors that Abelard might teach. This risk was far from imaginary since the new approach to scholarship introduced by Abelard in exegesis of Scripture could lead to a misunderstanding on the part of those who rejected the method.[15] Abelard departed for Paris, where he taught both philosophy and theology and drew large numbers of students.

During his Paris years, beginning in 1115, Abelard became a famous teacher. He was feared for his aggressive use of the dialectical method. His astuteness in logic allowed him to win every debate. This in turn led his opponents, who received little or no opportunity to voice their objections to his theological method, which they regarded as quite valid, to search for other ways to attack him. Abelard gave them sufficient opportunity by publishing treatises that originated in the course of his teaching. Since these treatises developed during the teaching process, Abelard wanted to

14. M. M. Tweedale, *Abelard on Universals* (Amsterdam, 1976).
15. J. Jolivet, *Arts du language et théologie chez Abélard* (Paris, 1969), 229-335.

revise them constantly. But other versions of what he taught, some even based on hearsay, also began to circulate. Though he was not the direct author of such versions, he was nevertheless held responsible for them.

The misunderstandings regarding Abelard's approach to theology that arose from this situation provided more than enough opportunity to accuse him of heresy before the ecclesiastical authorities. By condemning a number of propositions derived from his writings, an attempt was made to silence him. In 1211 a council in Soissons condemned his views, or, perhaps more correctly, his attempt to provide more clarity about the Trinity and the relationships among the three persons of the Godhead. His opponents, who had brought charges against him with the church authorities, had been his enemies already for a long time.

Abelard soon recovered from this condemnation, because his students remained loyal toward him, and was soon able to resume his teaching. But he remained hampered by the condemnation. Finally, with the assistance of friends and students, he acquired a building where he could teach without being disturbed and where his students could live. But he left this building again in 1125, even though he had dedicated it to the Holy Spirit, the Paraclete. Because he felt threatened by the kind of enemies he had had to face in Soissons, he then accepted an appointment in an obscure Breton monastery. This appointment gave him the possibility to return to the region of his birth, but it was soon apparent that he no longer felt at home there.

It is remarkable how Abelard in his *Historia calamitatum* blames the hostility of his opponents for all the problems he has to face as a teacher. He excludes every possibility that motives other than lack of appreciation for his approach could play a role. At a later stage he was often criticized for the popularity of his teaching, which was seen as a real danger. Propositions that he accepted as hypotheses for further theological study were elsewhere presented as articles of faith. Fear of another round of persecutions did not make him less provocative when he believed he had to criticize generally accepted opinions. Apparently he did not sufficiently realize how much he damaged his own position through his play with dialectics and his exposure of uncritically accepted traditions.

What happened after his condemnation at Soissons is typical of Abelard's insensitivity to possible problems. At Soissons the bishops decided to put him away in the monastery of Saint-Medard in order to silence him. This decision was not implemented and Abelard was allowed to return to the abbey of Saint-Denis near Paris, where he had been living for a few years. He had entered this monastery as a monk after his affair with Heloise had ended with his castration by her uncle. He taught his students, who had followed him there, until he was condemned in Soissons. On his return to the abbey he did not resume his teaching, though he did find another way of upsetting those around him.

The abbey of Saint-Denis was highly regarded, in particular at the French royal court. For centuries the kings of France were buried there. The fame of the monastery was based partly on the story of its supposed establishment by Dionysius the Areopagite, who according to some traditions was the bishop of Athens in apostolic times. Abelard dared to raise doubts with regard to this legend by pointing to the writings of the Venerable Bede. He suggested that Dionysius never was the bishop of Athens, but had only been bishop of Corinth.[16] Abelard thus unnecessarily injured the reputations of both Dionysius and the monastery. This was inexcusable. The abbot had him detained and brought charges against him at court. Abelard escaped condemnation by fleeing from the monastery and through the death of the abbot. The next abbot, Suger, tried to calm the emotions of the situation, but under no circumstance could Abelard return to Saint-Denis. He lived for some time as a hermit near Troyes until his friends and students built the oratory of the Paraclete for him there.

※　　　　　　　　※

ABELARD'S CRITICAL undermining of traditional beliefs may have been an important, if not the most important, reason for his calamities. It could not but call forth reactions on the part of those who felt threatened by it. But in part Abelard's misfortunes arose from a matter of a totally different nature, namely, his love affair with Heloise. We have seen how the affair gave great fame to the *Historia calamitatum*. As a result of this fame, many have seen Abelard's involvement in this affair as the apex of his misfortunes. Undoubtedly many will regard castration as worse than the constant threat of being silenced. But I believe that Abelard would have experienced the latter threat as worse.

The facts of the affair are well known. Heloise was seventeen years old and Abelard almost forty. She had been educated in a convent and had recently come to live with her uncle, the canon Fulbert, who wanted

16. E. R. Smits, *Peter Abelard, Letters IX-XIV* (Groningen, 1983), 137-53, 249-53 (letter XI).

someone to teach her further. As a scholar Abelard belonged to the clergy. But at the time he was only a deacon and could have married. According to his own words, he had until then never been involved with a woman, not primarily because he had accepted celibacy as inevitable, but because he had been totally immersed in his studies. But Heloise aroused his passions and things were made easy for him when Fulbert offered him lodging in exchange for his teaching. He even entrusted Abelard with full supervision of Heloise. And Heloise not only saw Abelard as a famous teacher, but also found herself attracted to him.

The lovemaking in which they soon lost themselves had a definite impact on Abelard's lectures. Their quality decreased considerably, and his students knew the reason. They, too, sang the songs that he wrote for his mistress. Unfortunately these songs have not been preserved. Fulbert was the last to know about the affair. When at last he caught the couple and ended their relationship, Heloise was already pregnant. Abelard sent her to relatives in Brittany, where she could give birth in all secrecy. The son she gave birth to remained there. The sources do not inform us whether this separation caused distress to either Heloise or Abelard.

Before Heloise returned to Paris, Abelard came to an understanding with Fulbert. They agreed that Abelard would marry Heloise secretly. Public knowledge of their marriage could impede Abelard's teaching career. But the canon publicized the marriage as widely as he could as soon as it had been concluded. Abelard then demanded that Heloise enter the convent of Argentueil, where she had been brought up. She obeyed and he insisted that she be dressed as a nun, but without the veil. Fulbert regarded this as a betrayal of the marriage arrangement. He took revenge by having Abelard ambushed and castrated. As a result Heloise had no further reason to remain without the veil.

In his *Historia calamitatum* Abelard gives ample attention to his affair with Heloise. But Heloise's arguments against marriage receive as much attention as the events themselves. She preferred, Abelard writes, to be his mistress rather than his wife, since marriage, with all its consequences, would mean the end of his scholarly career. Abelard summarizes her many arguments and the examples that she derived from Scripture, from classical antiquity, and from the Fathers, most having to do with philosophers of the past. It is impossible to establish which precisely are Heloise's own words in what Abelard wrote ten years later. But it is clear that Abelard's major concern was his pursuit of scholarship. This seems to me to be a further argument for the proposition that his real calamity was the continuous threat that his scholarly career could come to an untimely end.

This danger existed in 1125 when he left the Paraclete. His reason for leaving, he says, was that his old enemies then dispatched two new apostles, who were generally believed. He remains vague about their identity and only remarks that one of them had brought a revival among the regular canons and the other among the monks. It has been suggested that the two men were Norbert of Xanten, who founded the order of the Premonstratensians, and Bernard of Clairvaux, who had brought fame to the Cistercian order. Indeed, Abelard did have troubles with both. But the difficulties with Bernard, whom he first met in 1131, did not begin until 1139.

Abelard must have had problems with Norbert before 1126, the year in which this founder of a monastic order became bishop of Magdeburg. It is usually assumed that Norbert participated in the Council of Soissons, and we know that Abelard ridiculed him rather strongly: In a sermon about John the Baptist, Norbert is depicted as an unsuccessful healer who has tried to bring a dead person back to life.[17]

Abelard's decision in 1125 to leave the Paraclete and accept an appointment as abbot in the Breton monastery of St.-Gildas soon proved to be unfortunate. On that occasion — if not earlier — he must have been ordained as a priest. The problem was that he now found himself in charge of a community for which he felt no affinity. The monks were behaving in an undisciplined way, and the material situation of the monastery was precarious. The duke of Brittany, who had approved Abelard's appointment, seems to have demanded more tax money from the monastery than he usually demanded even from Jews in his realm. Not surprisingly, Abelard's account of his time as an abbot is a continuous lamentation.

He found some comfort in the opportunity to pursue his scholarly interests to some extent. During that time he worked on several of his writings. He also found a new purpose for the Paraclete. In 1128-29 Heloise and her nuns were forced to leave the convent of Argenteuil, where she had been the prioress. The convent was the property of the abbey of Saint-Denis, and Abbot Suger required it back on forged rights.[18] Abelard

---

17. *Sermo XXXIII: De sancto Joanne Baptista* = *PL* CLXXVIII, 605. Cf. A. Borst, "Abälard und Bernhard," *Historische Zeitschrift* 186 (1958), 502.

18. Cf. T. G. Waldman, "Abbot Suger and the Nuns of Argenteuil," *Traditio* 41 (1985), 239-72.

then offered the Paraclete to Heloise and the nuns who were still with her. This building, or one could say monastery, was Abelard's property. He put the building at the disposal of the community of nuns as an irrevocable gift and began to go there from time to time to meet Heloise.

This transfer of ownership must have gone through official channels. During the sojourn of Pope Innocent II in France, he confirmed the donation in a charter dated November, 1132. The nuns were fully accepted in this new environment, and the Paraclete acquired a good reputation, in which Heloise, who had in the meantime become its abbess, shared. She was also held in high regard by the bishops and abbots of the region. Among them was Bernard of Clairvaux. In 1131 Bernard and Abelard had met for the first time in the abbey of Morigny. When Bernard later visited the Paraclete he made a remark about the text of the Lord's Prayer that was used in the Paraclete. Heloise informed Abelard, who then sent a letter to Bernard, in which he offered a clever defense of the use of the textual variant.[19]

Neither the letter nor the visit is mentioned in the *Historia calamitatum,* probably because at that time Bernard did not yet constitute a threat for Abelard and therefore did not yet belong to those whom Abelard held responsible for his calamities. The visits Abelard paid to the Paraclete while he was still abbot of St.-Gildas, are, however, mentioned. These visits still caused problems for him, as some suspected that he was still attracted to Heloise in spite of his castration.

A more formidable problem at that particular time was the task facing Abelard as abbot of St.-Gildas. He was not at all equal to it and met with much opposition. He complains bitterly about this in the *Historia calamitatum.* His attempts to reform the life of the monks led only to death threats, even after he had been able to banish from the community those who had been most vocal in their threats. Abelard mentions that they went so far as to attempt to poison the wine that he was to consecrate and drink during the Mass. He refers to a similar experience in the life of St. Benedict, possibly to dramatize the conflict between himself and the monks, though the monks surely also knew the story, and Abelard was not the first medieval abbot who, as a result of his attempts at reform, was threatened with death or even killed by his monks.

Abelard mentions in passing in the last part of his *Historia* that during his stay in St.-Gildas he fell off a horse and broke a cervical vertebra and that

19. Smits, 120-36, 234-47.

this fracture gave him more discomfort and weakened him more than the physical calamity he had experienced earlier. The reference is, of course, to his castration, which, at least in retrospect, seemed less traumatic to him.

⅔   ⅔

WE HAVE POINTED OUT that Abelard downplayed his physical misfortunes, though he did mention them in his *Historia calamitatum.* He saw his real calamity in the repeated attempts to silence him as a theologian because of his application of dialectic to theology. He was merciless in his criticism of his opponents, immediately assuming that they knew or understood nothing of dialectic. In an open letter on this subject he attacked them as ignorant. This letter began with a fable about some foxes who saw cherries on a tree, but did not know how to climb the tree. They then said that they did not like cherries and hated their taste. The same was true, Abelard continued, in the case of the doctors who were unable to use dialectic.[20]

Abelard saw these scholars as the ones who caused his misfortunes, and we may thus assume that these calamities continued during the period of Abelard's life that is not dealt with in the *Historia calamitatum.* That much of his life is not dealt with there can be seen as an argument for the authenticity of the *Historia.* Had it been written after his death, the misfortunes that befell him later in life might not have remained unrecorded. But however much the authenticity of this work may once again be a matter of discussion, the work does concern itself particularly with the misfortunes that struck Abelard as a dialectical theologian. For that reason we must also look at the story of his later life.

When he wrote his *Historia calamitatum,* Abelard had already left the monastery of St.-Gildas. He left with the approval of the bishop under whose authority the monastery fell and was thus able to keep his title of abbot. We know from a later unkind insinuation by Bernard of Clairvaux that he continued to keep the title.[21] It appears that Abelard took a period of rest after his departure from St.-Gildas, during which he not only wrote his autobiographical letter but also carried on his correspondence with Heloise. The duration of this period of rest is unknown. But we learn from

20. Smits, 271 (letter XIII, lines 1-8).
21. "Master Peter Abelard is a monk without a rule, a prelate without responsibility. He is neither in order nor of an Order." Letter 193, written about 1141 = *SBO* VIII, 44 = James, 321 (letter 241).

237

John of Salisbury, who came to Paris to study in 1136, that by that time Abelard was teaching on the mountain of Sainte-Geneviève. The Englishman followed Abelard's lectures and noted with appreciation that Abelard surpassed all his contemporaries in the use of logic.[22]

Abelard's resumption of theological instruction using dialectic was bound to create new difficulties for him. He could imagine himself to be somewhat safer, since he now had some noteworthy students and could even claim to have supporters at the papal court. But he also had followers with dubious reputations, some of whom were regarded as threats to the church for their social activities, such as Arnold of Brescia, or for their preaching, such as Henry of Lausanne. The latter was an illiterate lay person whose brand of revolutionary fervor was by then no longer appreciated by the ecclesiastical authorities. His preaching included a number of ideas gotten from Abelard, but only through hearsay (see chapter VII in the present volume). It was this sort of effect of Abelard's teaching and writing that caused trouble for the master, and even more than before.

Three written reactions to the theological activities of Abelard have been preserved from this later period. The first is from Walter of Mortagne, who wrote a letter to Abelard before 1139, asking for clarification regarding some of Abelard's teachings. Walter, at that time a scholar at the cathedral school of Laon, began his letter by referring to the praises of their master sung by Abelard's students. They were deeply impressed by Abelard's enormous knowledge of the mystery of the Trinity. Walter had not immediately felt any concern about what the students reported. Teachers were often blamed for what their students misunderstood. But Walter became more worried when he read Abelard's tractate on the subject, because Abelard indicated that he did not intend to deal with the article of faith as such, but only to set out his own ideas on the subject.[23]

Here we have a demonstration of a profound difference of opinion concerning the nature and purpose of theology that had its origin in the first half of the twelfth century and that later proved ineradicable. Following current beliefs, Walter established a direct and unconditional link between theology and revealed truth. Theology must confirm the faith, and the Fathers were to provide the necessary support, since they were the

---

22. D. E. Luscombe, *The School of Peter Abelard* (Cambridge, 1970), 52, n. 4 and 9, n. 5.

23. H. Ostlender, *Sententiae Floriacenses* (Florilegium Patristicum 19; Bonn, 1929), 34.

ones who possessed authority. Abelard, however, saw theology as an intellectual exercise dealing with the difficulties arising from human thought in regard to the Christian faith. Its task was to develop hypotheses to help solve these problems. But he regarded these hypotheses as always relative and revocable. In this way theology served as a means toward a deeper understanding of individual articles of faith. Proper use of logic and dialectic enable the theologian to defend the articles of faith against those who attack or doubt them, particularly heretics who abuse dialectic.

Walter only wrote a letter for information, but both other reactions against Abelard from this period — those of William of Saint-Thierry and Bernard of Clairvaux, who was alerted by William — were intended to deprive Abelard of every opportunity for writing and teaching. They both saw a much greater danger in his work. This, of course, had to do with the monastic milieu to which both men belonged and with their receptivity to a mystical approach to the divine. To them theology and spirituality were inseparable. The important thing was not to know more about God through human reason, but to acquire a more intimate relationship with God through a mystical understanding of his essence and attributes. They were utterly convinced that God only reveals himself as a mystery and thus remains inaccessible to human reason.

For these two men, attempts to understand God through human reason were not only attacks on faith in God, but also detrimental to monastic spirituality. On that basis William was able to persuade Bernard to act. William exercised a strong influence over Bernard, having introduced Bernard to the mystical experience of God when Bernard was still a young abbot. Early in 1139 William sent Bernard a *Disputatio* against Abelard with a letter in which he listed thirteen errors he had noted in Abelard's *Theologia*. An important argument for action in the letter was that Abelard could now do as he pleased, since all his former opponents had died and all others had chosen to remain silent.[24]

Bernard responded that he shared William's concern and would soon visit him for further discussion on how to proceed. Regarding this discussion we know only that Bernard apparently consented to write a letter to the pope giving thorough explanations of Abelard's errors together with arguments against them. He sent a draft of this letter to William for his evaluation. Since this draft has been found among the manuscripts in

---

24. P. Zerbi, "William of Saint Thierry and His Dispute with Abelard," in *William, Abbot of St. Thierry*, ed. J. Carfantan (Kalamazoo, 1987), 181-203.

the Cistercian monastery of Signy, where William had gone after his abdication as abbot of Saint-Thierry, it is possible to determine in what ways William sharpened the letter, at least inasmuch as Bernard adopted his suggestions: It has been established that William succeeded in inserting several insults directed against Abelard.[25]

Later Bernard sent two or three other letters about Abelard to Pope Innocent and also nine letters to others, most of them also in Rome. Each of the letters was delivered by a temporary secretary of the abbot, and the secretary also gave an oral report.

❧   ❧

THE POPE ALSO received a letter from all the French bishops informing him of the council they had held in Sens on June 2, 1140, where they had condemned a number of Abelard's propositions.[26] In this letter they also explained how the council had been convened: Abelard had pressed the bishops for a public debate between himself and Bernard. He wanted to defend himself in their presence against Bernard's accusations and had also appealed to his students to come to Sens to lend support. But Bernard declined to enter into any discussion with Abelard, though he did agree to come to the council. The bishops planned to listen to the arguments of both sides in the presence of King Louis VII. The day after Bernard spoke, Abelard refused to defend himself, stating that he wanted to appeal to Rome. The bishops, then, on the basis of what Bernard had argued, condemned a number of propositions in Abelard's writings as heretical.

Most likely the bishops had already reached this decision before Abelard was given any opportunity to speak. Because of his decision to appeal to Rome the council could not — at least not at that moment — condemn him as a heretic, and thus he could not yet be silenced. Immediately after the council Bernard sent his other two letters to the pope. He succeeded in getting a papal reply within two months, in which Abelard was condemned for heresy and was prohibited from any further writing or teaching.[27] By that time Abelard had left for Rome, but had stopped

25. J. Leclercq, "Les formes successives de la lettre-traité de saint Bernard contre Abélard," *Recueil* IV, 265-83. Abelard reacted to this treatise with a letter to Bernard written before the Council of Sens. See R. Klibansky, "Peter Abailard and Bernard of Clairvaux," *Mediaeval and Renaissance Studies* 5 (1961), 1-27.

26. *Inter Bernardinas*, letter 327 = *PL* CLXXXIII, 540-52. Cf. James, 327, n.

27. *Inter Bernardinas*, letter 194 = *PL* CLXXXII, 359-61.

in Cluny because he was ill. The abbot of Cluny, Peter the Venerable, welcomed him with open arms and protected him until his death in 1142.

The bishops' letter reporting on the council gives some idea how Bernard, before the council, had attempted to deal with Abelard. The Gospel of Matthew (18:15-17) describes how to deal with an erring brother: Such a brother must first be admonished in private conversation. If that does not help, he must be spoken to in the presence of witnesses. Only then is it proper to involve the church. The bishops reported that Bernard had followed this procedure. When Bernard arranged to meet with Abelard before the council, he also — much to Abelard's displeasure — met with Abelard's students and preached to them on contrition and conversion.[28] This had some success, since some of these students followed Bernard to Clairvaux.

These encounters between Bernard and Abelard before the council completely destroyed any understanding between the two men, partly because Abelard thus learned about Bernard's comments on his own *Theologia* and of Bernard's plan to send these comments to the pope. Abelard decided to send the pope a written defense and, as mentioned above, urged the bishops to agree to a public debate. He was convinced that, with the support of his students, he would be able to defeat the abbot with the weapon of dialectic. But later he supposedly feared that the situation would get out of hand because of the presence of his students. At least Otto of Freising mentions that as the reason that Abelard declined to give any defense at the council.[29] But his account may imply that Bernard had also arranged to have supporters present; he was undoubtedly a gifted and popular preacher. But it has also been suggested that Abelard did not want to defend himself because he was already too ill to engage in battle.[30]

The bishops' letter to the pope clearly indicates that Abelard was not allowed to speak until they had listened to Bernard the evening before.

28. *SBO* IV, 69-116 = *Of Conversion: A Sermon to the Clergy by Saint Bernard of Clairvaux*, trans. W. Williams (London, 1938).

29. *Gesta Frederici* I.53, *Ausgewählte Quellen zur deutschen Geschichte des Mittelalters* XVII (Darmstadt, 1965), 228. There is some difference of opinion on what exactly happened at the Council of Sens. Cf. A. W. Murray, *Abelard and St. Bernard* (Manchester and New York, 1967), 35-46; P. Zerbi, "San Bernardo e il Concilio di Sens," *Studi su S. Bernardo di Chiaravalle* (Rome, 1975), 49-73. Cf. also L. Crane, *Peter Abelard* (London, 1970), 140-42.

30. J. Jeannin, "La dernière maladie d'Abèlard. Une alliée imprévue de saint Bernard," *Mélanges Saint Bernard* (XXVIe congrès de l'association bourguignonne des sociétés savantes; Dijon, 1954), 109-15.

It is quite possible, as we have noted, that they had already reached their decision, making any response by Abelard meaningless. A satirical account of the evening meeting during which Bernard addressed the council fathers was written by Berengar, a student of Abelard: The bishops listened to the abbot after they had eaten much and drunk more, so that they could hardly stay awake. Every time they were asked to respond to Bernard's arguments and to state their opinion of one of Abelard's propositions by answering the question *damnatis?* (do you condemn?), they could only say *namus,* thus indicating that they were swimming.[31] It is likely that Berengar thus parodies Bernard's remarks in his Apology about wine consumption in Cluny.

After the council, the protection offered by Peter the Venerable could not prevent further deterioration of Abelard's health. After some time the abbot of Cluny sent Abelard to a priory near Chalon-sur-Saône, where the climate was supposed to be better. There Abelard died on April 21, 1142. According to tradition Peter absolved Abelard's sins after his death and sent a document to that effect to Heloise on her request. She had asked not only for this document but also for Peter to say how Abelard's last years had been. The abbot described to Heloise the humility that had characterized Abelard in his life among the monks. No one demanded less in terms of clothing and food than he had. He had spent his time in prayer and reading, but had always been ready to enter into theological discussion if someone had asked him to.[32]

PETER THE Venerable succeeded in restoring Abelard's honor to a remarkable degree, but this was not widely publicized. Soon after he had welcomed Abelard in Cluny, Peter wrote a letter to Pope Innocent II, even before the papal confirmation of the condemnation of Sens had arrived in France. Peter's letter shows his diplomatic talent, which he used in full measure on behalf of his guest.

Peter supported unconditionally Abelard's appeal to the papal court.

31. Berengarius Scholasticus, *Apologeticus pro Petro Abaelardo;* R. M. Thomson, ed., "The Satirical Works of Berengar of Poitiers," *Mediaeval Studies* 42 (1980), 114; D. E. Luscombe, "Berenger, Defender of Peter Abelard," *Recherches de théologie ancienne et médiévale* 32 (1966), 322; *The School of Abelard,* 32.
32. Letter 115 = Constable I, 303-8.

From this court, surely, he could expect justice. He also described how Abelard suffered from being regarded as a heretic. Moreover — partly through the intervention of the abbot of Cîteaux — a meeting had taken place between Bernard and Abelard, during which they had made their peace. This remark of Peter the Venerable speaks for itself. Had Abelard indeed been a heretic, he would have been stubborn and this reconciliation could never have occurred. For the sake of those who could not come to this conclusion, Peter further stated that Abelard was prepared to eliminate any heresy from his writings that might be detected.

In this letter the abbot of Cluny went on to discuss Abelard's immediate future. Considering the great influence of Bernard with Pope Innocent due to his decisive role in the ending of the schism with which Innocent's pontificate had begun and the elimination of the counter-pope, it was to be expected that Rome would confirm Abelard's condemnation by the Council of Sens. Such a confirmation would not only imply that Abelard should be silenced, but also that he should be confined to some particular monastery.[33] With no allusion to all this, Peter suggested that Abelard would, because of his old age, poor health, and piety, choose Cluny as his permanent abode. In his summation, Peter asked the pope on behalf of Abelard, who now had put aside all the unrest caused by his teaching and scholarship, to permit him to spend what little time he had left in Cluny.[34]

When Abelard arrived in Cluny he was not unknown to Peter the Venerable. There are two undated letters written by Peter to a *Petrus scholasticus,* a successful teacher totally dedicated to his teaching and studies, without much renumeration, both material and immaterial. Peter invited this scholar, who is usually identified as Abelard, to enter Cluny.[35] It had finally come to that: For Abelard it was the only remaining option.

This abbot of Cluny was at that time the only person who could resist Bernard and who could hope to make him see reason. He had known Bernard for many years. They met first when Bernard, instigated by William of Saint-Thierry, had involved himself unilaterally in Cluny's internal problems and had thus ignited a violent quarrel.[36] Subsequently,

---

33. In a letter of Innocent II dated July 16, 1140, addressed to the archbishop of Reims, the bishop of Sens, and Bernard, the pope orders the imprisonment of Abelard in a monastery of their choosing (*PL* CLXXIX, 517 = letter 448).

34. Letter 98 = Constable I, 258f. Cf. P. Zerbi, "Remarques sur l'*Epistola* 98 de Pierre le Vénérable," in *Pierre Abélard, Pierre le Vénérable,* 101f.

35. Letters 9 and 10 = Constable I, 14-17; II, 101f.

36. *PL* CLXXVIII, 105-8, 375-78.

when he had to restore order among the Cluniacs, Peter the Venerable had dealt with Bernard in such a way that he had no choice but to treat Peter with complete friendliness. For that reason he could afford to offer Abelard protection against the abbot of Clairvaux.

We do not have Rome's response to Peter's letter to Innocent II. But Abelard could stay in Cluny and was even allowed to do some writing. This indicates that the pope had somewhat softened his condemnation. There is no agreement on which of Abelard's writings originated in this period. Some think that it was here that he finally wrote his *Apology* to Bernard. But, along with other arguments for dating it before the Council of Sens, that its full text has not been preserved points in the same direction. Abelard's writings in these last years were less subject to suspicion and have therefore been better preserved.

We have better reason to believe that it was in Cluny that Abelard wrote two short confessional statements intended to free himself from accusations that he had turned away from the Christian faith or had perverted the faith. One of these creeds is quite general and was written for all who might be interested. The other he wrote for Heloise.

Abelard's most important work from this final period — also the most mature of all of his writings, though it is incomplete — is the imaginary dialogue of a philosopher, a Jew, and a Christian. This work uses dialectic, but in a manner that contrasts with Abelard's other writings, having acquired a more meditative dimension.[37]

Nevertheless, it has been said about this text, that Abelard exhibits there his immodest pride as a philosopher and continues to regard himself as unsurpassed in this respect. For that reason some feel that this treatise cannot have been written in Cluny (or in the priory of Saint-Marcel lez Chalon). The contrast between the image he paints of himself in this *Dialogue* and the way in which he is depicted in Peter the Venerable's letter to Innocent II and in Abelard's own long letter to Heloise is simply too great. If Abelard wrote the dialogue in Cluny, we must conclude that the abbot of Cluny painted a highly flattering portrait of his guest and that the last and most terrible calamity that had befallen Abelard had done less to purify him than these letters suggest.

But it has also been pointed out that this work has three characters

---

37. *Petrus Abaelardus: Dialogus inter Philosophum, Judaeum et Christianum,* ed. R. Thomas (Stuttgart, 1970); *PL* CLXXVIII, 1611-82. Cf. Thomas, "Die meditative Dialektik im *Dialogus* . . . ," in *Peter Abelard,* ed. E. M. Buytaert (Louvain, 1970), 99-115.

and that Abelard should not too quickly be identified with the philosopher, who might rather represent his past. Abelard himself, it is suggested, speaks when the Christian takes the floor. From that perspective, this work may well be dated in the last period of his life. And on this same basis we may evaluate Abelard as a theologian in accord with an adage of Augustine, which seems to have been, in spite of his *fautes de qualité* — his arrogance and his bias — a guiding principle for Abelard: "I have desired to understand with my mind what I have accepted in faith."[38]

---

38. *De Trinitate* XV: Oratio = *CC* 50A, 534: 'Desideravi, intellectu videre quod credidi." Cf. R. Thomas, "Die Persönlichkeit Peter Abaelards im Dialogus inter Philosophum, Judaeum et Christianum und in den Epistulae des Petrus Venerabilis — Widerspruch oder Uebereinstimmung?" in *Pierre Abélard, Pierre le Vénérable*, 255-69.

IX

The Beginnings of the Franciscan Movement and the Canonization of Its Founder [1]

ᓀ   ᓀ

1. THE STRUCTURE OF THE BROTHERHOOD

AT THE DEATH of Francis of Assisi in 1226, direction of the Order of Lesser Brothers (or Friars Minor), in which the Franciscan movement then took form, was placed in the hands of Brother Elias. This Lesser Brother, known since the seventeenth century as Elias of Cortona, has been viewed as the evil genius of the Franciscan movement since its formative period. He has been reproached for distorting the ideals of Francis by changing a movement of illiterate penitents, essentially a brotherhood voluntarily living in poverty, into an order of well-educated clergy that came to be an instrument of power in the service of the popes. Although closer research has improved his reputation and rehabilitated him, it cannot be denied that Elias's position in the order after the death of Francis has always been controversial.

It is certain that Francis was very fond of Brother Elias. In 1217, Francis sent him to Syria. Two years later, when Francis went there himself, Elias became his constant traveling companion, and they later returned together. In 1221, after Francis had withdrawn from leadership of the movement that had grown around him, he appointed Elias as his vicar general.

---

1. This study was first published in Dutch in H. Noltenius and A. H. Bredero, eds., *Franciscus, verhaal en werkelykheid* (Franciskaanse Studies 3, 1988), 20-30.

Since the leadership of the order had rested on him for a long time, it seemed that Elias was therefore the logical successor. Nevertheless, he did not become the minister general when the assembled General Chapter met.

Elias was not chosen probably because he was unavailable for this function at that moment. Hugolinus of Segni, the cardinal bishop of Ostia, who at the request of Francis was appointed by Pope Honorius III as protector of the brothers, had given Elias a different task, one to which Hugolinus definitely wished to give priority, certainly after he was chosen pope. Hugolinus's election took place two weeks before the General Chapter session began. The new pope charged Elias with the task of building a basilica in Assisi in which the mortal remains of Brother Francis should be placed.

How greatly the new pope, who called himself Gregory IX, was involved in this project can be seen from the fact that he himself bought the ground where the basilica was to be built — a solution that prevented this church building from violating the restriction against the Lesser Brothers' owning property. The involvement of the pope in this project proved to be even greater when he went to Assisi to proclaim the canonization of Francis in 1228. Gregory decided to do this, even though the *Vita* of Francis was not yet written; he therefore acted in contradiction of the curial rules and prescriptions customary in the process of canonization. On this visit, the pope laid the first stone of the basilica of Francis. The mortal remains of the saint could not be placed there until 1230, at which ceremony the pope himself was not present, in accord with canonization protocol.

The building of the church has later been interpreted as a treason by Elias against the ideals of Francis, at least by the Spiritual Franciscans, who proposed a radical following of the rule. When the building was started, some discussion about this arose within the order. At any rate, at the General Chapter of 1230 Elias was reproached for bringing the saint's mortal remains to the crypt of this still uncompleted basilica. The vast plan of this building was not in harmony with the statement that Francis had given in his testament shortly before his death:

> The friars must be very careful not to accept churches or poor dwellings for themselves, or anything else built for them, unless they are in harmony with the poverty which we have promised in the Rule; and they should occupy these places only as strangers and pilgrims.[2]

2. Ch. 24. The translation of the testament in M. A. Habig, ed., *St. Francis of Assisi: Writings and Early Biographies* (4th ed.; Chicago, 1983), is faulty. For the Latin text, see *Opuscula sancti patris Francisci Assisiensis,* ed. K. Esser (Grottaferrata, 1978), 305-17.

It is not known in what context the building of this sepulchral basilica and the interring of Francis's body were discussed at the Chapter meeting. It is certainly imaginable that these matters were addressed there, because before this Chapter was also placed the question of the extent to which the testament of Francis had to be considered as a binding guideline for the rule of the order as it was approved in 1223 by Honorius III. The Chapter appeared unable to answer this question, probably because the members did not consider themselves competent in the matter. At any rate, they placed the question before Gregory IX. Among the delegation who visited the pope for this purpose was Antony of Padua, who himself did not favor the more literal understanding of the rule. The pope answered the question in his bull *Quo elongati*, which he published some months later on 22 September 1230. With this he chose the moderate position within the order.

In his letter Gregory called this testament a *mandatum*, which the friars were not to follow as if it were a juridical contract. He stated that the commandment — contained in the rule as well as the testament — to live according to the gospel and the vow of holy poverty could not be taken absolutely literally, for one reason, because of the numerous provisions that had to be taken in connection with the quick growth of the order. What was meant, the pope asked, by the stipulation that one had to live without property? The brothers had to have clothing, and if they had this, why then not houses and books? Of course, they could not claim ownership of these things, but use of them was certainly permissible as long as they could thereby edify others.

For this explanation of the life of poverty, Gregory appealed to Francis himself. He referred to the lengthy personal friendship that he had shared with him. In this way, the pope had learned firsthand of Francis's intentions, and he thought that his explanation was in accord with those intentions. Even if one assumes that this explanation is totally accurate, the letter still clearly shows that many alterations had occurred in the more than twenty years since the beginning of the movement initiated by Francis, similar to the evolution that had taken place in the thinking of Il Poverello (Francis) himself concerning the realization of his ideal.

The first indication of this is offered by what has been quoted above concerning the use of churches, houses, and other structures built for the use of the brothers. This text is a further explanation of the prescription dealing with this from the rule that Honorius III approved and published in 1223. In this *Regula bullata* (Reg.b. 6.1) it is only said that the friars could not appropriate a house or a place of abode, whereas in the older, merely orally approved rule, continually adapted by further developments and known as the *Regula non bullata,* this matter was not yet so expressly stated. There it was only said:

> No matter where they are, in hermitages or elsewhere, the friars must be careful not to claim the ownership of any place, or try to hold it against someone else. (Reg.n.b. 7.13)[3]

The respective stipulation in the *Regula bullata,* which Francis included in his testament, is an indication that the life of poverty was at this point differently understood and practiced. At this later time, the friars usually lived in houses. The word "monastery" was not yet in use. This change was due to the enormous increase in the number of friars who had joined Francis's movement. It was also partially connected with the adjustments and provisions which had to be made because of the task of preaching given to the friars. Originally, they had all taken up this task without further preparation, but over the years more exact prescriptions had been laid down for this preaching. The *Regula non bullata* determined that no brother might preach in contradiction with the church order and the regulations of the Holy Church, and could preach only when permitted by his minister (cf. Reg.n.b. 17).

It appears that this stipulation was not originally included in the *Regula non bullata,* because it is connected to the decision of the Fourth Lateran Council concerning preaching. Still, one should remember that prescriptions of the Council were often a reinforcement of stipulations already in existence. Therefore, it is rather probable that this task, originally given to all the friars, was inserted in very summary form in this rule, in the stipulation that the friars may give to all people, together with the blessing and laud of God, this or a similar admonition whenever they so feel and say: "Fear and honor, praise and blessing, thank and worship the Lord the Almighty God, three in one . . ." (Reg.n.b. 21.2ff.), as well as in the statement that they could summon people to do penance.

In the *Regula bullata,* the regulation for preaching that was given by the Lateran Council was worked out further, with consideration of the instructions that had long been in force: The brothers were not permitted to preach in any diocese where the bishop had forbidden them to do so.

3. For the English translation of the *Regula non bullata* in its 1221 version and the *Regula bullata* of 1223, cf. Habig, 31-66.

Moreover, none of the friars should even dare to preach if he had not first been judged and found suitable by the minister general and entrusted by him with the office of preacher (Reg.b. 9.32). Preaching required very earnest preparation, meaning study, and this placed requirements on the brothers' housing.

The spontaneous joining of this brotherhood, composed of those who had earlier entered the movement of Francis, was replaced by acceptance into an order, with detailed requirements for entrance. In this matter we see a slower development. The *Regula non bullata* already contained prescriptions about joining. It also mentioned a trial period, a novitiate, and the decision concerning the acceptance of a postulant was laid in the hands of the minister of the province of the order, to whom he applied. In the *Regula bullata* the decision about one's admission lay also within the jurisdiction of the provincial minister. Apparently, there was no difference in this regard between the two rules. However, the establishment of a year-long novitiate for postulants, as well as the injunction that once one had been accepted into the order he could not leave it during that first year, is known to date from 1220. In that year, Honorius III pronounced the bull *Cum secundum consilium,* in which he set forth these prescriptions. Only following this privilege were these regulations assimilated into the *Regula non bullata.*

The transition from brotherhood to order was the primary change that took place in Francis's movement. As a result, the charismatic aspect of that movement, on which the brotherhood had placed great importance, became subordinate to the hierarchical structure that they had to accept as an order. The transition started unavoidably at the point where a rule had to be formulated in order for the Franciscan movement to be given papal authorization; the friars especially valued this authorization, since through it the church bestowed confirmation for their mode of life. One can read about this first transition from a brotherhood to a hierarchically structured order in the Prologue of the *Regula non bullata,* where Francis and his successors demand obedience and respect for Pope Innocent III and his successors, equal to that which the brothers owed Francis and his successors.

In the final version in which the *Regula non bullata* has been preserved, the word "brotherhood" appears several times in passages where it is clear that this movement already had the hierarchical character of an order (Reg.n.b. 5.4; 18.2; 19.1; in 19.2 the word "order" is used). From this use of "brotherhood," we may deduce that, even though there was mention of a hierarchical subordination, the idea of a brotherhood was not abandoned easily. This is evident in the stipulation that the term "prior" could not be used for any friar who was the head of a house (Reg.n.b. 6.3). Rather, the one holding such leadership was called "minister." The term "brotherhood" appears similarly in the *Regula bullata,* in the chapter about the election of one of the brothers of the order to minister general, thus the "general servant" of the whole brotherhood (Reg.b. 8.28). In his first *Vita,* Thomas of Celano puts these words in the mouth of Francis: "I want this brotherhood to be called the Order of Lesser Brothers."[4] On the basis of Thomas's text, attributed only much later to Francis, the terms "brotherhood" and "order" cannot be seen as synonyms. A brotherhood does not have a hierarchical structure; an order, on the contrary, does. With this change Francis could not easily agree. For him the order remained a brotherhood. Thus, he mentions in his testament a minister general of his brotherhood.[5]

2. THE "FAILURE" OF BROTHER ELIAS

IT IS UNJUST to place full responsibility for these developments, by which the movement of Francis departed from his original ideals, on Brother Elias because of his behavior within the Order of Lesser Brothers. Francis himself had evolved with the changes that the movement had undergone in the years prior to 1221. Elias's role in the later changes can be seen as a necessary adjustment on his part to the further development of this movement. He wanted to remain faithful to Francis's dream. His zeal for building the sepulchre basilica was not, in his opinion, detrimental to these ideals. One must understand that Elias worked toward revering Francis as a saint in the manner in which saints were worshipped in those days.

This explains Elias's ambition to build the largest sepulchre basilica and to embellish it accordingly. As a child of his time he could not escape from or view critically the customary cult of saints. Therefore, he could not conceive that he was going against what Francis would have wanted, at least in respect to himself. Furthermore, in the beginning, when Elias's main attention was on this project, he did not meet much opposition within the order to his fervor for the sepulchre basilica. This is apparent

4. *Vita prima S. Francisci,* 38; Habig, 260.
5. Ch. 28. Cf. T. Desbonnets, *De l'intuition à l'institution* (Paris, 1983), 90-94.

from the fact that he was chosen minister general at the General Chapter of 1232.

It was only much later, in the fourteenth century, that Elias was reproached for this building project. Moreover, this reproach was an appendage to a different recrimination made against him: As minister general he was said to have been unfaithful in his policies to the ideals of Francis, whereby the order as a whole had also departed from those ideals. The latter charge, which was brought against Elias by the Spirituals as well, should be understood as their rejection of the development that the order had gone through in its beginning stage.

This charge directly counters that for which Elias as minister general was blamed after 1232, namely, that he had insufficiently stimulated this very development of the order. This deficiency in Elias, if one can judge his actions in this way, is closely linked with his honest attempt to respect the ideals of Francis as much as possible. Because of the quick growth of his movement, Francis himself had already realized that the ideal of the absolute life of poverty, as he had first proposed it, was not attainable — that it was impossible to let this fast-growing movement live only in and from the wind. This problem, which as a result of this tempestuous development begged for a solution, was compounded by the fact that in his last years Francis's health declined and he was no longer able to lead the movement. Therefore, he had withdrawn from actual leadership, even though he was still considered minister general.

As related above, Francis learned to accept the fact that the brotherhood he had set up was transformed into an order, that a novitiate was established for the initiation of the friars, and that they were housed in orderly monasteries where more serious attention could be given to the requirements the church laid on those friars who were qualified to preach and wanted to do so. Nevertheless, it can be concluded from his testament that Francis was worried about this development. These cares were the legacy of Brother Elias. As minister general, he experienced the sequel to this development in increased measure. The order indeed not only grew in numbers, but also spread farther and farther outside of Italy. Francis himself had strongly stimulated the spread of his movement. At the time, the vast majority of the friars still originated in what corresponds to modern Italy, but later the ratio changed in increasingly greater proportions.

Another drastic change in the order involved the numerical ratio of lay persons to clergy. This occurred most strongly in the periphery, in

France and England, where increasingly more clergy joined the order. The high regard held for priests, which Francis himself possessed and which he required from his followers, made it easier for the lay brothers to accept these changes. The literate among them would have found it more difficult to accept this. According to the *Regula bullata,* the lay brothers were no longer allowed to pray with the clergy, at least not the hours. Their prayer was restricted to saying a number of Our Fathers (Reg.b. 3.2).

Changes of this nature affected the preaching as well. As far as the clergy among the friars were concerned, it went without saying that the task of preaching could not be entrusted to the laity, since one had to equip oneself for this by study, and the church authorities had rejected lay preaching. With regard to changes within the Franciscan movement, it was of great importance that beginning in 1224, when the first establishments of the brotherhood were founded in France, several doctors who had taught at the universities entered the order and came to have considerable influence.

This very development led to sharp controversies within the order during the years that Elias was minister general. These concerned not only the relationship between the clergy and the laity, but also the conflict between Assisi and the non-Italian periphery of the order. This periphery desired greater decentralization in the leadership of the order. Evidence of this controversy can be found in the chronicles which relate the fortunes of the Lesser Brothers in the various provinces, especially the chronicles of Jordanus of Giano and Thomas of Eccleston for the German and the English provinces, respectively, and, to an extent, the later chronicle by Salimbene of Adam, a Lesser Brother originally from Parma who had close contacts with the province in France.

In these writings Elias was accused, among other things, of having led these provinces of the order without giving any say to the members. Between 1232 and 1239 he did not summon a General Chapter, he divided the provinces, and he appointed the provincial ministers himself. These officials often changed places, and Elias made them subordinate to the visitors who were sent to examine them. The Lesser Brothers from the "periphery" charged that Elias himself was merely a lay brother and continued to give top positions to other lay brothers.

These accusations were already aimed at Elias before the chronicles were written. They were repeated in the chronicles, when after his dismissal as minister general in 1239 Elias was compromised because of his political interference. He became estranged from the order and was even excommunicated by the pope. This scandal explains why Thomas of Celano, who was very positive about Elias in his first *Vita* of Francis, does not mention him by name in the second *Vita,* written around 1247-48, but only speaks of him as the vicar general and in this indirect manner judges him unfavorably. The background of these reproaches against Elias was his position in the conflict between the pope and the emperor. After his forced abdication, in which Pope Gregory IX finally let him fall, Elias hoped to arbitrate in this conflict. He gradually took the side of Emperor Frederick II, which led to his excommunication.

Elias had been accused of much worse behavior, such as ostentation and excessive show more suited to an abbot of a Benedictine monastery. In addition, he was accounted responsible for the conflicts that occurred in the order after 1240. These conflicts resulted from the increasingly strong desire to return to the ideals of Francis, at least to the image of those ideals that the friars possessed. In the circles of these *zelanti* (zealots), the story circulated that Elias had discarded these ideals, especially by building and embellishing the sepulchre basilica, by his cooperation with the clericaliz-ing of the order, by the priority that he gave to study above the life of poverty, and by his promotion of well-furnished monasteries.

It remains true that as minister general Elias did not reject these developments. But, as has been said, in the earlier days he was reproached for not having stimulated sufficiently these very developments, something that was impossible for him as a lay person. In addition, his policies of centralization were criticized. This is immediately apparent in the decisions made at the General Chapter of 1239. The number of provinces in the order was greatly decreased — to thirty-two, of which sixteen were in Italy. The Chapter also decided that the provincial ministers were no longer to receive their appointment from the minister general but were to be chosen by the provincial chapters. Furthermore, lay persons could no longer hold posts of leadership. Elias's successor as minister general was a priest and a non-Italian. It is possible that the Chapter had decided that from then on only clergy could be admitted to the order and that these must be well versed in grammar and logic; exceptions to this stipulation could be made for lay people and clergy whose behavior was a clear example for the people and the clergy.

Thus, the rule was one-sidedly interpreted from an intellectual, clerical perspective concerning the admission of postulants into the order. This interpretation of the rule found wide acceptance. In 1241, it was decided at a chapter in Montpellier that a commission must be set up in each province for the study of the rule. These commissions had to report to the General Chapter all problems of interpretation concerning the rule. Although this stipulation was a dead letter elsewere, in Paris it led to the first commentary upon the rule, composed by four friars who also served as doctors of the university. This commentary summarized questions that could arise about the rule. The simple words that Francis, as he mentioned in his testament, had written for the "Lord Pope" in his day later turned out to be problematic.

3. THE LONGING FOR THE RETURN TO THE TIME OF ST. FRANCIS

AGAINST THIS increasing estrangement from the ideals of Francis — at least the traditional image of them — a sharp reaction arose within the order in the fourth decade of the thirteenth century. The gradual legendizing of Francis as a saint contributed to this. Characteristic of this reaction is, for example, the vision described in the chronicle of Thomas of Eccleston, written around 1258:

> In that very night St. Francis appeared to Brother John Bannister and showed him a deep well. Brother John said to him: "Father, behold, the fathers want to explain the Rule; much better would it be for you to explain it to us." The saint replied: "Son, go to the lay brothers and let them explain the Rule for you."[6]

In those years many friars desired to know more about Francis. Those who had known him in life and who remembered him formed a minority in the order. For them, the *Life* of Francis, written by Thomas of Celano in 1228 in connection with his canonization, would suffice. For the less factual portions of this *Vita* they could substitute their own remembrances. However, for the younger friars who did not have such recollections, the *Vita* was deficient, so they had great interest in the oral narratives that circulated about Francis. These narratives came from the earlier companions of the saint, but over time they had became more subjectively colored.

6. *De adventu Fratrum Minorum in Angliam*, 13, quoted in M.-T. Laureilhe, *Sur les routes d'Europe au XIIIe siècle* (Paris, 1959), 123, and translated in P. Hermann, *XIIIth Century Chronicles* (Chicago, 1961), 158.

Because of the growing differences within the order, such devout stories could foster the development of factions, and it was important that the friars who had not known Francis have access to more detailed, factual information about the saint. This is probably the underlying reason for the summons with which the newly appointed minister general Crescentius of Jesi reacted to a request by the Chapter assembled in 1244 for more information about the life of Francis. Crescentius responded by inviting all the friars who had any real knowledge about Francis's life or knew of wonders and signs that he had done to submit a report.

This request did not remain unanswered, but the information concerning the stories we have is incomplete and has only a relative degree of trustworthiness. It is known that in answer to this appeal *The Story of the Three Companions* was written in 1246 or at least submitted then.[7] There must have been other, subsequent reactions. These remaining stories, however, are only related in later versions, such as the *Scripta Leonis* and the *Speculum perfectionis*. The letter with which *The Story of the Three Companions* is introduced could, with a variation in the text, be used as the preface to various other writings, at least in some of the manuscripts in which they have been handed down.[8] Unfortunately, the best-known companions of Francis who could have responded to Crescentius's request are for the most part known in name only.

To what extent these later texts can be regarded as valid witnesses is certainly not answered unanimously by the various investigators. Since the end of the nineteenth century, the attempt to reconstruct the history of the formative period of the Franciscan movement has led to divergent opinions, accompanied by some passionate polemics regarding the dating of the writings. It is clear that these writings, said to be those of Francis's companions — which they most likely are — betray a strong nostalgia for the fraternal relations as they were in the first days of the order but that later were lost. However, that aspect can certainly not be used as a method of dating these writings and of discovering later textual interpolations.

The response to the summons that Crescentius had made to the General Chapter was not meant — in spite of all those witnesses to the beginning period — to introduce a reform of the order aimed at returning

7. S. Clasen, *Die Dreigefährtenlegende des heiligen Franziskus* (Werl, 1972); translated in Habig, 855-956.

8. *Scripta Leonis, Rufini et Angeli, sociorum s. Francisci: The Writings of Leo, Rufino and Angelo, Companions of St. Francis,* ed. and trans. R. B. Brooke (Oxford, 1970), 69-72 (text of the letter, 86-88).

to those first years. Furthermore, the bull *Ordinem vestrum,* published by Innocent IV in 1245, once again forced the observance of poverty within the order into the background. The possibilities for social modification of the order regarding property and the receiving of grants became more far-reaching. Crescentius did not allow any resistance to this adjustment, which was required by the pope. As minister general he acted strictly against this resistance. He dismissed seventy friars from the order because of their zeal for the original experience of poverty.

Crescentius tried to curb the confirmation and approval that these written witnesses provided in favor of the zealots' views by writing a *Life* of St. Francis himself. When he was unsuccessful because of poor health, he assigned the task to Thomas of Celano. It is unlikely that Thomas's *Vita secunda* totally fulfilled the expectations of the minister general. At any rate, the author of this second *Life* had already shown himself to be moderate in the *Vita prima,* written directly after the canonization of Francis. It is likely that this is part of the reason Pope Gregory IX chose Thomas for this first *Life,* and not only because he wrote good Latin.

Crescentius was deposed as minister general by the General Chapter in 1248. This was due partly to the insufficient role the order had played in the Council of Lyons in 1245, causing great disapproval from Innocent IV, and partly to the growing nostalgic interest in the initial period of Francis's movement within the order. The successor of Crescentius, John of Parma, was at least a kindred spirit of the zealots, even though he had lectured for a time in Paris. Previously he had taught in Naples, where he had come into contact with new eschatological ideas. As minister general John brought those who had been dismissed by his predecessor back into the order and demonstrated a desire to return to observance of the rule, as Francis would have wished. In the opinion of the new minister, Francis's testament contained the most authoritative regulations for the brothers because he had written it after receiving his stigmata.

With this in mind, John of Parma agreed with the perspective of the zealots, who began to call themselves Spirituals. John thought he could support his ideas by philosophical arguments. It turned out that he was also influenced by Joachim of Fiore, a Cistercian abbot from Calabria. This monk divided history into three periods of salvation: that of the Father, which ended with the coming of Christ; that of the Son; and that of the Holy Spirit. This last period would lead to the destruction of the antichrist, who was already present in the world, and also to a charismatic renewal of the church. The period of the Holy Spirit was just beginning at that time with the renewal of the monastic system, which Joachim, as a Cistercian, tried to bring about. Joachim's ideas, explained in many writings, received much enthusiasm after his death in 1202, something the Fourth Lateran Council's condemnation of his teaching on the Trinity could not change.[9]

While teaching in Naples, John of Parma had come into contact with these ideas of Joachim. As a result, he had developed the conviction that the Franciscan movement must return to the ideals of Francis in order to be able to fulfill its charismatic role in the Age of the Spirit. John's strong preference for the Apocalypse of John, a result of his affinity with these visionary ideas, led him to identify Francis with the angel of the seventh seal in the book of Revelation. This identification was later a recurring theme in the *Vita* of Francis written by Bonaventure.[10] As a result of this apocalyptical understanding of Francis, John of Parma was suspected of supporting the very Joachimian concepts that were condemned — a suspicion inspired by a writing in 1254 by the Lesser Brother Gerard of Borgo San Donnino, entitled *Introduction into the Eternal Gospel*. For this reason, Rome demanded in 1255 that John step down as minister general. He was not, however, condemned.

Considering the manner in which John had fulfilled his duties, and especially because of his efforts toward a return to the ideals that Francis had in mind for his movement, this abdication caused a strong feeling of crisis within the order. The question of how Francis had lived and how he had envisaged the life of poverty became a burning issue for many of the friars. For this reason, the polarization grew increasingly. Need the developments the order had already gone through lead to conformity to other religious orders — especially the Augustinian friars and the Dominicans, as Rome had originally wished — or must the original radicality of Francis's ideal of poverty be determinative of the character of the order?

This internal division was felt more painfully after 1250, when the ideal of poverty fell under sharp criticism from the secular clergy in the university milieu, especially in Paris where the theologians explicitly attacked the ideal of a voluntary life of poverty as an authentic part of Christian doctrine. Neither Christ nor his disciples had lived without property. Because of this tarnishing of the central tenet of the order, it was

9. Cf. B. McGinn, *Visions of the End* (New York, 1979), 126-30, 158-61.
10. Revelation 8–9. Cf. S. Bihel, "S. Francis fuitne Angelus Sexti Sigili?" *Antonianum* 2 (1927), 59-90.

of vital importance for the Franciscan movement after the abdication of John of Parma that a definite end be made to escalation of the internal struggle over the direction to be taken by the order.

This task was left to Bonaventure. At a General Chapter held at Rome in early 1257, he was chosen as minister general by the intervention of Pope Alexander IV. Bonaventure was then thirty-six years old and was waiting to be appointed as doctor at the University of Paris, where until then he had studied and lectured. In order to bridge the controversy, the friars needed an image of Francis that showed more coherence than that offered by the often contradictory writings about him circulating at that time. For that reason, the General Chapter ordered Bonaventure in 1260 to write a new *Vita* of Francis. In 1263, the Chapter decided that this *Vita* must be considered the only authentic *Vita* of Francis and that it should replace all other writings about his life. In 1266, the friars were charged with the destruction of all those other writings. From that time on, there was only one available witness to consult in resolving controversies over Francis's memory or in discussing a return to the formative period of the order. Although Bonaventure was only partially successful, he is regarded for this reason as the second founder of the Order of the Lesser Brothers.

From what has already been said about the subsequent rediscovery of these suppressed writings, it can be concluded that the General Council's instruction, at the instigation of Bonaventure, that they be destroyed was only partially carried out. These writings did indeed disappear from official distribution, but they continued to circulate among the Spirituals. There they gained further additions and amendments, so that many variant versions have been preserved. It is possible that new texts were also written and attributed to the time of Francis. Since the end of the nineteenth century, when these writings were given renewed attention through the studies of Auguste Sabatier and the scholarly reaction thereto, they have become the subject of learned polemics. Much research has been conducted into these texts, but differences of opinion and interpretation remain.[11]

---

11. J.R. H. Moormann, *The Sources for the Life of S. Francis of Assisi* (Manchester, 1940); S. Clasen, *Legenda antiqua S. Francisci* (Studia et Documenta Francisciana 5; Leiden, 1967); R. Manselli, *Nos qui cum eo fuimus* (Rome, 1980). Cf. also R. B. Brooke, *Early Franciscan Government: Elias to Bonaventura* (Cambridge, 1959).

4. THE MEANING OF THE CANONIZATION
OF ST. FRANCIS

As A CONSEQUENCE of the attention required by these differences of opinion, for many the domain of research examined in their study of the beginnings of the Franciscan movement remained rather limited and restrained. Certainly the objections thrown up by Auguste Sabatier because he considered Francis more a victim than a son of the church have influenced these limitations of research. At the same time, some investigators have nevertheless dared to tread a broader territory. Accordingly, they have examined the ways in which the Franciscan movement was praised or distrusted during Francis's lifetime. Those changing opinions make clear that the actions of Francis and his followers developed gradually according to the adjustments necessary for the situation at hand.

However, such research has never taken place in a systematic or exhaustive way, just as extensive attention has never been given to the totality of new religious movements at that time in which the life of poverty and lay preaching were considered central. To what extent these movements were treated in such a broader framework, it was done — especially by scholars who were themselves Lesser Brothers — with the intention of accentuating clearly the fundamental differences between the efforts of the Franciscan movement and the ideals for which the other currents strove. Primarily, these studies emphasized that the Lesser Brothers had always sought their place within the church and were therefore not comparable with the other movements.

Departing from these expositions, one must conclude that the earlier impulse by Herbert Grundmann for a broader approach to these movements[12] mostly met with a modest response. Too few scholars wished to study all of these movements as both a component of and a concluding episode in the long and turbulent process of renewal and adjustment experienced by the medieval church in the drastic social changes of those days — an adjustment that meant, for many believers, that the ever present, unavoidable discrepancy between charisma and ecclesiastical institutions escalated into a painful and sometimes even violent conflict with the official church. The Franciscan movement has practically never been placed in this broader framework, and the internal problems that troubled this movement in its beginnings have been too dominant in later research.

12. *Religiöse Bewegungen im Mittelalter* (Berlin, 1935; 2nd ed., Darmstadt, 1961).

This can even be illustrated by the lack of attention given to the unusual circumstances surrounding the canonization of Francis in 1228. As already noted, it was remarkable that Pope Gregory IX departed from the procedure that had been standard for papal canonization trials for at least a century. Since the beginning of the twelfth century, it was required that the petitioner submit a written *Vita*. There were two main reasons for this requirement. Such a text had to contain the reasons why the petitioner regarded this person as suitable for this papal canonization. It could also indicate how great a chance of success the cult of the prospective saint might expect. In the case of the canonization of Francis, it is clear that this customary rule, otherwise considered as fixed by law, had been disregarded. Only in retrospect, after the canonization, did Thomas of Celano write the first *Vita* of Francis, and he did so at the request of Gregory IX himself.

As has been said, this course of events can be seen as very unusual and even exceptional. One may ascribe this departure from standard procedure to the fact that Gregory IX knew Francis so well that in his case the normal process of investigation could be omitted. But then the question remains unanswered: who had requested the canonization of Francis at that time? It appears that the pope himself took the initiative for this. This was absolutely against the customary rules, and therefore it is conceivable that Gregory himself, before his papal election, had already conceived the plan to request the canonization of Francis. But because he was chosen pope, he could not ask himself to start the procedure for this canonization.[13] He had already, before his election, given Elias the assignment of erecting a sepulchre basilica.

This exposition concerning the pope's actions does not explain why he found it opportune to depart from the usual canonization procedure and not charge someone else with the petitioning. Even though he was convinced of the sanctity of Francis, there may have been another reason for his haste in effecting its official recognition. This is demonstrated by the absence of Gregory IX in 1230 at the translation of the mortal remains of the saint. This ceremony was usually performed by a bishop after the pope had pronounced the canonization of the respective saint.

Before the beginning of the twelfth century, a canonization was still generally carried out by the bishops, and the elevation or translation of the

13. About this canonization cf. M. Bihl, "De Canonisatione S. Francisci," *Archivum Franciscanum Historicum* 21 (1928): 468-514.

body or of the relics of the new saint was then the central event of the canonization. The difference between an episcopal and a papal canonization was actually the interval that separated a liturgical act, the translation, and a legal decision. After a papal canonization, a translation performed by a bishop still took place as the liturgical confirmation of this canonization. If Pope Gregory IX was so hasty in canonizing Francis merely because he wished to be able to venerate him as a saint, then he would certainly also have desired to be present at the translation of the body of Francis, and Brother Elias certainly would have chosen a date at which the pope could have assisted. Considering the absence of Gregory at the translation, his haste in this canonization must have had a different reason.

This haste is shown by the fact that at the canonization there was no *Vita* to submit for judgment, which otherwise was a strict requirement for a papal canonization. That only at the canonization of Francis was this writing commissioned would subsequently prove a stumbling block for the Franciscan movement. Since there was no *Vita* at this session, there would also be no *Vita* which could be considered authoritative because of its role in achieving the canonization. This departure from the normal prescriptions meant that later various hagiographic writings with somewhat variant contents could circulate with the pretensions of giving an authentic portrayal of Francis as saint.

Pope Gregory certainly did not suspect at that time that pronouncement of the canonization of Francis before his *Vita* was written and authorized would later bring about so much hagiographic commotion within the Franciscan order. However, from previous experience the Roman Curia had learned that performing a canonization before there was a written *Vita* could lead to divergence in the cult of a saint. This had been the case after the canonization of Thomas à Becket in 1173. The procedure for his canonization was carried out before a *Vita* had been submitted. The reason for this exceptional canonization was that Thomas à Becket was counted among the martyrs and therefore should be canonized. The haste of Pope Alexander III in that case also had an external motive. The canonization of Becket had to make it impossible for the English King Henry II to choose the side of the schismatic pope supported by Emperor Frederick Barbarossa. The absence of a written *Vita* at the canonization of Becket was certainly regretted later by the Curia, if one considers the variety of hagiographic texts that were written afterward. In this case, however, the diversity led to less consequential controversies concerning the remembrance of Becket.

Considering these facts, there is reason to suppose that Gregory IX, who as protector of the Order of Lesser Brothers had already shielded them from difficulties within the church, intended to canonize Francis hastily in order to prevent other troubles for this order which might lead to its expulsion from the church. Concerning the course taken by the pope after the death of Francis whereby he tried to check all radicalism within the order, one can suppose that the problems that this movement of voluntary poverty encountered within the church remained after the death of its founder in 1226. It is even possible that the objections against them had multiplied, since the authority that Francis had enjoyed among his friars dwindled.

Undoubtedly, there were still ecclesiastical officials who did not have good feelings toward the friars and were even suspicious of them, as they had distrusted earlier movements of voluntary poverty. That earlier distrust, so they had discovered, had been justified. However, they did not realize that it was their own distrust that caused those movements to deviate and that promoted the very development of which these dignitaries were afraid. It is true that Innocent III and both of his successors, Honorius III and Gregory IX, granted Francis and his followers a better opportunity than earlier mendicant movements had received from the papacy. Still, this was not an absolute guarantee that after the death of Francis new suspicions and objections would not arise against his Lesser Brothers. We must keep in mind that the definite split in the Waldensian movement between those who took a heretical direction and those who wanted to be faithful to the church took place only after the death of Peter Waldo.[14] Therefore, surprises concerning the further development of the Order of Lesser Brothers were not precluded in spite of the great loyalty Francis himself had always demonstrated to the church of Rome.

Pope Gregory wanted to prevent this conceivable threat to the Franciscan movement after 1226, which is why after he was chosen pope he hastened the canonization of Francis. Afterward he continued this policy. For the same reasons he canonized Antony of Padua in 1232, ten months after that friar's death. Nevertheless, there is a difference between these two canonizations. The request for Antony's canonization came from Padua, and the petitioners were able to provide a written *Life* of the saint, the *Legenda prima sancti Antonii,* when they submitted their petition to Gregory. Nevertheless, the goodwill and haste with which the pope granted the request remain quite remarkable.

14. K. V. Selge, *Die ersten Waldenser* I (Berlin, 1967), 293-303.

By way of contrast, one could point out that the canonization of the Franciscan Benvenutus of Gubbio, who died in 1232, was not granted until 1236; however, his canonization was proclaimed in the same year in which the canonization process was introduced, and the canonization of the Franciscan Ambrose of Massa, pronounced in 1241, also took place within a year of his death. Moreover, we must note that at the canonizations of these two saints the pope strongly emphasized just how much following the Franciscan rule was valid as a precise criterion for their striving toward perfection.[15] Also striking is the fact that the interval between the death of Dominic in 1221 and his canonization in 1234 contrasts with the short period between the death and canonization of the four Franciscans proclaimed by Gregory IX. Therefore, Gregory's specific canonization policy for these Franciscan saints is more than just a coincidence.

The absence of a written *Life* at the canonization of Francis also provides some curious information about the Franciscan movement in the time directly after the death of its founder. Considering the sanctity of Francis's way of life, the miracles he had already performed during his life, and especially the wounds of Christ he received in his body, it is evident that during his life Il Poverello was already regarded as a saint by his friars. In the case of others who were also considered saints before their deaths, their fellow monks had already begun to write their *Lives,* so that the texts of those *Vitae* were available soon afterward. A good example is the manner in which the first *Life* of Bernard of Clairvaux, who died in 1153, was prepared.[16]

Every initiative of this kind was lacking in the case of Francis. This seems to me to be a strong indication that in the Order of Lesser Brothers, certainly in Italy, the clerics, who knew Latin well, still formed a small minority. Moreover, it shows that these clerics, at least since 1221, were not among the intimates of these saints, an indication that may help also to explain why Gregory IX did not rule out the possibility that after the death of Francis new problems with the ecclesiastical authorities could arise for the still young Franciscan movement. Thus, Gregory's haste in canonizing Francis and the other Franciscan brothers must be related to his care to protect the order against distrust and hostility, which despite his papal protection had not yet disappeared.

15. A. Vauchez, *La sainteté en Occident* (Rome, 1981), 396 and n. 298.
16. Cf. A. H. Bredero, "The Canonization of Bernard of Clairvaux," in *Saint Bernard of Clairvaux,* ed. B. Pennington (Kalamazoo, 1977), 63-100; cf. section 3 of ch. VI above; idem, *Bernardus van Clairvaux. Tussen cultus en historie* (Kampen, 1993), 57-68.

Gregory IX's canonization of Francis did not immediately lead to the addition of his holy day to the various ecclesiastical calendars, in spite of the bull *Sicut phialae aureae,* with which the pope sought to introduce the liturgical commemoration of this new saint to the bishops, abbots, and more distant prelates. An investigation of the various breviaries current outside the Franciscan order makes clear that in many cases the office commemorating Francis as a saint was lacking or that there was at the utmost a mere mention.[17] It seems that the English bishops originally ignored the papal exhortation about celebration of this holy day, whereas in 1284 the Lesser Brother Walter of Bruges, as bishop of Poitiers, made the Benedictine abbeys within that diocese celebrate this feast annually by offering them money.

Remarkable information comes also from Thomas of Celano, who records miracles that took place after the death of Francis: For example, people who showed disrespect for the Feast of St. Francis by doing physical work during that holy day were miraculously hindered in their efforts. Bonaventure, who in his *Legenda maior* repeats several of the incidents mentioned by Thomas, tells of more active resistance to the commemoration of this feast. Of course, this resistance was broken by the interference of the saint himself. Included were a soldier who paid for his resistance with death and a judge who was stricken mute for six years because of his oral protest against this festival.[18] This sort of story makes clear that there must have been resistance to the recognition of Francis as a saint at that time and that the proclamation of his canonization by Pope Gregory IX was not immediately greeted with joy everywhere in the church.[19]

5. THE BEGINNINGS OF THE FRANCISCAN MOVEMENT IN THE CONTEXT OF ITS TIME

As MENTIONED above, very little attention has been given to a more direct connection between the rise of the Franciscan movement and the activities of those who had earlier advocated voluntary poverty and lay preaching. Research into this has not seemed important. Francis was faithful to the

17. T. Desbonnets, "La diffusion du culte de saint François d'après les bréviaires manuscrits étrangers à l'Ordre," *Archivum Franciscanum Historicum* 75 (1982), 155-215.

18. *Tractatus de Miraculis beati Francisci* XII.99-103; *Miracula* X; *Analecta Franciscana* 10, 306f., 647f.

19. A. Vauchez, "Les stigmates de S. François et leurs détracteurs aux derniers siècles du Moyen Age," *Mélanges de l'Ecole française de Rome* 80 (1968): 595-625.

church, accepted the authority of the pope and the bishop without reserve, respected the clergy, and did not associate the validity of the sacramental acts with the dignity of a priest's life. Francis also opposed confession being heard or the sacraments dispensed by the laity. In this, he and his Lesser Brothers differed from many other advocates of voluntary poverty and popular preaching. The degree to which there was a difference between these groups remains largely undiscussed in scholarly studies. To what extent this difference existed from the beginning or increased as the Franciscan movement gained more and more adherents has not been sufficiently explored.

It also remains unanswered how much those differences that can indeed be seen between the Franciscan movement and earlier movements were due to what appeared later, that is, the image of the order as sketched by Thomas of Celano in his *Vita prima,* written under papal commission. Should not his account be regarded as something of a euphoria, in which the author conformed his sketch in all ways to the wishes of the pope, who took the initiative of canonizing Francis and commissioning Thomas to write this *Vita?* Should this work, considering the circumstances under which it was written, not also be seen as an apologia for the Order of the Lesser Brothers, from which it might appear that the bishops had little to fear from them? In any case, Gregory IX wanted a *Vita* that would ensure that the friars would not experience the same fate as other poverty movements, namely, being banned from the church. The members of these earlier movements had not left the church on their own.

The witness of Thomas of Celano to Francis's gentleness is not fully confirmed by all the hagiographic writings about this saint. In the *Scripta Leonis* one finds the following narrative:

> When St. Francis was at St. Mary of the Portiuncula for the General Chapter which was called the Chapter of Mats, where five thousand friars were present, a number of wise and well-educated friars said to the cardinal who was later Pope Gregory, who was present at the Chapter, that he should persuade St. Francis to follow the advice of wise brothers like themselves and allow himself to be sometimes guided by them. They cited the Rule of St. Benedict, of St. Augustine, and of St. Bernard which teach how to live thus, and thus, methodically. When he had listened to the cardinal's advocacy on this, St. Francis took him by the hand and led him to the friars assembled in Chapter and addressed them thus: "My brothers! My brothers! God has called

me by the way of simplicity and shown me the way of simplicity. I do not want you to name any Rule to me, not St. Augustine's, nor St. Bernard's, nor St. Benedict's. The Lord said to me that he wished that I should be a new-born simpleton in the world. God did not want to lead us by another way than by this kind of learning, but God will confound you through your learning and your wisdom. I have faith in God's constables, that through them he will punish you and you will return to your condition to your shame, whether you like or not." The cardinal was flabbergasted and said nothing, and all the friars were afraid.[20]

These *Scripta* date from the first half of the fourteenth century and circulated primarily among the Spirituals. A number of the tales told in them are supposedly based on real incidents. In the opinion of the editor of the texts, who gave great attention to the authenticity of the story quoted above, it is probably based upon a story of Brother Leo. The importance of the passage is that it diverges from the accepted image of Francis. The editor quotes this text in the preface of a later publication in which she wishes to illuminate the origin of the Lesser Brothers. For this reason, she precedes this anecdote with a review of all the earlier comparable poverty movements.[21] Not everything that she discusses in this book is vital to the core of the relationship between the earlier movements and the ideal that Francis had. In my opinion, the heart of that similarity, against which the church authorities had especially insurmountable objections and suspicions, was that lay people presumed to advocate reforms in the lives of Christians, both lay and clergy. These lay people were not qualified to offer such proposals, at least in the opinion of the authorities, and when they nevertheless advocated and strove toward reforms it unavoidably led to heresy. According to the judgment of the ecclesiastical authorities, who looked back on these earlier experiences, the *illiterati* were not able to be creative and at the same time have sensible ideas about spiritual life without even occupying themselves with theological questions and the exegesis of Scripture. For this reason, the gospel could not be placed in the hands of lay people and should therefore remain untranslated.

As has been remarked, the most likely heresy accompanying vol-

20. *Scripta Leonis, Rufini et Angeli*, 387-89 (no. 114).
21. R. B. Brooke, *The Coming of the Friars* (London and New York, 1975).

untary poverty had to do with a supposed correlation between the validity of the sacraments and the dignity of the dispenser. The validity of the sacrament was, in the opinion of many lay people, dependent upon more than the sacral status that the dispenser had received by his ordination. A certain amount of information has been preserved regarding this potential heresy for the laity. Already in the first half of the eleventh century, several lay people had felt themselves called to imitate the prophet Amos, to come out from behind the plow and go and preach the word of God, at the same time turning against the clergy. It is remarkable that practically nothing is known about the actions of such heretics from the second half of the eleventh century. This has been seen in connection with the Gregorian reform, which in a very radical manner directed itself against a number of abuses among the clergy and thereby gave the laity their own role. Thus the laity were encouraged not to attend the Mass or to receive the sacraments from unworthy priests. Inversely, advocates of this movement were accused of heresy and sometimes executed by those against whom the movement was directed.

In the same period, a kind of magnetism emanated from the eremitic existence that featured a more communal way of life than had been the case in the earlier Christian period.[22] It is known that Bruno, a canon from Cologne, founded the Grande Chartreuse in 1084. Still, not all hermits led a life characterized by *stabilitas loci,* the homeboundness long required of Benedictine monks. There were also itinerant hermits who preached and shared the poverty of the people. In their sermons they criticized the wealth and unworthiness of the higher clergy and they summoned the people to do what were often spectacular works of charity. These reformers also felt compassion for the fate of prostitutes and tried to give these women dowries and to take care that they were married, supposing that they would then be able to give up their sinful profession.

As long as the Gregorian reform movement received powerful support from Rome, the bishops did not take severe measures against the itinerant preachers, many of whom were lay people, at least when they requested permission to preach from the bishops in whose dioceses they were active. This may explain why reports about heresy are lacking for the second half of the eleventh century. The reports about these itinerant preachers date primarily from the end of that century, when zeal for the Gregorian reform began to wane. Nearly all those mentioned in the sources

22. Cf. H. Leyser, *Hermits and the New Monasticism* (London, 1984).

belonged to the clergy, such as Robert of Abrissel, Girald of Salles, Vitalis of Savigny, Bernard of Tiron, Norbert of Xanten, and the preacher of the Crusades, Peter of Amiens, also known as Peter the Hermit. Their followers were generally lay people, women as well as men.

Because of their criticism of the clergy and because some of them had little or no objection against confession being taken by lay followers, the itinerant preachers were distrusted by the ecclesiastical authorities. Most of the problems arose on account of the women who accompanied them on their preaching journeys. The bishops demanded that these women should be placed in cloisters, a requirement that the preaching hermits obeyed. Only one of them, Henry of Lausanne, rebelled. As we have seen, from the fragmentary information about his first preaching in the town of Le Mans and his later adventures, it can be assumed that his rebellion had its own cause. Henry took a very radical position in connection with the clergy. It was possible to place a ban on his preaching when it appeared that he was a lay person. Because he did not obey this injunction regarding lay preaching, he fell outside the church and was — not without reason — condemned as a heretic. Henry's transition from church reformer to heretic is closely linked to the fact that he was not allowed, as a lay person, to preach.[23]

It is remarkable that this preacher continued to consider himself part of the church, even long after the bishops had excluded him. The same can be seen in the case of the followers of Waldo at the end of the twelfth century. The very ideal for which they persisted in the poverty movement and popular preaching made them desire to belong to the church. However, the threat that the church felt regarding heresy — especially since the Cathari movement had gained importance and had influenced groups who in the meantime were excluded as heretics — was the reason that the doctrine proposed by newly arising religious lay movements did not receive enough notice. A shift took place in this attitude when, at the end of the twelfth century, some theologians paid attention to what these groups were actually teaching.

For the church authorities the combination of popular preaching and voluntary poverty remained an obstacle. Confirmation of this led, among other things, to this preaching being an implicit attack upon the manner of life of the clergy, especially that of the bishops and their canons. Furthermore, as a consequence of a rigorous following of the rule of

23. See section 2 of ch. VII above.

poverty, the material provisions necessary for schooling the members of such a lay movement were usually lacking. Still, such schooling needed to be modest, according to the church authorities, because of the restrictions that the church placed upon the content of lay preaching.

Nevertheless, more openness on the part of the church developed in this respect under the pontificate of Innocent III. Shortly after his election as pope in 1198, the Humiliati, a group of lay religious from Lombardy, had appealed to him. They had previously been excommunicated for heresy by Alexander III and Lucius III. They asked once again for recognition. Innocent then had their rule revised, resulting in a combination of the rules of Augustine and Benedict along with some additions, which did better justice to the characteristic life of this order. This led to reconciliation between the Humiliati and the pope. Similar was Innocent's attitude toward a group of Waldensians who also wished to reconcile themselves with the church. This was possible after a public debate that took place in Pamiers in 1207 between Diego, bishop of Osma, and Durandus of Osca, the leader of the Waldensian minority that desired reconciliation. In this way, Innocent III accepted the "Catholic Poor" into the church.[24]

These experiments — which fared better than Innocent's experiences in those years with the Cathari, against whom he finally summoned a crusade — contributed to the pope no longer viewing the resistance against and prevention of popular heresies as a hopeless matter. Thus, it is at least understandable that Francis was listened to and that the pope, when Francis visited him in 1210, gave his oral permission for the rule of his order. Furthermore, the pope prevented the decision of the Fourth Lateran Council of 1215 not to allow new orders to make their own rule from applying to this order. This altered decision led to the recognized oral rule of the Lesser Brothers being given a more far-reaching meaning than it originally had.

This course of events says very little concerning the relationship between the Franciscan order and the rest of those — within and outside the church, before it or even after it — with the same goal of giving a form to voluntary poverty and popular preaching. Externally, a relationship between these movements can be seen in such matters as the majority belonging to the laity; the desire to preach the gospel to a class of people

24. K. V. Selge, "L'aile droite du mouvement vaudois et naissance des pauvres catholiques," *Cahiers de Fanjeaux* 2 (1967), 227-43.

who, although they belonged to the church, knew little of the contents of the faith; and the longing for solidarity with the impoverished class by the voluntary and consequent choice of a life of poverty, in which one might imitate the life-style of the Lord himself.

Closer study concerning the relationship of the contents of these religious movements has now been initiated, especially regarding poverty and, in lesser measure, lay preaching. Also, closer attention has been given to the relationship between the Franciscan movement and the penitential brotherhoods of the time.[25] An exact description of this relationship is only possible on a small scale. Indeed, the starting points of the various movements are practically incomparable, yet at the same time the concrete situations in which each of these movements sought to give form to its religious motivation are different. Also, as persons Waldo, Durandus of Osca, and Francis are totally different. In this respect, the Franciscan movement is absolutely unique.

Of course, there has been an attempt to relate these movements by regarding them as forms of social protest, which lay partly in the heresies and partly in the movements accepted by the church. These attempts generally give attention to the religious dimension as if it were only an accident or at least a masking of a social problem. Thus, there is usually a misunderstanding, since one ignores religious reality as a historical fact and even violates this element.

Worthy of mentioning in this context is a work by David Flood, *Frère François et le mouvement franciscain.*[26] Here, the author connects the first appearance of Francis with some remarkable contemporary changes in the urban jurisdiction of Assisi, where the well-to-do citizens had placed newly arrived inhabitants in a lawless position. At the same time, this book offers a characterization of the uniqueness of the Franciscan movement in its origin. Flood does this by referring to the *Regula non bullata.* The regulations recorded there, frequently with several variants, supposedly demonstrate how this rule functioned in the Franciscan movement between 1210 and 1223 and how the friars lived at that time. However, various objections can be raised against both of these ideas. The first companions that Francis gathered around himself were of varied social origin, which makes it difficult to suppose that they remained together for years because

25. M. d'Alatri, ed., *Il movimento francescano della penitenza nella società medioevale* (Rome, 1980).

26. Paris, 1983.

of ideological reasons. Moreover, a characterization of this movement based upon the *Regula non bullata* is finally no more than a sketch of an ideal image, which could only partially have been satisfied by reality.

Therefore, every attempt at precisely describing the Franciscan movement in its beginnings seems to be an illusion, except to say that it was able to achieve more than previous movements with regard to the life of poverty and popular preaching. The difficulty remains that the internal development of this order in its earliest period when Francis was still alive cannot be clearly traced. It can be assumed that Francis wanted to accept compromises, on the one hand, because he desired to develop this movement within the church and, on the other hand, because it developed so rapidly that changes were unavoidable. To what extent he had made concessions in order to prevent this movement from meeting the same fate as earlier movements is also impossible to define precisely. It is certainly clear that Francis's thinking and actions were strongly influenced by his belonging to the church, however much his ideals were unavoidably in conflict with the interests fostered by the ecclesiastical institutions.

❧　　　❧

IN SUMMARY, the following may be stated. In the face of all the attempts exerted from outside the order as well as by a number of Lesser Brothers themselves, however often against great odds, to make the movement unacceptable for the church, the supposition seems to be justified that Francis did not show extreme readiness to make concessions in his wishes, in spite of his loyalty to the church. The narrative of the General Chapter of the Mats in the *Scripta Leonis* bears witness to this. Concerning this tension between charisma and institution experienced by Francis and his movement, stronger evidence may be concluded from the course of events at the canonization of Francis.

Gregory IX found it to be of great importance to give this young order its own saints, recognized by the church. In the matter of Francis, who was the most important saint, Gregory was even prepared to ignore the recognized rules of canonization which had been made by his predecessors. One gets the impression that the order at that moment was not yet able to take the initiative for the canonization itself and to compose a *Vita* of Francis themselves. From these hypotheses one may draw conclusions about the caution of this pope concerning the more radical feelings of a number of friars who were also a part of the movement of Francis.

Finally, it must be remembered that shortly before his death Francis had, by his testament, once again increased for his brothers the possibility of conflict with the church authorities. As long as he lived, the authorities did not have to be afraid of a conflict, due to Francis's loyalty to the church. But after his death, as has been mentioned, conflicts could still arise. Pope Gregory IX, who combated heretics vigorously, seems at least to have considered the possibility of such conflicts, as can be seen by his overhasty canonization of Francis. With this action he averted the danger, even though many bishops were not happy with the canonization. Gregory's accomplishment was this: Everyone who sought a radical explanation of the rule and who was willing to risk a conflict within the order or in the church for this purpose and to justify his attitude by appealing to Francis now had to remember that the one to whom he appealed belonged to the saints of the church. Loyalty to Francis meant, after 1228, that one had to remain faithful to the church and to the authority of Rome.

In elucidation of this argument, it must be remarked that in a comparable respect the sainthood of Francis remained vital within the order. All the later tumultuous controversies that put the Order of Lesser Brothers to the test, that scourged them and separated them, nevertheless did not lead to such divisions that controversial groups of Lesser Brothers found it necessary to leave the church of their own accord. From this perspective, it appears that the church also continued to need this saint.

X

Anti-Jewish Sentiment
in Medieval Society[1]

ૐ ૐ

HISTORIANS AND OTHERS are quite unanimous about the existence of anti-Jewish feelings in medieval society. That these feelings were current in those days is now generally recognized, though many textbooks of Western European medieval history deal with it only in passing and mention only a few facts related to the Black Death and the crusades.[2]

In the medieval world the Jews had a legal status that was unique and unfavorable to them. They lived in their own sections of the towns, first voluntarily, but later involuntarily. They were identified as Jews by signs on their clothing, except where this obligation could be bought off. The Jews' exceptional status was encouraged by the church and prescribed in canon law. The church prohibited Jews from having Christian slaves and from circumcising their slaves. They had to free slaves who decided to become Christians. Christians were not allowed to live in homes owned by Jews. Marriages between Jews and Christians were forbidden. Christians were not to share meals with Jews or to eat Jewish unleavened bread.

The Jews' distinct position in society was closely related to their

---

1. The Dutch original of this chapter appeared first in *Nederlands Archief voor kerkgeschiedenis* 64 (1984), 1-38. The excursus appeared in *Ter Herkonning* 14 (1986), 87-97.

2. A survey of Jewish and non-Jewish historians' writings on the place and importance of the Jews in medieval western Europe is in G. I. Langmuir, "Majority Historians and Post-biblical Jews," *Journal of the History of Ideas* 27 (1966), 343-64.

religion. Religion bound the Jews historically to Christians, but Jews also embodied rejection of the church by maintaining their separate religion. Moreover, the Jewish religion proved to be attractive to some Christians, even to priests. In order to prevent conversions of Christians to Judaism, Christians were not allowed to participate in any way in Jewish religious practices.

The church also sought to isolate Jews socially and to keep them out of social organizations. To this Jews did not object, because all social organizations had some Christian orientation, as was apparent from their banners, from their patron saints, and from their altars in churches. Consequently there were no Jewish guild members. Nor were there any Jews in local government, since they were forbidden from exercising authority over Christians. Jews were not permitted to acquire land since that would involve them in manorial structures or tenancy, both of which would imply a degree of dominance over Christian subjects and tenants.

This unique social position, in its turn, determined to a large extent what occupations were commonly held by Jews: trade in money and goods. The church contributed to this in yet another way. Christians had traditionally opposed charging interest on loans of money or food. Deuteronomy 23:19-20 permits charging interest of strangers, but not of brothers. The Third Lateran Council in 1179 formally prohibited Christians from charging interest when lending money. This for a time gave the Jews a monopoly as lenders. And even though they were forced out of the elite circles of moneylenders as early as the thirteenth century, they remained primarily moneylenders.[3] Their enormous profits from interest of course often inspired jealousy and evoked bitterness on the part of debtors. Interest rates were high, as much because of the relative scarcity of capital in this developmental phase of the monetary economy as because of the risks involved in lending money. High interest rates were related to the social insecurity that Jews continuously experienced. Jealousy and resentment repeatedly led to looting and bloody persecutions, to confiscations of Jewish possessions, and to temporary and permanent expulsions of Jews.

Moreover, some persecutions of Jews occurred when public opinion pointed to them as the scapegoat in times of calamity and disaster. This, too, was related to their unique position in society. They lived as strangers in the midst of the Christian population. Sometimes they fell victim to the personal vengefulness of powerful lords, as happened in Blois in 1171,

3. P. Elman, *Jewish Finance in Thirteenth Century England* (London, 1936).

when thirty-two Jews were burned and the Jewish community had to pay a large fine to Count Theobald, who had become spiteful when his relationship with his Jewish mistress had turned sour.[4]

The nature and intensity of these persecutions were often such that Jews took their own lives and the lives of other Jews in order to escape. Accepting baptism and thus converting to Christianity was sometimes a way of staying alive. At times the episcopal lord of a town would advise local Jews to avail themselves of this solution when he felt unable to stop an advancing armed crowd or when he refused to provide the Jews with tangible protection. But since Pope Gregory I had opposed coercion in conversion of Jews, church authorities usually did not encourage this method. And there was always the fear that converted Jews would fall back into their old religion. But such backsliding was punished. In the later Middle Ages this punishment was carried out by the Inquisition.[5] Reversion was punishable because conversion was supposedly voluntary, even though this often was not the case.

This general sketch may be supplemented in many ways. Later centuries heard accusations that Jews were involved in ritual killings of Christian children, that they desecrated the sacred host (the bread of the Eucharist), and that they poisoned wells, resulting in epidemics. On the other hand, Jewish children that had been baptized, by whatever means, could no longer be reared by their parents, while in some regions Jews were forced to listen to sermons designed to lead them to conversion, given by preachers specially trained for that purpose. In 1240 in France volumes of the Talmud were for the first time confiscated and burned, with the argument that the heretical corruption of the Talmud prevented Jews from understanding the Old Testament in the Christian way. The church's mission to the Jews, along with the general prejudice against Jews, did much to harm the Jews.

4. R. Chazan, *The Medieval Jewry in Northern France* (Baltimore and London, 1973), 56-60.
5. S. Katz, "Pope Gregory the Great and the Jews," *Jewish Quarterly Review* n.s. 24 (1933-34), 113-36; Y. Yerushalmi, "The Inquisition of the Jews in France in the Time of Bernard Gui," *Harvard Theological Review* 63 (1970), 317-77; S. Grayzel, "Popes, Jews and the Inquisition from *Sicut* to *Turbato*," in A. I. Katsch and L. Nemoy, ed., *Essays on the Occasion of the Seventieth Anniversary of Dropsie University* (Philadelphia, 1979), 151-88.

ว่ะ   ว่ะ

BUT A CATALOGUE of all that Jews had to endure, however complete it might be, will not automatically explain where the *origin* of this anti-Jewish sentiment is to be sought. It remains an open question to what extent it must be found in the church or in society. Yet, very often this choice is made with little discussion. It is self-evident that the church is not blameless in this matter. But does the guilt rest on the church as it manifested itself as a spiritual institution through the centuries, or mainly on the church in its concrete efforts to adapt itself to the medieval society in which it had to function?

The difficulty of answering this question and of distinguishing between the institutional church in abstract and its medieval manifestations must be blamed partly on the church of Rome, which tends to pay little attention to the distinction. In Rome's opinion the church is an institution of salvation with an unchanging mission in society from age to age. Although the church of Rome does not lack all historical reflection, it frequently fails to see the extent to which it has been shaped by the specific social forms that it has experienced in the past and that have given it its specific character.

This relationship to the past is itself historically conditioned. Since the days of the Counter-Reformation the church of Rome has, in general, no longer presented itself in terms of the metaphor used by Pope Gregory I, that of a ship endangered by storms. It has preferred to identify itself as the rock, which Scripture identified as the apostle Peter, on whom the church is built. The church itself has come to be viewed as this rock, that is to say, as an institution standing above history and in no way affected by changing times. This apologetic approach has strongly influenced the manner in which the church has viewed its place in history. Its doctrines, as reformulated by the Council of Trent, were to keep the same meaning for all ages, partly because it used a language that was not subject to time and was intelligible to all cultures: ecclesiastical Latin.

However unhistorical this image of the church may have been, it has been largely accepted by the church's adherents. It has also contributed to the usual emphasis of Roman Catholic medievalists on the church's influence on medieval society at the cost of consideration of the influence of medieval society on the medieval church. A clear example of this one-sided approach is seen in Gustav Schnürer's *Kirche und Kultur im*

Mittelalter, which was published between the World Wars.[6] Schnürer's main intention was to show how the medieval church brought Christianity and progress to society. That this society forced its character on the church remained outside the scope of this Swiss medievalist's vision, who gives not the slightest indication of having realized that the church failed in its dealings with the Jews.

A second reason that more attention is given to the church as an "everlasting" institution than to the church as a part of medieval society, especially with regard to anti-Jewish attitudes, is that it has been difficult to pinpoint how medieval society specifically contributed to these anti-Jewish attitudes. We will return to this problem. Here we must deal with other reasons why the attention of those who have studied these prejudices has usually focused on the role of the church, often to a large degree isolating it from its medieval context. The interest of such writers has been concentrated too much on the manifestations of anti-Jewish attitudes, neglecting the attitudes that gave rise to them, which have persisted beyond the Middle Ages. But then the church has also been drawn into more recent manifestations of anti-Semitism by society.

We should in this connection not fail to mention that Jewish historians see the Middle Ages as ending not in the sixteenth century, but at least as late as the seventeenth century. Renaissance and Reformation did not produce any real changes in the position of the Jews in Western European society. It is true that the fate of the Jews in northwestern Europe became much more bearable. But this was preceded by a massive immigration of Ashkenazi Jews into eastern Europe. The decrease in their numbers in the West undoubtedly helped to raise the threshold of tolerance there. The Sephardic Jews, on the other hand, though they had lived in medieval Spain in peaceful coexistence with Muslims and Christians, experiencing a period of cultural and intellectual progress, were faced with the choice between coerced conversion or exile after 1492, when the Reconquista of Spain was completed. This choice was all the more difficult because of their assimilation in the previous centuries of coexistence. Whatever choice they made, this was when their sufferings began. To whatever extent the Middle Ages ended with the sixteenth century, only the Enlightenment improved the social status of the Jews. But this improvement was to be less permanent than was probably anticipated when the laws establishing a separate and inferior status for Jews were taken off the books.

6. Translated as *Church and Culture in the Middle Ages* (Paterson, NJ, 1956).

When studying anti-Jewish sentiments through the centuries, one is inclined to concentrate more on the role of the church than on that of society because the church had already turned against the Jews in Christian antiquity. This hostility was often expressed in the same words in medieval polemics. Focus on the church as a transhistorical continuity on the part of those who have studied anti-Jewish attitudes through the centuries is not limited to a few Jewish historians, who, it must be added, have shown greater interest in the heritage being attacked than in the nature of the attack.

Some Christian authors have paid attention to harassment of Jews, though their approach has been rather one-sided. They are clearly motivated by deep shock about the fate the Jews of Western Europe suffered more recently and by a strong embarrassment over the acquiescence to this suffering on the part of the overwhelming majority that did not actually participate in these persecutions. In retrospect this passivity calls for some kind of response, and in a sense this present discussion is just such a response. But the response that I have in mind leads to a reflection on anti-Jewish sentiments in the European past with the aim of leaving aside the problems posed by the most recent past, for which our century must still give account. I am referring, of course, to the Holocaust, the genocide of the Jews executed by the Hitler regime and tolerated by other heads of state.

One of the first such responses appears in Friedrich Heer's *Gottes erste Liebe*. In a chapter dealing with the Middle Ages — a period he is familiar with, as his other publications show, Heer more or less overlooks the specific nature of medieval anti-Semitism as he extends this period into the twentieth century. He believes that "there exists side by side a Jewish and a Christian Middle Ages, which last almost into the present."[7] Anti-Semitism, he maintains, must not primarily be seen in a medieval context, but rather as a demonic force that continues to plague Europe, in which Christianity has repeatedly participated. Jews were persecuted less at the end of the Middle Ages not because of any change in mentality, but because so many Jews had left western Europe. These demonic forces came later to be directed against women in witchcraft trials. Heer's primary focus is on the continuity of this hostility, as is apparent from the subtitle of his book: "Two Thousand Years of Judaism and Christianity: The Emergence of Adolf Hitler, an Austrian Catholic." This approach implic-

7. *Gottes erste Liebe* (Munich, 1967), 85.

itly places responsibility for anti-Judaism on the church and Christianity, while ignoring the specific medieval social circumstances within which anti-Judaism manifested itself. Questions about the particular nature of anti-Semitism in the medieval world are left unasked.

Somewhat similar to this approach is the more recent work by Hans Jansen, *Christelijke Theologie na Auschwitz*. Jansen attempts to discover the theological and ecclesiastical roots of anti-Semitism. He is a theologian, not a historian. My objections against his methodology resemble those that I have to writings of historians who deal with theological problems of the past and refer to theological statements without consideration for their historical context. Neither seems to realize that the impact of a statement in a later period differs from its function in its original context. But my objection against this theologian goes even further. He often supports his arguments with facts, without worrying much about their historical setting.

Without exception, such a theological argument supported by historical facts will result in distortion. This is clearly the problem in Jansen's book, in which many facts are mentioned. The author also follows this method when dealing with the Middle Ages, taking these facts out of their historical context and isolating them from the ideology of the time. This enables him to draw forceful conclusions from his survey of the medieval church in relation to anti-Jewish sentiments. But on close examination, these conclusions do not hold.

The following example will illustrate this: "It is not difficult to prove the striking resemblance between the anti-Jewish laws the church promulgated 750 years ago," that is, in 1214 during the Fourth Lateran Council, "and the Nuremberg laws of 1935 and later Nazi legislation."[8] Such similarity can indeed be demonstrated if the intentions behind the discriminatory laws against Jews at these diverse dates are disregarded and no attention is paid to the different contexts in which these laws were enacted. The fact must be ignored that the Nazi laws were intended to restore the purity of the Aryan race — a myth that all school children were to be indoctrinated with — and to tie each Jew to his Jewish identity before destroying him. The aims of the discriminatory laws of the Fourth Lateran Council were to encourage Jews to abandon their religion and become Christians. The church thus tried to eliminate the protest against itself embodied by the Jews. If such "details" are disregarded, by a very

8. *Christelijke theologie na Auschwitz* I (The Hague, 1981), 105.

rough analogy the medieval church may be held *directly* responsible for the genocide of the Jews in the Hitler era.

But it would be more correct to relate the laws of the Fourth Lateran Council regarding Jews to earlier stipulations against Jews, which may be found in part in decisions of earlier local councils and can clearly be linked to ordinances against the Jews in the *Codex Theodosianus.* This late Roman compilation of laws, dating from 438, contains a number of *novellae* that Christian emperors had decreed against the Jews since 315. The church had a limited share in their origin. These laws should be compared with stipulations against other religions and movements that the church of the time regarded as threats: When compared to the decrees against pagans and heretics, the laws regarding Jews are rather moderate. The society of the time rather than the church deserves credit for this moderation. The Roman Empire had a tradition of recognizing Judaism as a *religio licita,* a permitted religion, even though Jewish proselytism was prohibited.

The church played a more direct role in the transmission of these injunctions to medieval society. The provisions of the *Codex Theodosianus* were restated in the decisions of a series of councils held in Toledo, in the Visigothic kingdom, during the sixth and the seventh centuries. These statutes were officially promulgated by the bishops, but were forced on them by the Visogothic kings, who hoped in this way to limit the influence of Jews. The kings chose to work through the bishops because they had no other means of enacting legislation.[9]

It should be remembered that earlier the Visigothic rulers had been Aryans, and thus the leaders of a national church. This did not really change when they converted to the church of Rome. The church synods took care of legislation for them, but would only enact laws that confirmed older legal traditions. For that reason, when taking measures to limit the influence of Jews in their kingdom, the Visigoths fell back on the provisions of the *Codex Theodosianus* and of decisions of local ecclesiastical synods, which prohibited contacts between Christians and Jews for fear of losing Christians to Jewish proselytizing.

These decisions were, as time went by, recorded in collections of canon law — notably around 1143 in Gratian's *Decretum* — and thus received general validity. They were then absorbed, as canon XXVI, into the decisions of Third Lateran Council, held in 1179. The inclusion of these

9. B. S. Bachrach, *Early Medieval Jewish Policy in Western Europe* (Minneapolis, 1977), 3-26.

stipulations in the decrees of the Third Lateran Council was more than just a legal mechanism. For alongside this de jure anti-Semitism, de facto anti-Jewish sentiments had developed, as witnessed by the often bloody persecutions of Jews beginning in the eleventh century.

The presence of anti-Semitism in canon law is even more strongly felt in the four constitutions on the Jews issued at the Fourth Lateran Council thirty-five years later. To some extent these constitutions were an outgrowth of earlier canonical decisions regarding Jews. But this council also included new measures, including the requirement that, like some other minorities, Jews wear distinctive clothing.[10] The continuity with earlier legislation shown, nonetheless, by the Fourth Lateran Council has caused some to see it as the link between the *Codex Theodosianus* and the Nuremberg laws. This continuity was, at any rate, already thought of by Montesquieu in a reference in *De l'esprit des lois* to the synodical decisions of the Visigothic bishops: "All norms, principles, and ideas of the present inquisition are based on the laws of the Visigoths; the monks only copied the laws that the bishops enacted in earlier times."[11] In this view, the medieval church, because of the zeal of its monastic copyists, became a channel for the anti-Semitic legislation that had been formulated by the institutional church during the transition from antiquity to the Middle Ages.

This same pattern is seen in the many purely literary polemics between Christians and Jews. For this polemical material, with its characteristic barrage of abuse directed against the Jews, also goes back to the time of the early church, the oldest being, as far as we know, from the middle of the second century. The arguments of early Christian authors were simply repeated by medieval theologians. The authority of the ancient Fathers was such that it was unthinkable to diverge from their views. But mere repetition of old statements does not guarantee that the same ideas are communicated, since meaning depends partly on the context in which a statement is made. During the Middle Ages this context underwent a gradual but substantial change because of changes in relationships between Christians and Jews, which in turn resulted from changes in society at large. And other kinds of polemics against Jews developed in the late Middle Ages, often with different characteristics.[12]

10. A. Cutler, "Innocent III and the Distinctive Clothing of Jews and Muslims," in J. R. Sommerfeldt, ed., *Studies in Medieval Culture* I/2 (Kalamazoo, 1970), 92-116.

11. XXVIII.1; ed. J. Brethe de la Grassage, vol. IV (Paris, 1961), 34.

12. A. Funkenstein, "Basic Types of Christian Anti-Jewish Polemics in the Later Middle Ages," *Viator* 2 (1971), 373-82; A. L. Williams, *Adversus Judaeos: A Bird's-eye View of Christian Apologiae* (Cambridge, 1935).

THE PROBLEM of this ongoing polemic, with medieval authors merely repeating what their predecessors had said, deserves closer attention. The polemic between Christians and Jews dates from the moment when the birth of the church created a schism in Israel. The Jewish authors of the New Testament already engaged in polemics against fellow Jews who rejected Jesus as the Messiah. The two groups came to be distinct communities. From the beginning the Jews were accused of killing Jesus, because they had refused to acknowledge him as the Messiah.

At first the Jews did not object to this accusation, since they believed Christ's punishment had been deserved. But later they became more prudent on this point, when they found themselves in a minority position in a Christian world, while in the Middle Ages the stereotypical accusation of Jews as "murderers of God" took on a life of its own. When the crusades began, the crusaders believed this accusation gave them the right to kill Jews before leaving for the Holy Land.

Historians still disagree whether these persecutions resulted from desire to loot on the part of poor, undisciplined soldiers or from religious fanaticism incited by the church.[13] The church disapproved of the violence, partly perhaps out of fear of anarchy, but it also encouraged it to some degree by demanding that Jews pay part of the expenses of the crusades. At times intense emotions were involved. We know of a letter from Peter the Venerable, the abbot of Cluny, to King Louis VII, written in 1147 at the beginning of the Second Crusade, possibly in response to a request of the king to contribute to the expenses of this expedition. The abbot refers to Jews living among Christians as a greater evil than the Saracens, and he protests vigorously against the custom of Jewish moneylenders demanding liturgical treasures as collateral for loans. He, and probably others with him, considered this sacrilegious. He mentions this practice as an added argument for forcing Jews to pay for the crusade.[14]

The rejection of violence against Jews had, of course, a theological

13. G. I. Langmuir, "From Ambrose of Milan to Enicho of Leiningen: The Transformation of Hostility against the Jews in Northern Christendom," in *Gli Ebrei nell' Alto Medioevo* (Spoleto, 1980), 313-68.

14. Letter 30 = Constable I, 327-30. For a more extensive interpretation of the attitude of this abbot, see G. I. Langmuir, *American Historical Review* 91 (1986), 620f.

basis. Society did not yet resemble a constitutional state providing protection for all its members. Theologians based their arguments on the situation of the early church: At that time violence against Jews had been approved in that destruction and confiscation of synagogues was tolerated. The church argued against further violence because the apostle Paul had argued that the hardening that had come on part of Israel, resulting in their rejection of Jesus as the Messiah, would end when the great mass of Gentile nations had entered. And then all Israel would be saved (Rom. 11:25f.). This statement implied that the Jews had to survive until the end of time and that extermination of them was therefore to be avoided.

The church's official view was that the punishment of the Jews was to be limited to their dispersion among the nations. This led to the fable (at present still popular among Palestinians) that Palestine was devoid of Jews after its Jewish population had been destroyed by Rome. Because they were guilty of the death of Christ, diaspora Jews were to be subject to the peoples among whom they lived. At the beginning of the Second Crusade, for which Bernard of Clairvaux launched the appeal, the seriousness with which this line of thought was taken becomes apparent. Bernard used it in letters promoting the crusade, and during his preaching of the crusade in the Rhineland he prevented a massacre of the Jews in that region.[15]

The main point of contention in the polemics between Jews and Christians had to do with their differing understandings of the Torah. How were the predictions of the Messiah's coming in the Law and the Prophets to be interpreted? For Christians these passages clearly referred to Jesus Christ. From the beginning Jews opposed this view and therefore soon rejected the Septuagint as biased. And they regarded Jerome, who made a Latin translation based on the Hebrew text — the Vulgate — as a deceiver.

In addition to their exegetically based rejection of faith in Christ, the Jews developed philosophical and rational arguments against other Christian beliefs, in particular against the divine incarnation, the birth of Christ from the virgin Mary, his resurrection from the dead, the transformation of bread and wine into the body and blood of Christ during the celebration of the Eucharist (transubstantiation), and the Christians' trinitarian concept of

15. D. Berger, "The Attitude of Saint Bernard towards the Jews," *Proceedings of the American Academy for Jewish Research* 40 (1972), 89-108; G. Dahan, "Saint Bernard et les Juifs," *Sens* 43 (N.S. 157, 1991), 163-70.

God.[16] Jewish objections increased where these fundamental beliefs were experienced and interpreted in liturgy and theology in ways that went beyond Scripture. To debate such points on a rational basis became more and more difficult, since ordinary Christians saw rejection of these truths as blasphemy. For that reason Christians soon added a number of invectives to the reproaches they addressed to the Jews concerning Jewish unbelief *(perfidia Judaeorum)* and blindness, which had already become stereotyped in the early church and remained so among medieval theologians. Even theologians who never met any Jews called them criminals and murderers because of their guilt in the crucifixion. When in the thirteenth century medieval theologians in fact began to encounter Jews and their polemics were therefore no longer merely literary, the organization of public disputations was repeatedly forbidden or discouraged.

As in so many other areas of medieval theology, Augustine played an important role in the written polemics of medieval theologians. Today so much is known about the way in which medieval theology dealt with the ideas of this Church Father that a distinction is usually made between Augustine and medieval Augustinianism. As a result of Bernhard Blumenkranz's study of Jewish-Christian relations in antiquity and the Middle Ages, a similar distinction can be made regarding Augustine's views of the Jews and their influence in the medieval period. Blumenkranz showed in his 1946 Basel dissertation, *Die Judenpredigt Augustins,* that the bishop of Hippo entertained good relationships with Jews and listened to what they had to say. In many of his writings Augustine discussed Judaism, in particular when he defended the Christian faith against pagan or heretical authors. He believed that it was important to underline that Christianity was no new invention, but was grafted on the Jewish religion.

But Augustine did reject Judaism unequivocally. In doing so, he sometimes used rather harsh words, which was to be expected in the missionary competition between Jews and Christians of those days. And he did use abusive terms against Jews when dealing with Christ's passion. But — contrary to what some modern authors have suggested — his choice of language was more prudent, moderate, and even sympathetic, in his *Adversus Judaeos* — the treatise, or rather sermon, in which he addressed the Jews and spoke of their rejection by God as foretold by several Old Testament prophets.

16. D. J. Lasker, *Jewish Philosophical Polemics against Christianity in the Middle Ages* (New York, 1977).

In his further research Blumenkranz has paid attention to the manner in which these statements of Augustine were received in the Middle Ages.[17] He discovered a few discrepancies. It appears that, besides Augustine's sermon about the Jews, there were two other treatises in which he supposedly addressed the Jews. However, one of these was not written by Augustine, while the other is an abbreviated and mutilated version of what he wrote against pagans and heretics. Both of these treatises contain more invective against Jews than the sermon referred to above. But medieval authors, such as the Venerable Bede, Alcuin, Hrabanus Maurus, and Hincmar of Reims, who dutifully quoted from Augustine's writings, reproduced this more vehement rejection of the Jews and its corresponding terminology, although, like Augustine, they were not consumed by anti-Semitism. One does not find any hatred for Jews among authors who wrote before the twelfth century. They simply repeated a conviction that was handed on by tradition and was therefore sacrosanct.

The one exception that must be noted is Agobard, bishop of Lyon in the first half of the ninth century. In several of his writings Agobard fiercely opposed the favors bestowed on the Jews by the Carolingian rulers, who apparently disregarded the canonical precepts concerning Jews and granted them special privileges. Agobard insisted that Jews should continue to live in isolation and should be prevented from seeking converts. He also said that Jewish children should be coerced to join the church. Some believe that Agobard's attitude may have been due to his Spanish background. In any case, there is no doubt that he was acquainted with Judaism and with the Talmudic writings. Converts from Judaism may have assisted him in acquiring such information. His familiarity with the Talmud, or at least with parts of it, makes him an exception among authors before 1100 who dealt with Jews and Judaism.

We learn from Agobard's treatise *De iudaicis superstitionibus* that he was acquainted with an early version of the *Toledoth Yeshu,* which relates the story of Christ's birth, life, and death in a way that must have been particularly offensive to Christians. Knowledge of this document, perhaps far more than Agobard's Spanish background, explains the hostility toward Jews that is evident in many of his writings. But since Christians did not

17. Blumenkranz's articles on this subject are brought together in *Juifs et Chrétiens. Patristique et Moyen Age* (London, 1977). His complete bibliography is given in G. Dahan, ed., *Les Juifs au regard de l'histoire. Mélanges en honneur de Bernard Blumenkranz* (Paris, 1985).

yet study the Talmud, the way in which Agobard turned against the Jews remained an isolated phenomenon, in spite of the many reproaches later hurled against medieval Christendom because of his views.[18]

Production of stereotyped writings against Jews even decreased sharply in the ninth century. The polemics revived in the eleventh century, and in the twelfth century the tone of these writings became sharper and their accusations went further. This escalation may, for instance, be found in an almost interminable treatise of Peter the Venerable against the Jews. His invective reached new depths of crudity. Using biblical terminology, he repeatedly referred to the Jews as the synagogue of Satan (Rev. 2:9). He called their intellect beastly and held them to be inferior to demons. He further doubted whether a Jew could be regarded as a human being.[19] He used, of course, the standard insults of Jews, such as scandalousness, hardness, blindness, and wicked unbelief.

The financial crisis at Cluny may explain Peter's more hostile attitude, which was already present in his letter to Louis VII concerning the Jewish financial contribution to the Second Crusade. Through the years Peter continued to face financial problems, and we learn from one of his other writings that the Cluniac monasteries were repeatedly at the mercy of Jewish moneylenders. But this harsher tone against the Jews probably also has to do with his familiarity with the Talmud, against which he reacts in the last section of his polemic, in a long chapter on "the ridiculous and stupid fables of the Jews." We know that he acquired his knowledge of the Talmud from Peter Alfonsus, a convert from Judaism who himself had written a dialogue with a Jew — perhaps himself before his conversion.

Malicious stories about Jews became more common during the twelfth century. The papal schism of Anacletus (1130-39) may have contributed to this. The schism was caused by the election of two popes after the death of Honorius II. Cardinal Pierleone, the candidate who eventually lost, came from a family of Roman bankers that half a century earlier, during the pontificate of Gregory VII, had left the Jewish faith. But the family had continued its dubious financial practices, and probably for that reason Pierleone's opponents vigorously denounced him for his Jewish

18. Cf. A. Chabaniss, *Agobard of Lyon: Churchman and Critic* (Syracuse, 1953); A. J. Zuckerman, "The Political Uses of Theology: The Conflict of Bishop Agobard and the Jews of Lyons," *Studies in Medieval Culture* 1/2, 23-51. On the Toledoth, see M. Goldstein, *Jesus in the Jewish Tradition* (New York, 1950).

19. *Petri Venerabilis adversus Iudeorum inveteram duritiam,* ed. Y. Friedman (*CCCM* 58; Turnhout, 1985), vii-xxv.

background after he had been elected pope and had ruled in Rome, as Anacletus, for a number of years with the financial support of his family.[20] Informing Peter the Venerable about the death of Pierleone/Anacletus, whom they had both opposed, Bernard of Clairvaux wrote, "That impious one, who made Israel to sin, has been swallowed up in death and gone down into the pit. In the words of the Prophet he 'made terms with death and a contract with hell.' "[21]

The most objectionable story about Jews from that time is found in the autobiography of Guibert of Nogent: A monk who wanted to engage in black magic sold his soul to the devil. He was assisted by a Jewish physician, who made the monk perform some obscene act in order to effect the transaction.[22] Neither this story nor any variant of it is found anywhere else. And it is not found in preaching *exempla* in which Jews play a role. But the more offensive tone of derision and ridicule seen in Guibert's story was also increasingly present in historical accounts. All this indicates that a change was happening in the relationship between Jews and Christians.

These changes in the attitudes of literary Christians toward Jews were, of course, related to the increased hostility against the Jews on the part of Christian lay people from the eleventh century on. But another factor was the greater familiarity of Christian authors with the content of the Talmud, especially the sections about Christ and Mary, which they considered blasphemous. The constitution of the Fourth Lateran Council points in that direction: It stipulates that Jews had to be identified by a symbol on their clothing, that Jews were not to be seen in public on Christian fast days, particularly during commemoration of Christ's passion, so that they would not ridicule the Christians, and that ridiculing the Savior or cursing the cross was prohibited. This prohibition probably had to do with something in the Talmud, for which Christians usually manifested a rather one-sided interest, emphasizing only those elements that were against their religion. They found such passages with the aid of Christianized Jews.

The Talmudic legends regarding Christ and Mary also gave rise to some controversies within Judaism, notably in Spain. But Jewish op-

---

20. M. Stroll, *The Jewish Pope: Ideology and Politics in the Papal Schism of 1130* (Leiden and New York, 1987).

21. Letter 147.2 = *SBO* VII, 351 = James, 216 (letter 147).

22. *Self and Society in Medieval France*, ed. J. F. Benton (New York, 1970), 115.

ponents of the legends remained a minority, and this contributed to the conversion of some members of that minority to Christianity. Nicholas Donin of La Rochelle fits into this category. Because of his objections to the Talmud, he was expelled by the Jewish community in 1225. In 1235 he asked for baptism, possibly with the aim of continuing his opposition to the Talmud. It was at his prompting that the church began its hunt for Talmud codices.[23]

Increased understanding of Jewish views, ideas, and standpoints did not always lead to greater hostility. At times it led to rapprochement. An early example of this countermovement is found in the *Disputation* by Gilbert Crispin, written at the end of the eleventh century. In this work the author, abbot of Westminster and a student of Anselm of Canterbury, allows the Jew to speak for himself and puts the Christian in the defensive role. This approach was so different that this treatise has often been regarded as an account of a real discussion, but this is doubted by others. The *Disputatio* must be classified somewhere between monastic and scholastic theology. Besides offering an intellectual renewal, this work also pays attention to moral values, which was one of the hallmarks of monastic theology.

This duality is also present in a twelfth-century dialogue between a Jew, a philosopher, and a Christian, in which each of the three participants manifests a positive attitude toward the others. This dialogue was written by Peter Abelard toward the end of his life, as he was searching for a balance between the two approaches to theology represented by the philosopher and the Christian (see ch. VIII above).

In these two writings the Christian is not always right, as was invariably the case in earlier polemics and as would usually be the case in later writings.[24] But Gilbert and Abelard were not alone in their more open attitude toward the Jews. There were other signs in the twelfth century of a greater interest on the part of Christians in the *Hebraica veritas*, which was centered in particular on the Jewish understanding of the Old Testament, in

---

23. J. M. Rosenthal, "The Talmud on Trial," *Jewish Quarterly Review* 47 (1956-57), 58-76, 145-69.

24. A. Sapir Abulafia, "An Attempt by Gilbert Crispin, Abbot of Westminster, at Rational Argument in the Jewish-Christian Debate," *Studia Monastica* 26 (1984), 55-74; H. Liebeschütz, "The Significance of Judaism in Peter Abelard's *Dialogus*," *Journal of Jewish Studies* 12 (1961), 1-18; cf. above, ch. IX, nn. 36f.; D. Berger, "Mission to the Jews and Jewish-Christian Contacts in the Polemical Literature of the High Middle Ages," *American Historical Review* 91 (1986), 576-91.

an attempt at arriving at more profound exegesis. The significant role of Rashi in Jewish exegesis must be mentioned in this context. He lived in Troyes in the eleventh century, but was just as influential after his death as during his lifetime. His commentaries on the Scriptures as well as his writings on the administration of justice among the Jews were so authoritative that later generations referred to the school of Rashi.[25]

Some Christians in the Carolingian era had already shown an interest in Jewish Bible exegesis. Among them was Alcuin, who was entrusted with the task of imposing some uniformity on the Latin Bible versions that were circulating. This interest revived at the end of the eleventh century. Stephen Harding, abbot of Cîteaux and creator of a Bible manuscript that is famous for its illuminations (†1134), showed great interest in the original Hebrew text and therefore consulted Jewish scholars. The emergence of cathedral schools in the towns provided a favorable climate for this technique of Bible study. Jewish exegetes were available in the towns for consultation. The best-known school of this kind was at the monastery of Augustinian canons at St. Victor in Paris, founded by William of Champeaux. The Victorines learned Hebrew, and their biblical exegesis created considerable excitement.[26]

From the twelfth century on study of the Old Testament thus brought together Christian and Jewish intellectuals. This cooperation proved to be of more than temporary importance. It laid the groundwork for the work of Nicholas of Lyra, a late medieval Bible exegete who also consulted Jewish scholars.[27] His biblical commentaries, *Postillae perpetuae*, remained authoritative for a long time and continue to impress readers for the straightforwardness with which the biblical texts are understood.

But this rapprochement of Jewish and Christian scholars remained marginal when compared to the theological rejection of Judaism, which scholastic theology developed further, and to the church's often violent opposition to Jews from the twelfth century until after the Middle Ages. Indeed, this rapprochement could almost be regarded as the strange hobby of some who dared to be ecclesiastical nonconformists. Numerous documents, especially declarations and council reports, show how different the position of the church authorities was from the twelfth century on.

25. H. Hailperich, *Rashi and the Christian Scholars* (Pittsburgh, 1963).
26. B. Smalley, *The Study of the Bible in the Middle Ages* (1941; repr. Notre Dame, 1964), 83-195.
27. A. Grabois, "The *Hebraica Veritas* and Jewish-Christian Intellectual Relations in the Twelfth Century," *Speculum* 50 (1975), 613-34.

One such statement must be singled out for further discussion. It was written at the end of the fifteenth century by Bishop Giovanni Baptista dei Giudici of Ventimiglia. Bishop Giovanni opposed an accusation of ritual murder brought against Jews in a trial at Trent,[28] and in a treatise on veneration of saints he criticized the popular custom of venerating murdered children as saints. In that treatise, though, he also expressed regret for the church's tolerance of Jewish worship, adding that tolerance did not imply approval: "The church tolerates in the towns many things of which it does not approve, such as the presence of brothels and Jews."[29] This remark is remarkably ambiguous: It joins a fixed point of view with a perspective conditioned by time and place: It is clear that the church has never had, nor will it ever, any position regarding the presence of brothels that is not negative. But rejection of Jews in an urban society seems typical of the church as a *medieval* institution, even though the church had not yet relinquished this standpoint when the sixteenth century began.

⁂   ⁂

AND SO Bishop Giovanni's statement takes us back to the fundamental question posed in this chapter: To what extent must the anti-Jewish sentiments of medieval society be blamed on that society, and to what extent must we blame the church in its character as the timeless instrument of salvation? The distinction is important, unless we want to see the institutional church as a relic from the past, a medieval phenomenon that tries to maintain itself in our time though it is merely antiquarian. It almost appears as if the Church of Rome, through some of its statements, invites Christian historians to that position.

I am convinced that the question we are asking amounts to more than a minor detail. But, as indicated above, it is difficult to answer. I have referred to the biased way in which the church of the Counter-Reformation is often portrayed in isolation from its historical context, as if it were simply a continuation of the medieval church. Other difficulties to be faced are the continuing existence of anti-Judaism after the Middle Ages and the inclination of some authors to base Christian responsibility for the Holocaust simplistically on anti-Jewish attitudes that persisted through

28. W. P. Eckert, "Aus den Akten der Trienter Judenprozesses," in *Judentum im Mittelalter* (Miscellanea Mediaevalia 4; Berlin, 1966), 97-305.

29. A. Vauchez, *La sainteté en Occident* (Rome, 1981), 484, n. 15.

the centuries. And some trace the continuity of anti-Semitism through the transition from the early to the medieval church, similarly eliminating society's role.

There is another difficulty that I have not yet mentioned: Is there any way today for us to trace the distinction between church and society, recognizing that this distinction continued in the Middle Ages? Can we still discover how the church was influenced by the medieval world, considering that most of the written documentation of that society came from the hands of the clergy? Or to put it more concretely, can we differentiate between ecclesiastical and social aspects when dealing with topics such as the harassment of the Jews just before the First Crusade and at the time of later crusades, or with the persecution of Jews as a response to alleged desecrations of the sacred host?

Even if study of these themes fails to provide an answer to this question, we are left with one remarkable fact that may give us some idea what our answer could be. I am referring to expressions of anti-Jewish sentiments, which often developed into persecutions, for which social factors can definitely be blamed. We may think of fiscal violence of rulers against Jews, of accusations of ritual murder, and of the fourteenth-century blaming of the Black Death on Jews supposedly poisoning wells. This last accusation claimed a great number of victims in areas where Jews were still permitted to live, that is, in the towns of the German Empire.

The medieval church must accept part of the blame for the fiscal violence by the princes. The claims of the princes on Jewish possessions were derived from ideas, developed by theologians, that, because of their culpability in the death of Christ, Jews were to live in subjection to Christians. A pope like Gregory IX might protest against some of the excesses to which this subjection led, but in 1233 he demanded strict compliance with it.[30] By this time the princes had developed their own ideas as to what subjection meant: They believed that the property and income of Jews was at their own free disposal.

Of course it began more subtly. Beginning with Henry IV, the German emperors regarded the Jews as belonging to their *camera,* in the same way as others who fell under their immediate protection. Frederick Barbarossa gave a more explicit explanation of this principle in a privilege granted to the Jews of Regensburg. His duty to protect them implied that

---

30. Cf. S. Grayzel, *The Church and the Jews in the XIIIth Century* (rev. ed.; New York, 1966), 198-203.

they were to recognize no other authority but his. Fifty years later, in 1236, this exceptional status was formalized in a *Kammer-Knechtschaft*, which implied an eternal submission of the Jews to the emperor, particularly in regard to taxes. When imperial authority declined, local rulers and towns assumed this royal privilege of taxing Jews.[31]

In this connection the question that Countess Aleyda of Brabant posed to Thomas Aquinas in the 1360s concerning the right to impose taxes on the Jews is of special interest. He answered her question with a small treatise, *De regimine Judaeorum,* in which he argued that, because of their guilt, Jews ought to live in eternal submission to the princes, and that a prince may consider Jewish property as his own.[32] In this respect the developments in the relationship between the authority of the princes and the Jews was different in England and France. These developments were tied to the emergence of royal authority in those countries. As their authority grew, kings were able to tax the Jews ever more heavily, under the illusion that this might to some extent cover their growing deficits. The common people, who depended on the Jews when they needed to borrow money, suffered the most from this royal policy.

Under the constantly rising taxes and the uncertainty of their own future, Jews increasingly passed on the burden. Resentment of them grew because of this, and they were eventually banned from these countries. Hatred of Jews was also stimulated by accusations of a different kind: They were charged with counterfeiting money, since they often profited from the limitations imposed by the princes on the minting of coins. When at last they were expelled — from England in 1290 and from France in 1306 — leaving, of course, their possessions behind, the common people were happy with the expulsion of these Shylocks *avant la lettre,* for whose creation not Shakespeare but medieval society must largely be credited.

The situation is quite different with regard to the role of society in the development of the ritual murder accusations. The earliest such charge dates from 1144: The body of a young man was found buried in unconsecrated ground in Norwich on the Saturday before Easter. A month later

31. G. Kisch, *The Jews in Medieval Germany: A Study of Their Legal and Social Status* (1949; repr. New York, 1970).

32. H. Liebeschütz, "Judaism and Jewry in the Social Doctrine of Thomas Aquinas," *Journal of Jewish Studies* 13 (1962), 57-81; B. Alexander, "Medieval Jewry through the Eyes of Aquinas," in G. Verbeke and D. Verhelst, ed., *Aquinas and Problems of His Time* (Louvain, 1976), 57-68.

an uncle of the deceased accused the Jews of murdering the boy. The local bishop was eager to have the tomb of a saint in his cathedral because of the money it would bring in. He saw reason enough in the uncle's accusation to have the body reburied in the church. A *Vita* for this new saint was written: It reported that the boy had been crucified.[33] Similar stories came to be told elsewhere. When in 1163 the body of a boy was discovered in Pontoise, France, the accusation subsequently directed against the Jews received particular attention because the body was buried in Paris, in the church dedicated to the Holy Innocents. Popular belief gave a biblical dimension to the sainthood attributed to these martyrs who had supposedly fallen victim to Jews. Sometimes the accusation of ritual murder simply served as an excuse. This was the case in 1171 when it was used in Blois to legitimize the revenge of Count Theobald on the local Jews that we have already described.

Most of the particular accusations and the ensuing killings of Jews took place in the German Empire, though not before the thirteenth century. The legendary Jewish custom of killing a Christian child during Passover to commemorate the death of Christ also developed into more general charges. It was rumored that in 1308 the Jews had murdered a woman in Tienen. The chronicle reports that the woman, whose body was found, *fuit miserabiliter martyrizata:* "was mercilessly tortured." Charges against Jews even degenerated into accusations of cannibalism.

These sorts of charges continued to live on, more or less underground, in Germany. When anti-Judaism reemerged in the nineteenth century as anti-Semitism, several authors repeated them in numerous uncritical *Belegstellen.* The Nazis had only to copy from these "scholars." The persistence of prejudice against the Jews in Germany was undoubtedly also influenced by what Luther — as a medieval person, rather than as a reformer — wrote against the Jews. His hatred for Jews did not, however, have the racist dimension that was to be so prominent in later anti-Semitism.[34]

The church cannot be fully exonerated in regard to the ritual murder accusations, but its contribution is clearly related to the social circumstances of the time, which, in the context of the general prejudice

33. G. I. Langmuir, "Thomas of Monmouth, Detector of Ritual Murder," *Speculum* 59 (1984), 820-46.
34. H. A. Oberman, "Martin Luther: Heil und Unheil aus den Juden," *Würzelen der Antisemitismus* (Berlin, 1981), 127-83.

against the Jews, lent credibility to the accusations in the minds of the common people. The role of the church has to do with this credibility, mainly because the church regarded Jews as "murderers of God." This was clearly expressed in ordinances that Jews were not to be seen in public in the period before Easter, so as not to add to the grief of Christians commemorating the death of Christ.

This credibility was also supported by stories about Jews desecrating the host. The church implicitly confirmed these stories by tolerating and even promoting the cults of the miraculous hosts, sometimes forcing Jews to pay to build chapels devoted to such miraculous hosts. The same applies to the desire of the common people — as part of the strongly promoted cult of the saints — to venerate murdered children as martyrs. Such children had to have been murdered for their faith in order to be recognized, and that recognition could be obtained by accusing Jews of murder, even with no proof.

The popes never fully agreed with these practices and at times even attempted to protect Jews against such charges. We have two letters of Pope Innocent IV written in 1247 to the German and the French bishops respectively in which he vigorously opposes such accusations. He notes that the Jews' own laws prohibit them from touching corpses during Passover, so that it is ridiculous to charge them with such crimes when a body has been found.[35] Remarkably enough, in these letters the pope held the princes, and sometimes also the bishops, responsible for these accusations. In their greed they were looking for profit, since the possessions of condemned Jews would fall to them in accordance with their rights over the Jews.

Finally there is the charge that Jews poisoned wells and thereby caused the Black Death. When the plague broke out, many, in their fear and consternation, sought a scapegoat, as they had when other calamities had struck. People saw no use in the explanations of the intellectuals, in particular the medical experts, of those days, who looked for the cause in the influences of heavenly bodies on the earth. The experts wondered about contagion, but not about impure water, and certainly not about a premeditated attempt to generate and spread the plague.

Where the idea that the Jews were to blame came from is unclear. At first the accusation was not pointed just at them. In Spain Saracens and foreign pilgrims were blamed. In England lepers were considered the

---

35. Grayzel, *The Church and the Jews*, 268-70.

culprits. This accusation was already made before 1321 in a continuation of the chronicle of William of Nangis. Many lepers were executed in Aquitaine. They were supposed to have poisoned wells and springs with the intention of spreading sickness over all of France and Germany. But a rich Jew was also implicated: It was said that he had paid a substantial amount of money to incite the lepers to their evil deeds and had given them the poison, which consisted of human blood, urine, three unknown herbs, and a pulverized consecrated host. Witnesses had actually seen the lepers transporting this concoction. Jews were included in the subsequent executions at the stake. In fact, this last detail is probably the only credible part of the report, for the negative image of the Jews made them automatically culpable for problems beyond human power to change.

The accusation itself proved to be beyond the power of the pope, Clement VI, who resided in Avignon. As early as 1338, before the persecutions of the Jews started, he had rejected the accusation as utter nonsense and had opposed profiting from Jews by coercing them to be baptized or by cheating them out of their money. Later he also condemned the persecutions and stated that those who made these accusations were misled by Satan.[36]

When Clement made this last statement in September 1348, the persecutions had already begun. At the outbreak of the plague in Savoy, the count had imprisoned a number of Jews, who under torture had confessed being part of an international plot, based in Toledo, to poison springs. In this "confession" the poison was again a weird concoction. Eleven Jews were burned at the stake and the others were condemned to pay heavy fines, which they could not pay since their possessions had already been confiscated. Persecution spread in epidemic proportions from Savoy to other places as those who were responsible exploited the fear of the people.

The property of Jews was safe nowhere. In some cases town magistrates assumed the claims of the Jewish moneylenders, but waited for the executions of the Jews since they otherwise might have had to forfeit these claims to the emperor, particularly when they fell outside their jurisdictions. Elsewhere the guilds were behind the persecutions, intent as they were to get their hands on the Jews' possessions. Sometimes, as in Strasbourg, the bishop was to blame. But whatever the case, the fate of

36. E. A. Synan, *The Popes and the Jews in the Middle Ages* (New York and London, 1965), 133f., 211, n. 53.

the Jews in these persecutions was always the same: executions at the stake in great numbers. The role of the flagellants, the bands of men who scourged themselves during the epidemic, appears — contrary to what has often been said — to have been rather limited. Their religious fanaticism can hardly be considered the cause of these persecutions.

It remains difficult to explain the persecutions, but it must be remembered that Jews were killed frequently, though more often by gangs than by the authorities: In many towns a Jew on a stake was not a totally unknown sight. Further explanations must be sought in the social relationships and tensions of the time. Frantiček Graus, for example, has suggested that this explanation is to be found in the social and economic problems of the time.

Considering their ferocity and the scale on which they occurred, these persecutions do seem to fit in a society characterized by instability, insecurity, and consequent panic and hysteria. People were no longer sure of traditional ideas and values, the economic security of many was undermined, and society was becoming more and more complex. Economics, politics, and the whole social fabric seemed to be driven by anonymous forces. In such a situation there would be a natural urge to put the blame somewhere. The Jews were a likely target, since they had had the scapegoat role for centuries. And putting the blame on them had the added advantage of annulments of debts, even for the common people. That the Jew as scapegoat had often been portrayed as a demonized being led to easy acceptance of the accusations of well poisoning and host desecration, especially in this situation of insecurity and the desperate search for protection.

The consequences of these persecutions were unpredictable where the fear and hostility of the people were allowed free rein. Town magistrates therefore often thought it best to orchestrate the discharge of these emotions — which some of them may have regarded as inevitable and therefore acceptable — in such a way that their local communities would experience as little damage as possible. Thus they cynically organized mass executions with this purpose in mind, erecting the stakes in isolated places such as Jewish cemeteries or on river islands.[37]

In such persecutions the role of medieval society is clearly evident. The responsibility of the church was only of secondary importance. But

37. F. Graus, "Judenpogromme in 14. Jahrhundert: Der Schwarze Tod," in B. Martin and E. Schulz, *Die Juden als Minderheit in der Geschichte* (Munich, 1981), 68-84.

this indirect responsibility cannot be overlooked, especially since persecuting Jews began in the course of the eleventh century and became a common practice then, and in this period the church was more involved than is often admitted. In any case, these persecutions changed the relationship between Jews and Christians irrevocably, and later persecutions must be understood first of all as escalations of earlier measures against the Jews.

꙲   ꙲

THE BEGINNING of these earlier persecutions is usually dated to the beginning of the crusades. The persecutions are in this view interpreted as an expression of the eschatological fanaticism to which the church had educated medieval society. But many historians dealing with the crusades have minimized the eschatological aspect, even if they see the crusades, especially in their early phases, as a religious event and do not share the opinion of those who explain the crusades primarily from economic motives. But the relationship between the crusades and the persecutions of Jews remains a matter of debate. Even Lea Dasberg's interpretation, which linked the reduced legal and social status of the Jews in the eleventh century to the Cluniac movement and the Gregorian reforms, has not convinced everyone.[38]

Others have argued for an explanation that ties the hostility toward the Jews to the development of a new form of unity in medieval society, which took the place of the older kinship communities. The older communities had disintegrated when they were incorporated into the Carolingian Empire. The shaping of this new bond — Christendom — which was to take the place of kinship loyalties, was the goal of Charlemagne's political strategies, particularly his dealings with the church. He wanted an empire unified by church and faith. What he attempted became a social process — *the formation of Christendom* — that continued even after his empire had collapsed. This unity was to be realized in the eleventh century, and some feel that this may explain the emergence at that time of intolerance toward groups that remained outside Christendom or who refused to conform to it: heretics, Muslims, and Jews. The difference between this view and that of Dasberg is that in the evolution spoken of here the very

38. *Untersuchungen über die Entstehung des Judenstatuts im 11. Jahrhundert* (Paris and The Hague, 1965). Cf. the review by H. Liebeschütz in *Cahiers de Civilisation Médiévale* 11 (1968), 227f.

foundation, that is, the common people who belonged to the church and determined the kind of society they wanted, is attributed a more specific role of its own.

But this line of argumentation goes no farther in establishing an incontrovertible link between social development — which at the same time implies a further growth of the church in society — and persecution of the Jews at the beginning of the crusades. It fails in this way for three reasons:

First, it downplays the importance of the persecutions of Jews that took place around 1010 in different places, which may have manifested a clearer pattern than has often been acknowledged. And it should be remembered that even before that period situations of panic prompted acts of violence against Jews.

Second, this view generally disregards the anti-Jewish sentiments that had developed on the part of the illiterate masses. Where did these prejudices come from? Did they find their origin just in the ancient injunctions of the church against the Jews that were codified in medieval canon law and in the writings of medieval theologians who, in a distorted way, repeated the statements of Augustine? Or did this anti-Judaism develop rather in the day-to-day interactions of the people with Jews? How this relationship evolved is quite difficult to determine. Any evaluation will have to take into account the social position of the Jews in early medieval society, which was largely agricultural and gave little attention to trade. Trading was in the hands of foreigners, who were not integrated into society and remained suspect. Among these were the Jews, who also had a different religion and, as a result, a different culture. They lived in their own communities, since they wanted to maintain their religion and its accompanying manner of life. This could only be realized in an urban setting. This, in turn, explains why many Jews chose to live in southern France, where urban life manifested stronger continuity. And it also explains why so many Jews, from Roman days onward, settled in the Rhineland.

As a result of the privileged position of the Jews as the traders of the Carolingian Empire, some of them in southern France came to belong to the wealthy landowning class. In spite of the protests of Bishop Agobard, the stipulations of the church with regard to Jews were not adhered to during the reign of Charlemagne and Louis the Pious. The privileged position of the Jews probably depended not only on their importance for trade in the empire, but also on their numerical insignificance. They were no social threat to a majority that was hardly involved in their monetary economy. This situation changed when Jews began to settle outside the older urbanized areas, notably in northwestern Europe. They became dependent on the landowning elite, who claimed to have seignorial rights that they wanted to see accepted by the populations of the pre-urban settlements. That even in these regions the Jews wanted to live in their own communities made their relationships with these landowners complex since the degree of dependence on a landowner could differ among members of a single Jewish community. This made it natural for Jews to participate in attempts of those pre-urban settlements to resist the claims of these lords. It also explains why the opposition of the seignorial class to urban autonomy was accompanied by feelings of animosity toward Jews. We may therefore conclude that the anti-Jewish sentiment was strengthened by conflicts between landholders and urban communities.

In addition, we must realize that the populations of the emerging towns were viewed with suspicion by the people in the countryside. Clear indications of this are found in the writings of Alpertus of Metz concerning eleventh-century events in the town of Tiel, a merchant settlement in the Netherlands, and in the autobiography of Abbot Guibert of Nogent, writing about the population of Laon.[39] As a result the eleventh century experienced a contemporaneity of incontemporaneities, with all the inherent tensions and contrasts. In such a situation feelings of hatred on the part of the majority could easily develop, especially in a context of ecclesiastical protests against Jews; and that context became more familiar to the people as Christianization proceeded.

Among the avant-garde of traders, whom the peasants regarded with great suspicion, the Jews occupied a special place. Even though their profession gave them much in common with other traders, they also differed from them in their literacy and their culture, as well as in language and religion. Therefore the opposition of the non-urban population against the trading profession, however diverse this class may have been, must have developed a special focus on the Jews, since they were the most distinct group.

The Jews were very conscious of these differences between themselves and others among whom they lived and considered themselves somewhat as an elite. When toward the end of the eleventh century persecutions broke out, many, if not most, of the Jews expressed their

39. *Self and Society in Medieval France,* ed. Benton, 115.

religiosity in thought and deed by preferring death to baptism. By accepting baptism they would have given up their unique position, at least in the minds of their oppressors and feeble protectors. But the differences in culture also played a role, and contributed to the fact that baptism was not an acceptable alternative in spite of the threat of death.[40]

The third obstacle to constructing a direct link between the social development of the church in the eleventh century — which among other things found expression in the response to the appeals for the crusades — and the persecutions of Jews that were taking place, is found in what actually happened. The persecutions were not the work of the crusader armies themselves, not even of the popular forces led by Peter of Amiens. The armies did contribute to the persecutions by demanding financial support from Jewish communities in several towns, and the Jews in some German towns tried to buy off the threat of violence by giving this support. But for the least disciplined among the crusaders, mostly from the northern part of France — who, due to their profession, were accustomed to equating plunder with warfare — these financial compensations provided a further incentive. These crusaders often belonged to small bands, mostly under the command of Count Emicho of Leiningen, a rather obscure figure who had gradually moved away from the discipline and idealism of the crusader armies. We know of incidents in which his followers abducted Jewish children. These children were then baptized so that they would grow up as Christians. Whatever may have been the background for this kind of action, it does not indicate a direct link between the church's influence on society and the manifestations of strong anti-Jewish sentiment in the eleventh century. The intentions of these bandits in having Jewish children baptized might be seen as reflecting such influence, but it may also be interpreted as a strong protest against a group that was unwilling to conform.

Gavin Langmuir, who has written a number of studies of this anti-Jewish feeling in the Middle Ages, has strongly emphasized the important role of such bands in these persecutions of Jews in the context of the early crusades. He distinguishes three aspects in this anti-Jewish sentiment: doctrinal, legal, and popular. Doctrinal anti-Judaism existed from the beginning of Christianity and consisted of the attempt to prove that Christians were the true Israel.

40. Cf. K. W. Deutsch, "Anti-Semitic Ideas in the Middle Ages," *Journal of the History of Ideas* 6 (1945), 239-54.

Legal anti-Judaism became prominent when Christians were able to influence or control secular authority. It consisted of the enforcing of doctrinal anti-Judaism by sanctions aimed at depriving Jews of any control over Christians, at preventing Jewish proselytism, and at excluding Jews from the rights and advantages enjoyed by Christians.

Without popular anti-Judaism, neither doctrinal nor legal anti-Judaism could be fully realized, and this had to wait until the majority of the population identified itself profoundly with Christianity, accepting its cosmology enough to result in a desire to attack Judaism and degrade Jews. Evidence of such a broad popular anti-Judaism is lacking before the eleventh century. And even then anti-Jewish sentiments among the common people occurred not in Mediterranean Europe, but in the northwest, where the number of Jews was far smaller. Jews had settled in that region at a later date, and their professions showed less diversity than in the Mediterranean region.

In northwestern Europe Christianity itself was also of later date and had only recently penetrated the broader classes of society. Langmuir believes that the Christianization of northwestern Europe was accompanied by a change in the nature of religion itself, particularly in the way it was experienced. Inspired by views current in the sociology of religion, he distinguishes between empirical religiosity and supraempirical religiosity, which does not try to relate to social phenomena and may be considered universal. The empirical form of religious experience is above all directed toward the concrete reality of this world. It is, for instance, directly related to the kinship community and nobility and is expressed in extended rituals. When religion is experienced in such a way, there is nothing problematic in praying that one's own community may conquer its enemies. The anti-Jewish policies of the Visigothic kings, formulated in church synods, may be seen as expressing an empirical experience of religion. And this way of experiencing religion existed among all the Germanic tribes, even after they had been Christianized and had become part of the Carolingian Empire, where Jews were in a privileged position.[41]

But Langmuir believes that Christianity in the Roman Empire tended toward supraempirical experience and that this was a factor in the anti-Jewish sentiments in the ancient experience of religion. He maintains that the Jewish community would not have been able to develop further

---

41. G. I. Langmuir, "Anti-Judaism as the Necessary Preparation for Anti-Semitism," *Viator* 2 (1971), 383-89.

in western Europe if the post-Constantinian Roman Empire had survived. To support this view, Langmuir points to the attitude of Bishop Ambrose toward the Jews.

Langmuir acknowledges that all varieties of religious experience manifest a blending of empirical and supraempirical aspects. Nevertheless, there was a marked difference in the balance of these aspects of religious experience between Roman and Germanic Christianity. In northwestern Europe we do not find the supraempirical religious experience before the eleventh century, and then the blending of supraempirical experience with empirical experience there resulted in a Christianity that differed from what already existed in the Mediterranean region.[42]

This difference in the manner in which religion was experienced may explain why a group of undisciplined crusaders would be prompted by their religious experience, with its empirical and nonempirical aspects, to persecute Jews. And we already saw how this persecution effected a drastic change in the relationship between Jews and Christians, even though there were earlier acts of violence against Jews. Langmuir emphasizes that the anti-Jewish sentiments manifested in such persecutions were most frequent in that part of northwestern Europe where Christianity was least influenced by its earlier Roman context. He believes that the reason that persecutions broke out and continued in this area in particular must be sought in the way in which the two forms of religious experience were blended there. He continues by pointing out that Luther was the only

---

42. Langmuir, "From Ambrose," 331-35, 358-61. In a personal communication (May 22, 1983), Langmuir offers further explication:

What I emphasized at Spoleto [where he lectured on this matter] was not so much the change from a primarily supra-empirical religiosity to a heavily empirical one, but rather the change from a rational-legal society to a traditional or tribal society. That change, I believe, altered people's understanding of the nature of human identity, making the "tribal" collectivity both the basis of individual identity and the fundamental human unity which was in communication with God and with which God was concerned. . . . In other words, what I was arguing was that the way people conceived of their identity in relation to God and the kind of pre-scribable and observable ways in which they believe in God . . . varies depending on the nature of the prevailing social organization or disorganization. Consequently, I believe that any religiosity reflects the prevailing social relations, either by accepting them or by reacting against them. I therefore also believe that Christian religiosity has varied remarkably through history in the extent to which it has been the "tribe," the role-differentiated rationally organized society, or the individual as the essential basis of human identity and the unit of humanity that is in contact with God. Hence, any drastic change in the way individuals are related to a collectivity will affect that dimension of people's religiosity.

reformer who vigorously persisted in the anti-Jewish attitude expressed in northwestern Europe.[43]

As far as I have been able to follow these fascinating, but rather complex, arguments, it seems that they ignore a few things. For instance, I believe that the reasoning regarding the supraempirical character of Ambrose's religious experience with regard to the Jews is questionable. Ambrose was simply defending concrete, this-worldly interests in his opposition to the rebuilding of the synagogue in Callinicium. Moreover, his loyalty to the Roman Empire, to which he attributes a role in the economy of salvation, leads him to be susceptible to an empirical religious experience.

A second objection arises from the romanizing of the Rhineland by the Romans themselves. In Trier, for example, Christianity originated and spread within the context of Roman civilization. And the absence of persecutions in England and France at the time of the Black Death — in contrast to what happened in the German Empire — must to a greater extent be related to the fact that Jews had been expelled from England and France. It seems a rather bold presupposition to think that there the persecutions would have been less cruel and less bloody. For we also know that the first burning of Jews because of the plague epidemic did not occur in northwestern Europe, and that in the later Middle Ages cruel persecutions of Jews also took place in the Mediterranean region. We may think of the activities of the Pastoreux against the Jews in Languedoc in 1320 and of the burning of some Jews in Toulouse in 1348.

But Langmuir's explanation of the escalation of medieval persecutions of Jews does not pretend to give a final answer to our present question: What is the relationship between church and society with respect to the diverse expressions of anti-Jewish sentiments in the Middle Ages? Our conclusion is that, in spite of all the anti-Jewish traditions that the church carried with it when it addressed medieval society, it can be held responsible for neither such manifestations of anti-Jewish feeling nor for the persecutions to which Jews fell victim. In some of the persecutions society itself, the Jews included, played a decisive role. In some other cases it remains uncertain what part society played. More will certainly depend on further study — provided there is enough interest in continued research.

43. Langmuir does not totally resist the temptation to continue the line of that anti-Judaism up to the recent past. See his "Medieval Anti-Semitism," in H. Friedlander and S. Milton, ed., *The Holocaust: Ideology, Bureaucracy and Genocide* (New York, 1981), 34f.

꙰   ꙰

IN CONCLUDING THIS *tour d'horizon,* I would like to make some remarks about the possible form such research could take. It would require a method that differs from the traditional approach to medieval church history, though a method that, in dealing with this segment of history, focuses attention on the manner in which members of the medieval church experienced their faith in daily life is not totally new. It has been practiced by the *Annales* group in Paris, which proposes to move from church history to a history of religion, without, however, limiting itself to the Middle Ages. But the members of this group are not the only historians practicing *histoire religieuse.* Langmuir, in a sense, also supports such a historical project in relation to anti-Judaism, though in my opinion he is somewhat impeded by presuppositions from the sociology of religion, which threaten the impartiality of such research if they influence it too strongly and at too early a stage.

A similar objection has at times been raised against the research into religious experience undertaken by the *Annales* group.[44] Nevertheless, the plea of this group for a change in approach deserves attention. In this connection one can point to the consistent relationship between a particular type of religious experience and the kind of society in which it exists and to its particular, though changing, functions within that society. One can point, that is, to the concrete way in which religion is experienced by all classes of a society. This implies a shift in focus away from traditional church history. Instead of studying a series of events that occurred during a certain period in history, the focus shifts to a number of aspects of religious life within a given time frame: The emphasis is on what is constant, rather than on changes that happen to occur.

Such an approach carries with it the danger of underestimating the value of written sources and the appropriate philological methodology in a desire to apply the methods of the social sciences, which are treated as paradigmatic. Such an approach, which only substitutes for philological methods those of the social sciences, also leads to no real broadening of historical research.[45] This danger is of particular significance in an attempt

---

44. Cf. my extensive reaction to J. Le Goff, *The Birth of Purgatory* (Chicago, 1984) in *Revue d'Histoire ecclésiastique* 94 (1983), 429-53.

45. Cf. A. H. Bredero, "L'empirisme d'un médiéviste et le renouveau des méthodes

to study how the church is influenced by society at large with regard to the prejudices of any given time. For such a study written statements, placed within their origin and context, are indispensable, regardless of how they have been transmitted. Without them it remains impossible to understand either the constant features of these prejudices or how they developed in and through the ties between the church and its members' socially conditioned experience of faith.

It is less difficult to trace these developments than has sometimes been suggested. It is true that we have to depend on statements of a literate elite, which usually represented the church in society. But this elite was not completely isolated from popular culture or withdrawn into a *culture savante*. In expressing the official views of the church, this group often, and certainly in the case of anti-Judaism, echoed popular culture. Emotion often played an important role in this popular culture, particularly in actual contacts with Jews. We have already seen how these confrontations not only had negative effects — as many writings indicate — but also led to some positive results. These more positive effects are more difficult to trace, but the interpretation of the negative statements is also far from easy. They often merely repeat older viewpoints and stereotypes.

For that reason they must always be read in the context in which they were written or reiterated. We only need to look at the many fictional accounts of desecrations of the host. Further material is found in the increasingly harsh polemics against Jews in chronicles, which give inhumanly matter-of-fact accounts of persecutions of Jews, and, of course, in legal documents. We also have material on Jews in the collections of sermon *exempla,* which in part are of ancient vintage and contain stereotypical ideas, but at times also present new elements. And we must also mention the stereotypical portrayals of medieval Jews in passion plays and literary narrations, which kept unwarranted prejudices alive, for instance, the *Canterbury Tales.*

This list is far from complete. We could, for example, refer to statements in hagiographical sources and to many passing remarks about Jews in other sources. The method and execution of such research would be far from simple, even though some Jewish historians have already published studies of limited scope. This type of study remains inconceivable unless it is embedded in a larger framework. But it would be extremely

---

d'interprétation," in *L'histoire et ses méthodes* (Travaux et Mémoires de la Maison Descartes, Amsterdam 4; Lille, 1981), 78-85.

worthwhile, since it could make a real contribution in making this ever sensitive chapter of western European history a subject for more careful discussion.

EXCURSUS:
THE ROLE OF THEOLOGY IN THE VILIFICATION
OF THE JEWS IN THE LATE MIDDLE AGES

IN 1984 Nico Oudejans, a scholar of Dutch language and literature, published an article on "The Jew in Middle Dutch Literature."[46] His examination of the texts of this period led to the hardly surprising conclusion that the image of the Jew in this literature is characterized by anti-Jewish statements. Oudejans made a survey of these statements and tried to explain their origin. He believed they could not have been grounded in actual feelings against the Jews at that time, as there were very few Jews in the region where this literature originated. He maintained that the image of the Jew had a life of its own in medieval literature and that it closely resembled the New Testament portrayal of the Jew. Having stated this, he concluded his article with the following statement concerning this concept of the Jew:

> It grew into an aggregate of faults and shortcomings, a top-heavy complex that gave the Christian a conceptual framework in which to place the phenomenon of the "Jew." This conceptual framework was not grounded in social conflict or in a historical perspective, but was anchored in a Christian theology that attempted to win the community of believers for itself by creating a common enemy. Through the centuries this theology, as expressed in a "catechesis of defamation," tried to force an image of the demonic, totally corrupt Jew on the Christian mind. It is astonishing to see how well it succeeded.

In this statement theology becomes the scapegoat. It apparently deserves that role, since it carries the sole responsibility for the fact that late medieval Jews had the role that they had. As we have shown above, there can be no doubt that from the start the theology of the church was extremely hostile against Judaism and Jews. It developed a view, or perhaps even a doctrine, of Jews which was accepted by the medieval world and

46. "De jood in de middelnederlandse literatuur," *Literatuur* I (1984), 246-53.

by Christendom of later centuries. But still it seems that the origin of the often virulent anti-Jewish sentiments that were manifested in the later Middle Ages cannot be found so simply in catechetical appropriation of that theology. It is known, at least among medievalists familiar with these matters, that late medieval theology in fact avoided the various social manifestations of contemporary anti-Jewish sentiments.

Any attempt to determine more precisely the role of Christian theology in late medieval anti-Judaism and its manifestations will have to show more subtlety than Oudejans does in the statement quoted above. One will have to ask whether early Christian theology continued to have an impact on the Middle Ages in other areas besides those of Judaism and Jews. If it did, one will then have to ask whether this abiding influence of early Christian theology on medieval society might be seen as a social rather than a theological phenomenon. Moreover, it is useful to distinguish between what medieval theology says about Judaism and the picture medieval folklore paints of Jews. This will make it possible to more clearly delineate how the two are interrelated. This, understandably, went beyond Oudejans's intentions. But that he nonetheless made such a sweeping statement is, then, all the more difficult to accept.

The superficiality of his approach is immediately apparent in his reference to a "catechesis of defamation." He borrowed this terminology from the Dutch title of Jules Isaac's *L'Enseignement de mépris,* the title of which may best be translated as "The Theological Teaching of Contempt."[47] "Catechesis" carries the specific connotation of instruction for the common people. The Dutch title is therefore misleading, and this is reflected in Oudejans's understanding of theology as catechesis. Theology and catechesis are usually closely related. But medieval catechesis on Jews and Judaism contained a number of other aspects that were not so clearly provided by medieval theology.

Isaac's book deals rather with doctrinal themes that were prominent in Christian theological instruction concerning the Jews from early times on, namely, the dispersion of Israel as a providential punishment of the Jews, the supposed degeneracy of the Jews and Judaism in the time of Jesus, and the Jews as murderers of God. Under these headings Isaac dealt with the teachings concerning Judaism of Jerome, Ambrose, Augustine, and others in Roman Christian antiquity. These teachings denied the Jews any continued election, accused them of being murderers of God, and

47. The English title is *The Teaching of Contempt* (New York, 1965).

stated that as a punishment they were to live in submission to Christians — in such a way that they would eventually no longer exist, since they were the involuntary witnesses of the salvation that Christ had brought. This line of thought was accepted with no major modifications by medieval theologians.

But the late medieval accusations against the Jews have nothing to do with this pattern of teachings. The clergy may well have had a substantial part in the dissemination of the later accusations against the Jews, by referring in sermons and miracle stories to desecrations of the host or ritual murders. But the origin of these accusations is not to be found in theology. They were part of medieval folklore and expressions of society itself, in particular of its craving for sacralization and demonization. These accusations were never absorbed into Christian theology. The popes explicitly condemned the charge of Jewish cannibalism, as well as the accusation that the Jews had caused and spread the Black Death. And never did the popes — except by remaining silent — agree with the allegation that Jews killed Christian children in ritual crucifixions in preparation for Passover.

That such accusations and figments of the popular imagination are found in sermon collections and elsewhere, as in the *Canterbury Tales,* does not prove that they were part of medieval theology. They have much more to do with the popular sentiments that led to such actions as the destruction of Jewish synagogues and cemeteries, extortions, and laws requiring distinctive clothing. Failure to make this distinction would enable us to blame the anti-Jewish sentiments that were so prominent in late medieval society on theology. And it must be acknowledged that the appearance in the late Middle Ages of the popular preachers, who attempted to bridge the distance between church doctrine and the common people, has made it more difficult to make this distinction between the teachings of Christian theology regarding the Jews and what the common people heard about them. These popular preachers — in particular those of the mendicant orders — often referred to these folk tales.

Jeremy Cohen's book *The Friars and the Jews,* published in 1982, shows how the activities of the popular preachers continues to present a challenge to historians. Cohen places blame on the mendicant orders, especially the Dominicans and the Franciscans. They contributed in a determinative way to the further development of anti-Jewish sentiments, since in their missionary zeal they sought to eliminate the Jews from Christian Europe or to force their conversion. According to Cohen their intentions were particularly transparent in their disputations with the Jews, which were designed to discredit the Talmud. Their study of Hebrew was almost exclusively inspired by that motive. Cohen believes, in fact, that the most famous late medieval Christian biblical scholar, the Franciscan Nicholas of Lyra, who in his interpretation of the Old Testament gave considerable attention to Jewish exegesis, had only one aim: to contribute to this anti-Jewish polemic. In brief, the mendicant orders supposedly brought a radical change in the polemical dialogue between Jews and Christians. They no longer adhered to the relative tolerance manifested by theologians who followed Augustine's example.

So far this view has not met with unconditional agreement. One critic, who is not unsympathetic to it, has remarked that this theory remains unproven as long as we have no sure evidence that those who attempted to expel the Jews from western Europe acted from theological motives, that the Dominicans' and Franciscans' disputations with Jews were primarily aimed at encouraging tolerant Christians toward a more anti-Jewish attitude, and that the polemicists consciously moved away from Augustinian tolerance.[48]

Such evidence cannot be provided. But there is reason to think that the thirteenth-century polemicists were motivated by a desire to eliminate the Jews from Europe by either conversion or expulsion. The mendicant friars undoubtedly tried to arouse further hostility against the Jews. Their preaching may, in fact, be understood as a "catechesis of defamation." But this preaching was not part of official theology as taught to all and every-where. The friars were not motivated by official theology in their anti-Jewish preaching. They simply hoped, through their treatment of the Jews, to increase their authority with those who listened to them. But their hostility toward the Jews was also a source of frustration for these preachers, since the people refused to accept their arguments as truthful and convincing. Psychological rather than theological motives played a key role in their opposition to Jews. From this perspective, it is difficult to agree with the idea that the "catechesis of defamation" was a translation of the early Christian and medieval theological position regarding Judaism and Jews. This catechesis cannot be related just to the theological views concerning

48. Review of Cohen, *The Friars and the Jews*, by D. J. Lasker in *Speculum* 58 (1983), 743-45. Cohen completed and summarized his perspective in "Scholarship and Intolerance in the Medieval Academy: The Study and Evaluation of Judaism in European Christendom," *American Historical Review* 91 (1986), 592-613. See there also the "Comment" by G. I. Langmuir, 614-24.

Jews that had been developing from early Christian times on, since it clearly consisted of a number of components. A factor in the approach of the popular preachers who manifested such hostility toward the Jews was undoubtedly also their ambition to appear more important than they in fact were or could hope to be. This was directly related to their lack of education, at least in the field that their ambition led them to enter. The church's restrictions on participation in disputations with Jews was inspired not only by fear that people would be misled by Jews but also by prudence, to prevent escalation. This caution was disregarded by these popular preachers, whom we should probably consider pseudo-intellectuals and might compare with journalists who use sensationalism as a means of drawing attention, without caring much about the truth of what they present.[49]

But it cannot be denied that the theological ideas of the Church Fathers concerning Judaism and the Jews did have a permanent effect. The supposedly more tolerant attitude of theology, to a large extent based on Augustine, made the status of the Jews in the Middle Ages already quite difficult. Augustine's theological position regarding the Jews in society is succinctly expressed in *The City of God:*

> The Jews who killed [Christ] and refused to believe in him, to believe that he had to die and rise again, suffered a more wretched devastation at the hands of the Romans and were utterly uprooted from their kingdom, where they had already been under the dominion of foreigners. They were dispersed all over the world — for indeed there is no part of the earth where they are not to be found — and thus by the evidence of their own Scriptures they bear witness for us that we have not fabricated the prophecies about Christ. In fact, very many of the Jews, thinking over those prophecies both before his passion and more particularly after his resurrection, have come to believe in him. About them this prediction was made: "Even if the number of the sons of Israel shall be like the sand of the sea, it is only a remnant that will be saved" [Isa. 10:20]. But the rest of them were blinded; and of them it was predicted: "Let their own table prove a snare in their presence, and a retribution and a stumbling-block. Let their eyes be darkened, so that they may not see. Bend down their back always"

---

49. In these comments I am indebted to Professor Langmuir, who responded to my questions on the new preaching of the friars in a personal communication (March 2, 1985).

[Ps. 69:22]. It follows that when the Jews do not believe in our Scriptures, their own Scriptures are fulfilled in them, while they read them with blind eyes. . . . God has thus shown to the Church the grace of his mercy in the case of her enemies the Jews, since, as the Apostle says, "their failure means salvation for the Gentiles" [Rom. 11:11]. And this is the reason for his forbearing to slay them — that is for not putting an end to their existence as Jews, although they have been conquered and oppressed by the Romans; it is for fear that they should forget the Law of God and thus fail to bear convincing witness on the point I am now dealing with. Thus it was not enough for the psalmist to say, "Do not slay them, lest at some time they forget your Law", without adding, "Scatter them." For if they lived with that testimony of the Scriptures only in their own land, and not everywhere, the obvious result would be that the Church, which is everywhere, would not have them available among all nations as witnesses to the prophecies which were given beforehand concerning Christ.[50]

This theological argument concerning the place of the Jews in western Christian society was generally accepted in medieval theology. Augustine built it on a number of biblical passages, carefully selected to support his view. The shape of the argument was determined by the relationships among Christians and Jews in his time. But an important aspect remained the manner in which theology was based on the Scriptures. The Bible was not interpreted historically or literally, but allegorically. A theological concept was developed on the basis of allegories that were selected and elaborated as needed.

At that time theology was still largely coextensive with interpretation of Scripture and was regarded simply as an extension of the Bible. As a result it could share in the authority attributed to Scripture, which made the interpretation of the Bible by early Christian authors — the Fathers — almost as normative as the Scriptures themselves. This authority was further enhanced by the fact that tradition to a large extent determined medieval conduct and thought. The writings of the Fathers were therefore of extreme importance in medieval theology, an aspect which — as already mentioned — must be seen as social rather than as theological. As a result statements by the Fathers, thus related to the Scriptures, were considered inspired, in particular in the period prior to Scholasticism.

This phenomenon is somewhat comparable to what happened to

50. XVIII.46; trans. H. Bettenson (Harmondsworth, 1972), 827f.

the Torah in Judaism. The midrashic and haggadic commentaries on the Torah were also considered inspired. Within Judaism this development went even further. When these commentaries were put in writing in the Talmudic literature, they were accepted as a new series of inspired writings. The patristic writings did not attain quite the same status in medieval Christendom. But throughout the Middle Ages statements by Church Fathers were quoted as authoritative. This was notably the case with their statements about Judaism and the Jews.

A striking example of this is found in a letter written by Bernard of Clairvaux in 1147, when he was promoting the Second Crusade. The text of this letter was distributed all over Europe, with minor variations. All versions of the letter contain the following passage about the Jews:

> The Jews are not to be persecuted, killed, or even expelled. Ask all who know the Holy Scriptures about the prophecies concerning the Jews in the Psalms. "God has informed me about my enemies, says the church: do not kill them, lest my people will be forgotten." The Jews are for us like the living words of the Holy Scriptures, because they forever remind us of the Passion of the Lord. For that reason they have been dispersed in all directions so that they may, while bearing the punishment for their enormous crime, be living witnesses of our redemption. Therefore the church adds these words on behalf of the church: "Make them totter by your power, and bring them down, O Lord, our shield" (Ps. 59:12). And that is what has happened: Everywhere they have been dispersed; they have been brought down. Christian princes have submitted them to harsh slavery. But they will return when the evening begins (Ps. 59:7), and the time will come when they will receive attention. And finally, when the great heathen masses have entered the church, "all Israel," according to the words of the apostle, "will be saved" (Rom. 11:25). But those who die will remain in death. . . .
>
> What would happen to our hope for their salvation, for their conversion, which has been promised for the end of time, if the Jews were to be totally eradicated?[51]

This passage from Bernard's encyclical on the crusade agrees with the view that Augustine developed seven centuries earlier. But it was

---

51. Letter 363.6-7 = *SBO* VIII, 31. James, 462-643, translates another version of this encyclical, the one addressed to the English people.

written in a totally different context and, as a result, meant something quite different. We may find this text rather uncongenial. But Bernard wrote it to protect the Jews against the excesses to be expected during the buildup to the crusade. Augustine wrote under different circumstances. He was not involved in any conflicts between Jews and Christians and never undertook any actions against Jews. He reflected — rather abstractly — on the theological results others had arrived at in actual confrontations. Medieval theology repeated his views and elaborated them, depending on the concrete circumstances of the times. Sometimes this elaboration was favorable to the Jews, as in Bernard's letter, and sometimes it was not. Unfavorable application became the norm in the late Middle Ages, when Augustinian texts of this nature were almost exclusively used as weapons against the Jews.

The time in which Augustine lived marked the end of a period in which anti-Jewish sentiment among Christians had become much more pronounced. This was a result of problems that the church was facing at that time in its relationship to the Jews. Since Constantine (†337) the church had been officially recognized in the Roman Empire and found itself more and more privileged. This prompted many to join the church without any genuine conversion. Their entry into the church gave them, among other things, more knowledge of Judaism, of the history of the Jews as a chosen people, and of their religious practices.

At that very time Judaism was developing a stronger missionary attitude. Jewish worship proved to be more attractive for many than Christian worship. And Jewish communities enjoyed a cultural level that was considerably higher than that of the Christian churches. As a result of all these factors the church was in danger of simply becoming for a number of newly converted Christians an intermediate stage on the way to Judaism. The Jewish religion was recognized in the Roman Empire, and its status changed hardly at all when the church received its privileged position. Therefore Judaism could only be attacked in writing.[52]

This sort of attack became one of the themes of Christian theology at the time, with full emphasis on the contribution of the Scriptures. Jerome's interpretation of the metaphor of the vineyard in his commentary on Isaiah (5:1-7) provides a striking example of such a theological attack. The metaphor was already paraphrased in the Gospels (Matt. 21:33-43 and the parallels). Isaiah tells of the owner of a plot of land who planted a vineyard with great

52. Cf. M. Simon, *Verus Israel* (2nd ed.; Paris, 1964), 315-55.

care and built a wall around it, but subsequently destroyed it when it failed to bear fruit: "For the vineyard of the Lord of hosts is the house of Israel, and the people of Judah are his pleasant planting; he expected justice, but saw bloodshed; righteousness, but heard a cry!" The Gospel writers extended the metaphor by introducing Christ as the landowner's son who is killed by the tenants of the vineyard. Matthew's version concludes: "The kingdom of God will be taken away from you and given to a people that produces the fruits of the kingdom" (Matt. 21:43).

It is still debated whether this extension of the metaphor originated when the conflict between Jews and Christians was still a conflict among Jews or when the church had begun its mission to the Gentiles. It seems obvious that Gentile Christians understood the Gospel writers' interpretation as a rejection of Judaism. This interpretation paved the way for the "theology of substitution," according to which the Jews' election had passed to the Christians, with the church as the new, or true, Israel. This theology was developed in the early church and passed on to the medieval church, which accepted it easily and even gratefully.

Jerome considered Matthew's interpretation of the metaphor so important that he wanted to see it already predicted in Isaiah's passage. This required some exegetical gymnastics, but the allegorical approach to Scripture provided a solution. The key was found in the last word of Isaiah's passage: *cry* or *clamor*. Jerome saw a connection here with the cries of the Jews mentioned in the Passion story in John's Gospel: "They cried out, 'Away with Him! Away with Him! Crucify Him!'" (19:15). And in his comments Jerome then links this text with Ephesians 4:31: "Put away from you all bitterness and wrath and anger and wrangling [i.e., cries] and slander, together with all malice." And he continues: "Because the righteous have shed blood, the blood of the Lord's Passion cried to the Lord, since they answered righteousness with cries, as we read in Genesis (4:10), 'Your brother's blood is crying out to me from the ground'."[53] Thus Isaiah's metaphor could also be interpreted as a rejection of the Jews.

Augustine was not the only theologian to remain known in the Middle Ages. Jerome was also read, particularly his commentaries. His interpretation of Isaiah has been preserved in a fifteenth-century manuscript from the Carthusian monastery of Utrecht. The houses of the Brethren of the Common Life were familiar with Jerome. Many of these "brethren" adopted his name. Other sources also indicate that he was read

53. *PL* XXIV, 79.

by many in the Middle Ages. This would certainly justify interest in an analysis of anti-Jewish statements in his biblical commentaries.

There were also other ways in which Jerome's biblical commentaries reached medieval exegetes. His interpretation of the vineyard metaphor is also found in the *Glossa ordinaria,* a collection of short comments on biblical passages begun in the Carolingian era and expanded and widely used in later times.[54] Other collections of commentaries that were popular at that time contain statements against the Jews. One is the list of scriptural allegories that was compiled in the Carolingian era by Hrabanus Maurus (†856) but, as the author himself acknowledges, borrowed from the Fathers. This list includes under the word *impius* (godless) four comments referring to the devil, the antichrist, and the Jewish people, even though Hrabanus was assisted in his exegesis by a Jewish scholar and did not cherish anti-Jewish feelings himself.[55] Considering how he refers to Jews in other entries, we may conclude that this juxtaposition of Jews with the forces of evil seems not to be done out of any evil intent. Moreover, each of the images alluded to is in an Old Testament passage. But in the later Middle Ages it was quite common to lump these images together, and the picture of the godless Jew, the devil's henchman and the antichrist's herald, was known only too well.

The issue with respect to this borrowing from patristic commentaries is that the repetition — with no malicious intent — of what the Fathers had written about the Jews had disastrous consequences when the social climate of the later Middle Ages had deteriorated for the Jews. The commentaries were used and reread in changed situations and applied in new settings. The resulting change in their meaning was, I believe, primarily a social phenomenon rather than a conscious theological reflection on the Jews. But this is not to deny that theology contributed to the deteriorating position of the Jews in that later period, even though theologians did not support the accusations that were made.

But it is impossible to maintain that from the thirteenth century on theologians did not participate in what was written, preached, or otherwise initiated against the Jews, even if we leave aside the *exempla* literature with its more or less stereotypical anti-Jewish anecdotes. To be sure, there were theologians who did not swerve from the Augustinian

54. Isa. 5:7; *PL* CXII, 1241: *Ecce Clamor.* Cf. B. Smalley, "La Glossa Ordinaria," *Recherches de Théologie ancienne et médiévale* 9 (1937), 365-400.
55. *Allegoriae in Sacram Scripturam, PL* CXII, 970.

tolerance, such as Thomas Aquinas, though he developed some thoughts of his own on the Jews. But theologians played a major role in the disputations that were sometimes forced on Jews in the thirteenth century. These disputations, for example, in 1240 in Paris and in 1263 in Barcelona, were intended to discredit the Talmud, even among the Jews themselves.[56]

Attention in these disputations was focused primarily on the relationship between the Talmud and the Torah, the document in which God had revealed his covenant with the Jewish people. This relationship was alleged to be false and contradictory. The attacks on the Talmud were accompanied by confiscations and burnings of Talmud volumes. Why they were confiscated and why their content and tenor were under so much attack remain unclear. Initially they were confiscated on instigation of a "convert" from Judaism who had convinced the pope that the Jews — once they were deprived of the Talmud — would read the Torah in such a way that they would be receptive to the Christian truth.

But it may well be asked whether these confiscations and disputations were not inspired by a desire to coerce Jews into the church and to expel those who refused to be coerced. Some theologians who were involved in the disputations probably thought along those lines. But such thoughts may have been a result of the disputations rather than their basis. Still, this pattern of thought did not fail to have effect. It led to the further questions about Judaism, whether, with the important place it gave to the Talmud, it had not deviated so far from the original Jewish religion that the Jews of those times were no longer to be equated with those of the Old Testament. Could the statements of Paul in Romans 10–11 about the salvation of the Jews still be applied to the Jews of late medieval times?

This last question came to receive a definite answer among many preachers and catechists. Since the thirteenth century catechesis had become extremely important. Its anti-Jewish tendency is apparent in, for example, the fourteenth-century catechetical treatise of the Franciscan Marquard of Lindau. In his comments on the fifth commandment, "Thou shalt not kill," he permits himself a venomous anti-Jewish statement.[57] Other statements by catechists were undoubtedly also partly responsible for the later defamation and persecution of the Jews. But they do not

56. *Judaism on Trial: Jewish-Christian Disputations in the Middle Ages,* ed. and trans. by H. Maccoby (Rutherford, NJ and London, 1982).

57. *Das Buch Die Zehn Gebote* (Venice, 1483), ed. J. W. van Maren (Amsterdam, 1984), 66.

belong to the cumulative tradition to which theology, in a completely different way, contributed.

At first the early Christian hostility toward the Jews was passed on rather naively, with no idea of forging Christian solidarity. But the content of what was transmitted had a different effect when medieval society, for its own social and economic reasons, decided to banish the Jews and to make them a scapegoat in the face of the threats it experienced. When that happened, theology mirrored, both in spite of and because of its firm links with tradition, the countenance of its own time.

Nonetheless, theology never completely identified itself with that time and that society, as can be illustrated by many examples. One is found in a canon law collection preserved in the Frisian language and entitled *Thet Autentica Riocht*.[58] It mentions three reasons that Jews are to be left alive: because of the ancient law, because of the forebears from whom Christ was born, and because of the text *Convertuntur ad vesperam* ("*Each evening they come back,* howling like dogs and prowling about the city," Ps. 59:6, 14). These words are interpreted as meaning that the Jews will eventually, before the Last Day, be converted, though in the meantime they have to go hungry like dogs as they wander about in the world. Here we have an example of the relative tolerance of theology, reflected in canon law. It shows how theology did not fully identify with the animosity toward the Jews that was current in society. That animosity had developed for nontheological reasons, though prevailing sentiments seem to have influenced some theologians to the extent that they accommodated themselves to it.

58. J. Brouwer, *Thet Autentica Riocht* (Assen, 1941), 69.

XI

Religious Life in the Low Countries
(ca. 1050-1384)[1]

❧   ❧

1. INTRODUCTION

FROM 1050 TO 1384, the year in which Gerhard Groote died, religious life
in the Low Countries was generally equated with the pattern of the
Christian religion tied to the Church of Rome. This bond with Rome
underwent a gradual change, in particular because it was to some extent
determined by the degree of authority of Rome in the Latin Church, which
was also subject to change. At first this authority was rather weak, and
most monasteries and episcopal sees were under lay control. The later
expansion of papal power, which resulted in an exemption of monasteries
from episcopal jurisdiction and later in the reservation of appointment of
bishops, sparked resistance, which also affected the bond with Rome.
Increased papal authority became especially tangible in the financial obligations of the bishops, which they in turn passed on to the faithful in
their care.

Throughout this period, however, the authority of the pope was
recognized. It also functioned in religious experience, where faith in the
church itself was an integral part. On the whole papal authority was not
felt to be onerous, at least not until the thirteenth century. In a sense it

1. This chapter is revised from "Het godsdienstig leven (circa 1050-1384)," *Algemene
Geschiedenis der Nederlanden* III (Haarlem, 1982), 221-48.

was even liberating. Following medieval legal custom, papal authority mitigated the weight of obligations, suspending the normal rules by granting privileges. Thus papal authority defined the norms of religious life.

Confusions surrounding papal authority resulting from the Western Schism, which began in 1378, had in most cases, the Low Countries included, little impact on the religious experience of the people. The power of the Burgundians, who took the side of Avignon, did introduce conflicts into acceptance of papal authority, but this did little to change the customs and canons regulating religious practice. This does not mean that there were no changes in the religious life of the people. From the beginning of the thirteenth century movements of religious renewal manifested themselves, particularly in the Low Countries. But these reform movements had a character of their own, independent of the problems brought by the Schism.

But the distinctive character of these reform movements has often been overemphasized. As a result more traditional forms of religious life have been judged in the light of these movements, which have been seen as reactions against the older traditions. Such a narrow view of religious life has usually led to a distorted picture, particularly because historians have been too eager to find in these movements precursors of the Reformation. And the way in which the church of Rome usually painted its own medieval past has contributed to this distortion.

That portrayal of the medieval church was idealized and suggested that the church never changed. It was thought that there were no essential changes in doctrine or liturgy after the time of the Council of Trent (1545-63). It was simply ignored how concepts and ideas tend to change, even when an established terminology is maintained. It was also emphasized that Trent did not constitute a break with medieval Catholicism. This may seem true when Trent is compared to the Protestant Reformation, but not in any absolute sense. Trent was regarded as a confirmation of the course in which the faith and the religious experience of medieval Christians had developed under the leadership of Rome. As a result of this view there was only minimal attention to the development of religious life during the Middle Ages. It appeared to differ only slightly from the faith and the religious practice of present-day Catholics. And therefore it seemed superfluous to deal with medieval religious life in historical studies of a more general nature. Even in surveys of church history religious life usually received little explicit attention. Such books dealt more with religious doctrine than religious practice.

This notion of unchangeability has now been overcome as a result of developments in the Church of Rome. Moreover, the interest of historians has shifted from the bare facts to the people behind those facts. The modern historian wonders what motivated people materially and spiritually and wants to find out how they integrated their actual day-to-day life in their experience of reality. Their religious experience, insofar as it was determined by the time in which they lived, is an important element in historical study. For that reason historiography not only deals with structures and developments in religious life, but also with the experience of religion itself. Depending on the approach of the historian, this area of special attention is usually defined as the domain of *popular religion* or *popular piety.* And the approach of the historian is partly determined by the value that he or she attributes to religion. This means that we will look in vain for a consensus on this subject among historians.[2]

The study of the history of the church in the Low Countries in this period should not limit itself to providing a list of the special features of the church in those regions. The history of religious life ought to be placed in a broader context. For the unique aspects of religious experience recorded in the sources only stand out when they are placed in a wider context. This context is to a large degree the religious experience of medieval Christendom as a whole, since people in the Low Countries shared in this broader community experience, recognized the same ecclesiastical precepts, and belonged to a community in which the borders within the Low Countries had no meaning: The dioceses in the southern and northern Low Countries all belonged to the church provinces of Reims, Trier, and Cologne.

Religion did not always play the same role in society through the Middle Ages, but that role was always more extensive than it is now. We find manifestations of religious life in numerous matters that today are totally detached from religion. In some of these areas of life religion even held a central place. Religious and social life were so closely intertwined that no clear distinction could be made in the way that it is now. Medieval people did not distinguish the social and religious components of their religious and social conduct, even though they often made a sharp distinction between church and state, since church and state competed in attempting to monopolize religious and social life.

2. Cf. J. Van Enghen, "The Christian Middle Ages as an Historiographical Problem," *American Historical Review* 91 (1986), 519-52.

This lack of separation between religious and social dimensions of life is visible when we visit a medieval cathedral. There we see the functions of the cathedral's many chapels, altars, and images and realize that those who used this consecrated space did not form a single closely knit community of believers. They did belong to the same church, but they did so as members of distinct social interest groups, all of which had their own sanctuaries within the church. Their unity was symbolized by the one building and was based on their membership in one church, which served as an umbrella for specific organizations.

It is still a matter of debate whether the religious brotherhoods, which coincided with the medieval guilds, began earlier or later than the guilds themselves. Many of the social tasks that are now cared for by civil authorities belonged then to the domain of the church, particularly education and care for the poor and the sick. In the eleventh century, concluding and enforcing a peace was a matter demanding the direct involvement of bishops. At first, secular authorities were often unable to protect those who did not participate in hostilities — the clergy, peasants, and merchants — from the consequences of warfare. But then the appearance of seigneurial authority and the town magistrate made this possible. For that reason some then no longer regarded education and care for the poor and the sick as concerns of the church. But whether this really amounted to a reduction of the church's role is debatable, since such a conclusion rests to a large extent on a narrowly spiritualized understanding of the church that fails to see lay initiatives inspired in part by nonspiritual considerations as an involvement of the church with society. This, however, does injustice to the status of the church in medieval society.

Work toward social reforms, or even toward mild ameliorations, was understood in those days as religious renewal. It carried the intent of returning to the ideal situation of the imaginary primeval age when church and society had originated. In this primitivist approach to action no one asked whether the emphasis in motivation was on the religious or social side. The distinction was not made, partly because of the place of the church in society. More interest was devoted to what would happen to a person after death. Life after death was generally accepted, but there was concern about what one should expect. To a considerable degree this concern determined a person's conduct during earthly life, the nature of which depended on one's relationship to God. But that relationship was in turn partly determined by one's attitude toward other people. And thus social reform and religious renewal were almost completely intertwined.

But town authorities not only were responsible for administering justice, providing protection, and collecting taxes, but also had to ward off famine and prevent outbreaks of contagious diseases. And they were not always compelled by religious motives in the execution of these duties. But when a lack of supply disrupted food distribution, or when physicians were unable to cope with the numbers of victims of an epidemic, the authorities would fall back on church institutions, on monasteries and hospitals. The monasteries usually kept supplies for distribution among the poor, while the church was often involved in establishing and operating hospitals. St. John's Hospital in Bruges was established before 1188 and thus is among the oldest civic hospitals in Europe. It was founded by the chapter of the Lieve-Vrouwekerk (Church of Our Lady). The Biloke of Ghent, established in 1228, was built adjacent to the convent of the Cistercian nuns, who from the very first were entrusted with care of the sick. The names of hospitals are quite revealing. St. Elizabeth's Hospital in Haarlem dates from the thirteenth century. St. Joris's Hospital in Delft and the Catherine Hospital in Gouda were founded in the fourteenth century.

These activities were not regarded by the church as "humanitarian work." That concept was still unknown. The involvement of the church was primarily religious in nature. The church unfailingly admonished the faithful about the abiding value of works of mercy, such as feeding the hungry, clothing the naked, visiting the sick and prisoners, providing hospitality, refreshing the thirsty, and burying the dead — works that are all rooted in a Gospel commission (Matt. 25:34-40). The context in which Scripture commanded these duties to the faithful made them the most important legal ground for one's claim to eternal life. This implied *a fortiori* that there was no real separation between religious and social engagement, and it called for religious life to extend itself over a broad range of social issues. But though it might be possible to some extent to quantify this social aspect of religious life, it remains impossible to determine the intensity of religious commitment, as the left hand was not supposed to know what the right hand was doing.

2. CHURCH MEMBERSHIP

DURING THIS PERIOD every inhabitant of the Low Countries was expected to be a member of the Church of Rome. Membership began with baptism, which was received shortly after birth. Baptism was a sacramental act. It was preceded by an adjuration or exorcism of the devil and was concluded with a blessing and the presentation of a baptismal candle and a christening dress. The actual baptismal ceremony was no longer necessarily done, as in the early church, by immersion in flowing water; often the water was simply poured over the head of the person receiving baptism. The infant's acceptance of baptism was expressed by godparents: They spoke on the child's behalf, renouncing the devil and worldly vanities and confessing the child's faith and loyalty to the church. Thus they accepted responsibility for guiding the child into a Christian life. And they were expected to teach the child the appropriate prayers.

Church membership was a matter of course. Hardly anyone rebelled against it later in life. This may partly be explained from the collective character of medieval society. But more important was the fact that baptism, whatever other meanings were attached to it, was considered protection against the ever-present power of evil. Evil was something quite tangible; it could, so people believed, act independently and was easily personified in demonic figures and depicted in wood carvings and sculptures in and on medieval churches. The threat of evil was encountered in those realities of life that people felt powerless against: sickness, famine, war, floods, and other natural calamities. Society was characterized by a dualistic understanding of good and evil, spirit and matter. The introduction of Aristotle by Scholasticism, which brought a more positive interpretation of earthly reality, could not prevent the continued popularity of this dualistic view. It manifested itself time and again in the urge to seek deliverance from the power of evil. Several purification rituals helped to achieve this, for instance the rites for women who had given birth. Baptism was thought of primarily as a purification ritual, as it began with an exorcism, providing deliverance from the devil. Refusing baptism was an affront to God, who would pour out his wrath over the parents and the newborn child.

Baptism was only refused when parents did not want a child to live. But Christianity had made infanticide rare by the eleventh century.[3] Children were more often abandoned. This change seems to be reflected in the softening of the penalties attached in church laws to infanticide and abortion beginning with the canon collection of Bonizo of Sutri, dating from 1050. The earlier punishment of lifelong excommunication was re-

3. Cf. E. Coleman, "Infanticide in the Early Middle Ages," in S. M. Stuart, ed., *Women in Medieval Society* (Philadelphia, 1976), 47-70.

duced to a period of ten years, accompanied by acts of penance.[4] This remained the established disciplinary norm apart from indulgences, which might bring further mitigation.

ə⃛ ə⃛

To be excommunicated meant to be deprived of church membership, and thus also of the sacraments.[5] This measure was already known in the early church. But enforcing the excommunication of one diocese in another presented a major problem. Decrees regarding this matter were repeated at the first two general councils of the Latin church, held in the Lateran papal residence in 1123 and 1139. But the Third Lateran Council of 1179 found itself confronted with a different issue. It appeared that some religious orders, which as beneficiaries of papal privileges were no longer under episcopal jurisdiction, tended to take excommunications by bishops less seriously; they would often admit the excommunicated to the sacraments and allow them church burials. This undermining of excommunications had also to do with rash overuse of the disciplinary rite. The Fourth Lateran Council of 1215 tried to rectify this situation.[6]

But it did not bring an end to abuses of excommunication. We find such abuses time and again, including in the Low Countries. At times expulsion from the church was in essence politically motivated. For example, Jan of Enghien, bishop of Liège, excommunicated his canons in 1278, taking the side of the burgers of Liège in their conflict with his chapter. Even more dubious was the Avignon popes' acquiescence in the use by Philip V and Philip VI of France of excommunication as a weapon in the struggle against Flanders. They did so repeatedly. Since the excommunication in this case involved a whole population, it could only be effective in the form of an interdict. This forced the clergy to close the churches and not administer any sacraments, except extreme unction. The dead could not receive church burials or be buried in consecrated ground. Many corpses were left unburied for considerable lengths of time. Besides the ban and the interdict there was also the suspension, which prohibited a member of the clergy from performing sacred acts without risking his

4. *Liber de vita Christiana* IX.32, ed. E. Perels (Berlin, 1950), 291.
5. Cf. E. Vodola, *Excommunication in the Middle Ages* (Berkeley, 1986).
6. Lateran I, canon 1; Lateran II, canon 3; Lateran III, canon 9; Lateran IV, constitutions 47f. Cf. *COD* 190, 197, 216, 255-57.

325

ecclesiastical status. For example, in 1383 the bishop of Utrecht, largely from political motives, forbade Gerhard Groote to preach.[7] The abuse of excommunication did partly destroy its effectiveness, but less than has often been suggested. At the time of the Utrecht Schism of 1421, when Rudolf of Diepholt and Zweder of Kuilenburg contested the bishop's see, excommunication and interdict were taken very seriously by the faithful.

Although the curse, the anathema, pronounced over the excommunicated person delivered him into the power of Satan, this was usually considered a temporary matter. Frequent confession offered a way back into the church, even if absolution was not sufficient. This change from the way excommunication was practiced in the early church carried with it a risk of inflation. From the twelfth century on, therefore, theologians pleaded for excommunication to be reserved for hardened sinners and not applied to the repentant.[8]

In the case of remorseless sinners, excommunication was usually solemnly promulgated, with the bishop, accompanied by twelve priests carrying burning candles, pronouncing the anathema. After the anathema had thus been pronounced, the candles were thrown to the ground and extinguished. The anathema would then be repeated publicly at regular intervals.

An excommunication could only be lifted by the one who had pronounced it or by his successor, unless the excommunicated person could appeal to a higher level of authority, usually Rome. Some offenses resulted in excommunication that could only be lifted by the pope, such as crimes against members of the clergy or the religious or falsification of papal letters in order to acquire offices, prebends, or privileges.[9] Another such offense was burning down church buildings in which people in flight from violence, war, or other dangers had sought refuge: In 1139 the Second Lateran Council decreed that any infringement of the right of asylum was to be punished by excommunication.[10] This prescript was taken very seriously. In 1322 it was decided in the diocese of Utrecht — following an earlier decision by the ecclesiastical province of Cologne — to suspend all

7. R. R. Post, *The Modern Devotion: Confrontation with Reformation and Humanism* (Leiden, 1968), 137-49.

8. J. W. Baldwin, *Masters, Princes and Merchants: The Social Views of Peter the Chanter and His Circle I* (Princeton, 1970), 151.

9. Robert of Flamborough (canon-penitentiary of St.-Victor at Paris), *Liber Poenitentialis* III.141-58, ed. J. J. F. Firth (Toronto, 1971), 144-58.

10. Canon 15; cf. *COD* 200.

services in a church where the right of asylum had been violated, while the town or region from which the perpetrator came was placed under an interdict.[11]

Besides the solemn excommunication there was a simpler version that could be pronounced by a priest, or could even take effect with no precise formula, in response to an offense that according to canon law called for excommunication. This often involved offenses that had traditionally been followed by excommunication, such as dishonoring a virgin, a married woman, or a widow. A woman who refused to return to her lawful husband was also excommunicated, as was a widow who broke her promise to remain unmarried under a bishop's protection. Lay persons who attempted to procure spiritual offices were in principle also expelled from the church. The same fate befell apostate priests, when, for instance, they converted to Judaism. The anathema was also pronounced over anyone who married a priest, monk, or nun.[12]

But excommunications were no longer irrevocable, even when the offense had been abortion, murder, or self-castration. A person who committed suicide did remain excommunicated.[13] But church authorities claimed the right, on the basis of the power of the keys given to St. Peter, to excommunicate or to lift the ban on a person after his death. In 1076, for example, the bishop of Liège asked Pope Gregory VII to annul the excommunication of his colleague in Utrecht, who had died an excommunicant. In the case of suicide, if the person did not die immediately, he could receive extreme unction, but was denied a church burial. This rule also applied to those who died from wounds suffered during tournaments. Participation in tournaments was prohibited under penalty of excommunication.

Here we touch on the reason that the medieval church insisted that people be excommunicated. It had less to with the particular sin than with its social impact. This was an outgrowth of the church's struggle against breaches of the peace. The church continued to claim the right to establish social order that it had acquired during the anarchy of the post-Carolingian era. Church leaders believed they had the prerogative to judge and discipline any conduct that had social consequences.

---

11. *Statuta Ecclesie Trajectensis* CV.6; S. Muller, ed., *Het Rechtsboek van den Dom van Utrecht* (The Hague, 1895), 273.

12. *Liber de Vita Christiana* VIII.19, 22, 55, 56; IX.34, 46.

13. Robert of Flamborough, 21 (V.243).

At first this involved only the elite, the nobility and the princes. But when the rise of the money economy brought radical changes to society, the church began to apply its excommunication policies also to the merchant class and focused on the offense of charging interest. All of this happened gradually. The Second Lateran Council added the possibility of excommunication to the church's long-time disapproval of interest. The Council of Tours, in 1163, prohibited the clergy from asking interest and from lending against any collateral that yielded income. The Third Lateran Council in 1179 simply made demanding interest punishable by excommunication.[14] In this way the church took the initiative with regard to this social problem. Twenty years later Baldwin IX of Flanders issued a general prohibition against asking interest in his jurisdiction. This conformity to the church's standpoint clearly illustrates to what extent church and society overlapped. The church in fact excommunicated people as a service to society. Those who disobeyed this injunction, which was considered of major importance for society, were thus expelled from the community by the church.

The church followed the same policy with regard to breaches of the peace. Here, of course, the church had a stronger self-interest, because of its defenselessness. It prohibited the clergy from bearing arms, while permitting this to other groups classified in law as free. But the church protected its clergy against acts of violence by punishing the offenders with excommunication. This protection was also extended to religious orders, such as the Knights of St. John, the Templars, and the Lazarites, who cared for lepers, and to those who belonged to households of parish priests.[15]

But not all acts of violence against these categories of people resulted in excommunication. The rule did not apply to offenders below the age of fourteen. And an offender would go free if the victim was not recognizable as a clergyman by his clothing and tonsure. Nor would excommunication result if the incident was the result of jest, or when death resulted from the administration of a penitential chastisement. Likewise there would be no excommunication when violence was used against a member of the clergy who was caught in improper conduct with the offender's daughter, sister, or wife or in the case of acts of violence between members of the clergy, a rule that also applied to students.

14. Lateran II, canon 10; Lateran III, canon 25; *COD* 199, 223. On the Council of Tours, cf. Mansi XXI, 176.

15. Robert of Flamborough, 150f. (III.148).

This effort to prevent violence was not limited to protecting the clergy, even though the church, through many additional precepts, strongly emphasized that aspect. Excommunication would also, as we have mentioned, follow other forms of breaches of the peace, such as participation in tournaments, which was made subject to excommunication by the different Lateran councils, and violations of the right of asylum. The Second Lateran Council also determined that those who used the crossbow in combat were to be excommunicated, and the Third Lateran Council pronounced an anathema over a number of mercenary armies, including the Brabangons, who were feared for their practice of setting churches afire and attacking defenseless people. The same council excommunicated merchants who sold arms or merchandise to the Saracens.[16]

The church also used excommunication to promote peace in other ways. A warring prince or lord who had been excommunicated lost the support of his vassals and allies and was thereby forced to cease hostilities. But this measure repeatedly made the church a party in conflicts, often after it had been pressured by one side to excommunicate the other. In the period of the Avignon popes Flanders in particular experienced how the position of the church depended on the social interests of the curia. This dubious use of excommunication illustrates the problems inherent in the blending of society and church, of social issues and religion, in the Middle Ages. For by annulling the church membership of the opponents of its political allies, the church impeded them from a full experience of their religion.

Depriving people of their church membership could also bring conflict between the clergy and the laity. Almost all the early synod decisions of the dioceses of Liège and Utrecht that have been preserved, dating from 1288 and 1292 respectively, were accompanied by threats of excommunication. As a result a great many of the laity were at risk of falling outside the life of their religion, while many measures were explicitly designed to protect the extensive privileges and possessions of the clergy. An indication of this distinction between clergy and laity is found in the preface of a bull published by Boniface VIII in 1296:

> That laymen have been very hostile to the clergy antiquity relates; and it is clearly proved by the experiences of the present time. For not content with what is their own the laity strive for what is forbidden

16. Lateran III, canon 24; *COD* 223. Baldwin I, 267.

and loose the reins for things unlawful. Nor do they prudently realize that power over clerks or ecclesiastical persons or goods is forbidden them: they impose heavy burdens on the prelates of the churches and ecclesiastical persons regular and secular, and tax them, and impose collections: they exact and demand from the same the half, tithe, or twentieth, or any other portion or proportion of their revenues or goods; and in many ways they try to bring them into slavery.[17]

In Liège opposition by the laity forced the bishop in 1292 to mitigate some of the regulations. This growing resistance did not mean that excommunications, often followed by interdicts, lost their effect. The place of religion in society and the fact that religion was experienced almost wholly in the church inevitably resulted in a refusal of the people to accept any protracted closing of church doors. To prevent such from happening, they submitted to many measures that were enforced by the threat of excommunication.[18]

3. GOD AND HIS SAINTS

How DID THE FAITHFUL of the eleventh to fourteenth centuries imagine the God they worshipped? Sculptures, miniatures, and church windows allow us to answer that question from an iconographic perspective. But a survey of these artistic representations does not tell us about the concept of God that was most familiar to the Christians of those days. Since the concept of God is so all-inclusive, we may expect that people do not always think of God in the same way. And for Christian believers God is not just an abstract concept, as they believe in a living God, who not only became a man at a specific point in history, but whose incarnation is continuously realized and therefore occupies a central place in their cult, in the sacrifice of the Mass.

But that Christians have changed their concept of God over time and under changing circumstances is manifest in the ways in which they have confessed their faith, and this is true for the high Middle Ages. We read, for instance, in the preamble of a charter from 1050 in which Bishop

17. B. Tierney, *The Crisis of Church and State, 1050-1300* (Englewood Cliffs, NJ, 1964), 175.

18. R. R. Post, *Kerkgeschiedenis van Nederland in de Middeleeuwen* (Utrecht and Antwerp, 1957) I, 87-189, 255.

Bernulfus of Utrecht lists the land holdings of St. Paul's abbey, "in the name of the holy and indivisible Trinity." We find this opening line time and again throughout this period. Sometimes, as in the statutes of the city of Middelburg of 1217, we find "in the name of the Father, of the Son, and of the Holy Spirit."[19] The faithful were familiar with these trinitarian invocations. They were used in many liturgical prayers and blessings, as for instance when knighthood was conferred. They said these words when they crossed themselves. They confessed their faith in the Trinity at baptism in the creed, which was also part of every Mass from the beginning of the eleventh century, and in the threefold *Kyrie eleison*, taken over in about 600 from the liturgy of the Greek Church.

But people felt more at ease with the concept of the incarnate Son of God, the Christ. This concept of God is also found in the charters referred to above. The most common formula for dating events was, "in the year . . . of the incarnation of the Lord." Often a charter was addressed to "all who believe in Christ," or "who worship Christ."

But Christ was not always pictured in exactly the same way.[20] In the beginning of this period there was strong affinity with the Byzantine portrayal of Christ on the cross, which emphasized his kingship and presented him in unimpeachable majesty. This representation changed in the transition from Romanesque to Gothic style, which, though it dated from the beginning of the twelfth century, found only gradual acceptance in the Low Countries. Gothic artists tended to depict Christ as a suffering man. This fit well with the emphasis of the time on imitation of the human Christ. Later in this period this humanizing of Christ led to an emphasis on his birth and childhood, to representations of the *Ecce homo,* the man of sorrows, and of Veronica's sudarium with the face of Christ — representations that would become popular in medieval piety all the more as many late medieval pilgrims to Rome brought them home with them.

Besides the concept of God as the Trinity and as the Son of God, there was also a more general and distant concept of the divine inspired by the Old Testament. Often the term "God" was used without further explanation. The rule of St. Benedict refers explicitly to the Trinity only once. There are six references to the Holy Spirit in the rule and nineteen

19. A. C. F. Koch, *Oorkondenboek van Holland en Zeeland tot 1299* I (The Hague, 1970), nos. 81, 386.

20. On the iconography, cf. F. van der Meer and H. Sibbelee, *Imago Christi* (Antwerp, 1980).

to Christ, while the term "God" is used exactly one hundred times. This designation occurs eleven times each in Old Testament and New Testament contexts, while the other occurrences often refer to "God's work," "the fear of God," "God's commandments," and "God's help." In such instances the concept of God is rather less specific.

In the eleventh century this less specific concept of God is most often related to the Old Testament. Carolingian spirituality was intensely concentrated on the Old Testament.[21] This strongly influenced traditional Benedictine, and in particular Cluniac, monasticism. This understanding of God was maintained by daily recitation of the Psalms in larger numbers than was prescribed by the rule. Indications of this emphasis on Old Testament aspects in the Christian concept of God are found in those instances where New Testament aspects, such as the Trinity and the Son of God, are denied. Such situations arose, for instance, when a priest converted to Judaism, which seems to have happened repeatedly in the eleventh century.[22]

Such a conversion is mentioned in the oldest piece of historical writing from the Northern Low Countries: In De diversitate temporum ("Events of Our Time") Alpertus of Metz tells of the conversion to Judaism of Wecelinus, a priest. Toward the end of his treatise Alpertus includes a letter of this "apostate" about his change in religion along with the response of another priest. The argument between the two is, in fact, centered on the concept of God. The response to Wecelinus is intended to refute his rejection of the deity of Christ. In defense of Judaism, Wecelinus rejects any attempt to equate the God of Israel with the God of all nations, appealing to the Old Testament text, "I the Lord do not change" (Mal. 3:6).[23]

But both Old Testament and New Testament elements may be discerned in the general concept of God in the eleventh century. A clear biblical example is the image of the Good Shepherd, which was used in the Middle Ages in the liturgies of baptism and public penance. This blending of Old Testament and New Testament aspects is also found in the hymn Te Deum Laudamus. This hymn was widely used in the western

21. Cf. A. Vauchez, La spiritualité du Moyen Âge occidental (Paris, 1975), 10-14.

22. B. Blumenkranz, "La conversion au Judaisme d'André, Archevêque de Bari," Journal of Jewish Studies 14 (1963), 33-36.

23. Alpertus Mettensis, De diversitate temporum I.7; II.22-24, ed. H. van Rij (Amsterdam, 1980), 16-18, 88-105.

Latin church from the sixth century on, perhaps partly as a result of Benedict's injunction that it be sung during matins on Sundays and holy days. The Benedictine rule also required monks to take their vows "before God and his saints"[24] — a formula derived from the Old Testament but interpreted quite differently in the Middle Ages, when the veneration of saints had developed.

In eleventh-century texts from the Low Countries the place of Christ and the Trinity in the concept of God were rather modest. The *Vita* of Poppo, a reform-minded abbot of Stavelot (†1048), mentions a few times that Poppo acted on promptings by the Holy Spirit. And in the account of Poppo's journey during his youth to Jerusalem, the tomb of the risen Christ assumes a central place. But these testimonies must be regarded as clichés, given the hagiographic genre to which this document belongs. The same is true of expressions like "priest of Christ," "soldiers in the phalanx of Christ," "friends and poor of Christ," and "Christ's yoke." The prayers mentioned in the *Vita* of Poppo are directed more generally, simply to "God." Poppo is called God's servant, but no direct relationship is established between God and his sainthood, which is primarily measured by comparison to the example of other saints — of Benedict, Martin, Remaclus, and Lambert.[25]

❧   ❧

WRITINGS OF THIS PERIOD often refer to God together with his saints. The *Gesta abbatum* of the monastery of St. Trond, written by Abbot Rudolf (†1138), begins with a letter by the author. In this letter Rudolf states that he had become the abbot of their monastery through the grace of God and of Saints Trudo and Eucherius, to whom the monastery was dedicated.[26] The opening of the *Vita* of the tenth-century monastic reformer Gerhard of Brogne, written around 1030, is likewise revealing:

> The glorious power of the Lord is the more loudly proclaimed the more wonderfully it expresses itself in the saints. For God works through the saints, so that he may be seen in them and in their miracles. Therefore the prophet exclaims in wonder: "God is glorious in his

24. *RSB* 11, 58.
25. *MGH Scriptores* XI, 310. Cf. H. Glaesener, "Saint Poppon, abbé de Stavelot-Malmédy," *Revue bénédictine* 60 (1950), 163-79.
26. *MGH Scriptores* X, 228.

saints!" Giving honor to a saint may therefore, without any doubt, be interpreted as paying honor to God. For that reason the saints must be honored, so that God may be more and more praised.[27]

By the eleventh century veneration of saints had already a long history of development behind it. It began in the early church as a veneration of the martyrs, who were distinguished from the other saints, that is, other Christians who were honored after their death. When the local books of martyrs were replaced by books in which the martyrs of a number of churches were recorded, the difference between saints and martyrs disappeared. As a result, monks and bishops who had died were promoted to the status of authentic sainthood and were now commemorated in cults of their own. This change took place in the sixth and the seventh centuries, after the cult of the saints had increased in importance in the church's liturgy.[28]

A second change concerned saints' relics. At first relics were not the physical remains of martyrs but objects that they had touched. The tombs of martyrs remained unopened. This changed in the eighth and ninth centuries, when tombs of martyrs outside Rome were in danger of desecration. From that time on it became customary in the Latin church to bring the physical remains of saints to shrines where they could be venerated. These first translations were supposed to have been to the basilicas of Rome, but many of the new relics actually found their way to shrines beyond the Alps. The *Vita* of Remaclus tells us how the founder of the monasteries of Stavelot and Malmedy, after much prayer and fasting, succeeded in returning from Rome with relics of St. Peter, which he considered necessary to the foundation of his monasteries.[29]

In chapter VI we discussed how churches and monasteries acquired relics. Because of the practices being employed it was necessary to establish some control over who was to be venerated as a saint. Charlemagne issued regulations to that end, but due to the Viking invasions these measures had little result. Indeed, the invasions worsened the chaotic situation regarding the veneration of saints in another way: The *Vitae* of many saints were lost — in any case, their written forms — when the Vikings came and people were forced to flee.

This was a serious misfortune, since a *Vita* was indispensable for

27. *MGH Scriptores* XV, 656.
28. A. Vauchez, *La sainteté en Occident* (Rome, 1981), 20f.
29. Ch. 21 = *PL* CXXXIX, 166.

the cult of a saint. The *Vitae* were the source for the liturgical readings on the feast days of these saints and for the *exempla,* the sermons in which the saint was presented as a model. Thus many *Vitae* had to be rewritten.

And there were other reasons for rewriting *Vitae:* Accounts of miracles occurring near the tomb of a dead saint had to be added, and new facts had to be added to the biography in order to establish links between the saint and other saints of the time or between possessions of a particular church and the saint, especially when the saint had founded the church. Sometimes literary revisions were made or rhymed versions produced. In the tenth century the bishop of Liège revised the original *Vita* of St. Lambert, the bishop of Maastricht (†706), since the original version was said to make people laugh.

These needs led in Flanders and in the duchy of Lower Lorraine to extensive hagiographic production in the eleventh century, which reflected both moral restoration and a revitalization of literary life.[30] The rebuilding of the monasteries encouraged the revival of the cults of saints who had been venerated at these places and revision or rewriting of *Vitae* and *miracula* and translations of relics. More than a hundred new or revised texts were produced. Founders and patron saints of monasteries were the prominent heroes in these writings — not only because of their accomplishments during their lives, but also because of the protective power ascribed to the relics kept in the monasteries — together with bishops and abbots who had worked for church reform.

The eleventh-century *Vitae* of these "heroes" possess little biographical value. They were edifying, but full of clichés and passages copied from other similar writings. *Vitae* were intended first of all to foster the cults of the respective saints. Some bishops and abbots who had been supporters of church reform in the eleventh century, though without questioning the imperial authority over the church, were also considered saints. But *Vitae* were not written for all of them. One was written for Bishop Bernulfus of Utrecht (†1054), but none was written for his predecessor Adalbold, who was also venerated as a saint, nor for Wolbodo, the bishop of Liège (†1021).

The writing of a *Vita* was seen as extremely important, as is evident from the large number that were written in this period. Sigebert of Gem-

---

30. Cf. B. de Gaiffier, "L'hagiographie dans le Marquisat de Flandre et le duché de Basse-Lotharingie au XIe siècle," in *Études critiques d'hagiographie et d'iconologie* (Brussels, 1967), 415-507.

bloux, who lived in the monastery of Gembloux from 1071 to 1112 and is known for his chronicle of world history and his *Gesta abbatum* (Acts of the Abbots), wrote no less than eight *Vitae*. Abbot Olbert had reformed Gembloux in 1020-21 and was therefore venerated as a saint. Sigebert's biography of Olbert refers to Olbert's initiatives in the production of several *Vitae* as one of his heroic virtues. Sigebert also mentions that the record of the deeds of these saints, performed for the glory of God, could be sung to agreeable melodies — an indication of the cultic function of *Vitae*.[31]

Later these hagiographic biographies played a broader role: They came to be considered when judgments were made as to whether particular dead persons should be venerated as saints. A *Vita* played an important role in determining whether a new cult for which permission was requested would serve a useful purpose. From the middle of the twelfth century on the popes exercised the prerogative of canonizing saints and granting them their places in the liturgical calendar. These canonizations were legal rather than cultic events. Earlier canonizations had been performed by bishops, who approved of and participated in the cults. A bishop would be present at the solemn exhumation of the new saint and participated in the translation, the transfer of the physical remains to the shrine. Often bishops from neighboring dioceses were also present. These translations developed into processions of the saints, in which the relics were carried about.

The Flemish count Charles the Good, murdered in 1127, was canonized by a bishop. His first translation from the desecrated St. Donatian's church at Bruges, where he had been killed, did not yet amount to canonization. But his canonization did not come as a surprise. Charles was seen as a martyr, and a miraculous healing had already taken place at his temporary resting place. Fifteen days later his body was exhumed again, followed by a solemn translation. The grave was opened by Simon of Vernandois, the bishop of Noyons-Tournai. During the canonization itself the count's sainthood was further confirmed by a flood of miracles. And the two abbots who assisted the bishop found that the physical remains did not give off the usual odor of a corpse.[32]

The cult of Charles remained local in character, as was the case with most saints in the Low Countries. They were primarily venerated

---

31. *MGH Scriptores* VIII, 540.
32. Galbert of Bruges, *The Murder of Charles the Good, Count of Flanders*, chs. 23, 78, ed. and tr. J. B. Ross (rev. ed.; New York, 1967), 141, 247.

where they were buried. But the cult of some saints did spread. Amandus, Remaclus, and Willibrord were venerated in many places. Veneration of Boniface and of Bishop Lambert of Maastricht, both martyrs, extended beyond the Low Countries. The same was true of saints from the northern Low Countries, though they were far fewer in number. There were also fewer revisions of their *Vitae,* since there were fewer monasteries there where such revisions could be written.

Some of the saints were legendary, such as Cunera, who was believed to have belonged to the eleven thousand virgins of St. Ursula, and Oda, a recluse in St. Oedenrode. Others were preachers of Hiberno-Scottish descent or of local origin, martyrs who had died at the hand of the Vikings, and bishops of Deventer and Utrecht. No founders of monasteries were canonized, except perhaps St. Adelbert, whose relics played a role in the founding and early development of the abbey of Egmond from the tenth to the twelfth centuries. Because of his dual function two *Vitae* were written for him.

During the period under consideration in this chapter, the Low Countries did not provide the church with any saints officially recognized by Rome once canonization had become the monopoly of the pope and the curia. Albert of Louvain, who was murdered in 1192 shortly after he had become bishop of Liège, and the mystic Marie of Oignies, who died in 1213 and whose *Vita* was written by Jacques de Vitry, received papal canonization at the beginning of the seventeenth century, which opened the possibility for a regional cult on a limited scale. Attempts by the monastery of Aduard to have one of their monks of the thirteenth century canonized, the Englishman Richard, remained unsuccessful, partly because of a reluctance to pay the high costs of the canonization process.

Moreover, papal canonization offered little to a saint's devotees. They were much more interested in the exhumation or subsequent translation by the bishop. Translations of saints who were already venerated, such as the translation of St. Trudo in 1169, were important events. The day of Trudo's translation continued to be commemorated in the diocese of Liège. Among the obligatory holy days listed by the bishop of Utrecht in 1346 were the translations of Saints Lebuin and Martin.

The cult of formally canonized saints prescribed by the Roman liturgy (which was not yet binding on the whole church) was only gradually accepted. A saint like Bernard of Clairvaux found acceptance as a result of the spread of the Cistercian order. The same is true of Francis, because of the Franciscans. But here we have a different situation, since the mendicant orders observed the Roman liturgy and thus introduced the cults of newly canonized saints such as Saint Louis. The cult of Elizabeth of Thuringia (†1231 and canonized in 1235) followed in the wake of the development of care for the sick. Elizabeth was the patron saint of hospitals in Antwerp, Haarlem, and Utrecht. There were other examples of veneration of saints centering on acts of charity. The most striking instance is the cult of Dympna in Gheel, which was focused on care of the mentally impaired.

Information about the spread of cults of saints can also be gathered from the naming of churches after patron saints. But it must be emphasized that this is a very complex area of research, partly because churches belonging to monasteries or located on their land often adopted the same patron. Little research has been done on this topic in regard to the Low Countries. But it has been established that in the northern Low Countries refuge was often sought with early Christian, often Roman saints, such as Catherine, Cecilia, Laurence, Sebastian, and Pancras. Apostles were also venerated, in particular Peter, John, and Batholomew, as were saints with their own medieval traditions, such as Martin, the patron saint of the Frankish kingdom, and Nicholas, who owed much of his popularity to the fact that Bari, where his relics were kept, became an exit port for crusader armies. Another such saint was Mary Magdalene, who, together with her relics, belonged mainly to the realm of legend, though she was extremely popular with the medieval faithful because of her association with Christ while he was on earth and because she was a penitent sinner, one whose sins people could identify with.

THE PREFERENCE for legendary saints in the later Middle Ages is related to a change in the function of saints. Their task of leading the faithful to God became less pronounced. A new spirituality was introduced with the rise of the new religious orders in the early twelfth century. It focused in particular on the humanity of Christ and on imitation of him. This new spirituality brought a change in the understanding of God, and this modification was also discernible in the lives of saints. Before the thirteenth century, for example, one finds no stigmatic saints.[33]

The change in spirituality also affected Marian devotion. The feasts

33. Vauchez, *Sainteté*, 514-18.

of the Virgin — Purification, Annunciation, Assumption, Nativity, and Conception — were already known in the Latin church. But Bernard of Clairvaux had rejected the idea of an immaculate conception. His view had found some acceptance, for instance with the recluse Gheraert Appelmans (†1325), who in his *Glose op den Pater Noster* repeated Bernard's opinion that Mary had been sanctified only in her mother's womb. But Bernard also did much to stimulate veneration of Mary. All Cistercian monasteries were under her patronage.

Devotion to Mary was directly linked to devotion to Christ and developed in the wake of the stronger emphasis on Christ. She appeared in many visions with the Christ child, whom she allowed the visionaries to hold. This sort of vision was experienced by two monks of the Cistercian monastery of Villers and by Ida van Leeuwen (†1260), a Cistercian nun. The Ave Maria became a popular prayer in Cistercian circles, which led to the gradual development of the rosary, though the term rosary dates only from the fifteenth century. A choral office was also introduced in Mary's honor. Beatrice of Nazareth (†1231) as a novice already prayed an office of Mary. But we do not know whether this was the same as the office of Mary that Gerhard Groote translated into Middle Dutch around 1380. The cult of Mary was also promoted by the mendicant orders. The Franciscans made every Saturday into a day of Mary with its own office for the Mass and introduced the devotion of the seven sorrows and seven joys of Mary — all related to her close ties with Jesus. Marian devotion was equally elaborated among the Beguines. In Ghent the Beguines were obliged to have communion on her feast days and to begin preparations on the vigil, the day before the feast.

The sainthood of Mary was also commemorated in magical ways. In 1090 an image of the Mother of God was carried through the streets of Tournai to plead for the end of an epidemic. We are told of a nobleman from Brabant, Walter of Bierbach, who missed a tournament because he tarried to attend Mass. Mary took his place and gained the victory for him. There are many stories about souls saved by Mary. Whoever prayed to her was saved from perdition. There is a story of a devil who entered the service of a rich man, waiting in vain for the day when the man would forget to pray to Mary. Many asked for Mary's intercession. In 1349 — the year of the Black Death — flagellants, that is, penitents who flogged themselves in public, revealed that Mary had succeeded in preventing the end of the world, which God had scheduled for September 10 of that year. This had been disclosed in a letter deposited in Jerusalem by an angel sent by Christ. There are countless examples of Mary's intervention. Prominent among these is the Beatrice legend.

There was a gradual change in the veneration of saints when their function of mediation had lost some of its importance to the new emphasis on imitation of Christ. The result was a specialization in the saints' functions. This change particularly affected early Christian saints, whose legendary biographies lent themselves more easily to such specialization than did the *Vitae* of later officially canonized saints. It is remarkable to see how little space is given to these later *Vitae* in the *legendaria* — the hagiographic collections of texts not directly related to the liturgical calendar. The early saints also dominated the greatly condensed collections of saints' lives that were composed when the legends of saints had become folk stories. Their martyrdom appealed more to the imagination than did the heroic pursuit of virtue that in later times led to sainthood. Even the *Legenda Aurea,* written by James of Voragine around 1255, which belong to the more balanced examples of the hagiographic genre, give the early saints most attention.

We find in the fourteenth century, on the other hand, in addition to this preference for legendary saints, the development of a new genre of lives of saints, in which virtue underwent a drastic redefinition. In their asceticism the saints of that period opted — at least in the *Vita* model of contemporary hagiographers — for a much more intense imitation of the sufferings of the martyrs, of the rigorism of the hermits of the desert, and of the poverty of the mendicant friars. In the tradition of fourteenth-century hagiography, the biography of a contemporary saint, whether canonized or not, was no longer intended as a feasible example for the virtue-loving faithful. Heroic virtues of the fourteenth century had to exceed the limit of what was attainable, sometimes even grotesquely. Alongside the early legendary saints this new kind of saint enjoyed a remarkable popularity, in a strange combination of horror and fascination.[34]

The specialization of the saints had to do with matters for which the faithful invoked their intercession. The saints became protectors against all kinds of ailments. The help of St. Appolonia was sought for toothaches, because she had lost teeth when she was tortured. St. Agatha was

34. R. Kieckhefer, *Unquiet Souls* (Chicago, 1984), 1-15. Cf. A. H. Bredero, "De Delftse Begijn Gertrui van Oosten en haar niet-erkende heiligheid," in D. E. H. de Boer and J. W. Marsilje, ed., *De Nederlanden in de Late Middeleeuwen* (Utrecht, 1987), 83-97.

called on in cases of chest pain, and St. Laurence in cases of back pain. This specialization represented a less than completely healthy development. Huizinga comments in his classic study of fourteenth- and fifteenth-century modes of thought:

> Every saint, by the possession of a distinct and vivid outward shape, had his own marked individuality, quite contrary to the angels, who, with the exception of the three famous archangels, acquired no definite appearance. This individual character of each saint was still more strongly accentuated by the special functions attributed to many of them. Now this specialization of the kind of aid given by the various saints was apt to introduce a mechanical element into the veneration paid to them. If, for instance, Saint Roch is especially invoked against the plague, almost inevitably too much stress came to be laid on his part in the healing, and the idea required by sound doctrine, that the saint wrought the cure only by means of his intercession with God, came in danger of being lost sight of.[35]

Those who wanted to have full protection venerated all the healing saints. This resulted in the cult of the Fourteen Holy Helpers, who even received their own place in some liturgical calendars. This phenomenon must be explained not only on the basis of the extreme social conditions people had to face in the fourteenth century. The veneration of saints had become so deeply entrenched that it could by itself lead to far-reaching consequences.

The most bizarre example in the Low Countries may have been the veneration of St. Ontkommer ("Unburden" or "Uncumber," that is, one who escapes). The oldest traces seem to lead to Steenbergen. St. Ontkommer is depicted as a woman with a beard, hanging on a cross. She was regarded as the helper of all who were suffering distress, as the one who could free them from their sadness. In this peculiar cult it appears at first as if a female Christ were being venerated as a saint. The cult probably originated when a crucifix with a Christ who was not wearing just a loincloth, but was fully dressed, was misunderstood. Such portrayals were intended to emphasize the majesty of Christ, even on the cross.

This misunderstanding led to the legend of Wilgefortis, the virgin daughter of a Portuguese king, who had given her in marriage to the king

---

35. J. Huizinga, *The Waning of the Middle Ages* (Harmondsworth, 1955), 115. The first Dutch edition appeared in 1919.

of Sicily. Wilgefortis became a Christian and rejected this marriage because she wanted to belong to God. When she was imprisoned by her father, she prayed for an effective antidote against being desired by men. Her prayer was answered: During the night she grew a beard, and the king of Sicily then withdrew his marriage proposal. Her father had her crucified.

A Middle Dutch text explains why Wilgefortis was also venerated as St. Ontkommer: As she hung on the cross, a voice was heard, saying, "Wilgefortis, bride and daughter of God, rejoice in God, for he has heard your prayer. And he wants you to have another name. Henceforth your name will be Ontkommer. You will be a mother of all whose hearts are burdened with sadness, but who will escape their sadness through your prayers."[36]

THE INFLUENCE of the veneration of saints is also apparent in the rise of eucharistic devotion in the late Middle Ages. The first accounts of a display of the Holy Sacrament in large monstrances date from the thirteenth century. At the same time the cult of the real presence of Christ in the host, which was also to be worshipped outside the Mass, rose to prominence. As a result there developed the "lauds" with their eucharistic hymns, including the *Adoro te* of Thomas Aquinas. Eucharistic devotion resembled in some ways veneration of the relics of saints. The Low Countries, particularly the diocese of Liège, played a significant role in the development of eucharistic devotion.

The Eucharist is an essential part of the Mass. Because of the Eucharist the Mass is referred to as the *sacrifice* of the Mass. It is a repetition of the Last Supper and also an unbloody reenactment of the sacrifice on the cross. Bread and wine are consecrated to be the body and blood of Christ, which are then considered inseparably present in both symbols. Communion under both kinds, that is, with the laity receiving the wine as well as the bread, was relatively rare. Before 1100 the Eucharist outside the sacrifice of the Mass was limited to keeping consecrated hosts for the sick. Charlemagne ordered the churches to do so, and his directive remained in force.

The presence of Christ was not always understood in exactly the

36. J. Gessler, *De Vlaamse baardheilige Wilgefortis of Ontcommer* (Antwerp, 1937), 50.

same way. The community of the faithful partaking in the liturgy of the Mass was also described as the body of Christ, an identification that had been strongly emphasized in the early church. From the eighth century on the role of the laity in the Mass became more passive. One reason was that the decline in the knowledge of Latin, which was undergoing a revival in its classical form, resulted in less participation in the liturgy of the Mass, and much of the earlier understanding of the presence of Christ in the Eucharist was lost. The presence was now more literally understood as relating to the symbols of bread and wine. Berengar of Tours (†1088) opposed this trend rather radically and thereby provoked a eucharistic controversy in the West. The resulting condemnation of Berengar led to a view of the transubstantiation that takes place during the consecration of the bread and the wine as resulting in an almost physical presence.

The participation of the laity in the celebration of the Eucharist was further reduced when, besides the concelebrated Mass, the Low Mass came into use. In the Low Mass the participation of the clergy was limited to one priest, while the laity could be represented by one acolyte. Thus the meaning of the celebration of the Eucharist was no longer linked to the community of the faithful and came to be interpreted by many as primarily magical in nature. It could then happen that some of the laity would be present at the celebration of the Mass only during the consecration and elevation of the elements of bread and wine, once the latter act of adoration had become standard.[37] After that moment they left the church building in order to be present in another parish church at the same magical moment.

This magical understanding of transubtantiation greatly influenced the manner in which the Eucharist was experienced: The elements acquired great significance even apart from the Sacrifice of the Mass. Candles were now burned in churches near the consecrated host, just as was done near relics. This was the origin of the sanctuary lamp in the eleventh century, followed by eucharistic fraternities to care for this ever-burning lamp. The first mention of this type of worship in the Low Countries is found in connection with the collegiate church of Harelbeke and dates from 1190. It became quite common in the Low Countries during the thirteenth century.[38] Even earlier we find the practices of kneeling and burning

37. L. Kennedy, "The Moment of Consecration and the Elevation of the Host," *Mediaeval Studies* 6 (1944), 121-50.

38. P. Browe, *Die Verehrung der Eucharistie im Mittelalter* (1933; repr. Munich, 1967), 4.

incense before the place where the consecrated hosts were kept. The resulting identification of the symbol with what was symbolized led to the practice that we have mentioned of elevating the host and the chalice in adoration immediately after the consecration.[39]

Frequent communion was, however, rare. The Fourth Lateran Council required the faithful to receive communion in their own parish churches at least once a year. Often some monetary offering was required. Many were afraid to receive communion out of fear of being impure and unworthy. The common understanding of God as a distant figure, with its Old Testament aura, remained common and contributed to this fear. The twelfth-century sequence *Dies Irae,* which came into general use in the liturgy of the Mass for the dead, referred, for instance, to "the King of terrifying majesty." The common notion of the sinfulness of the body was another cause for fear. Married couples were to refrain from sexual intercourse for some time before receiving Communion. Children who were too young to confess sins were not allowed to receive communion since they might already carry a burden of guilt for their sins. In the diocese of Liège the faithful were required to fast more intensely during the vigils preceding the Assumption of Mary, All Saints' Day, and Christmas, since these feasts were communion days. In monasteries communion was also rather infrequent. Once a week was already considered extreme. A counterbalance to the eucharistic fear became spiritual communion, mostly among beguines and nuns, but also among other laypeople.[40]

The reticence of the church in regard to frequent communion was also related to abuses. Because of their alleged magical powers, hosts were sometimes stolen or taken away during communion. They were buried or put in beehives or stables to ensure increased yields. Information about these abuses is found in those sections of the *exempla* that deal with the Eucharist and were intended to help preachers criticize and prevent abuses. These *exempla* also chide another abuse, that of kissing someone while holding the host in one's mouth. This had to do with the power of love ascribed to the host. But in spite of pastoral prudence, it became customary at the end of the fourteenth century to carry the sacrament in processions of prayer and penitence on the rogation days, that is, the three days

39. N. Mitchell, *Cult and Controversy: The Worship of the Eucharist Outside Mass* (New York, 1982).

40. P. Browe, *Die häufige Kommunion im Mittelalter* (Münster, 1938), 71-73; C. M. A. Caspers, *De eucharistische vroomheid en het feest van sacramentsdag in de Nederlanden tijdens de late middeleeuwen* (Louvain, 1992).

preceding Ascension Day. These processions were intended to improve the fertility of the land.

The reluctance of the clergy with regard to the participation of the laity in the Eucharist was focused most of all on the prayers in the canon of the Mass dealing with the consecration of the host and the wine. Since the Eucharist was often interpreted by the people magically, the clergy feared that these texts might be abused. The magic formula "hocus pocus" indicates that this did occur, based as it is on the words of consecration, *Hoc est corpus meum,* "This is my body." In missals for the laity these words of consecration were omitted. Matthew 7:6, "Do not give what is holy to dogs; and do not throw your pearls before swine," was specifically applied to the canon of the Mass in the late Middle Ages. Johannes Busch of Windesheim (†1479) burned a missal that he had found in a house of nuns, because it included the canon prayers of the Mass.

Many *exempla* stories circulated about the miraculous powers of the host. Several such accounts, collected by Caesarius of Heisterbach (†1240) in the ninth book of his *Dialogus Miraculorum,* were said to have taken place in the Low Countries. The "Book of Bees" of Thomas of Cantimpré (†1263), a Dominican from the southern Low Countries, also contained a number of eucharistic *exempla.*[41] But it was originally written in Latin and was only translated into Middle Dutch around 1450, in which form it became especially popular in convents for nuns in the northern Low Countries.

But several Middle Dutch versions of the *Graelqueste* (The Search for the Grail), which cannot be characterized as an *exemplum,* existed from the thirteenth century on. The oldest version was written by Jacob van Maerlant, who used Robert of Borron as his source. The object of the "quest" was the holy grail, the vessel used to serve the paschal lamb during the Last Supper and then to catch the blood from the wounds of the crucified Christ. The grail was, so the story goes, brought to the West by Joseph of Arimathea.

Eucharistic miracles occurred in many churches of the Low Countries. It was sometimes regarded as miraculous when hosts survived a fire or a flood. These hosts then became miracle hosts. Jews were usually charged in any case of willful desecration of the host. Such stories were, however, also told because eucharistic miracles were seen as the best re-

---

41. "Distinctio nona: *De Sacramento Corporis et Sanguinis Christi,*" in *Dialogus Miraculorum,* ed. J. Strange (1851; repr. Ridgewood, NJ, 1966) II, 164-217; C. M. Stutvoet-Joanknecht, *Der byen boeck* (Amsterdam, 1990), 172-75.

buttal of Jewish unbelief. In the Low Countries we know of only one case where Jews were accused of desecrating the host — in Brussels in 1369-70. The story is that Jews in Brussels had prompted a converted Jewess to steal a number of hosts. When during Good Friday of the following year they pierced the hosts with their daggers, the hosts bled profusely. The woman told what had happened, the accused were tortured and burned alive, and the miracle hosts were kept in a chapel especially built for the purpose adjacent to St. Michael's Cathedral,[42] which now also contains a memorial for the innocent Jewish victims.

The account of a host desecration by Jews in Remagen in Germany, reported at length in the chronicle of William Procurator (†1333), also shows the susceptibility of the people to such tales. In Bruges this credulity gave birth to an altered version of a story originating from Cologne about the murder of a maidservant by a Jew. The Jew had discovered that Christians who failed to receive communion on the three golden Fridays, that is, the Fridays following the feast of the Circumcision, of Ascension, and of Mary's Assumption, could not die without making their confession. The Jew did not want Christians to know this, but the girl did seem to know. So he killed her and buried her in his cellar. The crime was miraculously discovered, and the girl remained alive until she had made her confession. The Bruges variant of the story identifies the third golden Friday as the Friday after Ascension, which corresponded with the celebration of the feast of the Holy Blood in Bruges. Since 1128 a relic of Christ's blood had been venerated in Bruges.[43]

The proliferation of eucharistic miracles commemorated annually and drawing pilgrims to the churches where they had taken place was related to the creation of the Corpus Christi feast, which was observed on the second Thursday after Pentecost. This relationship is particularly apparent in the Low Countries, where Corpus Christi was first celebrated. The institution of the feast in 1246 followed the occurrence of a number of eucharistic miracles. More — a total of nineteen — occurred subsequently farther north. The feast was first instituted in the diocese of Liège by Bishop Robert of Thourotte at the instigation of Juliana of Cornillion. Juliana, who at the time was still a Beguine, was said to have received revelations about the creation of the feast.

42. P. Browe, *Die eucharistische Wunder im Mittelalter* (Wroclaw, 1938), 137, n. 4.
43. *Wihelmi . . . Procuratoris Egmondensis Chronicon,* ed. C. Pijnacker Hordijk (Amsterdam, 1904), 132f. Bruges Municipal Library manuscript 494.

The new feast no doubt promoted devotional interest in the Eucharist outside the Mass, but the question remains whether Juliana, who subsequently found refuge among the Cistercians, did not have other intentions. The fact is that she wanted to receive communion more often. In this she represented the desire of many female religious, including Beguines.[44] But the church was not inclined to accommodate this wish.

The Corpus Christi feast did not immediately find acceptance. In 1264 Pope Urban IV, who had earlier been archdeacon in Liège, prescribed it for the whole Latin church. But in 1288 it was still not yet considered obligatory in the diocese of Liège itself. Moreover, the introduction of the feast in the Latin church remained a dead letter. It did not find broad acceptance until after 1317, when Pope John XXII decreed it anew. We must therefore not exclude the possibility that a different sort of interest in the Eucharist existed among female religious in the second half of the thirteenth century, which enabled them to distance themselves from a eucharistic devotion intertwined with veneration of saints.

4. BLESSINGS AND PENANCE

THE WAY in which the Christian religion is experienced is in many ways determined by social circumstances and structures. We dealt with this theme in chapter I and have referred to it repeatedly in the subsequent chapters. Christianization changed social circumstances and structures, but often not in any revolutionary way. And Christianity adapted to a large extent and became a product of its time, even though the human capacity for eternity remained central to the Christian religion. The inner need to be part of a large social unit allowed medieval Christendom to become a corporate entity replacing the kinship units that disintegrated as a result of Christianization. Baptism made belonging to a kinship unit much less important, as people now received membership in a wider collectivity — Christendom — which developed into a closed community, replacing the security of kinship relationships. As this community developed further it became less tolerant toward outsiders, that is, toward Jews, unbelievers, and those who insufficiently conformed to the prescribed thinking and were therefore branded as heretics.

44. S. Roisin, "L'efflorescense cistercienne et le courant féminin de piété au XIIIe siècle," *Revue d'Histoire Ecclésiastique* 39 (1943), 342-78.

Blessings or benedictions and the penitential system were two major aspects of religious life on which the contemporary social circumstances and structures had their impact. Both were related to forms of religion that had existed already before Christianization, in the Low Countries as elsewhere. Religion was primarily experienced in concrete, often ritualized, acts and gestures intended to conjure up otherworldly powers or to fend off threats by them. Medieval Christianity adapted itself to its circumstances and maintained these pre-Christian religious forms for a considerable time, even though Christian teaching differed on essential points from the earlier religions, particularly in its rejection of blood sacrifices and its denial of autonomy to the powers of nature (which eventually paved the way for a secularized and humanized society).

This continuity from the pre-Christian past is apparent in the sacral defense against calamities, sickness, and dangers by means of the formulas of ecclesiastical benedictions. These blessings concerned, among other things, the phenomena of nature — fertility and crop failure, bad weather and damage caused by it, and of course weather in general. They also concerned protection of and against animals. There were also blessings for marriage, pregnancy, childbirth, and for children as they grew older. These benedictions were rooted not just in the pre-Christian religious traditions of the Low Countries. They were geographically far more widespread and were, moreover, partly of Jewish origin.[45] They found as much acceptance in the Low Countries as elsewhere, and continued far beyond the end of the Middle Ages.

Many sayings and proverbs that remind us of these medieval benedictions have survived in written form in the Dutch vernacular, and many were first written down after they had long been in use. The Dutch language knew formulas to bless crops, to retrieve stolen or lost property, to discover the truth, and for luck in gambling. There were special prayers to protect hearth and home, especially during bad weather. Other prayers prevented bad dreams or oversleeping, or assured good weather or a bearable life. There were formulas to chase away demons, spirits, and witches or to adjure devils and sorcerers. Some formulas to liberate bewitched persons or animals consisted of long prayers ending with the first words of the Gospel of John. These prayers were often accompanied by invocations of saints, but in reality they were more dependent on religious

45. Cf. A. Franz, *Die kirchlichen Benediktionen im Mittelalter* (2 vols.; Freiburg and St. Louis, 1909).

traditions that must have been popular before these regions were Christianized. Indeed, among these incantations we also find magical phrases to win the love of a woman, to acquire fertility, or to discover the identity of a future lover.

Some of these benedictions acquired a more specialized character, at least when viewed in the context of a society familiar with a sacral, otherworldly experience of reality. These benedictions are usually called sacramentals, a term that gradually developed in the Middle Ages to distinguish such blessings and consecrations from full-fledged sacraments. But a clear definition of sacramentals was not given as yet, and at first no clear distinction was made between sacraments and sacramentals. In the eleventh century exorcism was regarded as a sacrament. Some lists of sacraments from the first half of the twelfth century include rituals such as the anointing of a king, the consecration of a church, or the confirmation of a person in a religious state of life other than priesthood (as a canon, monk, or nun).[46] Early Scholasticism listed the seven sacraments that have become customary, but it was only from the thirteenth century on that other sacraments were excluded. It was also in the thirteenth century that the term "sacramentals" became current. The main distinction was that sacraments sanctify *people,* while sacramentals confer holiness on *things,* which in turn contribute to the sanctification of persons. For that reason chalices used in the Mass, church buildings, Easter candles, and church bells were consecrated.

The domain of the sacramentals remained broader and included defense against demonic forces and liberation from evils. In this respect they were closely related to the literature of incantations, which has also been preserved in Dutch. Water played a special role. This is understandable considering the purifying and healing power that most religions attribute to water. From early times the church used consecrated baptismal water. But there was also miraculous water with power derived from consecration by persons with a reputation of holiness. The confusion between the two kinds of water began when baptism no longer required flowing water and quantities of consecrated baptismal water were kept in reserve. As a result this holy water began to acquire other functions. In the eighth century it was, for example, used in the diocese of Liège to exorcise demons.

46. Sermo 79, *in Dedicatione Ecclesiae* = *PL* CXLIV, 897-902. This sermon, previously ascribed to Peter Damiani, was composed by Nicholas of Clairvaux, one of Bernard's secretaries.

Holy water acquired many functions in the life of medieval Christians. After it had become customary in the ninth century to sprinkle the faithful with it before Sunday Mass as a reminder of baptism, people would often take some of the water home to sprinkle objects in and around the house that needed protection or special favor. The many benedictions that developed around such practices were forms of folk liturgy that had their origin with the people and were permitted by the church. The medieval church believed that holy water could be used to exorcise demons, to free the human spirit of bad dreams or delusions, to save the human heart from worldly desires and cares, to keep a person from carnal sins, and to prepare the heart for prayer and for worthy reception of the sacraments. It could also protect against infertility, increase harvests, provide protection against illnesses, and drive out the plague. Dutch incantation texts also refer to uses of holy water, mainly for the purposes just listed. Ecclesiastical tolerance of folk uses of holy water did, however, have its limits. The baptismal font in the church, present since the twelfth century — when pouring began to replace immersion — now had a lid, partly to prevent people from stealing and misusing its water.

❧ ❧

WE HAVE ALREADY discussed baptism and the Eucharist. Among the other sacraments, we must give special attention to penance, since its structure and the way in which it influenced society was largely determined by the nature of that society.

In the early church a Christian could receive forgiveness for sins only once after baptism. The medieval church's system of multiple confessions was first introduced in Gaul by Irish missionaries. Public penance, that is, the performance in the presence of the bishop of a penitential regimen imposed by the church, was increasingly replaced by private penance. The nature of the assigned penance depended on the nature of the misdemeanor, the status of the offender, and the status of the person who had been wronged. The Carolingian Renaissance tried to reverse this development toward private penance. The result was that from that time on both private and public penance were practiced. Public penance was, however, limited to sins and offenses committed in public. The clergy was exempt from public penance, since it would involve automatic suspension from office. Moreover, public penance was thought to be redundant for religious, as their way of life was characterized by continuous penance and self-mortification.

Public penance came in two forms. In the solemn form the reconciliation of the sinner occurred in the presence of the bishop on Maundy Thursday, at the end of Lent. The less solemn form was more common and required the sinner to make a pilgrimage.

Private penance also underwent an essential change. At first absolution — the remission of sins — was granted after works of penance had been completed. But the periods of penance could be so protracted, notably when there was an accumulation of sins, that they could exceed the duration of human life. To solve this problem, one could shorten the period of penance by making the works of penance more intense or by enlisting others in performance of them. These others generally included members of monastic communities, who could benefit a sinner with their prayers and self-mortification — normally in response to some material payment to the monastery. This allowed absolution to be given when the sins had been confessed and made it possible to continue prayer and penance even after the death of the sinner. This created a bond of prayer between the monasteries and the faithful in the world that went beyond death.

It is no wonder that in this setting the feast of All Souls, when every priest read three Masses for the Dead, became widely observed in the Low Countries in the eleventh century. These Masses were said for those who had died when only part of the penance for their sins had been completed and who were therefore in purgatory. This feast, immediately following All Saints' Day, was first observed in the diocese of Liège, on the instigation of Bishop Notker (†1008), who had earlier been a monk of St. Gall. The transfer of penance to monasteries had the additional result that eventually, due to the increased frequency in the reading of private Masses, all choir monks came to be ordained as priests.

Indulgences were a new element developing in the penitential system that came to play an important role in the religious experience of the people.[47] Initially indulgences were granted just to crusaders who, because of the dangers they faced, could receive full absolution for their sins on confession. In addition to these plenary indulgences, from the twelfth century on the bishops gave partial indulgences, in particular to promote the building of churches, or sometimes of bridges. In 1215 the Fourth

47. Cf. J. H. Crehan, "Indulgences," *Catholic Dictionary of Theology* (London, 1971) III, 84-90; J. van Herwaarden, "Middeleeuwse aflaten en Nederlandse devotie," in de Boer and Marsilje, ed., 31-68.

Lateran Council decreed that a partial indulgence could be given to whoever attended a church on the day of its consecration. This indulgence was not to exceed one year, regardless of whether the consecration had been performed by one or more bishops. Each year, on the day when the church's consecration was commemorated, an indulgence of no more than forty days could be given to all who came to church.[48] The forty-day maximum was not always observed, even though it was reemphasized by Boniface VIII at the end of the thirteenth century. In 1256 Arnold of Semgallen, the suffragan bishop of Liège, granted a church in Namur an indulgence of one hundred forty days, and when in 1288 Bishop-elect Jan of Nassau began the restoration of the cathedral in Utrecht, which had burned down in 1248, he gave an indulgence of one year and the forty days of Lent to all who came to church.[49]

There were understandable reasons for extending the duration of indulgences. In Maastricht a wooden bridge collapsed in 1275 just as a procession was passing over it, and four hundred people died. In 1284 four archbishops and fifteen bishops in Orvieto, where the curia was residing, granted a collective indulgence of nineteen times forty days to whoever helped build a new stone bridge. Arnold of Semgallen, as we have seen, used this method earlier in Liège.[50] Little attention was paid to the decision of the Fourth Lateran Council that prohibited this practice of lengthening indulgences. The restatement of the prohibition by Boniface VIII made hardly any difference, and Boniface himself promised a plenary (i.e., lifetime) jubilee indulgence to all who would visit Rome during the holy year of 1300.

Already in 1249 Maastricht had its first indulgences. In that year Pope Innocent IV confirmed that those who visited the church of St. Servatius in Maastricht during the feast of the Seven Brothers (July 10) or during the octave of that feast, could earn an indulgence of forty days. Later in that same year the pope granted a similar indulgence to all who went to the church of St. Servatius with pious intentions on the feasts of the Holy Virgin, of St. Servatius (May 13), or of St. Monulfus and St. Gondulfus (July 17), or on Easter or during the octave of Easter. Such indulgences were still exceptional and must be seen against the background of the pope's intense struggle with Frederick II, who had been excommunicated in 1245.

48. Lateran IV, constitution 62; *COD* 263f.
49. *Mendicatorium of the Bishop-elect Jan van Nassau*, 10; J. H. Vroom, *De Financiering van de Kathedraalbouw in de Middeleeuwen* (Maarssen, 1981), 503.
50. N. Paulus, *Geschichte des Ablasses im Mittelalter* (Paderborn, 1922) II, 260, 266.

The influence of the system of indulgences on religious life was not wholly negative. Sometimes indulgences were given to those who came to listen to a sermon. But indulgences that were partly intended to promote charitable or cultural projects, with a clear focus on monetary contributions, did have negative implications. The collection of these contributions led to a traffic in indulgences. One or more members of the clergy would be licensed by a bishop to travel through the region to collect the income from indulgences. Such begging expeditions were known as "quests" and its leaders as "questors." They carried relics with them to attract the people and would enter a town in a procession with the church bells ringing. The day of the collection was given the obligatory status of a church feast, with the threat of punishment for all who failed to attend.

This practice dates from the thirteenth century, as does the resistance against it. When the archbishop of Rheims wanted to have the questors in his suffragan dioceses welcomed in this manner, in an attempt to raise money to build the cathedral, some sought papal support for their resistance. In 1246 Innocent IV decided against the archbishop on one point: He had exceeded the limit of forty days for the building indulgence. Protests often came from the mendicant orders, who accused the bishops of profiting personally from this traffic. But the practice was also repeatedly condemned by episcopal synods, such as those of Liège in 1287 and of Utrecht in 1310.[51] These condemnations failed, however, to have lasting results.

The organization of a quest required the permission of the cathedral chapter of the particular diocese. This condition was also in effect in Utrecht, where the chapter sometimes leased the quests of other churches in an attempt to raise money for their own cathedral. Collecting money for other churches could damage the material interests of this cathedral, which had from early times been considered the most important church of the diocese. Prior approval by the chapter also implied some control over the quests.

There was, however, much less control over the actual practices of the questors. This can be deduced from the decretal of John XXII in 1317 stating that the questors did not always follow the rules. One of the rules stipulated that they could only promote indulgences in sermons. Bishops were supposed to verify the authenticity of the papal letters that authorized quests. It was specifically emphasized that questors could not release people

51. Ibid. II, 271, 281.

from vows or grant absolution to those who confessed to murder, perjury, or other reserved sins. They were not allowed to grant plenary indulgences, nor to claim that they could release family members of those who made donations from purgatory. They were not to keep for themselves any of the penitential payments they requested from those who confessed and were not to suggest that people could keep goods that were acquired illegitimately as long as they paid some specified amount.[52] John's decretal, which became part of canon law, had so little effect in the long run that quests came to be forbidden by the Council of Trent.

Plenary indulgences could only be granted by the pope and were only given to crusaders and holy year pilgrims to Rome. From the thirteenth century on a plenary indulgence could also be granted to special persons, often rulers, but only on request. Most common was the indulgence granted *in articulo mortis*. This was given in the form of a letter of confession that would in the hour of death procure forgiveness of sins and absolution of punishment from any confessor one might choose. The letter also covered sins committed from the moment it was issued up to the death of the beneficiary, but was no authorization to indulge in sin. In the fourteenth century this kind of indulgence did not yet require good works and did not involve questors. It was granted on individual request, which could be made by others. In 1350 Jan III of Brabant asked such an indulgence for his chancellor. In another case, a nobleman wanted such an indulgence for himself, his squire, and his two maidservants. In 1359 Bishop Jan of Arkel requested it for himself and for twelve persons that he would name later. This information may be gleaned from the petitions sent between 1342 and 1366 from the diocese of Utrecht to the popes at Avignon.

But temporary indulgences were also granted. Those who assisted in the restoration of the abbey of the Cistercian nuns in Mariendael, near Utrecht, which had been damaged by war, received an indulgence of two years and forty days. Visitors to the church of St. Peter in Chains in Axel, who came to venerate the relics of the cross and who contributed to the restoration of the church, received an indulgence of one hundred days. Visitors to the parish church of Vleuten could count on an indulgence of one year and forty days — one-third of what had been requested. This

---

52. *Clementiniarum* V.IX.2; A. E. Friedberg, *Corpus Iuris Canonici* part 2: *Decretalium collectiones* (1879; repr. Graz, 1959), 1190f. On the background of this decree of Pope John XXII, cf. Paulus II, 284-86.

church had also suffered from war. A total of eleven indulgences are recorded in these published petitions from Utrecht. This small number indicates clearly that the popular stories about the medieval traffic in indulgences are only partly true for the end of the period we are considering.

But the inflation of indulgences, whereby a pardon for one hundred days of penance could become a pardon of one hundred years or even multiples thereof, does indeed date from the period of the Avignon popes. But its origin must be sought in Rome, where relief was needed for the recession suffered by the important churches as a result of the absence of the pope. This inflation seems to have been only temporary, and it would appear that the late medieval abuse of indulgences was much less general than is often assumed. Still some Dutch texts of the fifteenth and sixteenth centuries do mention indulgences of many thousands of years.[53]

5. THE BILINGUALISM OF THE CHURCH AND ITS SOCIAL CONSEQUENCES

SCHOLARS WHO ARE interested in the history of mentality and who study religious life in the Middle Ages sometimes create a contrast between official religion and popular religion. They see a substantial distance between clergy and laity resulting from social differences and particularly from differences in language. The clergy used Latin and resisted the vernacular. Latin was the written language, while initially the vernacular was only used in speech. Such an approach to religious life in the Middle Ages, which looks for opportunities to trace the religious life of the common people and is intent on finding expressions of pre-Christian religiosity, has much to commend it. The historian engaged in this search for the life patterns of a people living in an oral culture transposes the research methods of social scientists into the past and focuses on aspects that before received only the attention of cultural anthropologists.

The problem with this method is that little or no consideration is given to what was *shared* in the religious life of the clergy and the laity in the Middle Ages. For both groups, insofar as they were believing Christians, the core of religious experience was belief in the living God who became incarnate, the hope of eternal salvation in the presence of God,

53. R. R. Post, *Supplieken gericht aan de pausen Clemens VI, Innocentius IV en Urbanus VI* (The Hague, 1936), 204, 248, 323, 98, 278, 433.

and the expression of love for God through care for other people. These principles took on a progressively sharper focus in religious life as Christianization advanced. It is, of course, clear that reality never fully reached the ideal. The reality was tied to social changes that occurred during the period we have been considering. If the common elements in the religious experience of both clergy and laity are disregarded, incidental conflicts, which admittedly did frequently arise, are easily interpreted as continuous friction, with all the ideological factors that are usually assumed to form the background of social conflict. But this approach leaves us with the question whether we will see anything but the mere surface of medieval religious life.

Another aspect of this issue is the increase in superstition in the late Middle Ages. But here we are perhaps faced with an illusion, since we have a much more complete picture of the religious and superstitious practices of those later centuries. We simply have more sources. Moreover, the church was coming closer to the common people as a result of Christianization and ecclesiastical preaching. This rapprochement is particularly mirrored in the constitutions of the Fourth Lateran Council regulating pastoral care. And the church was also coming closer to the people because of the development of the towns and the subsequent rise of the mendicant orders. Greater intimacy led the church to show greater tolerance for the influence of superstitious practices in the experience of the Christian faith. This development is in fact, I believe, an indication that the distinction between official religion and popular belief was less extensive and less sharp than some have supposed.

Nevertheless, it cannot be denied that there existed at the beginning of the period under consideration here a substantial gap between how the clergy and the laity experienced their religion. In the post-Carolingian era the role of the laity in the liturgy was utterly passive. The liturgy was completely ritualized and no longer expressed the sentiments of the community of the faithful, especially since the laity could no longer sing the Latin hymns. The value of these rituals strongly resembled that of the Germanic legal tradition: In the Germanic culture a wrong gesture or imprecise formula could invalidate a legal transaction and change a declaration of not guilty into its opposite. The value attributed to the ritual of the Mass led to the reading of the Mass with no one present except the one priest doing the reading.

Changes in the role of writing that began during the Carolingian era are also tied to this process of ritualization: Everything was written in

Latin and writing was a sacral act, performed mainly in the service of liturgy. A good liturgy depended on a precise use of language. This required a purification of Latin, which in turn necessitated a return to classical Latin and resulted in the alienation of liturgical Latin from vernacular Latin. The refinement of Latin for the liturgy was required in order to avoid answers to prayer that differed from what had been requested. Thus the Germanization of the church promoted its bilingualism.

The distance between liturgical Latin and vernacular Latin may have accelerated a change in the process of Christianization. The Christianization of the Germanic peoples had been preceded by a rudimentary Romanization. But this Romanization did not occur as the church moved farther north. In regions conquered by the Franks preachers were employed who could make themselves understood in the languages of the tribes among whom they worked. Romanization was no longer a prerequisite for Christianization. (Perhaps this deserves more attention in studies of the origin of the boundary between the Romance and the Germanic languages.) Moreover, an individual's entrance into the church was no longer preceded by a catechumenate. Christianization was no longer presupposed before baptism, but followed baptism. As a result baptism acquired the character of a magical act.

This change in the process of Christianization fostered bilingualism and increased the difference in religious experience between the clergy and the laity. The religion of the laity consisted mainly in a passive presence during liturgical events, the search for security in relics, obedience to concrete, moral precepts, and works of penance when those ordinances were disobeyed. The prescribed works of penance mentioned in penitentials resembled the rules regarding wergild by which Germanic law dealt with crimes and offenses. Moreover, the higher classes of the Germanic laity desired to continue their ancestor cults, which explains their willingness to found and favor monasteries where their ancestors had been buried.

In this lay experience of religion, Latin was dispensable. But that was not the case for those who wanted a deeper religious life. Such persons had to leave the world of the laity and undergo a conversion. That is, they had to enter monastic communities. The active participation by the monks in the liturgy required some knowledge of Latin.

Familiarity with Latin was less of a problem for the clergy involved in pastoral care. Their work was to a large extent limited to sacramental acts, and it was not considered vital for the priests to understand the exact meaning of the liturgical texts. Some of the clergy differed only slightly in birth status and way of life from the dependents living on estates. Such a priest would care for a church that belonged to the owner of an estate and would sometimes be succeeded in this function by his son. The higher clergy, the bishops of the realm, were of noble birth and had often been educated in monasteries or sometimes at imperial chancelleries.

Most of those who chose or were directed to a religious life outside the world came from the nobility. Often such a noble would enter the monastery already at a very early age, as an oblate, usually to honor a parental vow. For those coming from the lower classes, withdrawing from the world normally meant becoming a recluse or one of the numerous lay brothers in monasteries. For the latter, religion was experienced in terms of work and any knowledge of Latin would have been virtually superfluous. But things were different for those who fought a spiritual battle in their daily choral prayers. Those prayers were strongly ritualistic and were understood as a struggle against evil and a defense of the kingdom of God.

We need not discuss the development of clerical spirituality except in one respect. The rise of the Cistercian order from the twelfth century on largely ended the practice of boys entering monasteries before their fifteenth birthdays. Monks now learned their Latin at cathedral schools or chapter schools. In the Low Countries most went to Liège. If that was impossible, they could go to Rheims, as did, for instance, William of St.-Thierry. As a result the monk now had some experience of life in the world. Therefore monastic spirituality came to use many images derived from physical love in speaking of God's love, and many commentaries were written on the Song of Solomon.[54]

The status of women living a religious life outside the world was at first extremely problematic. Their position in religious life remained closer to that of the laity, since as women they were excluded from all sacred and sacramental acts. In the early Middle Ages, these prohibitions were less severe. Some abbesses who headed the monasteries of both men and women that existed at that time performed baptisms and heard confessions. In the Carolingian Renaissance there was an attempt under Germanic influence to conform religious life to Old Testament norms and prescriptions, and all participation of women in sacred acts was therefore ended. Exclusion of women from church office was defended with the argument (still accepted) that only men had been chosen as apostles and that no women were present at the Last Supper.

54. Cf. J. Leclercq, *Monks and Love in Twelfth-Century France* (Oxford, 1979).

We can grant that this development reflects its time, but it did not come out of the way in which the gospel was interpreted at the time. It had more to do with, broadly speaking, the dualistic worldview of the time. As I have pointed out in chapter VII, this dualistic view meant that the world was controlled by supernatural powers, some striving for good, some for evil. Good powers are directed toward what is spiritual, evil powers toward what is material and physical. In opposition to this viewpoint, which exists especially in religions with no written revelation, the church does teach that evil is not an independent power but a negation of good (so Augustine). But in practice, dualism had a strong effect on Christian teaching, particularly during the Middle Ages. This was the case until the revival of Aristotelian philosophy in Scholasticism, which made possible a positive appreciation for the material reality of creation. But this reevaluation did not include a reassessment of human physical nature. That remained sinful, and this sinfulness manifested itself primarily in sexuality.

This dualistic concept of sinfulness had far-reaching consequences for the position of women in the medieval Church. The sinfulness of sexuality led to the view that women were more sinful than men, since begetting children took much less time than pregnancy and childbirth. Women and their bodies, with which they aroused the lust of men, had a much greater part in sexuality. For these reasons and because of menstruation, which was caused by physical fertility, women were considered more depraved than men and were excluded from what was sacred, even if they did not marry. The greater depravity of women found confirmation in the biblical story of the seduction of Adam by Eve. Furthermore, the creation of Eve from Adam's rib was understood theologically as proof of the inferiority of women. Women were incomplete men, and for this reason were excluded from church office and administration of the sacraments.

The church also had greater reserve with respect to married women than married men. It expected from a woman who wanted to live a devout and modest life that, after the death of her husband and after she had completed her task of raising children, she lament her sinfulness arising from the married state by entering a convent, not a second marriage. No similar objections were raised to the second marriage of a man who desired to live a God-fearing life in the world. Rather, such a marriage was thought to protect him against seduction by women.

But the reorientation of the monastic system in the twelfth century, when various new orders took form, brought changes in how women acted out their religious devotion. Many women followed the itinerant preachers, who, in order to escape the suspicions of the ecclesiastical authorities, established new convents in which women might experience religiosity in a more positive sense than just as penitence for having been married. Norbert of Xanten, who originally traveled about the Low Countries as a popular preacher and had many women among his followers, thus established communities for women. But the order that he founded later disposed of most of these monasteries for women.

The Cistercian order also offered more to women. The Cistercian orientation toward a spirituality of the bride of Christ, developed primarily by Bernard of Clairvaux, attracted many women.[55] In the Low Countries many Cistercian nuns lived as mystics from the end of the twelfth century on. Some of them became well known: Ida of Nivelles (†1231), Lutgard of Aywières (†1247), Alice of Schaarbeek (†1250), Ida of Leeuw (†1260), Beatrice of Nazareth (†1268), and Ida of Louvain (†1300).[56]

The extant *Vitae* of these women are written in Latin. Thomas of Cantimpé, for instance, wrote the *Vita* of Lutgard. But women who wrote used the vernacular. This sheds additional light on the bilingualism of the church, but it leaves unexplained why these women's *Vitae* were written in Latin. In any case, it seems that the separation between the literate and the illiterate — and the latter included those who wrote only in the vernacular — did not fully coincide with that between clergy and laity. It is possible, however, that people insisted on regarding these women as mere lay sisters, along with other women religious, such as the Beguine Marie of Oignies (†1213), Margaret of Ypres (†1237), and Christina, a nun from St. Trond.

Their *Vitae* were written by contemporary authors of real authority, but these women must still have met with some suspicion, though not to the same degree as Margaret Porete of Valenciennes. Two propositions, which sounded absurd out of context, were lifted from her *Mirror of Simple Souls*, a treatise that was later highly appreciated in the church. On the basis of these propositions she was condemned and then in 1310 — one year before the

55. R. W. Southern, *Western Society and the Church in the Middle Ages* (Pelican History of the Church 2; Harmondworth and Grand Rapids, 1970), 312-18; S. Thompson, "The Problem of Cistercian Nuns in the Twelfth and Early Thirteenth Centuries," in D. Baker, ed., *Medieval Women* (Studies in Church History Subsidia 1 [Festschrift Rosalind M. T. Hill]; Oxford, 1978), 227-52.

56. S. Roisin, *L'hagiographie cistercienne dans le diocèse de Liège au XIIIe siècle* (Louvain and Brussels, 1947).

Council of Vienne — burned in Paris as a heretic.[57] Usually these women did not see themselves as standing in opposition to the official church; bilingualism did not therefore seem to pose much of a problem. The curious fact that only in 1373 was a Middle Dutch translation made of the rule of St. Benedict, which was followed by the Cistercian nuns, points in the same direction. The translation was made for one of the Cistercian houses.

಄ ಄

THE DIFFERENCE in religion as officially experienced by the latinized clergy and as practiced by the common people does not mean that the illiterate had a religion of their own. The relationship between Cistercian mysticism of the twelfth century, mostly inspired by the writings of Bernard of Clairvaux and William of St.-Thierry, and the later popular mysticism of the southern Low Countries, indicates that this contrast was more limited in scope. Cistercian mysticism is linked to that of Jan van Ruysbroeck (†1381) and came not only through the works of Bernard and William but even more through women such as Hadewijch († before 1275).

But there does seem to have been a deep cleft between ecclesiastical Latin and the vernacular with respect to Bible translations. In a letter of 1199 to the faithful of the diocese of Metz, Pope Innocent III opposed the reading of translated books of the Bible. His main concern was lay exegesis occurring outside the ecclesiastical context.[58] A synod of the diocese of Liège determined in 1203 that writings about the Bible in Walloon or Old Flemish had to be submitted to the bishop for approval. This stipulation, no doubt, also extended to translations of the Bible. From an apology written by Lambert le Bègue, a preacher from Liège, we learn about a Psalter translated by a Flemish master that circulated in Liège before 1177.[59]

The Bible was to occupy a distinct place in the religious life of illiterate people. Trends in the development of medieval spirituality indicate that the Bible became increasingly important. But for a long time it was deemed undesirable, and it was also impossible, to familiarize the illiterate with the written text. The people learned about the Bible through representations in art and through sermons. Since Latin was no longer generally

---

57. Margaret of Porete, *Speculum simplicium animarum* = *CCCM* 69 (Turnhout, 1986).

58. *PL* CCXIV, 695-99.

59. C. C. de Bruin, *De Statenbijbel en haar voorgangers* (Leiden, 1937), 51.

understood, the clergy were given the task of preaching in the vernacular. At a rather early date the library of the abbey of Egmond possessed a *Psalterium teutonice glosatum* — a psalter with translations added to the Latin text.[60]

As long as only oral translations were required, the standard for translations could remain relatively low. Difficulties began when lay people learned to read and write in the vernacular. The translator now had to master fully both the Latin and the vernacular. The vernacular posed the greatest number of problems, since it consisted of different local dialects, and there were hardly any definite rules for spelling and grammar. Another difficulty was the original text on which the translations were to be based. The Cathars, who had penetrated the Flemish towns as weavers migrated from the Languedoc region, had a translation of the New Testament not based on the Vulgate text. The oldest Middle Dutch version of the Diatessaron — an ancient harmony of texts from the four Gospels, with a commentary — was translated in Flanders or Brabant shortly after 1250.[61]

Ecclesiastical authorities remained somewhat reticent in their condemnation of the vernacular Bible, but there was great suspicion on the part of the clergy, possibly because it made their expositions less important. Even Jacob van Maerlant's rhymed Bible was regarded with misgivings. It was not really a translation of the Bible. Van Maerlant had translated and revised Peter Comestor's (†1179) *Historia Scolastica,* a Bible history based on the historical books of the Old Testament and the Apocrypha and on the Gospels. Van Maerlant, who completed his work in 1271, was a man of great erudition and unimpeachable orthodoxy. He wrote that he wanted to "uncouple the *Scolastica* from Latin by using Dutch words." But we learn from his *Spiegel Historiael* (Mirror of History) that he was criticized for making the "mysteries of the Bible" accessible to the laity. He tells us that the relationship between laity and clergy continued to be strained. He compared them with two kinds of ravens, unable to live together in peace.

But he made this comparison before he wrote his rhymed Bible, which seems to have been a turning point in his career. His *Historie van den Graele* (History of the Grail), written earlier, shows that he had long been interested in religion. His later works, however, manifest this religious interest most clearly. His criticism of the church in these later works in no way implied that his critical religiosity led him to abandon the church.

60. H. G. de Kleijn, "De catalogus van de boeken van de abdij van Egmond," *Archief der Nederlandse kerkgeschiedenis* (1887), 142.
61. C. C. de Bruin, *Het Luikse Diatessaron* (Leiden, 1970).

His decision to write *Vitae* of Saints Francis and Clare — the texts of which have been lost — indicates, as does his *Der Kerken Clage* (Complaint about the Church), his desire to see the institutional church reformed.[62]

Others who opposed the church as an institution also wanted to quit using the language of the official church. They were collectively labeled heretics. Compared to other regions, such people had little impact in the Low Countries. Moreover, there were some misconceptions about those who were identified as heretics. At the beginning of the twelfth century Tanchelm was accused of heresy by the canons of Utrecht, while in reality he was a champion of the Gregorian reforms.[63] A similar fate befell Lambert le Bègue, a preacher in Liège. Current scholarship assumes that Lambert wanted to protect Liège against error but was denounced because of his radicalism.[64]

A few heretics were burned at the stake in the twelfth century. Some of them were familiar with the Bible and did not give in during disputations. But the resistance of heretics was not always an expression of progressive opposition to the ecclesiastical status quo. Catharism, for instance, may well have begun precisely as resistance against changes in the church resulting from the church's increasing interaction with society, changes that the Cathars refused to come to terms with.[65]

Reports from the Low Countries concerning heresies in the thirteenth century are mainly from the south. These reports do not contain hard evidence, but show an increasing polarization between the official church and heretical movements. The initiative came mostly from the church. In the context of the Inquisition, ordered by Rome, the suppression of heresy in the Low Countries was taken up by Robert le Bougre, a sadist who allegedly employed black magic. We know little about Robert. Chroniclers mention him only in a negative light. He was not even appreciated in his own circles, and the picture that we do have of him misconstrues the beginning of the work of the Inquisition.[66] Whenever a closed society lacks the freedom of pluralism, Inquisition is inevitable: It is a cultural phenomenon, not just a religious phenomenon.

62. Cf. J. te Winkel, *Maerlant's werken beschouwd als spiegel van de dertiende eeuw* (1892; repr. Utrecht, 1979), 64, 66, 186.

63. See above, ch. VII, pp. 206f.

64. J. Goossens, *De kwestie Lambertus "li Beges" (†1177)* (Brussels, 1984).

65. Vauchez, *Spiritualité*, 120-24.

66. C. H. Haskins, *Robert le Bougre and the Beginnings of the Inquisition in Northern France* (Studies in Mediaeval Culture; Oxford, 1930).

At times the common people were so suspicious of renewal that the inquisitors had to prevent popular justice. No variations were tolerated from the normal experience of religion as we have been describing it in this chapter. For that reason many were suspicious of those who did not want to break with the world in the traditional way of pursuing a religious life. Such deviant people realized that they had to forsake the goods of this world, but they wanted to experience this process of detachment *in* the world, while seeking the monastic ideals and virtues.

The religious poverty movement, in which this desire became manifest, was closely linked to the development of urban life. Urbanization did not put an abrupt end to the predominantly agrarian character of society; in many areas it did not even have any major impact. But now there was besides the way of life of the agrarian population, with a religiosity largely determined by this manner of life, also an urban alternative, which would have to create new forms for urban religious life. These new forms were partly inspired by the poverty movement with its resistance to the social consequences of the monetary economy. The reaction embodied in that movement led to an ethic that was more adapted to the monetary economy and that also advanced the Christianization of the masses. The mendicant orders formed a third order — besides those of the clergy and the monks — of religious who remained in the world, that is, in the towns, as part of the laity. This third order developed from the poverty movement, that is, from already existing groups of penitents.[67]

The mendicant orders were officially recognized by the church after many in the poverty movement had fallen into heresy. The heretical wing of the poverty movement was largely a lay movement, and its leaders lacked the normal education of the clergy. Their training was usually unstructured. These leaders wanted to give the Bible to the people in the vernacular and wanted to preach as they saw fit. Recognition by the mendicant orders did not immediately take away all suspicion from this new form of religious life. The second order, founded by Clare of Assisi, a spiritual friend of Francis, was therefore restructured as a congregation of world-denying enclosed nuns, the Clares. This restructuring reflected the fear of the official church of the success of itinerant preachers, particularly among women.[68]

---

67. L. K. Little, *Religious Poverty and Profit Economy in Medieval Europe* (London, 1978), 197-217. See also ch. IX above.

68. G. Huyghe, "Histoire du clôture chez les religieuses," in *La séparation du monde* (Paris, 1961), 95-123.

Before the advent of the mendicant orders, women in the Low Countries had already been seeking religious renewal. Some became Beguines and thus placed themselves outside existing rules of orders. This caused misgivings, especially when the recognized convents were faced with an ever more stringent mode of religious life. As a result the Beguine communities unintentionally stood out even sharper. But the Beguine movement was too large to be accommodated within the Cistercian and Premonstratensian orders. The novices in those orders usually came from the higher social classes — young ladies with a dowry. The mendicant orders arrived a little too late on the scene in the Low Countries to provide spiritual guidance for the Beguines. Later, though, the Franciscans offered them protection. But that did not solve all their problems. Distrust for the Beguines remained.[69]

The church had no real understanding of the Beguines' loose organization. Consequently there was great fear that heretical ideas would find acceptance among them.[70] Nonetheless, the unique character of the Beguines in the Low Countries was semi-officially recognized by Rome. Some even survived the condemnation of "evil men and treacherous women popularly called Beguines and Beghards" issued by the Council of Vienne in 1311. This condemnation at first added to their difficulties, but after 1318 the Beguines gradually regained ecclesiastical recognition from the Low Country bishops.

The Beguines owed much to Jacques de Vitry, a canon in Liège, then from 1216 bishop of Akka, and eventually a cardinal (†1240). Shortly after 1213 he wrote the *Vita* of Marie of Oignies, whom he had known well. In an introductory letter he spoke of such women in general and characterized his treatise — his gathering of information about Marie — as the gathering of pieces after the miraculous feeding in the Gospels. He compared these women to the early Church Fathers about whom Jerome and Gregory the Great had written. While these fathers lived in the desert, these women, regardless of whether they were married or unmarried, had remained in the world. But they had freed themselves totally from the world. Jacques introduced them as mothers of the religious life and expected them to become of great significance for the church.

---

69. E. McDonnell, *The Beguines and Beghards in Medieval Culture* (New Brunswick, NJ, 1954).

70. F. Oakley, *The Western Church in the Later Middle Ages* (Ithaca and London, 1979), 92f.

But Jacques de Vitry failed to get more than an oral commitment from the pope with regard to the continued existence of the Beguine communities, in spite of his career in the church. All his life he remained impressed by the religiosity of these women, and many of his experiences in his contacts with them can be found in his *exempla*. Thomas of Cantimprè likewise did much to give publicity to the saints among these women.[71] But in spite of all this, with their eucharistic, Christ-oriented piety, they were tolerated rather than accepted by the official church, which nevertheless remained dear to them — possibly because it was more to them than just an institution.

Things were different for another religious movement, the flagellants, which came to the fore in the fourteenth century in a much more tumultuous manner. The flagellants should probably be seen as a phenomenon rather than as a religious movement; this "sect of the scourgers" had no overarching organization, even though they were most active in the more developed, urban regions of Western Europe. They constituted a reaction against social changes that because of the accompanying needs and injustices were more acute in urban regions. This reaction found extreme religious expression in the flagellants' public self-chastisement and penitential processions. An extensive report of these activities is found in the contemporary chronicle of Gillis Li Muisit, the abbot of St. Martin's in Tournai.[72] People of varying social status participated in these processions.

The radicalism of the flagellants differed from place to place, as did their part in the persecutions of Jews that erupted in many towns in 1349. Flagellant activity in the Low Countries was concentrated mainly in Flanders. It is unclear to what extent flagellant activity was stimulated by the Black Death, which was raging throughout most of Western Europe in the fourteenth century, and it remains debated how serious Flanders was affected by the plague. But even if the epidemic took only few victims there, it may well have caused a feeling of panic. Fear of the plague is, at any rate, evident in the graveyards that were laid out as a precautionary

71. B. Bolton, "*Vitae Matrum:* A Further Aspect of the *Frauenfrage,*" in Baker, *Medieval Women,* 253-73. For the text of Jacques de Vitry's introductory letter, cf. *Acta Sanctorum* 25, 23 June, IV, 547-49. For the supplement to this *Life* by Thomas de Cantimpré, cf. ibid. IV, 666-76.

72. *Chronicon,* ed. J. J. de Smet, *Corpus Chronicorum Flandriae* II (Brussels, 1877), 3-30.

measure.[73] A relationship between the flagellant movement and the proclamation of a holy year is also possible, but has not been proven. The flagellants viewed the calamities and distresses of their day as divine punishments. They sought through their penitential processions and their self-chastisements to entreat God to alter his plan to destroy the world. In this they claimed support from the intercession of Mary. And in their rites of penance they felt a union with the sufferings of Christ. Indeed, their processions were arranged to last exactly thirty-three and a half days.

The flagellants were extremely critical of the way in which religion was usually experienced. Most of this criticism was directed against the clergy. The clergy paid insufficient attention, the flagellants said, to proper Sunday observance and to the rules of fasting. They also fell short in the care of souls. These reproaches of the clergy were usually justified, but were at times accompanied by violence against priests, though not in Flanders. There the flagellants usually showed moderation, and some Flemish priests may have joined the movement, which would have facilitated the custom within the movement of confessing sins to each other and of giving absolution to one another.

The phenomenon of the flagellants was not revolutionary in all respects. Self-chastisement had been customary in the eremitical orders since the eleventh century. And others before the flagellants had appealed to the letter said to have been written in heaven by Christ and deposited on his tomb in Jerusalem. The version of this letter appealed to by the flagellants, which dated from 1349, has not been preserved. But other versions were circulated as early as 1260, and there were precursors from the sixth century.[74]

As was said above, the flagellants constituted a phenomenon rather than a movement. Their activity was too short-lived to become a movement. It ended soon when their activities were forbidden by Pope Clement VI, after they had organized a procession to Avignon. Participants in such penitential processions did not form any communities outside the church. Scourging took place during later penitential processions, but the flagellant phenomenon as we have described it was over.

The emergence of the flagellants has been explained in terms of

73. W. P. Blockmans, "The Social and Economic Effects of the Plague in the Low Countries," *Revue Belge de Philology et d'Histoire* 98 (1980), 833-63.

74. H. Delehaye, "Note sur la légende de la lettre du Christ, tombée du Ciel," in *Mélanges d'hagiographie grecque et latine* (Brussels, 1966), 150-78.

resistance of the oppressed lower classes against the church and as a manifestation of tumultuous eschatological expectations, which sup- posedly played a major role in the thought patterns of the medieval world. These expectations were focused on a thousand-year period of divine rule to be established on earth at the end of time.[75] But one analysis of the activities of the flagellants, which has served as an important source for our discussion here, concluded that the flagellant phenomenon cannot be satisfactorily explained either from the supposed millenarian context or as a reaction against the feudal church, while an explanation that combines both elements remains far too general. The two points of departure are perhaps too categorical to be combined in an interpretation of this phe- nomenon. Social and religious aspects are, here again, so inextricably related that it becomes impossible to explain the flagellants by employing these two points of departure as categories for the fourteenth century. Moreover, millenarianism was no more than marginal in the thinking of the time, so no definite validity can be attributed to it. This is also suggested by the letter from heaven, which with respect to eschatological expectations pointed to something other than this-worldly salvation. The letter was probably written in Latin, but it had a great appeal particularly for the truly illiterate.

᪣   ᪣

YET ANOTHER fourteenth-century threat to the practice of the religious life among the faithful was necromancy. In 1375, on the eve of an episcopal synod, Arnold of Hoorn, the bishop of Utrecht, issued four decrees. Three of them dealt with abuses that were apparently quite common, considering the shortness of the decrees and their moderate tone. These practices were usury, the wearing of worldly attire by members of the clergy, and cohab- itation of members of the clergy with concubines. But the first decree differs from the other three in scope and tone. It deals with necromancy, which was apparently a new problem. It has been remarked that this decree gives the impression

> that the whole diocese was full of superstitious and agnostic sectarians who were involved in all sorts of magic and sorcery. . . . The first signs of an obsession with witches appear here already, and the bishop is

75. N. Cohn, *The Pursuit of the Millennium* (rev. ed.; Oxford, 1970), 124-48.

ready to take measures. The clergy are to admonish those who are guilty of these practices, and the perpetrators are to stop these evils and do sufficient penance. If these injunctions are not followed, the cleric in question will face suspension and the lay members involved will be punished with excommunication. . . .[76]

The biography of Gerhard Groote by Dier van der Muiden and Thomas à Kempis sheds some light on this decree.[77] As a canon Gerhard lived in Deventer. There he became sick and wanted to receive communion. The priest of the Bergkerk was unwilling to grant this request until Gerhard had burned his books of magic, even though he was assured that Gerhard himself did not practice magic. At first Gerhard refused to comply, but when he had looked at his urine and had concluded that he was near death, he changed his mind, had the books burned on the Deventer Green, and received communion. He was subsequently fully restored and was a changed man.

The supposition that the medieval persecution of witches had begun by this time cannot be supported on the basis of this story about Gerhard Groote. Bishop Arnold's decree tells us that even members of the clergy were involved in necromancy. It would seem that this was the case with Groote, in spite of his biographers' assurances that he had not stooped to the frivolity of magic. But for Groote this was not a frivolous matter, nor was it for others who were involved in magic.

The bishop opposed magical practices, "since they mislead in a crafty way the simple Catholics, who are part of the working class (in-sudantes et simplices), drawing them away from the Catholic faith, with the result that most of them retain only a superficial faith and seem to deviate to the course of the heathen, or of the unbelievers."[78] The decree was not directed just against the superstition of the common people, but also against the natural sciences, in which necromancy played an important role. Naturally the bishop was alarmed by this faddish intellectualism of a literate elite — still consisting mainly of men who had been educated for the clergy — that would further incite the superstition already present among the common people, whose religion often lacked the desired fervor.

---

76. Post, *Kerkgeschiedenis,* 269.

77. R. Dier, "Scriptum de magistro Gherardo Grote," in G. Dumbar, *Analecta, seu vetera aliquot scripta inedita* I (Deventer, 1719), 2f.; Thomas à Kempis, *Vita Gerardi Magni,* in *Thomae Hemerken a Kempis opera omnia,* ed. M. J. Pohl (Freiburg, 1922) VII, 68f.

78. S. Muller, "Mandementen van bisschop Aernt van Hoern tot handhaving der kerkelijke tucht," *Archief voor de geschiedenis van het aartsbisdom Utrecht* 17 (1889), 128.

R. R. Post has emphasized this aspect in his *Kerkgeschiedenis van Nederland in de Middeleeuwen*. He points out that if Gerhard Groote meddled in necromancy, many others must have been doing the same. He also remarks that elsewhere black magic and astrology in particular were practiced with an almost scientific air, "even by prominent persons, of whom one would not expect it."[79] Nevertheless, Post misses the point implied in the reference in Groote's biography, even though he praises them for mentioning such a delicate thing in their essentially hagiographic work. The story of Groote's renunciation of necromancy constitutes the core of his conversion story. He thus renounced science as it existed in those days and as he himself had practiced it, because it endangered the true experience of religion. This threat could only be exposed unequivocally by speaking of its most objectionable feature, which was necromancy.

Here we also find the origin of the Devotio Moderna, a movement which has elicited strongly diverse interpretations. The relationship of this movement to Renaissance humanism and the Reformation has been adequately dealt with[80] and need not be addressed here. But we may well ask what motivated Gerhard Groote to give up his prebends and to withdraw for three years into the Carthusian monastery of Monnikshuizen near Arnhem. These three years are usually viewed as a period of uncertainty about what to do next. In this connection reference is made to Groote's contacts with Jan van Ruysbroeck in Groenendaal. Groote hesitated, perhaps, between a contemplative life and apostolic activity before deciding for the latter. But in his conversion he had already chosen to return to the old pattern of the church and of religious life that he had given up as a scientist. In Monnikshuizen he rediscovered the traditional theology in the library of the monastery. Subsequently he spent a fortune to acquire such theological works for his own library.

His relationship with Groenendaal was of a different sort. He admired the mystical thought of van Ruysbroeck, but had reservations about his use of language and his methodology. Here the differences between the two men stand out. Although Groote had lived with the Carthusians, he had not become primarily interested in mystical theology,

---

79. Post, *Kerkgeschiedenis* I, 272.

80. Post, *Modern Devotion;* A. Hyma, *The Brethren of the Common Life* (Grand Rapids, 1950). On the role of Gerhard de Groote in this reform movement, cf. G. Epiney-Burgard, *Gérard Grote et les débuts de la Dévotion moderne* (Wiesbaden, 1970). Cf. also the report of the congress commemorating the sixth centenary of the death of de Groote: *Geert Grote en Moderne Devotie,* ed. J. Andriessen, et al. (Antwerp and Nijmegen, 1985).

which had become marginal in theological discourse since the development of Scholasticism. Mystical theology did not operate with scholastic argumentation. It had, rather, survived and developed outside the scholarly milieu. In the Low Countries this had taken place mostly in the vernacular, and van Ruysbroeck had aligned himself with this recent tradition. Groote followed a different way. He had reservations regarding the work of van Ruysbroeck, among other reasons, because van Ruysbroeck used the vernacular. Groote did make Latin translations of three of van Ruysbroeck's writings, though he made corrections to the text, and he did exhort his friends in Groenendaal to translate their own works into Latin. But their writings needed to be "improved" before they were to reach a wider public. For those who knew no Latin Groote translated the office of Mary into the vernacular.

This apparent contradiction in Groote is a plain indication of his intention to set clearly defined boundaries for religious texts. His followers soon acquired a major share as copyists in the distribution of religious texts and treatises. It was only natural to want to know how far they could go in translating vernacular texts, and they discussed this matter more than once. Evidence of this is probably seen in *De libris Teutonalibus et de Precibus vernaculis* (About Books in Dutch and Prayers in the Vernacular) by Gerard Zerbold van Zutphen (†1398).[81]

Around 1380 Zerbold came to Deventer to attend the chapter school. There he came into contact with the Devotio Moderna. He joined the movement shortly before or just after the death of Groote. According to his later biographers Zerbold distinguished himself within the movement by his ambition for study and scholarship. In any case, he was one of the few brethren who eventually became priests. He loved books and became the librarian of the Florenshuis. It is therefore hardly surprising that he wanted to discuss the extent to which the vernacular could be used. In his treatise he defended restrictions that would give more scope to the vernacular than others were prepared to allow. This opposing view seems to have been shared by most of the brethren, considering the few books in the vernacular that could be found in their libraries.

The position taken by Zerbold in this treatise clearly agrees with Groote's actual practice. Groote stimulated the use of the vernacular for religious texts as such, while rejecting it for treatises that were more difficult

---

81. A. Hyma, "The 'De libris Teutonicalibus' by Gerard Zerbolt of Zutphen," *Nederlands Archief voor Kerkgeschiedenis* n.s. 17 (1924), 42-70.

to understand. Possibly Zerbold showed greater tolerance for the use of the vernacular. He pleaded for a Bible in the vernacular that would be made accessible to all. This was, in fact, the burden of the major part of his treatise, and he supports it with many arguments, some of them rather farfetched, though others are based on reality. He remarks, for instance, that the lay people have access to all kinds of worldly and evil books and wonders why they should be prevented from reading the Holy Scriptures, which kindle a love for God instead of a love for the world.

Zerbold believed that sophisticated books about such topics as the essence of the Godhead, the Trinity, predestination, and divine providence were unsuitable for the laity and for distribution in the vernacular. He regarded study of such subjects by lay people as meaningless. Moreover, it would put them at risk of falling into heresy. Neither were lay people to read purely scholarly books about articles of faith that they were simply supposed to know. He maintained the same reservation with regard to books with unfortunate expressions and deviations from the teachings of the saints. He mentioned in particular the books of the mystic Meister Eckhart. Zerbold also frowned on lay people who would read such works. Their knowledge of new and strange words could easily lead them to behave in a superior way and with disrespect for others. For that reason he agreed that such books ought to be condemned and burned. On this point his position probably closely resembled that of Groote.

Zerbold's view is clear evidence of the fact that Groote's Devotio Moderna was far from a revolutionary reform. But in evaluating Groote's return to the old ways, it should be remembered that reform and renewal were seen as a return to an ideal from which people had strayed. Groote opted for apostolic activity rather than for a contemplative life, and this choice was not without deeper meaning and gave his activities as a reformer a conservative character. His work was, in a sense, a prelude to the observantism of the fifteenth century, when many orders sought reformation through strict obedience to the traditional precepts, which had been neglected mostly for secondary reasons.[82]

But even though he did not teach anything new, Groote had the ability to make people listen to him, and his criticism of many aspects of church life and of the manner of life of many of the clergy made it inevitable that he — as a deacon — would be prohibited from further

82. Cf. H. Zschoch, *Klosterreform und monastische Spiritualität im 15. Jahrhundert* (Tübingen, 1988).

preaching. That occurred in 1383, a year before he died. His ventures with regard to the communities he established for his followers were more revolutionary. He did not incorporate these communities into any existing orders, as canon law required. In this respect he seems to have taken as his ideal the early church, in which religious orders did not yet have their own clearly defined domain. On this point he was unwilling to make concessions, but soon after his death his followers abandoned this position.

The question arises, of course, as to what Groote found objectionable in the existing orders. Perhaps he wanted to keep his options open for developments that he could not yet foresee. Most likely he did not intend to establish an institution for his followers. Some have hinted at a rivalry between him and the mendicant orders and have even suggested that there was a specific dispute between them. But this sort of dispute came up only later. It occurred for the first time in the fifteenth century as a result of some disagreements between the houses of the brethren and the monasteries of the mendicant orders. But later, in the nineteenth century, when Groote was depicted primarily as a precursor of the Reformation, it was suggested that this conflict had already begun during Groote's lifetime.

Another reason that Groote was unwilling to accept an existing rule was supposedly his own desire for reform. He wanted to avoid, it is said, any link between the life of his followers and the religious orders, which were in decline. But Groote was much more of a traditionalist than has often been thought, while religious life was not really deteriorating in the late Middle Ages. Why should we so easily speak of decline when the church was increasingly becoming the domain of the common people and was less exclusive than before, when it was focused on the Christianization of the nobility?

It remains impossible to explain Groote's attitude. Perhaps the matter should be placed in another context. Perhaps, that is, more attention than before should be paid to a particular aspect of religious life of the time in the Low Countries: the bilingualism of the church. In our discussion above we have mentioned this aspect only in a very general way. It is an area that has remained largely untouched by scholars. In the first phase of the period under discussion in this chapter bilingualism did not present major problems for religious life. The "illiterate" could neither read nor write, but they did not see this as a problem. They preferred to memorize what they had heard, and for this they were well trained. Latin was the written language, and writing was therefore something sacral, reserved for the mysteries of worship. Preaching was oral and for the literate approximated a translation, though it was not regarded by the illiterate as a derivative of what was written.

Only when the Low Countries were also affected by the slow process in which the written word gained ascendancy over what had been committed to memory did a new category of "illiterates" come into being, that of people who could read and write, but only in the vernacular.[83] This group wanted texts in the vernacular, particularly translations of the Bible, to enable a deeper experience of their religion. In the Low Countries these people had to wait considerably longer for such translations than, for example, in France. There rhymed Bibles were produced at an earlier date and in greater variety. And in France the rule of St. Benedict was translated a century earlier than in the Low Countries.

The need for a translation of St. Benedict's rule must have been felt long before 1373, in particular in the many convents of the Cistercian nuns, where it had been adopted. Most of the nuns knew too little Latin to understand the rule without translation. But the rule itself contains a stipulation that each day a passage from the rule was to be read to the community. It is remarkable that the *Vitae* of Marie of Oignies and other religious women, who themselves related their mystical experiences in the vernacular, were written in Latin, and, significantly enough, by authors who knew them intimately. Only the *Vita* of St. Lutgard was subsequently translated. For those who were conversant with Latin, translating into Middle Dutch must have been more difficult than into Old French, since the difference from Latin was greater. Even the clergy, who were most likely to perform this task, were often insufficiently educated for it. And it remains remarkable that in the Low Countries translation of religious texts from Latin only began in the fifteenth century. This was true even of sermon *exempla,* which were considered the most effective means of teaching the faith to the common people and which were highly appreciated by them. In this respect Groote and Zerbold belonged to the avant garde.

The role of educated lay people must also be mentioned in this discussion of the written use of the vernacular to foster religious life. In this connection we already referred to van Maerlant, and noted that the clergy did not fully appreciate his endeavors. He himself mentioned a

83. Cf. M. T. Clanchy, *From Memory to Written Record: England 1066-1307* (London, 1977).

conflict between clergy and laity. Half a century later, between 1325 and 1333, Jan van Boendale, a ship's clerk from Antwerp, wrote his *Der Leken Spieghel* (The Mirror of the Laity).[84] Among other things he dealt in this work with topics that a lay person was apparently supposed to know about: God, heaven, hell, purgatory, creation, the life of Christ, and everyday morality. He did not see the same contrast between clergy and laity as van Maerlant, but preferred the ordinary parish priests over members of the mendicant orders, even though the priests were usually no richer than mendicant monks. Other authors followed suit, such as Jan de Weert of Ypres, who based his *Spieghel van Sonden* (Mirror of Sins) on a Latin original.[85] But not all these authors belonged to the laity.

It must be said once more: We are dealing here with a topic that needs to be explored further, particularly with respect to the role of the clergy in the transition to the use of the vernacular for religious purposes — a change that was to remain limited, considering the continuing importance of Latin in the church. And what in particular was the contribution of the mendicant orders, which — as is usually assumed — intended to close the gap between the urban population and the church? That we possess hardly any mendicant sermon material from the fourteenth century does not simplify our investigations. But more work needs to be done. For we cannot hope to give a clear and accurate picture of the religious life of the time — including that of dissenting groups — as long as we know so little about the shift in the bilingualism of the church during the fourteenth century.

84. *Jan Boendale: Der Lekenspieghel, leerdicht van den jare 1330*, ed. M. de Vries (4 vols.; Leiden, 1844-48).

85. J. H. Jacobs, ed., *Jan de Weert's Nieuwe Doctrinael of Spieghel van Sonden* (The Hague, 1921).

Appendix: Reason in the Middle Ages[1]

❧   ❧

Alexander Murray, *Reason and Society in the Middle Ages* (Oxford: Clarendon, 1978; paperback ed., 1985).

IN REVIEWING this substantial work, a distinction must be made between
the arguments developed by the author in the numerous chapters with
historical expositions, and the intention of the book as a whole. Let us
begin with a survey of his historical expositions, which he divides into
four main sections. His main aim is to clarify how human reason gradually
prevailed in economic, mathematical, and intellectual activities. The
author discusses at length how in all these domains human reason acquired
a predominant place.

In the first part he deals in particular with the economy of the early
Middle Ages. He gives special emphasis to the emergence of the use of
money in the last phase of the Carolingian era. The rise of a monetary
economy brought a change in the mentality of society as a whole. It
stimulated greed, apparent in robberies and in the practice of simony (the
traffic in spiritual offices), and in the increasing number of moral complaints about stinginess. Another result of the growing circulation of

1. This book review appeared originally in *Tijdschrift voor Geschiedenis* 91 (1980),
605-8.

money was the deterioration in the relationship between Jews and Christians, mainly because the Jews were the most prominent representatives of this new wealth.

Yet another aspect of this development was increasing ambition to rise on the social ladder. This has usually been related to the greater social mobility brought by circulation of money. In this context the author also refers to the philosophy widely held at the time — and used by the establishment in its opposition to change — that society was, and should remain, divided into three classes. In this complexity of developments human reason must have played a major role, since these changes were intimately connected with the increasing power of humankind over nature, which surrounds and threatens people, while interpersonal relationships were also to a greater degree shaped by reason. In support of this thesis the author points to an increasingly rationalistic approach in government and military expeditions, while emphasizing the growing awareness of the usefulness of knowledge.

In the second part of his work the author deals in more detail with the rise of arithmetic and points to the new mentality that accompanied this development. New tools, the abacus and Arabic numerals, made possible faster calculations, which until then had been impeded by Roman numerals. The change in mentality that became manifest in this new arithmetic expressed itself, according to Murray, in the numerical precision seen, for example, in the *Domesdaybook,* a fiscal land registry of England commissioned by William the Conqueror in 1087, though at the same time many events continued to be noted with little or no chronological exactness and people continued to make highly exaggerated estimates. The rise of this new arithmetic also, of course, influenced the increase in trade.

The author supports his survey of all these trends with a variety and abundance of data. He uses manuscripts, and particularly illuminations; he gives a remarkable amount of attention to sermon literature, which gives evidence of changes in mentality; he refers repeatedly to hagiographic texts, to works dealing with chronology, and to what was said about the *quadrivium,* the arithmetic part of the *artes liberales.* Murray also points to the accounts of chroniclers, which tended to become more exact in quantitative statements. In brief, his arguments rest on a broad range of source materials. He does not, however, always refer to the primary sources. As a result the reader is left wondering whether many things that Murray appears to know only from secondary sources always had the same meanings in their original contexts.

The third part deals with the relationship between reason and learning as it developed at the cathedral schools and subsequently at the universities. The field of inquiry is very broad and more work was done here before Murray than in the area of arithmetic. As a result he argues at an even greater remove from the sources. By way of introduction he refers to the influence of the Gregorian reform movement on learning in the church. Not all of the movement's consequences were foreseen. Scholasticism originated within the church, but many chose an education in the church for non-ecclesiastical careers, often with an eye to serving a secular prince. The sources for this type of information are rather unique: satirical writings, which, however, also denounce the church careers that these studies led to.

Next the author deals with the social status of learning. Teachers often made a very good living. But peasants had a strong antipathy against learning. This aversion was partly the reason for the anticlericalism of the time. At the same time there was a widespread belief that philosophers came to a bad end. Only in some regions did intellectuals form a distinct and self-conscious class, particularly in cities such as Paris and Florence. Nonetheless, they were responsible for far-reaching social change.

This change began with an assault on the authority of the clergy and the nobility in high medieval society. The authority of the clergy was undermined by the rise of intellectual heresies, and philosophers saw their influence increased, or at least they claimed expertise in religious matters. This process was particularly visible in the shift of meaning in the term *clericus* from "clerk" to "scholar." The intellectuals were also involved in a continuous campaign against the nobility, although this began a little later. In this connection Murray refers, for instance, to *Le Roman de la Rose* by Jean de Meung and to the fourth book of Dante's *Convivio*. But the intellectuals' assault was not limited to theoretical criticism; in the process they also acquired social advantages of their own, that is, their own privileges granted at the universities. They also criticized the state of the church, and here the Goliardic poetry (the poetry of the wandering scholars) is the earliest known example. The later and more radical condemnation by the Franciscans directed itself, under the influence of the universities, against the lack of education of many of the clergy, while the attack of Marsilius of Padua on the social significance of the papacy preceded the conciliar movement, which opposed the authority of the pope in the church.

The fourth and last part of Murray's book, entitled *Nobility and*

Religion, supplements his arguments in a rather peculiar way. He wants to show how the twin intellectual currents, the mathematical and the literary, existed side by side. On the basis of considerable research he concludes that in those days a religious minority, which was able to detach itself from its own social origins, succeeded in realizing a classless society — a pattern we tend to regard in our time as resulting from the increasing rationality of our European society. This conclusion is presented to the reader after an extensive analysis of medieval nobility.

Murray refers to a 1909 study by Aloys Schulte,[2] which argues that noble birth was a necessary qualification for high church office. Murray points out that the nobility provided a remarkable majority of all the candidates for leading functions in the ecclesiastical hierarchy and monastic institutions. In his chapter entitled "Were Nobles Better Christians?" he also observes, on the basis of the *Vitae* of the saints and genealogical studies by others, that most medieval saints were of noble birth and that a greater percentage of religious celibates were from the nobility than from the other social classes. He does, of course, wonder about a possible influence of religion on the noble condition. Members of the nobility were subject to temptations of social status, wealth, and power. Against this, or in combination with this, an ethic of magnanimity was developed. This helped to bring many noble youths to a spiritual awakening, a *conversio,* which led them to renounce worldly careers and marriage. Murray further discusses the social determinants of such conversions. Preference for a celibate life was prompted both by the unattainable ideal of love and by the ease of arranging sexual encounters, which caused in some a loathing of sex. But the military life also, with its danger of death and its narrow escapes, led many to leave the world. Here Murray's argument seems a little strained, but once again he supports his thesis with a wealth of data gathered from the sources.

This fourth part, in which Murray's study goes off on a surprising tangent, ends with a chapter about the saint as a classless person. This ties in with the conclusion already referred to above that the ideal of a classless society has roots in our European past that are not altogether rationalistic. This leads the author to the real intention of his book. He discusses this intention already in his introduction, which I have thus far not mentioned. Murray believes that European history was characterized in its spiritual

---

2. *Der Adel und die deutsche Kirche: Studien zur Sozial-, Rechts- und Kirchengeschichte* (Darmstadt, 1909, 1922; repr. Stuttgart, 1958).

development by a constant tension between its Hebrew and Greek roots, which formed the basis, respectively, for religious and rationalistic development. These two currents continued to exist side by side in the medieval world. In later evaluations of the period this fact was obscured by the dominant role of medieval theology, which obstructed the progress of other scientific disciplines in a way comparable to the neglect of the humanities that is not uncommon in our time. This coexistence of two currents in the Middle Ages inspired Murray to write this study, in which his intention is to discuss the often neglected rationalistic currents of that time. He points out how today many too easily suppose that this tension between a Hebrew and a Greek heritage did not exist in the Middle Ages and that rationalism is to be regarded as something unique to our time.

In his treatment of these rationalistic currents in the Middle Ages, Murray uses the concept of *ratio* in different ways. He uses it first in the less strict and more ethical sense of "reasonable." As such, he suggests, we find *ratio* in the many compromises that even in the Middle Ages existed between opposing currents and powers. In that time we also find the concept of *ratio* used with a narrower meaning: argumentation based on reason. But it was not often used in this way, since only one philosophical school, known as Averroism, taught that *ratio* is the most suitable avenue to the truth. Finally, *ratio* was used in a sense that reflects the conviction that nature has its fixed laws, which prevailed in spite of all the faith in miracles that also existed. Without this belief in natural laws cathedrals could not have been built, and astronomy would have remained impossible without mathematical knowledge. Murray's concept of *ratio* in the Middle Ages does, however, to some extent lack this last meaning, in which *ratio* also included calculating and reasoning.

The preoccupation that led Murray to write this rather ambitious study is already present in an article entitled "Piety and Impiety in Thirteenth-Century Italy," which he wrote in 1972.[3] Taking as his point of departure the sermon literature, which he interpreted with great discernment, he argued in this article that there was not only much sinfulness among the medieval Italian urban population, but also much unbelief: Many doubted or even denied such articles of faith as the presence of Christ in the Eucharist, Christ's bodily resurrection, and a personal life after death. This led Murray even then to the conclusion, which he

3. G. J. Cuming and D. Baker, ed., *Popular Belief and Practice* (Studies in Church History 8; Oxford, 1972), 83-106.

emphasizes in the introduction of *Reason and Society in the Middle Ages*, that the characterization of the Middle Ages as an "age of faith" is incorrect. The idea that everything taught by the church was universally accepted is, according to Murray, a fabrication of the Enlightenment, according to which faith was not a virtue but an original sin, from which one could escape through rationalism. Opponents of the Enlightenment often accepted this fabrication just as eagerly as its proponents and also spoke of the Middle Ages as an "age of faith," to which all should return without delay.

From what has been said so far it will have become clear that, with respect to Murray's book, a distinction should indeed be made between his argument in the various chapters and what he, on that basis, concludes concerning the coexistence of faith and reason. I will limit myself to saying that Murray also intended his book for nonmedievalists who, either as supporters or contestants of the Enlightenment, still hold the wrong idea about the Middle Ages that his book combats.

Concerning Murray's views of the rationalistic currents in the Middle Ages and the development of a classless society, some details of his interpretation might be open to criticism, while other points could be further strengthened by additional material from the sources. But criticizing such a substantial study in every detail is nearly impossible. The author set himself a formidable task, which he has completed in a deserving way, even though his argumentation is not always convincing, as, for instance, in his discussion of the increase in moral complaints against avarice. In general the book displays critical and careful reasoning, but it suffers at times from an overload of facts and too detached a treatment of the source material. As a result it remains rough edged. Those who acquaint themselves with some of Murray's earlier monographs will perhaps regret that he did not publish a few more such studies in preparation for this book. His otherwise significant book would thereby have lost in quantity but gained in quality.

For Further Reading

⽊   ⽊

Auerbach, E. *Literary Language and Its Public in Late Latin Antiquity and in the Middle Ages.* Princeton, 1965.

Bachrach, B. S. *Early Medieval Jewish Policy in Western Europe.* Minneapolis, 1977.

Baldwin, J. W. *Masters, Princes and Merchants: The Social Views of Peter the Chanter and His Circle.* 2 vols. Princeton, 1969.

Barber, M. *The Two Cities: Medieval Europe 1050-1320.* London and New York, 1992.

Barber, R. *The Penguin Guide to Medieval Europe.* London, 1984.

Bartlett, R. *Trial by Fire and Water: The Medieval Judicial Ordeal.* Oxford, 1986.

Benson, R. L., and Constable, G., ed. *Renaissance and Renewal in the Twelfth Century.* 1982; repr. Oxford, 1985.

Bloch, M. *The Royal Touch: Sacred Monarchy and Scrofula in England and France.* London, 1973.

Bogin, M. *The Women Troubadors.* New York, 1976.

Boswell, J. *Christianity, Social Tolerance, and Homosexuality: Gay People in Western Europe from the Beginning of the Christian Era to the Fourteenth Century.* Chicago, 1980.

Bouchard, C. B. *Sword, Miter, and Cloister: Nobility and the Church in Burgundy, 980-1198.* Ithaca, 1987.

Boyle, L. *Pastoral Care, Clerical Education and Canon Law, 1200-1400.* London and New York, 1981.

Brentano, R. *Rome before Avignon: A Social History of Thirteenth-Century Rome*. New York and London, 1974.

Brett, E. T. *Humbart of Romans: His Life and Views of Thirteenth-Century Society*. Toronto, 1984.

Breukelaar, A. H. B. *Historiography and Episcopal Authority in Sixth-Century Gaul: The Histories of Gregory of Tours in Their Historical Context*. Amsterdam, 1991.

Brooke, C. N. L. *The Medieval Idea of Marriage,* Oxford, 1980.

———. The Monastic World, *1000-1300*. London, 1974.

Brooke, R. B. *The Coming of the Friars*. London, 1975.

———. *Early Franciscan Government: Elias to Bonaventure*. Cambridge, 1959.

———, and Brooke, C. N. L. *Popular Religion in the Middle Ages: Western Europe 1000-1300*. London, 1984.

Brown, P. *The Cult of the Saints: Its Rise and Function in Latin Christianity*. Chicago, 1980.

Brundage, J. A. *Law, Sex and Christian Society in Medieval Europe*. Chicago, 1987.

Bynum, C. W. *Holy Feast and Holy Fast: The Religious Significance of Food to Medieval Women*. Berkeley, 1987.

Cantor, Norman F. *Inventing the Middle Ages: The Lives, Works, and Ideas of the Great Medievalists of the Twentieth Century*. New York, 1991.

Chazan, R. *Daggers of Faith: Thirteenth-Century Christian Missionizing and Jewish Response*. Berkeley, 1989.

———. *European Jewry and the First Crusade*. Berkeley, 1987.

———. *Medieval Jewry in Northern France*. Ann Arbor, 1973.

Chenu, M.-D. *Nature, Man and Society in the Twelfth Century*. Chicago, 1968.

Chibnall, M. *The World of Orderic Vitalis*. Oxford, 1984.

Clanchy, M. T. *From Memory to Written Record: England 1066-1307*. London, 1977.

Clark, E., and Richardson, H., ed. *Women and Religion: A Feminist Sourcebook of Christian Thought*. New York, 1977.

Cobban, A. B. *The Mediaeval Universities*. London, 1975.

Cohen, J. *The Friars and the Jews: The Evolution of Medieval Anti-Judaism*. Ithaca, 1982.

Cohn, N. *The Pursuit of the Millennium*. Rev. ed. Oxford, 1970.

Collett, B. *Italian Benedictine Scholars and the Reformation: The Congregation of Santa Giustine of Padua*. Oxford, 1985.

Constable, G. *Cluniac Studies*. London, 1980.

————. *Monks, Hermits and Crusaders in Medieval Europe*. London and Brookfield, Vt., 1988.

Cowdrey, H. E. J. *The Cluniacs and the Gregorian Reform*. Oxford, 1970.

Deane, H. A. *The Political and Social Ideas of St. Augustine*. New York, 1963.

De Nie, G. *Views of a Many-windowed Tower: Studies of Imagination in the Works of Gregory of Tours*. Amsterdam, 1987.

Dronke, P. *Women Writers of the Middle Ages: A Critical Study of Texts from Perpetua (†203) to Marguerite Porete (†1310)*. Cambridge, 1984.

Duby, G. *The Chivalrous Society*. Berkeley, 1978.

————. *The Early Growth of the European Economy: Warriors and Peasants from the Seventh to the Twelfth Century*. London and Ithaca, 1974.

————. *The Knight, the Lady and the Priest: The Making of Modern Marriage in Medieval France*. New York, 1983.

————. *Medieval Marriage: Two Models from Twelfth-Century France*. Baltimore, 1978.

Elliott, A. G. *Roads to Paradise: Reading the Lives of the Early Saints*. Hanover, N.H., 1987, and London, 1988.

Erdmann, C. *The Origin of the Idea of Crusade*. Princeton, 1977.

Erickson, C. *The Medieval Vision: Essays in History and Perception*. New York, 1976.

Falco, G. *The Holy Roman Republic: A Historical Profile of the Middle Ages*. Cranbury, N.J., 1965.

Finucane, R. C. *Miracles and Pilgrims: Popular Beliefs in Medieval England*. London and Totowa, N.J., 1977.

————. *Soldiers of the Faith: Crusaders and Moslems at War*. London, 1983, and New York, 1984.

Fowler, D. C. *The Bible in Middle English Literature*. Seattle, 1984.

Freed, J. B. *The Friars and the German Society in the Thirteenth Century*. Cambridge, Mass., 1977.

Gardiner, E., ed. *Visions of Heaven and Hell before Dante*. New York, 1989.

Geary, P. J. *Furta Sacra: Thefts of Relics in the Central Middle Ages*. 1978; repr. Princeton, 1990.

————, ed. *Readings in Medieval History*. Petersborough and New York, 1989 (1991).

Gellrich, J. M. *The Idea of the Book in the Middle Ages*. Ithaca, 1985.

Gies, F., and Gies, J. *Marriage and the Family in the Middle Ages*. Rev. ed. New York, 1989.

Gilson, E. H. *Heloise and Abelard.* 1951; repr. Ann Arbor, 1963.

Goffart, W. *The Narratives of Barbarian History (A.D. 550-800): Jordanes, Gregory of Tours, Bede, and Paul the Deacon.* Princeton, 1988.

Goodich, M. *Vita perfecta: The Ideal of Sainthood in the Thirteenth Century.* Stuttgart, 1982.

Goody, J. *The Development of the Family and Marriage in Europe.* Cambridge, 1983.

Grayzel, S. *The Church and the Jews in the XIIIth Century.* New York, 1966.

Green, V. H. H. *Medieval Civilization in Western Europe.* London, 1971.

Gurevich, A. *Medieval Popular Culture: Problems of Belief and Perception.* Cambridge, 1990.

Habig, M. A., ed. *Francis of Assisi: Writings and Early Biographies.* 4th ed. Chicago, 1983.

Hamilton, B. *The Medieval Inquisition.* London and New York, 1981.

——. *Religion in the Medieval West.* London, 1986.

Hanning, R. W. *The Visions of History in Early Britain: From Gildas to Geoffrey of Monmouth.* New York, 1966.

Haskins, C. H. *The Renaissance of the Twelfth Century.* 5th ed. Cambridge, Mass., 1971.

Head, T., and Landes, R., ed. *Essays on the Peace of God: The Church and the People in the Eleventh Century.* Waterloo, Ont., 1987.

——. *The Peace of God: Social Violence and Religious Response in France around the Year 1000.* Ithaca and London, 1992.

Heffernan, T. J. *Sacred Biography: Saints and Their Biographers in the Middle Ages.* Oxford, 1988.

——, ed. *The Popular Literature of Medieval England.* Knoxville, 1985.

Herlihy, D. *Medieval Households.* Cambridge, Mass., 1985.

Herrin, J. *The Formation of Christendom.* Princeton, 1986.

Hillgarth, J. N., ed. *Christianity and Paganism, 350-750: The Conversion of the West; Documents.* Rev. ed. Philadelphia, 1986.

Hinnebusch, W. A. *The History of the Dominican Order.* Vol. 1: *Origins and Growth to 1500.* Staten Island, 1966.

Housley, N. *The Avignon Papacy and the Crusades, 1305-1378.* Oxford, 1986.

Howard, D. R. *The Three Temptations: Medieval Man in Search of the World.* Princeton, 1966.

Hunt, N., ed. *Cluniac Monasticism in the Central Middle Ages.* Hamden, Conn., 1972.

Hyma, A. *The Brethren of the Common Life.* Grand Rapids, 1950.

Jerusalem Pilgrims before the Crusades. Tr. J. Wilkinson. Warminster, 1977.

Kedar, B. Z. *Crusade and Mission: European Approaches towards the Muslims.* Princeton, 1984.

Kemp, E. W. *Canonization and Authority in the Western Church.* 1948; repr. New York, 1980.

Kenny, A., ed. *Wyclif in His Time.* Oxford, 1986.

Kibre, P. *Scholarly Privileges in the Middle Ages: The Rights, Privileges and Immunities of Scholars and Universities at Bologna, Padua, Paris, and Oxford.* London, 1961, and Cambridge, Mass., 1962.

Kieckhefer, R. *Unquiet Souls: Fourteenth-Century Saints and Their Religious Milieu.* Chicago, 1984.

Knowles, D. *Christian Monasticism.* London, 1969.

————. *Historian and Character and Other Essays.* Cambridge, 1963.

Krautheimer, R. *Rome, Profile of a City.* Princeton, 1980.

Labarge, M. W. *Women in Medieval Life: A Small Sound of the Trumpet.* London, 1986.

Lambert, M. D. *Franciscan Poverty.* London, 1961.

————. *Medieval Heresy: Popular Movements from Bogomil to Hus.* New York and London, 1977.

Lampe, G. H. W. *The West from the Fathers to the Reformation.* Cambridge History of the Bible, vol. 2. Cambridge, 1969.

Langmuir, G. I. *History, Religion, and Antisemitism.* Berkeley, 1990.

Lawrence, C. H. *Medieval Monasticism.* London, 1984.

Leclercq, J. *The Love of Learning and the Desire of God: A Study of Monastic Culture.* 2nd ed. New York, 1977.

————. *Women and Saint Bernard of Clairvaux.* Kalamazoo, 1989.

Leff, G. *Heresy in the Later Middle Ages.* Manchester and New York, 1967.

Le Goff, J. *Time, Work and Culture in the Middle Ages.* Chicago, 1980.

Lerner, R. *The Heresy of the Free Spirit in the Later Middle Ages.* Berkeley, 1972.

Levison, W. *England and the Continent in the Eighth Century.* Oxford, 1946.

Lewis, C. S. *The Allegory of Love: A Study in Medieval Tradition.* 1938; repr. Oxford, 1958.

Leyser, H. *Hermits and the New Monasticism.* London and New York, 1984.

Leyser, K. J. *Rule and Conflict in an Early Medieval Society: Ottonian Saxony.* Bloomington, Ind., 1980.

Little, L. K. *Religious Poverty and the Profit Economy in Medieval Europe.* Ithaca, 1978, and London, 1979.

Llewellyn, P. *Rome in the Dark Ages.* London, 1971.

Loos, M. *Dualist Heresy in the Middle Ages.* Prague and Amsterdam, 1974.

Lynch, J. H. *Simoniacal Entry into Religious Life from 1000 to 1260.* Columbus, 1976.

Maccoby, H., ed. *Judaism on Trial: Jewish-Christian Disputations in the Middle Ages.* London and East Brunswick, N.J., 1981.

McDonnell, E. W. *The Beguines and Beghards in Medieval Culture, with Special Emphasis on the Belgian Scene.* 1954; repr. New York, 1969.

McFarlane, K. B. *Wycliffe and English Nonconformity.* 1952; repr. Harmondsworth, 1972.

McGinn, B. *Visions of the End: Apocalyptic Traditions in the Middle Ages.* New York, 1979.

———, and Meyendorff, J., ed. *Christian Spirituality: Origins to the Twelfth Century.* New York, 1985, and London, 1986.

McKitterick, R. *The Carolingians and the Written Word.* Cambridge, 1989.

McLeish, A., ed. *The Medieval Monastery.* Lakeville, Minn., 1988.

McNeill, J. F., and Gamer, H. M. *Medieval Handbooks of Penance: A Translation of the Principal Libri Penitentiales and Selections from Related Documents.* 1938; repr. New York, 1965.

Medieval Latin Lyrics. Tr. H. Waddell. 1952; repr. Harmondsworth, 1962.

Metzger, T., and Metzger, M. *Jewish Life in the Middle Ages: Illuminated Hebrew Manuscripts of the Thirteenth to the Sixteenth Centuries.* New York, 1982.

Milis, L. J. R. *Angelic Monks and Earthly Men: Monasticism and Its Meaning to Medieval Society.* Woodbridge, 1992.

Mladenovic, P. Z. *John Hus at the Council of Constance.* New York, 1966.

Mollat, M. *The Poor in the Middle Ages.* New Haven, 1990.

———, and Wolff, P. *The Popular Revolutions of the Late Middle Ages.* Oxford, 1968.

Moorman, J. *A History of the Franciscan Order: From Its Origins to the Year 1517.* Oxford, 1968.

Morris, C. *The Discovery of the Individual, 1050-1200.* London, 1972, and New York, 1973.

Morrisson, K. F. *Tradition and Authority in the Western Church, 300-1140.* Princeton, 1969.

Oakley, F. *The Western Church in the Later Middle Ages.* Ithaca, 1979.

Olst, G. R. *Literature and Pulpit in Medieval England.* Oxford, 1966.

Packard, S. R. *Twelfth Century Europe: An Interpretive Essay.* Amherst, 1973.

Pakter, W. *Medieval Canon Law and the Jews.* Ebelsbach, 1988.

Payer, P. J. *Sex and the Penitentials: The Development of a Sexual Code, 550-1150.* Toronto, 1984.

Pelikan, J. J. *The Growth of Medieval Theology (600-1300)*. Chicago, 1978.

Pullan, B. S. *Sources of the History of Medieval Europe from the Mid-Eighth to the Mid-Thirteenth Century*. Oxford and New York, 1966.

Purcell, M. *Papal Crusading Policy*. Leiden, 1975.

Queller, D. E. *The Fourth Crusade: The Conquest of Constantinople*. Philadelphia, 1977, and Leicester, 1978.

Reeves, M. *The Influence of Prophecy in the Later Middle Ages: A Study in Joachimism*. Oxford, 1969.

Reynolds, S. *Kingdoms and Communities in Western Europe, 900-1300*. Oxford, 1984.

Richards, J. *The Popes and the Papacy in the Early Middle Ages, 476-752*. London, 1979.

Riché, P. *Daily Life in the World of Charlemagne*. Philadelphia, 1978.

————. *Education and Culture in the Barbarian West: Sixth through Eighth Centuries*. Columbia, S.C., 1978.

Riley-Smith, L., and Riley-Smith, J. S. C. *The Crusades, Idea and Reality, 1095-1274*. London, 1981.

Robinson, I. S. *Authority and Resistance in the Investiture Contest: The Polemical Literature of the Late Eleventh Century*. Manchester and New York, 1978.

Rosenwein, B. H. *Rhinoceros Bound: Cluny in the Tenth Century*. Philadelphia, 1982.

————. *To Be the Neighbor of Saint Peter: The Social Meaning of Cluny's Property, 909-1049*. Ithaca, 1989.

Ross, J. B., and McLaughlin, M. M., ed. *The Portable Medieval Reader*. 1958; repr. New York, 1973.

Russell, F. H. *The Just War in the Middle Ages*. Cambridge, 1975.

Russell, J. B. *Dissent and Reform in the Early Middle Ages*. Berkeley, 1965.

————. *Lucifer: The Devil in the Middle Ages*. Ithaca, 1984.

Sheils, W. J., ed. *Monks, Hermits and the Ascetic Tradition*. Oxford, 1985.

Siberry, E. *Criticism of Crusading, 1095-1274*. Oxford, 1985.

Simonsohn, S. *The Apostolic See and the Jews*. 1/1: *Documents 492-1404*. Toronto, 1988.

Smalley, B. *Historians in the Middle Ages*. 1953; repr. New York, 1975.

————. *The Study of the Bible in the Middle Ages*. 1941; repr. Notre Dame, 1964.

Southern, R. W. *The Making of the Middle Ages*. 1953; repr. New Haven, 1973.

————. *Western Society and the Church in the Middle Ages*. Grand Rapids and Harmondsworth, 1970.

————. *Western Views on Islam in the Middle Ages.* Cambridge, Mass., 1962.

Stock, B. *The Implication of Literacy: Written Language and Models of Interpretation in the Eleventh and Twelfth Centuries.* Princeton, 1982.

Strayer, J. R. *On the Medieval Origins of the Modern State.* Princeton, 1970.

Stroll, M. *The Jewish Pope: Ideology and Politics in the Papal Schism of 1130.* Leiden, 1987.

Stuard, S. M. *Women in Medieval History and Historiography.* Philadelphia, 1987.

Sumption, J. *The Albigensian Crusade.* London, 1978.

————. *Pilgrimage: An Image of Mediaeval Religion.* London and Lotowa, NJ, 1975.

Swanson, R. N. *Universities, Academics and the Great Schism.* Cambridge, 1979.

Synan, E. A. *The Popes and the Jews in the Middle Ages.* New York, 1965.

Tellenbach, G. *Church, State, and Christian Society at the Time of the Investiture Contest.* 1959; repr. New York, 1970.

Thomson, J. A. F. *The Later Lollards, 1414-1520.* Oxford, 1965.

Throop, P. A. *Criticism of the Crusade.* Amsterdam, 1940.

Tierney, B. *Foundations of the Conciliar Theory: The Contribution of the Medieval Canonists from Gratian to the Great Schism.* 1955; repr. Cambridge, 1968.

Tuchman, B. W. *A Distant Mirror: The Calamitous Fourteenth Century.* New York, 1978.

Vodola, E. *Excommunication in the Middle Ages.* Berkeley, 1986.

Waddell, H. *The Wandering Scholars.* 7th ed. 1934; repr. Ann Arbor, 1990.

Wakefield, W. L., and Evans, A. P. *Heresies in the High Middle Ages.* New York, 1969.

Walsh, K., and Wood, D., ed. *The Bible in the Medieval World.* Oxford, 1985.

Warner, M. *Joan of Arc: The Image of Female Heroism.* New York, 1981.

Wemple, S. F. *Women in Frankish Society: Marriage and the Cloister, 500-900.* Philadelphia, 1982.

White, L., Jr. *Medieval Religion and Technology.* Berkeley, 1978.

White, S. D. *Custom, Kinship and Gifts to Saints: The "Laudatio Parentium" in Western France, 1050-1150.* Chapel Hill, 1988.

Wilkinson, J., Hill, J., and Ryan, W. F., ed. *Jerusalem Pilgrimage, 1099-1185.* London, 1988.

Wilks, M., ed. *The World of John of Salisbury.* Oxford, 1985.

Index of Names

Abelard, Peter, 59, 102-3, 147, 188, 217, 222, 225-45, 289
Adalbold of Utrecht (St.), 335
Adalhard of Corbie (St.), 114-15, 122
Adelbert (St.), 153, 337
Adhemar of Chabannes, 122
Adman (Adomnan) (St.), 96
Adrian IV, Pope, 171
Adso of Montier-en-Dèr, 67, 68, 98, 166
Agatha (St.), 340
Agobard (St.), 98, 286-87, 299
Albert of Louvain (St.), 337
Alcuin, 64, 90, 286, 290
Alexander II, Pope, 107, 205
Alexander III, Pope, 170, 171, 172, 262, 270
Alexander IV, Pope, 259
Alexis (St.), 27
Alexius I Comnenus, Byzantine emperor, 81, 85-86
Aleyda of Brabant, 293
Alfred (the Great), king of Wessex, 14, 15
Alice of Schaarbeek, 360

Alpertus of Metz, 300, 332
Altman (St.), 97, 100
Amandus (St.), 337
Ambrose of Massa (St.), 264
Anacletus II, 127, 287-88
Andrew of Fleury, 113-14
Anselm of Canterbury (St.), 101, 172
Anselm of Laon, 231
Anthony of Padua (St.), 174, 248, 263
Appelmans, Gheraert, 339
Appolonia (St.), 340
Aquinas, Thomas. See Thomas Aquinas
Aristotle, 36, 230
Arnold of Brescia, 238
Arnold of Cologne, 80
Arnold of Hoorn, 368-69
Arnold of Semgallen, 352
Athenaïs-Eudochia, Eastern Roman empress, 91
Augustine of Hippo (St.), 15, 16-17, 71, 87-88, 89, 97, 209-10, 225, 285-86, 311-12, 314
Aymard of Cluny, 169

Baldwin II, emperor of Constantinople, 94
Baldwin I (of Boulogne), king of Jerusalem, 84
Baldwin IX of Flanders, 328
Bartholomew (apostle), 3, 338
Beatrice of Nazareth, 45, 339, 360
Bede (the Venerable), 58, 97, 286
Benedict VIII, Pope, 169
Benedict of Aniane, 15, 132
Benedict of Nursia (St.), 15, 20, 22, 113-14, 157
Benedict Biscop (St.), 14
Benton, J. F., 228, 229
Benvenutus of Gubbio (St.), 264
Berengar of Tours, 242, 343
Bernard of Clairvaux (St.), 24, 44, 57, 62, 73, 100, 101, 103, 132, 137-50, 156, 157-58, 171-73, 181-97, 212, 213, 215, 217, 219-20, 221, 235, 236, 237, 239-42, 284, 288, 313, 337, 339, 360, 361
Bernard of Morlass (of Cluny), 102
Bernard of Tiron, 213, 214
Berno of Cluny, 169
Bernold of St. Blasius, 100
Bernulfus of Utrecht, 331, 335
Bertrada of Montfort, 53
Blumenkranz, Bernhard, 285-86
Boendale, Jan van, 375
Bonaventure (St.), 258-59, 265
Boniface (St.), 17, 337
Boniface V, Pope, 16
Boniface VIII, Pope, 38, 39, 329-30, 352
Bonizo of Sutri, 324
Bridget of Sweden (St.), 176
Bruno of Cologne (St.), 23, 157, 268
Burchard of Worms, 165
Busch, Johannes, 345

Caesarius of Heisterbach, 101, 345
Callistus (Calixtus) II, Pope, 79, 169
Cantelupe, Thomas de (St.), 175
Canute (the Great), king of England, 3

Cassiodorus, Flavius Magnus Aurelius, 58, 65
Catherine of Siena (St.), 178
Celestine V, Pope, 37
Celsus of Trier, 166
Charlemagne, Holy Roman emperor, 15, 16, 17, 64, 68, 91, 123, 160, 161, 162, 342
Charles II (the Bald), Holy Roman emperor, 91, 124
Charles the Good (St.), 336
Chateaubriand, François-Auguste-René de, 75
Chopinel, Jean. See Meung, Jean de
Christina of St. Trond, 360
Christopher (St.), 158
Chrodegangus (St.), 162
Clare of Assisi (Clara di Offreducio) (St.), 33, 174, 363, 364
Clement VI, Pope, 169-70, 296, 367
Clement of Metz, 166
Cohen, Jeremy, 309-10
Constantine I (the Great), 72, 90
Cosmas and Damian (Sts.), 92
Crescentius of Jesi, 256-57
Cunefort (St.), 4, 180
Cunera (St.), 337

Damian, Peter (Pier Damiani), 101, 169, 185
Dasberg, Lea, 298
Diego of Osma, 270
Dionysius (the Areopagite), 233
Dominic (St.), 264
Duby, Georges, 121, 123
Dunstan (St.), 14
Durandus of Osca, 270
Duvenvoorde, Willem van, 43
Dympna (St.), 338

Eckhart, Johannes (Meister Eckhart), 42, 372
Edgar, king of the English, 14
Edward (the Confessor) (St.), king of the English, 171
Edward I, king of England, 175

Edward II, king of England, 175
Elias of Cortona (Brother Elias), 246-47, 251-55, 262
Elizabeth (St.), 157, 174, 338
Elving of Corbie, 101-2
Emicho of Leiningen, 301
Emma of Normandy (St.), 3
Eucherius (St.), 166, 333
Eudochia (Athenaïs), Eastern Roman empress, 91
Eugenius I (St.), Pope, 164
Eugenius II, Pope, 127
Eugenius III, Pope, 1, 171

Flood, David, 271
Fortunatus, Venantius Honorius Clementianus, 166
Foucher de Chartres. See Fulcher of Chartres
Foy (St.), 4, 164
Francis of Assisi (St.), 32-33, 35, 174, 246-65, 270, 271-73, 337, 363
Frederick I (Frederick Barbarossa), Holy Roman emperor, 68, 172, 292-93
Frederick II, Holy Roman emperor, 352
Fulbert (canon), 233-34
Fulcher of Chartres, 83, 85
Fulk III (Nerra), 93, 94
Fulk IV (the Surly), 53

Geert Groote (Groete). See Groote, Gerhard
Gerard of Borgo San Donnino, 258
Gerard of Brogne, 164
Gerard of Cambrai, 111-12, 202
Gerard of Saint-Saveur, 114-15
Gerard of Toul, 166, 168
Gerhard of Brogne, 333-34
Gerlach (St.), 99
Gheraert Appelmans, 339
Gilbert Crispin, 289
Gillis Li Muisit, 366
Gilson, Étienne-Henry, 228

Giovanni Baptista dei Giudici, 291
Girald of Salles, 213
Glaber, Radulfus, 96, 97, 112-13, 118, 200
Godfrey of Auxerre, 173, 182
Gorgonius (St.), 162
Gotschalk of Orbais, 199
Gratian, 128, 165, 216, 281
Graus, Frantiček, 297
Gregory I (the Great), Pope, 15, 66, 69, 89, 97, 210, 276, 277
Gregory VII, Pope, 19, 55, 106, 127, 170, 202, 204-6, 216
Gregory IX, Pope, 33, 170, 176, 247, 248, 254, 261, 262, 263, 264, 266, 272-73
Gregory of Tours, 66
Groote, Gerhard, 44, 51, 140, 157, 326, 339, 368-73, 374
Grundmann, Herbert, 207-8, 260
Guibert of Nogent, 68, 112, 225-26, 288, 300
Guillaume de Champeaux. See William of Champeaux
Guillaume de Lorris, 226
Guinefort (St.), 4, 180

Hadewijch, 45, 361
Haimo of Halberstadt, 90
Hardenberg, Friedrich Leopold von (Novalis), 75
Harding, Stephen (St.), 290
Haskins, Charles Homer, 228
Hedwig (St.), 174
Heer, Friedrich, 279
Hegesippus, 96
Heloise, 226-29, 233-34, 235-36, 242
Henry II (St.), Holy Roman emperor, 1-2, 171
Henry III, Holy Roman emperor, 20, 168, 203
Henry IV, Holy Roman emperor, 68, 204, 292
Henry II, king of England, 172
Henry of Lausanne, 26, 30, 211-24, 238, 269

Henry of Segusia, 176
Heraclius, Eastern Roman emperor, 93
Hildebert of Lavardin, 211, 215, 218, 220, 223-24
Hildegard of Bingen (St.), 174
Hildegonde (St.), 100
Hincmar of Reims, 199, 286
Holy Innocents, 180
Honorius III, Pope, 247, 248, 250, 263
Hrabanus Maurus, 210, 286
Hrosnate (St.), 100
Hugenholtz, F. W. N., 153-54
Hugh of Cluny (St.), 118, 169
Hugo of Amiens, 148
Hugolinus of Segni, 247
Huizinga, Johan, 72, 341
Hus, Jan (John Huss), 48-49

Ida of Leeuw, 339, 360
Ida of Louvain, 360
Ida of Nivelles, 360
Innocent II, Pope, 127, 171, 236, 242
Innocent III, Pope, 1, 31-32, 33, 250, 263, 270, 361
Innocent IV, Pope, 33, 257, 295, 352, 353
Isaac, Jules, 308
Isembold, 101
Isidore of Seville, 97
Ivo of Chartres, 111, 126, 127, 165

Jacques de Vitry, 337, 365-66
James (apostle), 5, 92
James of Voragine, 340
Jan of Arkel, 354
Jan of Brabant, 354
Jan of Enghien, 325
Jan of Nassau, 352
Jansen, Hans, 280
Jerome (St.), 90-91, 96, 284, 314-16
Jesus Christ, 5, 6, 22, 63, 92, 93-95, 283-85, 286, 331
Jimenez de Cisneros, Francisco, 52

Joachim of Fiore, 29, 37, 257-58
John (apostle), 338
John VIII, Pope, 18, 124
John XV, Pope, 167-68
John XXII, Pope, 38, 175, 347, 353
John XXIII, Pope, 48
John of Fécamp, 184
John of Parma, 257-59
John of Salisbury, 238
Jordanus of Giano, 253
Josephus, Flavius, 96
Juliana of Cornillion, 346-47

Kunigonde (St.), 1-2

Lambert le Bègue, 361
Lambert of Arras, 83, 85
Lambert of Maastricht (St.), 335, 337
Lampert of Hersfeld, 101
Landulf (St.), 165
Lanfranc, 55
Langmuir, Gavin, 301-4, 305
Laurence (St.), 341
Lazarus (St.), 6
Lebuin (St.), 337
Leclercq, Jean, 158, 181-97
Leeuwen, Jan van, 45
Leo IX (St.), Pope, 168
Lethbald, 96
Leutard, 200
Liotulf of Augsburg, 167
Lothar (II), king of Lotharingia, 124
Louis I (the Pious), Holy Roman emperor, 15, 20
Louis IV (the Bavarian), Holy Roman emperor, 38
Louis VI (the Fat), king of France, 128
Louis VII (the Young), king of France, 68, 128
Louis IX (St.), king of France, 94, 176
Louis II (the German), king of Germany, 124
Lucius III, Pope, 270

Ludolf of Saxony, 44
Lutgard of Aywières, 360, 374
Luther, Martin, 294, 303

Maerlant, Jacob van, 345, 362-63, 374-75
Magi, 91
Malachy of Armagh (St.), 173
Mansuetus (St.), 166, 168
Map, Walter, 61, 214-15
Margaret of Ypres, 360
Margaret Porete, 42, 360-61
Marie of Oignies (St.), 337, 360, 365, 374
Marquard of Lindau, 317
Marsilius of Padua, 38, 378
Martial (St.), 122
Martin (St.), 337
Martin of Tours (St.), 15
Mary (mother of Jesus), 5, 36, 62, 91, 92, 338-40
Mary Magdalene (St.), 5, 93, 338
Matthew of Albano, 61, 64-65, 69, 145, 148
Mauril (St.), 166
Mayeul of Cluny (St.), 169
Meinolf (St.), 162
Meinwerk (St.), 95
Meung, Jean de (Jean Chopinel), 226, 378
Michael (archangel), 180
Montfort, Simon de, 92
Muiden, Dier van der, 369
Murray, Alexander, 376-81

Nicholas I, Pope, 110
Nicholas V, Pope, 176
Nicholas of Clairvaux, 104
Nicholas of Cusa, 52, 71
Nicholas of Lyra, 290, 310
Nicholas of Myra (St.), 158
Nicholas of Tolentino, 178
Nicholas Donin, 289
Norbert of Xanten (St.), 157, 214, 235, 360
Notker of Liège, 351

Novalis (Friedrich Leopold von Hardenberg), 75

Ockham, William, 38
Oda (St.), 337
Odilo of Cluny (St.), 169
Odo of Cluny (St.), 69, 169
Ogier, 195
Olbert of Gembloux, 337
Olivi, Pietro, 37-38
Ontkommer (St.), 180, 341-42
Orderic Vitalis, 53-57, 69, 70, 83, 136, 144
Otto I (the Great), Holy Roman emperor, 68
Otto of Freising, 241
Oudejans, Nicholas, 307-8

Patiens (St.), 166-67
Paul (apostle), 58, 284
Paulus Diaconus, 166
Pelagia of Antioch (St.), 92
Pepin III (the Short), king of the Franks, 12, 15
Peter (apostle), 162, 327, 334, 338
Peter of Amiens. See Peter the Hermit
Peter of Bruys, 30, 212, 218, 220
Peter the Hermit, 81, 85, 213
Peter the Venerable, 61, 96, 135, 140-46, 184, 212, 218, 224, 241-44, 283, 287, 288
Peter Alfonsus, 287
Peter Comestor, 362
Petrarch, 72, 225
Philip I, king of France, 53
Philip IV (the Fair), king of France, 39
Philip V (the Tall), king of France, 325
Philip VI, king of France, 325
Phillibert (St.), 163
Plato, 36
Pons of Melgueil, 79-81, 140-46, 169
Poppo of Stavelot (St.), 99, 333

Post, R. R., 370

Rabanus Maurus. *See* Hrabanus
  Maurus
Radegunde (St.), 64, 66
Rainon of Angers, 166
Ramirhdus, 202
Rashi (Rabbi Shlomo Yitzhaqi), 290
Raymond of Pennafort (St.), 175
Remaclus (St.), 162, 334, 337
Richard of Aduard, 177, 337
Richard of Fourneaux, 55
Robert II (the Pious), king of
  France, 93
Robert le Bougre, 363
Robert of Abrissel, 213
Robert of Borron, 345
Robert of Châtillon, 138, 140
Robert of Molesme (St.), 177
Robert of Thourotte, 346
Roger of Chalons-sur-Marne, 201
Rudolf of Diepholt, 326
Rudolf of St. Trond, 333
Rupert of Deutz, 135
Ruysbroeck, Jan van, 45, 361, 370-
  71

Sabatier, Auguste, 259, 260
Salimbene of Parma (of Adam),
  179, 253
Savonarola, 51
Sebald of Nuremberg (St.), 176
Sergius and Bacchus (Sts.), 92
Shlomo Yitzhaqi (Rashi), 290
Sigebert of Gembloux, 336-37
Sigismund, Holy Roman emperor,
  48
Simeon (St.), 168
Simon of Montfort, 92
Simon of Vernandois, 336
Stephen (St.), 91
Steven of Tournai, 59
Suger, 233, 235
Sylvester (St.), 180

Tanchelm, 206-7

Tertullian, 208-9
Thaddeus (apostle), 92
Theobald (Thibaut) of Blois, 276,
  294
Thibald of Montmorency, 93-94
Thomas à Becket, 172, 262
Thomas à Kempis, 369
Thomas of Cantelupe (St.), 175
Thomas of Cantimpré, 345, 360,
  366
Thomas of Celano, 251, 254, 257,
  261, 265, 266
Thomas of Eccleston, 253, 255
Thomas Aquinas (St.), 36, 293, 317
Trudo (St.), 333, 337

Ulrich (St.), 167
Urban II, Pope, 19, 68, 80, 81, 83-
  86, 105-7, 127-28, 136, 169
Urban IV, Pope, 95, 347
Urban VIII, Pope, 177-78
Ursula (St.), 337

Vacandard, E., 156
Valdés, Pierre. *See* Waldo, Peter
Valentine (St.), 164
Venerable Bede. *See* Bede
Victor III, Pope, 127
Visconti, Galeazzo, 43
Vitalis of Savigny, 213

Walafrid Strabo, 87, 90
Waldo, Peter (Pierre Valdés), 27-29,
  31, 214-15, 263
Walter of Bierbach, 339
Walter of Bruges, 265
Walter of Mortagne, 238
Walter von der Vogelweide, 72
Wazo of Liège (St.), 201
Wecelinus, 332
Weert, Jan de, 375
Werner of St. Blaise, 222
Wilgefortis (St.), 341-42
William (monk in dispute with
  Henry of Lausanne), 212, 216-18,
  221, 224

William II (William Rufus), king of
England, 54, 55
William V Fier-à-Bras (the Great),
121-22, 123
William of Champeaux, 231, 290
William of Malmesbury, 106
William of Nangis, 296
William of Ockham, 38
William of Saint-Thierry, 44, 64,
139, 147, 148, 182, 186, 192,
193, 239-40, 358, 361

William Procurator, 346
Willibrord (St.), 337
Wolbodo of Liège (St.), 335
Wycliffe (Wyclif), John, 45-49

Ximenes, Francisco, 52

Yves de Chartres. See Ivo of Chartres

Zerbold, Gerard, 371-72, 374
Zweder of Kuilenburg, 326

Index of Subjects

❧   ❧

Abbeys. *See* Monasteries, abbeys, convents
Abortion, 324, 327
Abstinence. *See* Celibacy; Marriage
Afterlife, 6-7, 322
Albigensianism, 29, 35. *See also* Catharism
Allegory. *See* Exegesis
Anathema, 326
Ancestor worship, 10-11, 118, 357
Annales, 305
Annates, benefices, prebends, 40, 51, 117, 202, 216, 376
Antichrist, 48, 64-71, 97-98, 116-17, 210
Anticlericalism, 25, 28, 216, 378
Anti-Judaism, 274-318
Antiqui, antiquitas, 53-76
Anti-Semitism, 274-318
Aristotelian philosophy, 36, 59, 230-31, 324
Art, 16, 125, 331
Augustinians, 15, 51. *See also* Augustine of Hippo (name index)
Authority. *See* Ecclesiastical authori-

ty; Papal authority; Privatization of religion; Secular authority
Averroism, 380
Avignon (papal see), 39, 47, 48, 176

Baptism, 11, 216, 323-24, 357
Beatus, 177
Begging. *See* Mendicant orders; Poverty, voluntary
Beghards, 42, 363
Beguines, 35, 42, 339, 347, 365, 366
Benedictines, 14, 15, 20, 22, 51, 131-33, 135, 136-37, 268, 331-32, 333, 374. *See also* Cluniacs; Benedict of Nursia (name index)
Benedictions. *See* Liturgy, prayer
Benefices. *See* Annates, benefices, prebends
Bible, 27, 46, 289-90, 312, 314-15, 331-33, 361-63, 374
Bishops. *See* Peace of God; Ecclesiastical authority
Blessings. *See* Liturgy, prayer
Bogomilism, 30, 199-200

397

Bollandists, 152
Brethren of the Common Life, 44, 315
Brethren of the Free Spirit, 37
Brothers, religious. *See* Lay religious

Calendar, liturgical, 7-8, 158, 176, 336, 341
Canonization. *See* Saints, canonization
Canons Regular, 15, 138
Capitularies of Thionville, 162
Carmina Burana, 61
Carthusians, 23, 43-44
Catechesis, 308, 317
Catharism, 29-30, 200, 206, 269, 270, 362, 363
Celibacy, 2, 30, 203
Children, 12-13, 86, 120, 217, 286, 291, 294, 301, 324, 358
Christendom, Christianity (terms), 16-18, 298-99
Church (as institution), 8, 277-78, 291-92, 319-21, 323-30
Churches (buildings), 7, 16
Cistercians, 23-25, 51, 56, 101, 130-50, 172, 173, 177, 358, 360, 361, 374. *See also* Bernard of Clairvaux (name index)
Classes, social, 117, 299, 358, 377, 379. *See also* Laity and clergy; Military class; Nobility; Peasants, serfs
Clergy. *See* Laity and clergy
Cluniacs, 21-22, 57, 132-50, 169-70. *See also* Monasteries, abbeys, convents, Cluny
Codex Theodosianus, 281
Communion. *See* Eucharist
Confession, 11, 214, 222, 350. *See also* Penance
Convents, 24, 33, 213. For individual place names, *see* Monasteries, abbeys, convents
Conversi. See Lay religious
Conversio ad succurrendum, 12

Corpus Christi, 95, 346-47
Councils, synods: African, 165; Basel, 50; Carthage, 160, 161; Charroux, 108, 122; Clermont(-Ferrand), 19, 83-84, 105-7, 127; Constance, 48, 50; Fines, 108; Frankfurt, 162; Lateran, First, 127; Lateran, Second, 127, 326, 328, 329; Lateran, Third, 127, 214-15, 275, 281-82; Lateran, Fourth, 32, 159, 174, 249, 258, 270, 280, 281, 282, 288, 325, 352; Limoges, 122; Lyons, 257; Mainz, 162, 165; Metz, 108; Narbonne, 107, 108, 123; Nicea, 159; Pisa, 48, 218; Poitiers, 122; Reims, 127, 128; Sens, 240, 243; Soissons, 129, 230, 232, 235; Toledo, 281; Toulouges-Rousillon, 109, 116; Tours, 172, 328; Trent, 159, 320, 354; Troia, 126; Vatican II, 158; Vienne, 35, 108, 361, 363
Counter-Reformation. *See* Reform
Crime and punishment, 129. *See also* name of offense
Cross, 93-94, 96
Crown of thorns, 94
Crusades, 19-20, 80-86, 105-7, 189, 287, 298, 311. *See also* Jerusalem; Pilgrimages, pilgrims

Devotio Moderna, 51, 157, 370-72
Devotion. *See* Cross; Crown of thorns; Eucharist; Sepulchre; persons' names (name index)
Dialectic method. *See* Scholasticism
Domesdaybook, 377
Dominicans (Preaching Friars), 35-36, 37, 309, 310. *See also* Dominic (name index)
Donatism, 209
Dualism, duality, 30, 192, 199, 324, 359

Ecclesiastical authority, 26, 45, 46,

50, 123, 154, 158-81, 277-78, 291-92. *See also* Papal authority; Peace of God; Privatization of religion; Truce of God

Economy, 8-9, 18-19, 24, 26, 39, 119-20, 133, 198, 275, 299-300, 364, 376

Ecumenical councils. *See* Councils, synods

Enlightenment, 74, 156, 278, 381

Epidemics, 39, 51, 82, 366

Eremites. *See* Hermits

Eschatology, 29, 63-73, 95-98, 116, 298

Eucharist, 41, 49, 95, 342-47; desecration of host, 295, 345-46

Evil, 324

Excommunication, 11, 324, 325-30

Exegesis, 63-64, 87-91, 284, 290, 307-18

Exempla, 36, 309, 316, 345

Fashion, style, 54

Feast days. *See* Holy days

Feudalization, 120

Flagellation, flagellants, 339, 366-68

Franciscans, 32-33, 35-36, 37-38, 246-73, 309, 310, 365. *See also* Francis of Assisi (name index)

Friars Minor. *See* Franciscans

God, 330-33

Golden Fridays, 346

Guilds, 322

Hagiography. *See* Saints, Lives

Hagiotherapy, 154, 180-81

Heresy, heretics, 28-31, 35, 42, 124, 198-224, 267-68, 363-65. *See also* Schisms; persons' names (name index)

Hermits, 22-26, 37, 43, 100, 214-15, 268. *See also* Preaching, preachers

Historical research and interpretation, 63, 76-78, 152-54, 181-97,

305-7, 321, 376-81. *See also* historians' names (name index)

History, 53-78

Holy days: All Saints' Day, 180, 344, 351; All Souls Day, 351; Annunciation, 339; Ascension, 345; Assumption of Mary, 339, 344; Christmas, 344; Conception of Mary, 339; Corpus Christi, 95, 346-47; Holy Blood, 346; Nativity of Mary, 339; Purification of Mary, 339

Holy water, 349-50

Hospitals, 323

Host. *See* Eucharist

Humiliati, 270

Idiota, 15

Illiteracy. *See* Literacy, illiteracy

Immaculate Conception, 62, 339

Indulgence, 39-40, 107, 351-55

Infant abandonment, 120, 324

Infanticide, 13, 324

Inquisition, 10, 363-64

Interest, 26, 27

Investiture Conflict, 207, 211

Jerusalem (biblical interpretation), 87-89

Jerusalem (place), 5, 19, 79-104. *See also* Crusades; Pilgrimages, pilgrims

Jews, 35, 124, 274-318; accusations against, 276, 283, 285, 287-88, 292, 293-96, 309, 345-46; conversion, 276, 286, 289, 300-301; persecutions, pogroms, 276, 296-98, 301-4; polemics, 282-87, 289, 309-10; social position, 274-75, 298-300

Judaism, 275, 284-85, 290, 312-13, 314, 317, 327, 332

Knights. *See* Crusades; Military class

Laity and clergy, 13-16, 18, 19-20, 26, 35, 117, 206, 214-15, 343,

355-58, 361-63, 374-75. *See also* Lay religious; Literacy, illiteracy; Privatization of religion

Latin, 13, 15, 16, 58, 355-58, 361-63. *See also* Vernacular

Lay religious, 23, 34-35, 41-43, 133-34, 252-53, 322. *See also* Preaching, preachers

Lesser Brothers. *See* Franciscans

Life after death. *See* Afterlife

Limbo, 62

Literacy, illiteracy, 15, 26-27, 117, 206, 221-24, 267, 360, 374. *See also* Latin; Vernacular

Liturgy, prayer, 7, 12, 15, 16, 176, 348-49. *See also* Calendar, liturgical

Lives of the Saints. *See* Saints, Lives

Lollards, 47

Magic, 42, 154, 343, 344, 345, 348-50, 368-70

Manichaeism, 30

Marriage, 2, 16, 30, 119, 216, 274

Mendicant orders, 35-37, 51, 309, 364. *See also* Poverty, voluntary

Middle Ages (term), 74

Military class, 8, 19, 81, 105-7, 117, 119, 120-21, 328

Minorites. *See* Franciscans

Moderni, 53-76

Monasteries (history), 12-13, 14

Monasteries, abbeys, convents (sites): Aduard, 177, 337; Argentueil, 234, 235; Bavo, 165; Beaulieu, 94; Böddeke, 162; Brogne, 164; Chalon-sur-Saône, 242; Cîteaux, 23, 56, 131, 132, 149, 177; Clairvaux, 24, 57, 80, 132, 134, 138, 181; Cluny, 21-22, 79, 118, 133, 134, 149, 169, 202, 287; Conques, 4, 164; Corbie, 114; Egmond, 153, 154, 337; Fécamp, 92, 170; Grande Chartreuse, 23, Grande Chartreuse, 268; Hirsau, 132, 149 (*see*

also Cluniacs; Cluny); Jarrow, 14; Jumièges, 164; La Ferté, 132; Malmedy, 162; Molesme, 149; Monnikshuizen, 44, 370; Morimond, 80, 101, 132, 134; Noirmoutiers, 163; Paraclete, 226, 227, 235, 236; Petersborough, 6; Pontigny, 132; Portes, 195; Preaux, 55; Prémontré, 213; St. Blandina, 165; Saint-Denis, 164, 232, 233, 235; Saint-Evroul, 53, 136; St. Gavin sur Gartempe, 16; St.-Gildas, 235, 236, 237; Saint-Medard, 232; Saint-Thierry, 240; St. Victor, 290; San Damiano, 33; Signy, 240; Souvigny, 169; Stavelot, 162; Tournus, 163; Utrecht, 315; Villers, 339; Warmouth, 14

Monastic orders. *See* Reform, monastic; names of orders

Murder, 107, 123, 327; ritual, 293-95

Mysticism, 42, 44-45

Necromancy, 368-70

Nobility, 118-19, 205, 378-79

Nuns. *See* Convents; Women; names of orders

Observantism, 51

Paganism, 26, 179-81

Papal authority, 19, 21, 37-38, 40, 161, 167-76, 205, 319-20. *See also* Ecclesiastical authority

Pataria movement, 205

Peace. *See* Peace of God; Truce of God; War and peace

Peace of God, 4-5, 19, 105-29

Peasants, serfs, 119-20, 299, 300, 378

Penance, 11-12, 39, 350-51, 357. *See also* Confession

Philosophy. *See* Aristotelian philosophy; Platonic philosophy; Scholasticism

Pilgrimages, pilgrims, 5, 90, 96-97, 98-102, 352, 354. *See also* Crusades; Jerusalem
Pisa (papal see), 48
Plague. *See* Epidemics
Platonic philosophy, 36, 59
Poor Catholics, 29, 32, 270
Poor Clares, 33, 364
Poor of Lyon, 29
Pope. *See* Avignon; Papal authority; Pisa; Rome; popes' names (name index)
Poverty, voluntary, 22, 25, 27, 29, 32, 33, 37, 248-49, 265-72, 364. *See also* Mendicant orders
Prayer. *See* Liturgy, prayer
Preaching, preachers, 25-26, 28, 212-15, 265-72. *See also* Hermits; Laity and clergy; names of religious orders
Preaching Friars. *See* Dominicans
Prebends. *See* Annates, benefices, prebends
Privatization of religion, 40-44
Punishment. *See* Crime and punishment; Penance
Purgatory, 12, 39

Quests, questors, 353-54

Reason, rationality, 171, 376-81
Reform, church, 19-20, 25, 49-51, 124, 198-224; Counter-Reformation, 52, 74, 151; monastic, 15, 21-23, 56, 64-65, 118, 130-50, 256-58; Reformation, 52, 73, 151; social, 29, 322-23
Reformation. *See* Reform
Relics, 2-4, 5, 6, 91-95, 122, 162, 164, 174, 334. *See also* Saints; saints' names (name index)
Religion and society, 8-10, 133, 321-23, 327, 338, 364. *See also* Peace of God
Romanticism, 74-75
Rome (papal see), 39, 47, 48

Rosary, 339
Rule: Augustine, 15; Benedict, 15, 20, 22, 131-33, 136, 331-32, 333, 374; Cluny, 21; customs and, 22; Francis, 32-33, 248, 254-55; Irish, 15; Martin of Tours, 15; *Regula Bullata*, 248-51, 253; *Regula non bullata*, 249-51

Sacramentals, 349-50
Sainthood, 2, 155. *See also* Saints
Saints, 2, 99, 151-97, 333-42, 379; canonization, 41, 162-78, 260-65, 337-38; cult of, 3-4, 5-6, 156; legendary/unofficial, 179-81, 337-38, 340; Lives, 152-54, 156, 163, 334-36, 340; *sanctus, beatus,* 161, 177-78. *See also* Relics; saints' names (name index)
Salvation, 46, 96
Sanctus, 161
Schisms: Anacletus, 287; Jewish, 283; Rome-Byzantium, 105-6; Utrecht, 326; Western, 39, 47-49, 50, 178
Scholasticism, 59, 229-31, 324
Secular authority, 18, 21, 26, 117-29, 202-3, 293
Seigneurie banale, 129
Sepulchre (Jesus'), 93, 94-95, 96
Serfs. *See* Peasants, serfs
Simony. *See* Annates, benefices, prebends
Slavery, 9, 274
Society. *See* Reform, social; Religion and society; Secular authority
Suicide, 327
Superstition, 42-43, 356. *See also* Magic; Necromancy

Talmud, 286, 287, 288-89, 317
Templars, 189-90
Tertiary orders. *See* Lay religious
Theology, theologians, 62-63, 216-18, 222, 231, 307-18. *See also* theologians' names (name index)

Third orders. *See* Lay religious
Torah, 284, 313, 317
Translation. *See* Latin; Vernacular
Transubstantiation. *See* Eucharist
Trinity, 330-31
Truce of God, 106-7, 109-10, 111, 112, 116-17, 122, 125

Veneration. *See* Cross; Relics; Saints; Sepulchre; persons' names (name index)
Vernacular, 14-15, 27, 31, 44-45, 355-58, 361-63, 371, 374. *See*

also Laity and clergy; Latin; Literacy, illiteracy
Vita, vitae. See Saints, Lives

Waldensians, 27-29, 269, 270. *See also* Waldo, Peter (name index)
War and peace, 329. *See also* Crusades; Military class; Peace of God; Truce of God
Women, 23-24, 25, 28-29, 33-34, 100, 191, 213-14, 227, 228-29, 269, 358-61, 365-66